Learning JavaScript

Other resources from O'Reilly

SECOND EDITION

Learning JavaScript

Shelley Powers

O'REILLY®

Beijing · Cambridge · Farnham · Köln · Sebastopol · Taipei · Tokyo

Learning JavaScript, Second Edition
by Shelley Powers

Published by O'Reilly Media, Inc., 1005 Gravenstein Highway North, Sebastopol, CA 95472.

O'Reilly books may be purchased for educational, business, or sales promotional use. Online editions are also available for most titles (*http://safari.oreilly.com*). For more information, contact our corporate/institutional sales department: (800) 998-9938 or *corporate@oreilly.com*.

Editor: Simon St.Laurent	**Indexer:** Joe Wizda
Production Editor: Sumita Mukherji	**Cover Designer:** Karen Montgomery
Copyeditor: Audrey Doyle	**Interior Designer:** David Futato
Proofreader: Sumita Mukherji	**Illustrator:** Jessamyn Read

Printing History:

October 2006:	First Edition.
December 2008:	Second Edition.

 This book uses RepKover, a durable and flexible lay-flat binding.

ISBN: 978-0-596-52187-5

[M]   [11/09]

1256672864

Table of Contents

Preface

JavaScript was originally intended to be a scripting interface between a web page loaded in the browser client (Netscape Navigator at the time) and the application on the server. Since its introduction in 1995, JavaScript has become a key component of web development, and has found uses elsewhere as well.

This book covers the JavaScript language, from its most primitive data types that have been around since the beginning of the language, to its most complex features, including those that have to do with Ajax and dynamic page effects. After reading this book, you will have the basics you need to work with even the most sophisticated libraries and web applications.

Audience

Readers of this book should be familiar with web page technology, including Cascading Style Sheets (CSS) and HTML/XHTML. Previous programming experience isn't required, though some sections may require extra review if you have no previous exposure to programming.

This book should help:

- Anyone who wants, or needs, to integrate JavaScript into his own personal website or sites
- Anyone who uses a content-management tool, such as a weblogging tool, and wants to better understand the scripting components incorporated into her tool templates
- Web developers who seek to integrate JavaScript and some of the dynamic web page/Ajax features into their websites
- Web service developers who want to develop for a new market of clients
- Teachers who use web technologies as either the focus or a component of their courses

- Web page designers who wish to better understand how they can enliven their designs with interactive or animated effects
- Anyone interested in web technologies

Assumptions and Approach

As stated earlier, this book assumes you have experience with HTML and CSS, as well as a general understanding of how web applications work. Programming experience isn't necessary, but the book covers all aspects of JavaScript, some of which are relatively sophisticated. Though the heavier pieces are few, you will need to understand JavaScript well enough to work with the newer Ajax libraries.

The Development Environment

Working with JavaScript can be especially challenging because your applications have to work not only on different types of machines, but also in several different browsers. If you look at web server logfiles for a site, you can see accesses from modern browsers, such as Firefox 3 and IE8, as well as ancient browsers such as IE5.

You can get caught up in trying to create JavaScript for all possible variations of operating system and browser, but a better bet is to pick a group of target browsers that matches the browsers used by most of the people accessing your web pages, and use these to test your applications. You may find that your applications won't work with older browsers, but at some point, you won't be able to support all environments for all people.

Throughout this book, I'll be mentioning "target browsers" when I mention how a piece of JavaScript works. For the book, my target browsers are Firefox 3.x, Opera 9.x, Safari 3.x (including recent builds of WebKit, the infrastructure that forms the basis of Safari), and primarily IE8, the next version of Internet Explorer. Most of the examples for IE should also work with IE 7.x and IE 6.x, and I'll try to note otherwise. Here is a list of the URLs where you can access these browsers:

- You can download Firefox from *http://www.mozilla.com/en-US/firefox/*.
- Safari is installed with Mac OS X, but you can also access it for the Mac and Windows at *http://www.apple.com/safari/*. Safari is based on the open source WebKit project, which provides nightly builds for testing at *http://webkit.org/*.
- You can access Opera at *http://www.opera.com/*.
- Internet Explorer is built into Windows, but you can access the IE8 beta at *http://www.microsoft.com/windows/internet-explorer/beta/default.aspx*.

JavaScript and browser development is very dynamic, and this adds a unique challenge when writing a book on JavaScript. Though I tried to include the most updated coverage of JavaScript, both the JavaScript specification (the ECMAScript specification, to be more accurate) and the browsers themselves were undergoing significant changes. For instance, as I was in the editing phase of this book, the ECMAScript working group announced plans to abandon work on what was known as JavaScript 2 and focus on a new interim specification release, ECMAScript 3.1. However, most of the changes in the newer ECMAScript aren't implemented in many of the target browsers. In the cases where I was relatively confident that the specification introduced a functionality that will be implemented in future browsers, I made a note, at a minimum, of upcoming changes.

In addition, browser makers are always introducing new versions of their tools. The target browsers used to test examples in this book reflect the state of the browsers at the time I wrote the book, which may not quite reflect what you'll find when you read the book.

However, most of the material I've focused on is "classic" JavaScript, which not only is stable, but also will always form the platform on which new changes to both browser and scripting language are based. Most, if not all, of the examples in this book should work in older and future browsers, as well as the target browsers used to test the examples.

Knock on wood.

How the Book Is Organized

The book is organized into six loosely grouped sections.

Chapters 1 through 3 provide an introduction to the structure of a JavaScript application, including the simple data types supported in the language, as well as the basic statements and control structures. These establish a baseline of understanding of the language for the sections that follow.

Chapters 4 and 5 introduce the main JavaScript objects, `String`, `Number`, and `Boolean`, in addition to other built-in objects, such as `Math`, `RegExp` (for regular expressions), `Array`, and the all-important `Function`.

Chapter 6 takes a breather from the language bits and prepares the reader for the more complex scripting examples later in the book by introducing the browser debugging tools, as well as troubleshooting techniques.

Chapter 7 introduces event handling, and Chapter 8 then expands on the subject by covering form events and JavaScript applications with forms.

Chapters 9 through 11 delve into the more sophisticated aspects of web page development. These chapters cover the Browser Object Model (BOM) and the newer Document Object Model (DOM), and show how you can create your own custom objects. Understanding these models is essential if you wish to create new windows, or individually access, modify, or even dynamically create any page element. In addition, with custom objects, you can move beyond the capabilities that are pre-built into either language or browser. Also included in these chapters is a look at browser cookies and some of the more modern client-side storage techniques.

Chapters 12 through 15 finish the book by diving into the advanced uses of JavaScript, including dynamic page effects and Ajax, as well as a more detailed look at using XML or JavaScript Object Notation (JSON) with Ajax applications.

Though I try to follow a logical course when covering JavaScript, sometimes I'll need to use functionality in an example that I won't cover in detail until a later chapter. When this occurs, I'll try to make a note about which chapter includes coverage of the more advanced functionality.

A Chapter Breakdown

The following is a detailed breakdown of this book's contents, including a brief description of what each chapter covers:

Chapter 1, *Hello JavaScript!*
> Introduces JavaScript and provides a quick first look at a small web page application. This chapter also covers some issues associated with the use of JavaScript, including some good programming practices recommended for JavaScript applications.

Chapter 2, *JavaScript Data Types and Variables*
> Provides an overview of the basic data types in JavaScript, as well as an overview of language variables, identifiers, and the structure of a JavaScript statement.

Chapter 3, *Operators and Statements*
> Covers the basic statements of JavaScript, including assignment, conditional, and control statements, as well as the operators necessary for all three.

Chapter 4, *The JavaScript Objects*
> Introduces the three primary built-in JavaScript objects, including `Number`, `String`, and `Boolean`, as well as `Date` and `Math`. The chapter also introduces the `RegExp` object, which provides the facilities to do pattern matching.

Chapter 5, *Functions*
> Focuses on one other JavaScript built-in object: `Function`. `Function` is key to creating custom objects, as well as packaging blocks of JavaScript into reusable functionality that can be invoked more than once in an application.

Chapter 6, *Troubleshooting, Debugging, and Cross-Browser Issues*
> Briefly introduces the debugging environments for the book's target browsers (Internet Explorer, Safari, Firefox, and Opera), as well as covers basic cross-browser development.

Chapter 7, *Catching Events*
> Focuses on event handling, including both the original form of event handling (which is still commonly used in many applications) as well as the newer DOM-based event handling.

Chapter 8, *Forms, Form Events, and Validation*

Introduces using JavaScript with forms and form fields, including how to access each field type—such as text input fields and drop-down lists—and validate the data once retrieved. Form validation before the form is submitted to the web server helps prevent an unnecessary round trip to the server, and thus saves both time and resource use. This chapter also briefly introduces issues related to security and forms.

Chapter 9, *Browser As Puzzle Box*

Begins to look at object models accessible from JavaScript, starting with the Browser Object Model—a hierarchy of objects including the window, document, forms, history, location, and so on. Through the BOM, JavaScript can open windows; access page elements such as forms, links, and images; and even create some basic dynamic effects.

Chapter 10, *Cookies and Other Client-Side Storage Techniques*

Covers script-based cookies, which store small pieces of data on the client's machine. With cookies, you can store usernames, passwords, and other information so that users don't have to keep reentering data. In addition, this chapter provides a brief overview of new and upcoming client-side storage techniques, such as Google's Gears and HTML5 local storage that offer capabilities beyond what a cookie can provide. The chapter also includes a review of the JavaScript sandbox.

Chapter 11, *The DOM, or Web Page As Tree*

Focuses on the DOM, a straightforward, but not trivial, object model that provides access to all document elements and attributes. Though the model is comprehensive and its coverage is fairly straightforward, the chapter could present some challenging moments for new programmers.

Chapter 12, *Dynamic Pages*

Provides a general introduction to dynamically altering the web page, including modifying an individual element's style, as well as adding and removing elements from the page. Some of the effects we'll explore in this chapter include drag-and-drop, collapsing and expanding page sections, visibility, and movement. An understanding of CSS is required.

Chapter 13, *Creating Custom JavaScript Objects*

Demonstrates how to create custom objects in JavaScript and covers the prototype structure that enables such structures in the language. We'll discuss some programming language concepts, such as inheritance and encapsulation, but you don't need prior experience with these concepts to benefit from reading this chapter.

Chapter 14, *Moving Outside the Page with Ajax*

Introduces Ajax, which, despite all the excitement it has generated, is actually not a complicated use of JavaScript. The chapter walks through a complete example, including server-side code.

Chapter 15, *Ajax Data: XML or JSON?*

Expands on the example in Chapter 14 that demonstrated Ajax with an HTML fragment by demonstrating how to generate and process XML through an Ajax application, and then how to do the same with JSON. We'll cover the advantages of both techniques, as well as when to use one over the other.

Conventions Used in This Book

The following typographical conventions are used in this book:

Constant width

Used for command lines and options that should be typed verbatim, C# keywords, and code examples

Constant width italic

Used for replaceable items, such as variables or optional elements, within syntax lines or code

Constant width bold

Used for emphasis within program code

Italic

Used for pathnames, filenames, Internet addresses (such as domain names and URLs), and new terms where they are defined

Indicates a tip, suggestion, or general note.

Indicates a warning or caution.

Using Code Examples

This book is here to help you get your job done. In general, you may use the code in this book in your programs and documentation. You do not need to contact us for permission unless you're reproducing a significant portion of the code. For example, writing a program that uses several chunks of code from this book does not require permission. Selling or distributing a CD-ROM of examples from O'Reilly books *does* require permission. Answering a question by citing this book and quoting example code does not require permission. Incorporating a significant amount of example code from this book into your product's documentation *does* require permission.

We appreciate, but do not require, attribution. An attribution usually includes the title, author, publisher, and ISBN. For example: "*Learning JavaScript*, Second Edition, by Shelley Powers. Copyright 2009 Shelley Powers, 978-0-596-52187-5."

If you feel your use of code examples falls outside fair use or the permission given here, feel free to contact us at *permissions@oreilly.com*.

Safari® Books Online

When you see a Safari® Books Online icon on the cover of your favorite technology book, that means the book is available online through the O'Reilly Network Safari Bookshelf.

Safari offers a solution that's better than e-books. It's a virtual library that lets you easily search thousands of top tech books, cut and paste code samples, download chapters, and find quick answers when you need the most accurate, current information. Try it for free at *http://safari.oreilly.com*.

How to Contact Us

We have tested and verified the information in this book to the best of our ability, but you might find that features have changed (or even that we have made mistakes!). Please let us know about any errors you find, as well as your suggestions for future editions, by writing to:

O'Reilly Media, Inc.
1005 Gravenstein Highway North
Sebastopol, CA 95472
800-998-9938 (in the United States or Canada)
707-829-0515 (international/local)
707-829-0104 (fax)

To ask technical questions or comment on the book, send email to:

bookquestions@oreilly.com

We have a web page for this book where we list examples and any plans for future editions. You can access this information at:

http://www.oreilly.com/catalog/9780596521875

For more information about books, conferences, Resource Centers, and the O'Reilly Network, see the O'Reilly website at:

http://www.oreilly.com

Acknowledgments

I want to thank my editing and review team for helping me write a better book. This includes technical editors Tony Ruscoe, Jeni Tennison, Matthew Russell, and Trey Holdener, who did an excellent job reviewing the content, as well as my long-time editor, Simon St.Laurent. In addition, I'd like to thank the other members of the production team: Rachel Monaghan, Sumita Mukherji, Joe Wizda, and Jessamyn Read.

CHAPTER 1

Hello JavaScript!

One reason JavaScript is so popular is that it's relatively easy to add JavaScript to a web page. All you need to do, at a minimum, is include an HTML **script** element in the page, specify `"text/javascript"` for the **type** attribute, and add whatever JavaScript you want:

```
<script type="text/javascript">
...some JavaScript
</script>
```

Installation is not required, nor do you have to torturously work through any odd library path configurations. JavaScript works, straight out of the box and in most web browsers, including the big four: Firefox, Internet Explorer, Opera, and Safari. All you need to do is add a scripting block, and you're in business.

Traditionally, you add JavaScript blocks to the **head** element in the document (delimited by opening and closing **head** tags), but you also can include them in the **body** element— or even in both sections. However, adding script to the body is not usually considered a good technique, as it makes it more difficult to find the script when you're modifying it at a later time. The exception to this rule is when performance is an issue, which I'll cover in Chapter 6. All of the examples in this book add scripting blocks only to the web page head section.

Hello World!

Also traditionally, the first example when learning a new programming language is known as "Hello, World"—a simple application that prints out "Hello, World!" to the user interface, whatever it may be. In the case of JavaScript, the user interface is the web page. Example 1-1 shows a web page with a JavaScript block that, using only one line of JavaScript, pops open a small window commonly called an *alert box* with the words "Hello, World!"

Example 1-1. The smallest JavaScript application: "Hello, World!"

```
<!DOCTYPE html PUBLIC "-//W3C//DTD XHTML 1.0
Transitional//EN" "http://www.w3.org/TR/xhtml1/DTD/xhtml1-transitional.dtd">
```

```
<html xmlns="http://www.w3.org/1999/xhtml" xml:lang="en" lang="en">
<head>
<title>Hello, World!</title>
<meta http-equiv="Content-Type" content="text/html; charset=utf-8" />

<script type="text/javascript">

alert("Hello, World!");

</script>
</head>
<body>
</body>
</html>
```

Copying Example 1-1 into a file and opening the file in web browsers that support JavaScript should result in an alert box that reads "Hello, World!" If it doesn't, you might want to make sure you have JavaScript enabled.

 Older versions of Internet Explorer also disable script if you open the page via the File Open menu rather than by using a web page address such as *http://<somedomain.com>/index.html*.

This application, although very limited in functionality, more or less demonstrates the minimum components of a JavaScript application: you have a web page, you have a `script` element, and you have a line of JavaScript. Try it yourself, except edit the string by replacing "World" with your first name.

Of course, if you want to move beyond just outputting a static message to the browser, you'll need to extend the example somewhat.

Hello World! Once Again

Another variation of the "Hello, World!" application actually writes the message to the web page rather than in an alert box. To do so, it makes use of four important JavaScript application components: the built-in browser `document` object, JavaScript variables, a JavaScript function, and an event handler. As impressive as this may sound, you can still code the application in seven lines of JavaScript, as shown in Example 1-2.

Example 1-2. "Hello, World!" printed out to the web page

```
<!DOCTYPE html PUBLIC "-//W3C//DTD XHTML 1.1//EN"
"http://www.w3.org/TR/xhtml11/DTD/xhtml11.dtd">
<html xmlns="http://www.w3.org/1999/xhtml" xml:lang="en">
<head>
<title>Hello, World!</title>
<meta http-equiv="Content-Type" content="text/html; charset=utf-8" />
```

```
<script type="text/javascript">
function hello() {

    // say hello to the world
    var msg = "Hello, World!";
    document.open();
    document.write(msg);
    document.close();
}
</script>
</head>
<body onload="hello()">
<p>Hi</p>
</body>
</html>
```

Though Example 1-2 is a very small application, it does expose several of the basic components of most JavaScript applications in use today, each of which deserves a closer look. In the rest of this chapter, we'll take that closer look, one component at a time.

 Not covered in this chapter is the Document Type Declaration (DOC-TYPE) used in Examples 1-1 and 1-2, which can have an influence on how different browsers process the JavaScript. I'll cover the impact of a DOCTYPE in Chapter 6.

The script Tag

JavaScript is frequently used within the context of another language, such as markup languages like HTML and XHTML. However, you can't just plop JavaScript into the markup wherever and however you want.

In Example 1-2, the **script** element encloses the JavaScript. This lets the browser know that when it encounters the script element's opening tag, it shouldn't process the element's contents as HTML or XHTML. At this point, control over the content is turned over to the browser's scripting engine.

Not all script embedded in web pages is JavaScript, and the **script** element opening tag contains an attribute defining the type of script. In the example, this is given as **text/javascript**. Among other allowable values for the **type** attribute are:

- text/ecmascript
- text/jscript
- text/vbscript
- text/vbs

The first **type** value listed specifies that the script is interpreted as ECMAScript, based on the ECMA-262 scripting standard. The next value causes the script to be interpreted as JScript, a variation of ECMAScript that Microsoft implements in Internet Explorer. The last two values are for Microsoft's VBScript, a completely different scripting language.

All of these **type** values describe the MIME type of the content. *MIME*, or Multipurpose Internet Mail Extension, is a way to identify how the content is encoded (i.e., **text**), and its specific format (**javascript**). By providing a MIME type, those browsers capable of processing the type do so, whereas other browsers skip over the section. This ensures that only applications that can process the script actually access the script.

Earlier versions of the **script** tag took a **language** attribute, which was used to designate the version of the language, as well as the type: **javascript1.2** as compared to **javascript1.1**. However, the use of **language** was deprecated in HTML 4.01, though it still appears in many JavaScript examples. And therein lies one of the earliest cross-browser techniques.

 I use the term *cross-browser* to denote JavaScript that works across all target browsers, or uses functionality to manage any browser differences so that the application works "cross-browser."

Years ago, when working with cross-browser compatibility issues, it wasn't uncommon to create a specific script for each browser in a separate section or file and then use the **language** attribute to ensure that only a compatible browser could access the code. Looking through some of my old examples (circa 1997), I found the following:

```
<script src="ns4_obj.js" language="javascript1.2">
</script>
<script src="ie4_obj.js" language="jscript">
</script>
```

The philosophy of this approach was that only a browser capable of processing JavaScript 1.2 would pick up the first file (primarily Netscape Navigator 4.x at that time) and only a browser capable of processing JScript would pick up the second file (Internet Explorer 4). Kludgey? Sure, but it also worked through the early years of trying to deal with frequently broken cross-browser dynamic page effects.

Other valid script attributes are **src**, **defer**, and **charset**. The **charset** attribute defines the character encoding used with the script. It usually isn't set unless you need a different character encoding than what's defined for the document.

One attribute that can be quite useful is **defer**. If you set **defer** to a value of **"defer"**, it indicates to the browser that the script is not going to generate any document content, and the browser can continue processing the rest of the page's content, returning to the script when the page has been processed and displayed:

```
<script type="text/javascript" defer="defer">
...no content being generated
</script>
```

The defer attribute can help speed up page loading when you have a larger JavaScript block or include a larger JavaScript library.

The last attribute, src, has to do with loading external JavaScript files, which we'll explore a little later. First, though, we'll take a closer look at the text/javascript type attribute, and what this means for each browser.

Adding Script to the Document's Body

Earlier, I mentioned that the script element is usually added to the head element of a web page because it's easier to maintain web pages when the script elements are organized in one place. However, there is a legitimate reason for including script within the body element: performance.

When script is added to the head element, the rest of the document can be held back from downloading until the script is finished loading because browsers load only so many resources from the same domain in parallel. In addition, the browser may hold up rendering the rest of the page because of the possibility of document.write within the script. If the JavaScript files are large, the web page's images and other important information can be delayed, perhaps beyond what's feasible.

Even the use of the defer attribute in the script element won't have an impact on the problems with parallel resource loading, or page rendering.

In his book *High Performance Web Sites* (O'Reilly), Steve Souders recommends putting the script elements in the bottom of a document, to let the rest of the web page load first, before the script. Developers of more complex web applications favor this approach. The downside to putting the script at the bottom of the page is that the script is then more difficult to find, and the pages are harder to maintain.

Which is the best approach? I've found that most websites don't incorporate JavaScript libraries that are so large that script placement becomes an issue, not when compared to the importance of being able to ensure that the pages are easier to maintain. Still, if you develop more complex JavaScript libraries, you may want to consider making the switch to footer-based scripts.

Regardless of the approach you use, be consistent: place your scripts either always in the head element or always at the bottom of the body element.

JavaScript Versus ECMAScript Versus JScript

Example 1-2 used the text/javascript type with the script element, and the application works with Firefox, IE, Opera, and Safari. However, not all browsers implement JavaScript.

Although the name "JavaScript" has become ubiquitous for client-side browser-based scripting, only Mozilla and the popular Mozilla browser, Firefox, implement *JavaScript*, which is the actual name of an instance of a broader-based scripting specification, ECMAScript. ECMAScript is actually the industry-wide client-side scripting specification. The latest released version of ECMAScript is ECMA-262, Edition 3.

However, most browsers honor the `text/javascript` type, in addition to the more appropriate (though far less common) `text/ecmascript`, though there can be differences, even significant differences, in exactly what each browser or other application supports.

 ECMAScript isn't restricted to just browsers: Adobe's ActionScript support in Flash is based on ECMA-262, Edition 3.

All of the browsers used to test the applications in the book—Firefox 3.x, Safari 3.x, Opera 9.x, and IE8—support most, if not all, of ECMA-262, Edition 3, and even some of the next generation of ECMAScript, ECMAScript 3.1 (and beyond). In this book, I'll note whenever there are browser differences or provide cross-browser workarounds. I'll also be using the more familiar `text/javascript` for the `script` element's type attribute, as shown in Example 1-2.

Defining Functions in JavaScript

In Example 1-2, the part of the JavaScript that actually creates the "Hello, World!" message exists within a function named `hello`. Functions are ways of enclosing one or more lines of script so that they can be executed one or more times. You also use functions to control when the enclosed script is executed. For instance, in Example 1-2, the function is called only after the web page is loaded.

Here is the typical syntax for creating a function:

```
function functionname(params) {
    ...
}
```

The keyword `function` is followed by the function name and parentheses containing zero or more parameters (function arguments). In Example 1-2, there are no parameters, but we'll see plenty of examples with parameters throughout the book. The script that makes up the function is then enclosed in curly braces.

I say "typical" when providing the function syntax because this isn't the only syntax that you can use to create a function. However, we'll get into other variations starting in Chapter 5, which covers JavaScript functions in detail.

Of course, once you have a function, you have to invoke it to run the script it contains, which leads us to event handlers.

Event Handlers

In the opening body tag of Example 1-2, an HTML attribute named `onload` is assigned the `hello` function. The `onload` attribute is what's known as an *event handler*. This event handler, and others, is part of the underlying object model that each browser provides.

You use event handlers to map a function to a specific event so that when the event occurs, the function's script is processed. One of the more commonly used event handlers is the one just demonstrated, the `onload` event attached to the `body` element. When the web page has finished loading, the event is fired, and the handler calls the mapped function.

Here are some commonly used event handlers:

`onclick`
> Fired when the element receives a mouse click

`onmouseover`
> Fired when the mouse cursor is over the element

`onmouseout`
> Fired when the mouse cursor is no longer over the element

`onfocus`
> Fired when the element gains focus (through the mouse or keyboard)

`onblur`
> Fired when the element no longer has focus

These are only a few of the event handlers, and not all elements support all event handlers. The `onload` event handler is supported for only a few elements, such as the `body` and `img` elements—not surprising, as the event is associated with loading something.

Adding an event handler directly to the opening element tag is one way to attach an event handler. A second technique occurs directly within JavaScript using syntax such as the following:

```
<script type="text/javascript">
window.onload=hello;

function hello(??) {

   // say hello to the world
   var msg = "Hello, World!";
   document.open();
   document.writeln(msg);
   document.close();
}
</script>
```

The `onload` event handler is a property of another built-in browser object, the `window`. The first line of the script then assigns the function, `hello`, directly to the window's `onload` event handler.

 JavaScript functions are also objects in JavaScript, so you can assign a function, by name or directly, to a variable or another object's property.

Using the object property approach, you don't have to add event handlers as attributes into element tags, but instead can add them into the JavaScript itself. We'll get into more details on event handlers and more advanced forms of event handling beginning in Chapter 7. In the meantime, let's take a closer look at the `document` object.

The document Browser Object

Example 1-2, as small as it is, used one of the most powerful objects available in your browser: the `document` object. The `document` object is, for all intents and purposes, a representation of the page, including all of the elements within it. It's through the `document` that we can access the page contents, and as you've just seen, it's through the `document` that we can also modify the page contents.

The `document` has collections mapped to page elements, such as all the images or form elements in the page. It also has methods that you can use to both access and alter the web page, including the `open`, `writeln`, and `close` methods used in Example 1-2.

The `open` method opens the document for writing. In Example 1-2, the document opened was the same document with which the script is contained. The `writeln` method is a variation of the `write` method, which outputs a string of text to the document. The only difference between `write` and `writeln` is that `writeln` also appends a newline character following the text. The `close` method closes the document, and also forces the immediate rendering of the document contents.

An unfortunate consequence of writing to the existing document after the page is loaded is that the existing contents of the document are erased. That's why when you open the page you'll see the "Hello, World!" message but you won't see the "Hi" that's already in the page.

 Another consequence of writing over the existing document is that with IE, at least with the beta of IE8, you'll lose your back button functionality.

The `open` and `close` methods aren't required for Example 1-2, as browsers will automatically open and close the document when the `writeln` method is called after the document is already loaded. If you used the script in the body of the page, you would need to explicitly call the open method.

The document, as well as the window mentioned earlier, is part of a hierarchy of objects known as the Browser Object Model (BOM). The BOM is a basic set of objects implemented in most modern browsers. I cover the document and other BOM objects in Chapter 9.

> The BOM is the earliest version of the more formal Document Object Model (DOM), and is sometimes referred to as *DOM Level 0*.

The property Operator

In Example 1-2, you accessed the methods from the document object through one of the many operators supported in JavaScript: the property operator, represented by a single dot (.).

Several operators are available in JavaScript: those for arithmetic (+, -), those for conditional expressions (<, >), and others that I detail more fully later in the book. One of the most important, though, is the property operator. Data elements, event handlers, and object methods are all considered properties of objects within JavaScript, and you access all of them via the property operator.

You also use the property operator in a process called *method chaining*, or sometimes just *chaining*, whereby you can apply calls to multiple methods, one after another, all within the same statement. We'll see the following example in the book:

```
var tstValue = document.getElementById("test").style.backgroundColor="#ffffff";
```

In this example, a page element is accessed using the document method getElementById, and its style object is accessed to set the background color for that element. The backgroundColor is a property of the style object, which is a property of the page element, which is accessed through the method getElementById, which is a property of the document object.

I cover all of these methods and objects in future chapters, but I wanted to introduce you to method chaining now, as you'll see it frequently. You cannot chain all properties of all objects—only those that return an object.

> One of the more popular Ajax libraries, JQuery, makes extensive use of method chaining. I'll cover JQuery briefly in Chapter 14.

The var Keyword and Scope

The "Hello, World!" string I used in Example 1-2 is assigned to an object named msg, which is an example of a JavaScript *variable*. A variable is nothing more than a named reference to a piece of data. The data can be a string, as in Example 1-2, a number, or the boolean value of true or false. It can also be a function reference, an array, or another object.

In the example, I defined the variable with the var keyword. When you use var with a variable, you're defining the variable with local scope, which means you can access them only within the function in which you've defined them. If I didn't use var, the variable msg would be global and would have scope inside and outside the function. Using a global variable in a local context isn't a bad thing—and it may be necessary at times—but it isn't a good practice, and you should avoid it if possible.

The reason why you want to avoid global variables is because if the application is part of a larger JavaScript application, msg may be in use in another part of the code in another file, and you will have overridden whatever data it originally contained. Or, if you create a global variable called msg, some other library's script could override it by not correctly using the var keyword, and the data you were tracking will be lost.

Setting the scope of a variable is important if you have global and local variables with the same name. Example 1-2 doesn't have global variables of any name, but it's important to develop good JavaScript coding practices from the beginning.

Here are the rules regarding scope:

- If you declare a variable with the var keyword in a function or block of code, its use is local to that function.
- If you use a variable without declaring it with the var keyword, and a global variable of the same name exists, the local variable is assumed to be the already existing global variable.
- If you declare a variable locally with a var keyword, but you do not initialize it (i.e., assign it a value), it is local and accessible but not defined.
- If you declare a variable locally without the var keyword, or explicitly declare it globally but do not initialize it, it is accessible globally, but again, it is not defined.

By using var within a function, you can prevent problems when using global and local variables of the same name. This is especially critical when using JavaScript libraries—such as Dojo, jQuery, and Prototype—because you're not going to know what variable names the other JavaScript code is using.

Statements

JavaScript also supports different types of processing instruction types, known as *statements*. Example 1-2 demonstrated a basic type of JavaScript statement: the *assignment*, whereby a value is assigned to a variable. Other types of statements are `for` *loops*, which process a script block a given number of iterations; the `if...else` conditional statement, which checks a condition to see whether the script block is executed; the `switch` statement, which checks for a value in a given set and then executes the script block associated with that value; and so on.

Each type of statement has certain syntax requirements. In Example 1-2, the assignment statement ended with a semicolon. Using a semicolon to terminate a statement isn't a requirement in JavaScript unless you want to type many statements on the same line. If you do, you'll have to insert a semicolon to separate the individual statements.

When you type a complete statement on one line, you use a line break to terminate the statement. However, just as with the use of `var`, it's good practice to use semicolons to terminate all statements, if for no other reason than it makes the code easier to read. More on the semicolon, other operators, and statements in Chapter 3.

Comments

As this chapter hopefully demonstrates, there's quite a lot to the JavaScript in even a small application such as Example 1-2. Hold on, though, as we're not quite finished. Last, but certainly not least, a word on JavaScript comments.

Comments provide a summary or explanation of the code that follows. Comments in JavaScript are an extremely useful way of quickly noting what a block of code is doing and whatever dependencies it has. It makes the code more readable and more maintainable.

You can use two different types of comments in your own applications. The first, using the double slash (//), comments out whatever follows in the line:

```
// This line is commented out in the code
var i = 1; // this is a comment in the line
```

The second makes use of opening and closing JavaScript comment delimiters, /* and */, to mark a block of comments that can extend one or more lines:

```
/* This is a multiline comment
that extends through three lines.
Multiline comments are particularly useful for commenting on a function */
```

Single-line comments are relatively safe to use, but multiline comments can generate problems if the beginning or ending bracket character is accidentally deleted.

Typically, you use single-line comments before a block of script performing a specific process or creating a specific object; you use multiline comment blocks in the beginning of a JavaScript file. A good practice to get into with JavaScript is to begin every JavaScript block, function, or object definition with at least one line of comments. In addition, provide a more detailed comment block at the beginning of all JavaScript library files; include information about author, date, and dependencies, as well as a detailed purpose of the script.

We've explored what you saw in Example 1-2. Now let's take a look at what you didn't see.

What You Didn't See: HTML Comments and CDATA Sections

Ten years ago, when most browsers were in their first or second version, JavaScript support was sketchy, with each browser implementing a different version. When browsers, such as the text-based Lynx, encountered the `script` tag, they usually just printed the output to the page.

To prevent this, the script contents were enclosed in HTML comments: `<!--` and `-->`. When HTML comments were used, non-JavaScript-enabled browsers ignored the commented-out script, but newer browsers knew to execute the script.

It was a kludge, but it was a very widespread kludge. Most web pages with JavaScript nowadays feature the added HTML comments because the script is copied more often than not. Unfortunately, some new browsers today may process the web page as XHTML, and as strictly XML, which means the commented code is discarded. In these situations, the JavaScript is ignored. As a consequence, using HTML comments to "hide" the script is actively discouraged.

Another way to "hide" the script, however, is encouraged, and that's the use of the XML `CDATA` section, particularly if the script is going to be used in XHTML. Example 1-3 is a modification of Example 1-2 with the addition of a `CDATA` section, shown in bold.

Example 1-3. Modification of Example 1-2 to add a CDATA section to "hide" the script

```
<!DOCTYPE html PUBLIC "-//W3C//DTD XHTML 1.1//EN"
"http://www.w3.org/TR/xhtml11/DTD/xhtml11.dtd">
<html xmlns="http://www.w3.org/1999/xhtml" xml:lang="en">
<head>
<title>Hello, World!</title>
<meta http-equiv="Content-Type" content="text/html; charset=utf-8" />

<script type="text/javascript">
//<![CDATA[

function hello() {
    // say hello to the world
    var msg = "Hello, <em>World!</em>";
    document.open();
    document.write(msg);
    document.close();
}

//]]>
</script>
</head>
<body onload="hello()">
<p>Hi</p>
```

```
</body>
</html>
```

The reason for the CDATA section is that XHTML processors interpret markup, such as the em element opening and closing tags in this new example, even when they're contained within JavaScript strings. Though the script may process correctly and may display the page correctly, if you try to validate it without the CDATA section, you'll get validation errors, as shown in Figure 1-1.

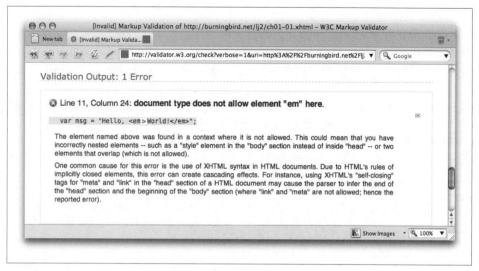

Figure 1-1. Validation error without using a CDATA section

JavaScript that is imported into the page using the script element's src attribute is assumed to be compatible with XHTML and doesn't require the CDATA section. You should delimit inline or embedded JavaScript with CDATA though, particularly if it's included within the body element. For most browsers, you'll also need to hide the CDATA section opening and closing tags with JavaScript comments (//), as shown previously in Example 1-3, or you'll get a JavaScript error.

Of course, the best way to keep your web pages uncluttered is to remove the JavaScript from the page entirely, through the use of JavaScript files.

Most of this book's examples are embedded into the page primarily to make them easier to read and follow. However, the Mozilla Foundation recommends (and I agree) that all inline or embedded JavaScript be removed from a page and placed in separate JavaScript files. Using a separate file, covered in the next section, prevents problems with validation and incorrect interpretation of text, regardless of whether the page is processed as HTML or XHTML.

JavaScript files are also more efficient, as the browser caches them the first time they're loaded. Additional references to the same file are pulled from the cache.

JavaScript Files

JavaScript usage is becoming more object-oriented and complex. To simplify their work, as well as share it, JavaScript developers are creating reusable JavaScript objects that they can incorporate into many applications, including those created by other developers. The only efficient way to share these objects is to create them in separate files and provide a link to each file in the web page. With the code now in files, all the developer needs to do is link the code into the web pages. If the code needs to change later, it's changed in only one place.

Nowadays, all but the simplest JavaScript is created in separate script files. Whatever overhead is incurred by using multiple files is more than offset by the benefits. To include a JavaScript library or script file in your web page, use this syntax:

```
<script type="text/javascript" src="somejavascript.js"></script>
```

The `script` element contains no content, but the closing tag is still required.

The browser loads script files into the page in the order in which they occur in the page and processes them in order unless `defer` is used. A script file should be treated as though the code is actually included in the page; the behavior is no different between script files and embedded JavaScript blocks.

Example 1-4 is yet another modification of our "Hello, World!" application, except this time the script is moved to a separate file, named *helloworld.js*. The *.js* file extension is required, unless you direct the web server to use some other extension to represent the JavaScript MIME type. However, because the *.js* has been used as the default for years, it's best not to get creative.

 Every rule always has exceptions, and the use of *.js* is one of them. If the JavaScript is being dynamically generated using a server-side application built in a language such as PHP, the file will have a different extension.

Example 1-4 contains the script, and Example 1-5 shows the now altered web page.

Example 1-4. The Hello World script, in a separate file

```
/*
    function: hello
    author: Shelley
    hello prints out the message, "Hello, World!"
*/
```

```
function hello() {

    // say hello to the world
    var msg = "Hello, <em>World!</em>";
    document.open();
    document.write(msg);
    document.close();
}
```

Example 1-5. The web page, now calling an external script file

```
<!DOCTYPE html PUBLIC "-//W3C//DTD XHTML 1.1//EN"
"http://www.w3.org/TR/xhtml11/DTD/xhtml11.dtd">
<html xmlns="http://www.w3.org/1999/xhtml" xml:lang="en">
<head>
<title>Hello, World!</title>
<meta http-equiv="Content-Type" content="text/html; charset=utf-8" />

<script type="text/javascript" src="helloworld.js">
</script>
</head>
<body onload="hello()">
<p>Hi</p>
</body>
</html>
```

As you can see, the page is much cleaner, and the application is more efficient from a maintenance perspective. Also, other applications can now reuse the code. Though it's unlikely that you'd reuse something as simple as the "Hello, World!" script, you'll be creating examples later in the book in which reuse becomes more important.

We have one last section of material to cover in this chapter before moving on to variables and data types in Chapter 2.

Accessibility and JavaScript Best Practices

In an ideal world, everyone who visits your website would use the same type of operating system and browser and would have JavaScript enabled. Your site would never be accessed via a mobile phone or some other oddly sized device, vision-impaired people wouldn't need screen readers, and the paralyzed wouldn't need voice-enabled navigation.

This isn't an ideal world, but too many JavaScript developers code as though it is. We get so caught up in the wonders of what we can create that we forget that not everyone can share them.

Many best practices are associated with JavaScript, but if there's one to take away from this book, it's the following: whatever JavaScript functionality you create, it must not come between your site and your site's visitors.

What do I mean by "come between your site and your site's visitors"? I mean that you should avoid using JavaScript in such a way that those who cannot, or will not, enable JavaScript are prevented from accessing essential site resources. If you create a drop-down menu using JavaScript, you also need to provide a script-free alternative. If your visitors are vision-impaired, JavaScript must not interfere with audio browsers, which happens when instructions are added to a page dynamically.

Many developers don't follow these practices because they assume the practices require extra work, and for the most part, they do. However, the work doesn't have to be a burden—not when the results can increase the accessibility of your site. In addition, many companies now require that their websites meet a certain level of accessibility. It's better to get into the habit of creating accessible pages in the beginning than to try to fix the pages, or your habits, later.

Accessibility Guidelines

The WebAIM site (*http://www.webaim.org*) has a wonderful tutorial on creating accessible JavaScript (available at *http://www.webaim.org/techniques/javascript/*). It covers the ways you shouldn't use JavaScript, such as using JavaScript for menus and other navigation. However, the site also provides ways you can use JavaScript to make a site more accessible.

One suggestion is to base feedback on events that can be triggered whether you use a mouse or not. For instance, rather than capture mouse clicks, you should capture events that are triggered if you use a keyboard or a mouse, such as `onfocus` and `onblur`. If you have a drop-down menu, add a link to a separate page, and then provide a static menu on the second page.

After reviewing the tutorial at WebAIM, you might want to spend some time at the World Wide Web Consortium's (W3C's) Web Accessibility Initiative (at *http://www.w3.org/WAI/*). From there, you can also access the U.S. government's Section 508 website (*http://www.section508.gov/*), which discusses what is known as "508 compliance." Sites that comply with Section 508 are accessible regardless of physical constraints. At that website, you can access various tools that evaluate your site for accessibility, such as Cynthia Says (at *http://www.cynthiasays.com/*).

Whether your site is located within the United States or elsewhere, you want it to be accessible; therefore, a visit to Section 508 is useful regardless of your locale.

Of course, not all accessibility issues are related to those browsers in which JavaScript is limited or disabled by default, such as with screen readers. Many people don't trust JavaScript, or don't care for it and choose to disable it. For both groups of people— those who prefer not to use JavaScript, and those who have no choice—it's important to provide alternatives when no script is present. One alternative is `noscript`.

noscript

Some browsers or other applications are not equipped to process JavaScript, or are limited in how they interpret the script. If the JavaScript is not essential to navigation or interaction, and the browser ignores the script, no harm. However, if the JavaScript is essential to access the site's resources and you don't provide alternatives, you're basically telling these folks to go away.

Years ago, when JavaScript was fairly new, one popular approach was to provide a plain or text-only page accessible through a link, usually placed at the top of the page. However, the amount of work to maintain the two sites could be prohibitive, and developers had to constantly worry about keeping the sites synchronized.

A better technique is to provide static alternatives to dynamic, script-generated content. When you use JavaScript to create a drop-down menu, also provide a standard hierarchical linked menu; when you use `script` to expose form elements for editing based on user interaction, provide the more traditional links to a second page to do the same.

The element that enables all of this is `noscript`. Wherever you need static content, add a `noscript` element with the content contained within the opening and closing tags. Then, if a browser or other application can't process the script (because JavaScript is not enabled for some reason), the `noscript` content is processed; otherwise, it's ignored.

Example 1-6 is one last variation of "Hello, World!" showing the `CDATA`-protected example modified with the addition of `noscript`. Accessing the page with a JavaScript-enabled browser should display a page with "Hello, World!" printed out. However, if you access the page with a script-disabled browser, a different message results.

Example 1-6. The use of noscript for non-JavaScript-enabled browsers

```
<!DOCTYPE html PUBLIC "-//W3C//DTD XHTML 1.1//EN"
"http://www.w3.org/TR/xhtml11/DTD/xhtml11.dtd">
<html xmlns="http://www.w3.org/1999/xhtml" xml:lang="en">
<head>
<title>Hello, World!</title>
<meta http-equiv="Content-Type" content="text/html; charset=utf-8" />

<script type="text/javascript">
//<![CDATA[

function hello() {
    // say hello to the world
    var msg = "Hello, <em>World!</em>";
    document.open();
    document.write(msg);
    document.close();
}

//]]>
</script>
</head>
<body onload="hello()">
```

```
<noscript>
  <p>I'm still here, World!</p>
</noscript>
</body>
</html>
```

Of course, Example 1-6 is just a simplified use of noscript; you'll see more sophisticated uses later in the book, as well as alternative script-safe methods.

To test Example 1-6, I used a Firefox extension called the Web Developer Toolbar. On this bar is an option to disable JavaScript support. When JavaScript is active, the original "Hello, World!" message displays. However, when I use the tool to deactivate JavaScript support, another message displays: I'm still here, World! Though you can turn scripting off directly in the browser, I've found that development tools such as the Web Developer Toolbar make testing a whole lot easier.

Which tools you use depends on the browser with which you prefer to develop. I prefer developing with Firefox, and make extensive use of the Web Developer Toolbar and Firebug, a sophisticated debugging tool. Later, in Chapter 6, which covers troubleshooting and debugging, we'll take a closer look at these, as well as tools and options available for other browsers.

CHAPTER 2

JavaScript Data Types and Variables

Variables in JavaScript are basically named buckets of data, a way of creating a reference to that data—regardless of whether the data is a string, number, boolean, array, or other object—so that you can access the same data again and again. More importantly, you can use variables to persist data from one process to another. For instance, your JavaScript application can store the value of a form element in a variable, and manipulate that value without having to actually manipulate the form element itself.

The variable's *data type* is the JavaScript scripting engine's interpretation of the type of data that variable is currently holding. A string variable holds a string; a number variable holds a number value, and so on. However, unlike many other languages, in JavaScript, the same variable can hold different types of data, all within the same application. This is a concept known by the terms *loose typing* and *dynamic typing*, both of which mean that a JavaScript variable can hold different data types at different times depending on context.

With a loosely typed language, you don't have to declare ahead of time that a variable will be a string or a number or a boolean, as the data type is actually determined while the application is being processed. If you start out with a string variable and then want to use it as a number, that's perfectly fine, as long as the string actually contains something that resembles a number and not something such as an email address. If you later want to treat it as a string again, that's fine, too.

The forgiving nature of loose typing can end up generating problems. If you try to add two numbers together, but the JavaScript engine interprets the variable holding one of them as a string data type, you end up with an odd string, rather than the sum you were expecting. Context is everything when it comes to variables and data types with JavaScript.

This chapter covers the JavaScript primitive data types of `string`, `boolean`, and `number`, as well as the built-in functions for modifying values of these types. In addition, we'll look at two special data types in JavaScript, `null` and `undefined`, toward the end of the chapter. Along the way, we'll explore escape sequences in strings and take a brief look at Unicode. The chapter also delves into the topic of variables, including what makes valid and meaningful variable identifiers.

Identifying Variables

JavaScript variables have an identifier, scope, and a specific data type. Because the language is loosely typed, the rest, as they say, is subject to change without notice.

Variables in JavaScript are much like those in any other language; you use them to hold values in such a way that the values can be explicitly accessed in different places in the code. Each has an identifier that is unique to the scope of use (more on this later), consisting of any combination of letters, digits, underscores, and dollar signs. An identifier doesn't have a required format, other than it must begin with a character, dollar sign, or underscore:

```
_variableidentifier
__variableidentifier
variableIdentifier
$variable_identifier
var-ident
```

Starting with JavaScript 1.5, you can also use Unicode letters (such as ü) and digits, as well as escape sequences (such as \u0009) in variable identifiers. The following are also valid variable identifiers for JavaScript:

```
_üvalid
T\u0009
```

Use special characters with caution, though, as some tools such as debuggers may have difficulty with them.

JavaScript is case-sensitive, which means it treats upper- and lowercase characters differently. For instance, JavaScript sees the following two variable identifiers as separate variables:

```
stringVariable
stringvariable
```

An additional restriction on variable identifiers is that they can't be a JavaScript keyword, a list of which appears in Table 2-1. Other keywords may be added over time, as new versions of JavaScript (well, technically, ECMAScript) are released.

Table 2-1. JavaScript keywords

break	else	new	var
case	finally	return	void
catch	for	switch	while
continue	function	this	with
default	if	throw	

delete	in	try
do	instanceof	typeof

Due to proposed extensions to the ECMA-262 specification, the words in Table 2-2 are also considered reserved words and can't be used as variable identifiers.

Table 2-2. ECMA-262 specification reserved words

abstract	enum	int	short
boolean	export	interface	static
byte	extends	long	super
char	final	native	synchronized
class	float	package	throws
const	goto	private	transient
debugger	implements	protected	volatile
double	import	public	public

In addition to the ECMAScript reserved words, certain JavaScript-specific words implemented in most browsers are considered reserved by implementation. Many are based on the Browser Object Model (BOM)—for example, objects such as document and window, which were briefly introduced in Chapter 1. Though not a definitive list, Table 2-3 includes the more common words.

Table 2-3. Typical reserved words in browsers

alert	eval	location	open
array	focus	math	outerHeight
blur	function	name	parent
boolean	history	navigator	parseFloat
date	image	number	regExp
document	isNaN	object	status
escape	length	onLoad	string

Naming Guidelines

Apart from the variable naming restrictions covered in the preceding section, you can use any identifier for variables and functions within code, but several naming practices—many inherited from Java and other programming languages—can make the code easier to follow and maintain.

First, use meaningful words rather than something you've thrown together quickly. For instance, the variable identifier interestRate is more descriptive than the variable `intRt` or even `ir`. The latter two names are too cryptic and too difficult to understand, even within a given context.

You can also provide a data type clue as part of the name, using something such as the following, which is a string, holding a first name:

```
var strFirstName = "Shelley";
```

This type of naming convention—using the data type as part of the variable name—is known as *Hungarian notation*, and is especially popular in Windows development. As such, you'll most likely see it used within the older JScript applications created for Internet Explorer, but less often in more modern JavaScript development.

Another naming convention is to use a plural for collections of items:

```
var customerNames = new Array();
```

Typically, variables are not capitalized because capitalization is usually reserved for objects such as `String`:

```
var firstName = String("Shelley");
```

Reserving capitalization for objects makes them easier to differentiate from simple variables.

Functions and variables frequently start with lowercase letters, and incorporate a verb representing what the function is doing. It's pretty easy to guess what the following function is doing:

```
function validateNameInRegister(firstName,lastName) ...
```

Many times, variables and functions have one or more words concatenated into a unique identifier, following a format popularized in other languages and frequently referred to as *CamelCase* because of the up-down nature of the name, like a camel's humps:

```
validateName
firstName
```

The CamelCase naming format makes the variable much more readable, though dashes or underscores between the variable "words" work as well:

```
validate-name
first_name
```

The newer JavaScript libraries invariably use CamelCase notation, which I also prefer for my own applications.

Though you can use a dollar sign, number, or underscore to begin a variable, your best bet is to start with a letter. Unnecessary use of unexpected characters in variable names can make the code harder to read and follow, especially for newer JavaScript developers. However, if you've looked at some of the newer JavaScript libraries and examples, you might have noticed some odd-looking variable names. The popular Ajax-based

Prototype JavaScript library is a strong influence in this regard—so much so that I think of the rise of new naming conventions as the "Prototype effect."

The following is an example of this effect:

```
var _break = someval;
```

The underscore is used in these libraries to signal a variable that's an object's private data member, a concept I'll cover in Chapter 13. Another interesting naming variation that Prototype has introduced is the following, which uses the dollar sign ($) to name a function that returns a reference to a page element:

```
$('test').invokeSomeMethod();
```

The use of the underscore or dollar sign doesn't change the behavior of the variable, even though such usage is relatively new. It's just another way of naming something.

 You can find the Prototype JavaScript library at *http://www.prototypejs .org/*.

Aside from the few JavaScript naming restrictions, nothing is mandatory or magical about the naming conventions I've outlined. They help to make JavaScript easier to read and debug.

Primitive Types

JavaScript is a trim language, with just enough functionality to do the job—no more, no less. However, as I've said before, it is a confusing language in some respects.

For instance, JavaScript has just three primitive data types: `string`, `numeric`, and `boolean`. Each is differentiated from the others by the type of value it contains: string, numeric, and boolean, respectively. However, JavaScript also has built-in objects known as `String`, `Number`, and `Boolean`. These would seem to be very different from each other: the first three are types of primitive values, whereas the latter three are objects, each one with its own built-in properties and methods.

In actuality, the two are connected. The `String` object *wraps* the string primitive—just as the `Number` and `Boolean` objects wrap their individual primitive types—when using the primitive type like an object. When you create a simple string variable in JavaScript, and then use one of the `String` methods, JavaScript implicitly wraps the string primitive in a `String` object, processes the `String` object property or method call, and then discards the object. In the following code snippet, when the method `toUpperCase` is called on `firstName`, an object is created to wrap the string and then process the method call before the object is discarded:

```
var firstName = "Shelley";
var cappedName = firstName.toUpperCase();
```

For all intents and purposes, `firstName` looks like an object, and it acts like an object when calling `toUpperCase`, but it is a primitive. If I call another `String` object method, the same thing will happen again: a `String` object is created and then wraps the primitive, processes the method call, and discards the object. As you can imagine, if you're going to be treating a string like an object, you'd be better off creating it as an object. At the same time, if all you need is a simple string to print a message or hold a value, you don't need all the functionality that accompanies an object, so creating a string primitive is the better option.

Rather than continue to mix primitive data types and objects in a confusing mishmash that wanders from primitive to object and back again, in the next three sections, we'll look at each of the primitive data types—how they're created and manipulated, and how you can convert values of one type to other type. In Chapter 4, I'll cover the data objects, their methods, and their properties.

 When I use the word *wrap* in the book, I'm talking about an object that typically encloses a simpler item, such as a `String` object wrapping a string primitive.

The String Data Type

Because JavaScript is a loosely typed language, nothing differentiates a string variable from a variable that's a number or a boolean, other than the literal value assigned to the string variable when it's initialized and the context of its use.

A string literal is a sequence of characters delimited by single or double quotes:

```
var strString = "This is a string";
var anotherString= 'But this is also a string';
```

No rule states which type of quote you use, except that the ending quote character must be the same as the beginning one. You can include any variation of characters in the string:

```
var thirdString = "This is 1 string.";
var stringFour = "This is--another string.";
var stringAsNumber = "543";
```

The last example of a string contains a number, but because it's surrounded by quotes, JavaScript creates the variable as a string.

A string can also include quotes. You can use single and double quotes interchangeably if you need to include a quote within a quoted string. All you have to do is be consistent—if the string contains a single quote, use double quotes around the string; the same is true with the double quote. For example:

```
var string_value = "This is a 'string' with a quote."
```

or:

```
var string_value = 'This is a "string" with a quote.'
```

The empty string is a special case: you'd commonly use it to initialize a string variable when it's defined. The following are examples of empty strings:

```
var string_value = '';
var anotherStringValue = "";
```

Which quote character you use makes no difference to the JavaScript engine. What's more important is to use one or the other consistently in your applications.

String Escape Sequences

Not all characters are treated equally within a string in JavaScript. A string can also contain an *escape sequence*, such as \n for the end-of-line terminator. An escape sequence is a pattern in which certain characters are encoded in certain ways in order to include them within a string.

The following snippet of code assigns a string literal containing a line-terminator escape sequence to a variable. When the string is used in a dialog window, the escape sequence, \n, is interpreted literally, and a newline is published:

```
var string_value = "This is the first line\nThis is the second line";
```

This results in:

```
This is the first line
This is the second line
```

You can also use the backslash to denote that the quote in the string is meant to be taken as a literal character, not as an end-of-string terminator:

```
var string_value = "This is a \"string\" with a quote."
```

By using the backslash with quotes, you can include single and double quotes within a string.

To include a backslash in a string, use two backslashes in a row:

```
var string_value = "This is a \\string\\ with a backslash."
```

The result of this line of code is a string with two backslashes, one on each side of the word "string".

You can also include Unicode characters in a string by preceding the four-digit hexadecimal value of the character with \u. For instance, the following outputs the Chinese (simplified) ideogram for "love":

```
document.writeln("\u7231");
```

What displays is somewhat browser-dependent; however, most of the more commonly used browsers now have adequate Unicode support.

You can learn more about Unicode, and access relevant charts, at *http: //www.unicode.org/*.

String Encoding

Using the backslash to escape characters is helpful when you're using ASCII characters that are normally control characters within a string. However, the backslash can't do anything with characters that are not ASCII; nor can it do anything if you want to make an entire string safe for HTML processing, which is necessary for Ajax-based applications (I'll touch on this at the end of the book).

You use the `encodeURI` and `encodeURIComponent` methods to escape, or more properly, to *encode* entire strings, converting ASCII and non-ASCII characters to URI encoding, which you can use in links and Ajax applications.

 URI stands for Uniform Resource Identifier, an example of which is a web page URL. An example of URI encoding is ISO Latin-1 (also known as ISO 8859-1).

The `encodeURI` makes an assumption that the string is a URI such as "*http://oreilly .com*", and reserves the following characters:

```
 ; , / ? : @ & = + $
```

Alphanumeric characters and the following punctuation are also not encoded:

```
 - _ . ! ~ * ' ( )
```

The page fragment symbol (#) is also not encoded.

The `encodeURIComponent`, however, encodes all characters except the alphanumeric and punctuation characters listed earlier. It assumes that the string being encoded is being used as a parameter to a URI, and therefore characters that are normally part of a URI, such as the following, are encoded:

```
 # & + =
```

Both functions also have their opposite member: `decodeURI`, to decode the `encodeURI` encoded string, and `decodeURIComponent`, to decode the `encodeURIComponent` string.

Example 2-1 shows a web page that uses all four functions to encode and then decode two strings, all of which are then printed out to the current web page using `document.writeln`.

Example 2-1. URI encoding two strings using the JavaScript encodeURI and encodeURIComponent methods

```
<!DOCTYPE html PUBLIC "-//W3C//DTD XHTML 1.1//EN"
"http://www.w3.org/TR/xhtml11/DTD/xhtml11.dtd">
<html xmlns="http://www.w3.org/1999/xhtml" xml:lang="en">
<head>
<title>URI Encoding</title>
<meta http-equiv="Content-Type" content="text/html; charset=utf-8" />
<script type="text/javascript">
//<![CDATA[

function encodeStrings() {
    var sOne =
encodeURIComponent("http://burningbird.net/index.php?pagename=$1&page=$2");
    var sTwo = encodeURI("http://someapplication.com/?catsname=Zöe&URL=");
    var sOutput = "<p>Link is " + sTwo + sOne + "</p>";
    document.write(sOutput);

    var sOneDecoded = decodeURI(sTwo);
    var sTwoDecoded = decodeURIComponent(sOne);

    var sOutputDecoded = "<p>" + sOneDecoded + "</p><p>" + sTwoDecoded + "</p>";
    document.write(sOutputDecoded);

}
//]]>
</script>
</head>
<body onload="encodeStrings()">
   <p></p>
</body>
</html>
```

Figure 2-1 shows the resultant page.

Figure 2-1. Result of encoding/decoding URI application

These are all demonstrations of how to explicitly create a string variable, and variations of string literals that incorporate special characters. You can also convert the values within a specific variable from other data types, depending on the context.

Converting to Strings

You can convert other data types, such as numbers and booleans, to a string; typically, the scripting engine will do the conversion automatically, based on the context. As an example, if a numeric or boolean variable is passed to a function that expects a string, the value is implicitly converted to a string first, before the value is processed:

```
var num_value = 35.00;
alert(num_value); // expects a string
```

In addition, when the plus sign (+) is used with two variables in an assignment statement, and one value is a string and the other a number, the number is converted to a string and then the two strings are concatenated:

```
var num_value = 35.00;
var string_value = "This is a number:" + num_value;
```

When the conversion from number to string occurs depends on when the JavaScript scripting engine encounters the string. For instance, if the string is the first in a sequence of values, all of the numbers that follow are treated as strings:

```
var strValue = "4" + 3 + 1; // becomes "431"
var strValueTwo = 4 + 3 + "1"; // becomes 71
```

However, if you use operators other than +, the opposite type of conversion is applied— the string is converted to a number:

```
var firstResult = "35" - 3; // subtraction is applied, resulting in 32
var secondResult = 30 / "3"; // division is applied, resulting in 10
var thirdResult = "3" * 3; // multiplication is applied, resulting in 9
```

This implicit conversion with its dependency on both operator and position demonstrates more fully the danger of loose typing: the values you end up with can vary widely, depending on something as simple as where in the sequence of operations you introduce a new data type, or what type of operator you use.

 I cover the addition and other operators demonstrated in this chapter, as well as others available in JavaScript, more fully in Chapter 3.

Rather than depend fully on happenstance data type conversion, you can explicitly convert a variable to a string using the **String** global function. If the value being converted is a boolean, the resultant string is a text representation of the boolean value: **"true"** for true; **"false"** for false. For numbers, the string is, again, a string representation of the number, such as **"-123.06"** for −123.06, depending on the number of digits and the precision (the placement of the decimal point). A value of NaN (Not a Number, discussed later) returns "NaN", whereas undefined or null variables will return "undefined" or "null", respectively.

Table 2-4 shows the results of using toString on different data types.

Table 2-4. toString conversion table

Input	Result
Undefined	"undefined"
Null	"null"
Boolean	If true, then "true"; if false, then "false"
Number	The string representation of the number, or NaN if the variable holds this latter value
String	No conversion
Object	A string representation of the default representation of the object

The last item in the table describes the ECMAScript rule for the result of toString with an object. The representation is:

```
"[object "+className+"]"
```

Example 2-2 shows explicit string conversion on several different variables and objects. New number and boolean variables are created and initialized to data-type-specific values and then both are converted explicitly to strings using String. The example applies the same conversion to a variable that's created without an initial value, and one initialized to null. Lastly, it passes the document object to String and the resultant string is also printed out to the page.

Example 2-2. Explicit and implicit string conversions

```
<!DOCTYPE html PUBLIC "-//W3C//DTD XHTML 1.1//EN"
"http://www.w3.org/TR/xhtml11/DTD/xhtml11.dtd">
<html xmlns="http://www.w3.org/1999/xhtml" xml:lang="en">
<head>
<title>Implicit and Explicit String Conversion</title>
<meta http-equiv="Content-Type" content="text/html; charset=utf-8" />
<script type="text/javascript">
//<![CDATA[

function convertToString() {
   var newNumber = 34.56;
   var newBoolean = true;
   var nothing;
   var newNull = null;

   var strNumber = String(newNumber); var strBoolean = String(newBoolean);
   var strUndefined = String(nothing); var strNull = String(newNull);

   var strOutput = "<p>" + strNumber + " " + strBoolean + " " + strUndefined + " "
+ strNull + "</p>";
```

```
    document.writeln(strOutput);

    var strOutput2 = String(document);
    document.writeln(strOutput2);

}
//]]>
</script>
</head>
<body onload="convertToString()">
    <p></p>
</body>
</html>
```

The output of this application varies among browsers. Firefox, Opera, IE, and Safari all output the first string in the same way:

```
34.56 true undefined null
```

However, only Opera and Firefox output the ECMAScript-specific object representation for document:

```
[object HTMLDocument]
```

IE outputs just [object] and Safari/WebKit doesn't output anything at all when using String with document.

The Boolean Data Type

The boolean data type has two possible values: true and false. They are not surrounded by quotes; in other words, "false" is not the same as false.

```
    var isMarried = true;
    var hasChildren = false;
```

An implicit boolean value is assigned to variables of different types, and it depends on whether the variable is set and, if it is set, what value it has. For instance, the following conditional block will be processed if the variable, testVariable, implicitly converts to a boolean true value; it will not be processed if it is implicitly converted to a boolean false:

```
    if (testVariable) {
        ...
    }
```

We'll see later how to use boolean values to manage the flow of control for an application, but for now, Table 2-5 shows how variables of different types would implicitly and explicitly convert to a boolean. I say "explicitly" because like the string data type, you can convert different data types into a boolean value explicitly using the Boolean function:

```
    var someValue = 0;
    var someBool = Boolean(someValue) // evaluates to false
```

Table 2-5. toBoolean conversion table

Input	Result
Undefined	false
Null	false
Boolean	Value of value
Number	Value of false if number is 0 or NaN; otherwise, true
String	Value of false if string is empty; otherwise, true
Object	true

You can also use *double negation* (the negation operator, !, used twice) to explicitly convert a number or string to a boolean:

```
var strValue = "1";
var numValue = 0;
var boolValue = !!strValue; // converts "1" to a true
boolValue = !!numValue; // converts 0 to false
```

The Number Data Type

Number data types in JavaScript are floating-point numbers, but they may or may not have a fractional component. If they don't have a decimal point or fractional component, they're treated as integers—base-10 whole numbers in a range of -2^{53} to 2^{53}.

The following are valid integers:

```
var negativeNumber = -1000;
var zero = 0;
var fourDigits = 2534;
```

The floating-point representation has a decimal, with a decimal component to the right. You also can represent the number as an exponent, using scientific notation. All of the following are valid floating-point numbers:

```
var someFloat = 0.3555
var anotherNumber = 144.006;
var negDecimal = -2.3;
var lastNum = 19.5e-2 //which is equivalent to .195
var zeroDecimal = 12.0;
```

Though larger numbers are supported, some functions can work only with numbers in a range of $-2e31$ to $2e31$ ($-2,147,483,648$ to $2,147,483,648$); as such, you should limit your number use to this range.

Two special numbers exist: positive and negative infinity. In JavaScript, they are represented by Infinity and -Infinity, respectively. A positive infinity is returned whenever a math overflow occurs in a JavaScript application. A negative infinity is returned when a number occurs that is smaller than the minimum value supported in JavaScript.

In addition to base-10 representation, you can use octal and hexadecimal notation with JavaScript numbers, though octal is newer and may be confused for hexadecimal with older browsers. A hexadecimal number begins with a zero, followed by an x:

```
var firstHex = -0xCCFF;
```

An octal value begins with a zero, but there is no leading x:

```
var firstOct = 0526;
```

What's interesting with both the octal and decimal representations is that if you convert either to a string using the String function (covered earlier), the scripting engine first converts the number to its base-10 (decimal) representation and then converts the result to a string. So, a string conversion of firstOct is "342", which is the string conversion of the decimal conversion of the octal number 0526.

In the preceding two sections, I demonstrated how to convert other types to a string or a boolean. In this section, I'm going to demonstrate two different functions you can use to convert a string to a number: parseInt and parseFloat. The parseInt function returns the integer portion of a number in a string, regardless of whether the string is formatted as an integer or as a floating-point number. The parseFloat function returns the floating-point value until a character that is not a sign (+ or -), decimal, number, or exponent is reached.

Example 2-3 passes three strings containing numeric values to either parseInt or parseFloat, and writes the values to the page.

Example 2-3. Converting strings to numbers using either parseInt or parseFloat

```
<!DOCTYPE html PUBLIC "-//W3C//DTD XHTML 1.1//EN"
"http://www.w3.org/TR/xhtml11/DTD/xhtml11.dtd">
<html xmlns="http://www.w3.org/1999/xhtml" xml:lang="en">
<head>
<title>Convert to Number</title>
<meta http-equiv="Content-Type" content="text/html; charset=utf-8" />
<script type="text/javascript">
//<![CDATA[

function convertToNumber() {
    var sNum = "1.23e-2";
    document.writeln("<p>" + parseFloat(sNum) + "</p>");
    document.writeln("<p>" + parseInt(sNum) + "</p>");

    var fValue = parseFloat("1.45 inch");
    document.writeln("<p>" + fValue + "</p>");

    var iValue = parseInt("-33.50");
    document.writeln("<p>" + iValue + "</p>");

}
//]]>
</script>
</head>
```

```
<body onload="convertToNumber()">
  <p></p>
</body>
</html>
```

The following is the output of the page using Firefox, Safari/WebKit, Opera, and IE8:

```
0.0123
1
1.45
-33
```

Notice with the resultant first value that the number is printed in decimal notation rather than the exponential notation of the original string value. The second printed value, which is the first string converted using parseInt, is truncated right at the decimal and before the exponent was applied to the number. Also, note that parseInt truncates the fractional component of the number in the fourth conversion result.

The third number conversion is the really interesting conversion. The parseFloat function grabbed the number from the string, "1.45 inch", up to the first nonnumber-specific value—in this case, the space between "1.45" and "inch". The function then converted the string "1.45" to the float, which was printed.

 Of course, the numbers shown in Example 2-3 are then converted back into a string for writing out to the page.

The parseInt function can convert a decimal to an octal or a hexadecimal and back again. A second parameter to the function, base, is equivalent to the number *radix*, and is 10 or base 10, by default. If any other base is specified in a range from 2 to 36, the string is interpreted accordingly. The following JavaScript:

```
var iValue = parseInt("266",16);
document.writeln("<p>" + iValue + "</p>");

var iValue = parseInt("55",8);
document.writeln("<p>" + iValue + "</p>");
```

results in the two converted values being printed to the page:

```
550

45
```

In addition to parseInt and parseFloat, the Number function also converts other data types to numbers. The type returned after conversion is dependent on the representation: floating-point strings return floating-point numbers; integer strings return integers. Table 2-6 shows the conversion to numbers from each type.

Table 2-6. Conversion from other data types to numbers

Input	Result
Undefined	NaN
Null	0 (note that IE returns NaN)
Boolean	If true, the result is 1; otherwise, 0 (note that IE returns NaN)
Number	Straight value
String	Integer or float, depending on representation
Object	NaN

In addition to converting strings to numbers, you can also test the value of a variable to see whether it's infinity through the `IsFinite` function. If the value is infinity or NaN, the function returns `false`; otherwise, it returns `true`.

Other functions work on numbers, but they're associated with the `Number` object, discussed in Chapter 4. For now, we'll continue to look at the primitive types with two special JavaScript types: `null` and `undefined`.

The null and undefined Variables

Nowhere in JavaScript is the line between literals, simple data types, and objects blurred more than it is when you're looking at two variables that represent nonexistence or incomplete existence: `null` and `undefined`.

A `null` variable is one that you have defined and to which you have assigned *null* as its value. The following is an example of a `null` variable:

```
var nullString = null;
```

If you have declared but not initialized the variable, it is considered undefined:

```
var undefString;
```

A variable is not null and is not undefined when you declare it and give it an initial value:

```
var sValue = "";
```

When you're using several JavaScript libraries and fairly complex code it's not unusual for a variable not to be set; if you try to use the variable in an expression, you can get an adverse result—usually a JavaScript error. One approach to testing variables if you're unsure of their state is to use the variable in a conditional test, such as the following:

```
if (sValue) ... // if not null and initialized, true; otherwise false
```

We'll look at conditional statements in Chapter 3, but for now, know that the expression consisting of just the variable `sValue` evaluates to `true` if `sValue` has been declared and initialized; otherwise, the result of the expression is `false`:

```
if (unknownVariable)// false, variable is not declared or assigned a value
```

```
if (undefinedString) // false, as variable has not been given a value

if (nullString) // variable has been defined and given a value, but that value is
null and so the result is false

if (sValue) // true if a variable is both defined and given a value (including
empty string)
```

Using the `null` keyword, you can specifically test to see whether a value is null:

```
if (sValue == null)
```

In JavaScript, a variable is undefined, even if it is declared, until it is initialized. A variable can be undeclared but initialized, in which case it is not null and is not undefined. However, in this instance, it's considered a global variable, and as discussed earlier, not specifically declaring variables with **var** causes problems more often than not.

 In some of the code snippets, comments that begin with // wrap to the next line because of the page width, not because the comments are actually multiple lines.

Though not related to existence, a third unique value is related to the type of a variable: NaN, or Not a Number. If a string or boolean variable cannot be coerced into a number, it's considered NaN and is treated accordingly:

```
var nValue = 1.0;
if (nValue == 'one' ) // false, the second operand is NaN
```

You can specifically test whether a variable is NaN with the `isNaN` function:

```
if (isNaN(sValue)) // if string cannot be implicitly converted into number, return
true
```

By its very nature, a null value is NaN.

 Author and respected technologist Simon Willison gave an excellent talk at O'Reilly's 2006 ETech conference, titled "A (Re)-Introduction to JavaScript." You can view his slides at his website, *http://simon.incutio .com/slides/2006/etech/javascript/js-tutorial.001.html*. The whole presentation is a very worthwhile read, but my favorite is the following line:

"In other words, zero, null, NaN, and the empty string are inherently false; everything else is inherently true."

For the most part, JavaScript developers create code in such a way that we know a variable is going to be defined ahead of time and/or given a value. In most instances, we don't explicitly test to see whether a variable is set, and if so, whether it's assigned a value.

However, when using large and complex JavaScript libraries, and applications that can incorporate web service responses, it becomes increasingly important to test variables that originate and/or are set outside our control. It is also increasingly important to be aware of how null and undefined variables behave when accessed in the application.

Constants: Named but Not Variables

Sometimes you'll want to define a value once, and then have it treated as a read-only value from that time forward. You use the keyword `const` to create a JavaScript constant:

```
const CURRENT_MONTH = 3.5;
```

The constant can be of any value, and because it can't be assigned or reassigned a value at a later time, it's initialized to its constant value when defined.

Just as with variables, a JavaScript constant has global and local scope. I use constants at a global level, primarily because they contain a value I want to be accessible (and unchanged) by a JavaScript block. Also, notice how the entire constant name is in uppercase. This isn't required, but it is a fairly standard naming convention, making constants easier to spot in code.

Test Your Knowledge: Quiz

1. Of the following identifiers, which are valid, which are not, and why?

   ```
   $someVariable
   _someVariable
   1Variable
   some_variable
   somëvariable
   function
   some*variable
   ```

2. Convert the following identifiers to CamelCase notation:

   ```
   var some_month;
   function theMonth // function to return current month
   current-month // a constant
   var summer_month; // an array of summer months
   MyLibrary-afunction // a function from a JavaScript package
   ```

3. Is the following string literal valid? If not, how would you fix it?

   ```
   var someString = 'Who once said, "Only two things are infinite, the universe and
   human stupidity, and I'm not sure about the former."'
   ```

4. Given a number, 432.54, what JavaScript function(s) returns the integer component of the number, and then finds the hexadecimal and octal conversions?

5. You're creating a JavaScript function in a library that other applications can use. A parameter, `someMonth`, is passed to the function. How would you determine whether it's null or undefined?

Test Your Knowledge: Answers

1. The following are valid:

   ```
   $someVariable
   _someVariable
   some_variable
   somëvariable
   ```

   The following are not valid:

   ```
   1Variable does not start with a valid character
   function is a reserved word
   some*variable uses an invalid character
   ```

2. The identifiers are converted as follows:

   ```
   var someMonth
   function getCurrentMonth
   CURRENT_MONTH
   summerMonths
   myLibraryFunction
   ```

3. The string is not valid. To make it valid, either use single quotes only within the double quote, or escape the double quotes:

   ```
   var someString = "Who once said, 'Only two things are infinite, the universe and
   human stupidity, and I'm not sure about the former'";
   ```

   or:

   ```
   var someString = 'Who once said, "Only two things are infinite, the universe and
   human stupidity, and I\'m not sure about the former"';
   ```

   Don't forget to escape the apostrophes in contractions.

4. The following code would work:

   ```
   var fltNumber = 432.54;
   var intNumber = parseInt(fltNumber);
   var octNumber = intNumber.toString(8);
   var hexNumber = intNumber.toString(16);
   ```

5. This is a trick question. Passing a variable that's not declared or defined to a function or object method results in a JavaScript error, so your function will not have to test the parameter.

   Use the following to test to see whether a variable has been set elsewhere in code:

   ```
   if (a) {
       ...
   }
   ```

CHAPTER 3

Operators and Statements

The examples I've shown you so far in the book have performed mostly simple tasks: we've defined a variable and set its value, printed a value in the page or in an alert box, and modified a variable through addition or multiplication or some other means. All of these examples use JavaScript statements and operators.

JavaScript features a number of different statement types: assignment, function call, conditional, and loop. Each is fairly intuitive, simple to use, and quick to learn. However, in JavaScript, as in other programming languages, although the statements are easy to learn, lining them up one after the other so that they do something useful can be tricky.

The Format of a JavaScript Statement

JavaScript statements usually end with a semicolon, but as I mentioned in earlier chapters, a semicolon is not required. If the application that processes the JavaScript determines that a statement is complete (by whatever criteria exist for each type of statement) and the line ends with a line break, you can omit the semicolon:

```
var bValue = true
var sValue = "this is also true"
```

If multiple statements appear on the same line, though, you must use the semicolon to terminate each one:

```
var bValue = true; var sValue = "this is also true"
```

However, not explicitly terminating each JavaScript statement is a bad habit to get into, and one that can result in unexpected consequences. For instance, if you use a tool to compress the whitespace in your JavaScript code, that tool can have problems with statements that are not explicitly terminated.

The use of whitespace in JavaScript has little impact on the processing of the code, though it can impact both the readability of the code and the size of the JavaScript file. For instance, the following two lines of code are interpreted in exactly the same way:

```
var firstName = 'Shelley'     ;
var firstName = 'Shelley';
```

Other than to separate words within quotes or to terminate statements, extra white-space—such as tabs, spaces, and newlines—is disregarded. In the following code, the variable assignment completes successfully, even though line breaks separate the statement:

```
var
firstName
= 'Shelley';
```

The line break isn't considered a statement terminator in this instance because JavaScript assignments require a variable name on the left, an assignment operator (=), and a value on the right. The processing application continues to process the Java-Script until either the semicolon is reached or the statement is completed.

The following code is also successful, because when a new variable is not assigned a value immediately, it is assigned a value of "undefined." The new variable assignment then triggers the processing application to finish processing the previous statement:

```
var firstName
var lastName;
```

In the following code, though, an error results because the JavaScript processing application recognizes that the **var** keyword begins a new statement, yet the previous statement is not complete:

```
var firstName =
var lastName = 'Powers';
```

Returning to the discussion of whitespace, I've used indentation throughout the book to make the examples more readable, but there's no functional reason to indent a line with a tab or spaces. The same holds true for whitespace surrounding operators such as the assignment operator (=) or one of the math operators (such as +). Whitespace isn't necessary. Whitespace and comments, as well as meaningful identifiers, are there to make the code easier to maintain.

Minify Your JavaScript

Whitespace helps an application's readability, but it also adds to the file size. Normally, this isn't a problem as most of our JavaScript files are relatively small. However, with some larger Ajax applications and more complex JavaScript libraries, the JavaScript can actually be quite large.

To compress a JavaScript file to the smallest it can be, you can *minify* the file using any number of freely available tools. Some tools, such as Dean Edwards' Packer (at *http://dean.edwards.name/packer/*), will minify your code online. Other tools, many which are listed in the Wikipedia entry for "minify" (at *http://en.wikipedia.org/wiki/Minify*), are libraries you'll need to install, either on your desktop or on your server.

Another use for tools such as these is to add a layer of copy protection to your JavaScript. The tools will not only strip out the extraneous whitespace, but also use a coded encryption to make the code more difficult to read.

The Assignment Statement

The most common JavaScript statement is the assignment statement. It's an expression consisting of a variable on the left side, an assignment operator (=), and whatever is being assigned on the right.

The expression on the right can be a literal value:

```
nValue = 35.00;
```

Or, it can be variables and literals combined with any number of operators:

```
nValue = nValue + 35.00;
```

The right side of the statement can also be a function call:

```
nValue = someFunction();
```

You can include more than one assignment on a line, as long as you separate the statements with a semicolon:

```
var firstName = 'Shelley'; var lastName = 'Powers';
```

You can also assign the same value to several variables at once:

```
var firstName = lastName = middleName = "";
```

However, with the following, where variables are lined up with commas between them, the first variable is set and the second ends up undefined:

```
var nValue1,nValue2 = 3; // nValue2 is undefined
```

You can concatenate assignments with commas, however:

```
var nValue1=3, nValue2=4, nValue3=5;
```

For readability and to ensure that no bugs creep in, I recommend that you separate your assignments with semicolons.

The Arithmetic Operators

You can use arithmetic operators to compute a value that is then assigned to a variable or is passed as a parameter to a function or method. An example of such an operation is the following, where two variables are added and are assigned a third:

```
var theResult = varValue1 + varValue2;
```

This operation is an example of a binary arithmetic expression, where two *operands* are separated by an arithmetic operator, leading to a new result. More complex examples can use any number of arithmetic operators, with any combination of literal values and variables:

```
nValue = nValue + 30.00 /  2 - nValue2 * 3;
```

An operand is nothing more than some value on which the mathematical operation is performed.

The operators used in the expression come from the following set, which is probably familiar to you from math classes and online calculators:

+

For addition

-

For subtraction

*

For multiplication

/

For division

%

To return the remainder after division

These are considered *binary* operators because they require two operands: one on each side of the operator. You can combine any number of these binary operators into one statement, and assign the result to a variable or pass it as a function parameter:

```
bigCalc = varA * 6.0 + 3.45 - varB / .05;
```

The examples I've shown you so far in this section show the binary operators working with numbers. How about if the values are strings?

In Chapter 2, I *concatenated* (joined) strings together using the plus sign (+), just as though I were adding two numbers together:

```
var newString = "This is an old " + oldString;
```

When you use + with a number, it functions as the addition operator. However, when you use it with a string, it functions as the concatenation operator. With all other binary operators, you can use a string as an operand, but the string has to contain a properly formatted number because, as we discussed in Chapter 2, the value is converted to a number before the expression is evaluated:

```
var newValue = 3.5 * 2.0; // result is 7
var newValue = 3.5 * "2.0"; // result is still 7
var newValue = "3.5" * "2.0"; // still 7
```

On the other hand (and it's important to be aware of the distinction), if you add a number literal or variable and a string, the number is the value that's converted from

---

number to string. In the following example, you might expect to get a value of 5.5, but instead you get a new string, "3.52.0":

```
var newValue = 3.5 + "2.0"; // result is a string, "3.52.0"
```

This one can trip you up quite frequently. Be careful when mixing types with implicit conversion; a simple accident in any of the values could lead to surprising results.

 Use caution when mixing number and string variables or you'll get un-expected results. In Chapter 4, I'll cover safer methods of data conversion.

The Unary Operators

In addition to the binary arithmetic operators we just covered, there are three *unary* operators. These differ from the binary operators in that they apply to only one operand:

++

Increments a value

--

Decrements a value

-

Represents a negative value

The following are examples of unary operators in action:

```
someValue = 34;
var iValue = -someValue;
iValue++;
document.writeln(iValue); // prints out -33
```

In the second line, the number is converted to a negative value through the use of the *negative* unary operator. The value is incremented by one using the double-plus sign, ++, which is a shorthand version of adding a value of 1 to a variable and then reassigning that value back to the same variable:

```
iValue=iValue + 1;
```

This operator is called the *increment* operator. The *decrement* operator is similar, except that 1 is subtracted from the value, not added.

The increment and decrement operators have another interesting aspect to them. In an expression, if the operator is *pre-increment* or listed first, the value is adjusted before the result is assigned. However, if the operator is *post-increment* or listed after the variable, the initial value in the variable is assigned first, and then the variable's value is adjusted:

```
var iValue = 3.0;

var iValue2 = ++iValue; //iValue is set to 4.0, and iValue2  is set
to the pre-incremented iValue and also is 4.0
```

```
var iValue3 = iValue++; //iValue3 is set to 4.0; iValue now has a
value of 5.0
```

Operator Precedence

Operators in JavaScript have precedence, which means that JavaScript processes some expressions containing some operators before others. In statements, expressions are evaluated left to right when all operators have the same precedence. If you use more than one type of operator with more than one type of precedence in a statement, the rule is that the operator with higher precedence is processed first, from left to right, and then the rest of the expression is processed.

Among the arithmetic operators, division, multiplication, and the remainder operators have precedence over the subtraction and addition operators. Let's consider the following code:

```
newValue = nValue + 30.00 /  2 - nValue2 * 3;
```

If the value of nValue is 3 and the value of nValue2 is 6, the result is 0. Breaking the statement down further, the division of 30.00 by 2 (resulting in 15) is processed first because division has higher precedence than addition. The multiplication operator has the same precedence as that of division, but it occurs to the right of the division. Because expressions are evaluated left to right when the precedence of the operators is the same, the leftmost division is done first.

The multiplication is performed next, and the value in the nValue2 variable is multiplied by 3, resulting in a value of 18. From that point on, the expression consists solely of addition and subtraction (equal precedence), and is evaluated left to right as:

```
newValue = nValue + 15 - 18;
```

The assignment operator has the lowest precedence, and once the arithmetic expression is evaluated completely, the result is assigned to newValue.

To control the impact of precedence, use parentheses around expressions you want processed first. Returning to the example, the use of parentheses can lead to widely different results:

```
newValue = ((nValue + 30.00) / (2 - nValue2)) * 3;
```

Now, the addition and subtraction within the parentheses are evaluated first, before division and multiplication. The result of this expression is –24.75.

You all knew this from your basic math classes. However, it doesn't hurt to get a little reaffirmation that although it's in JavaScript, the rules are the same.

In JavaScript, unlike in other languages, division results in a floating-point result, not a truncated whole number. The following results in a value of 1.5 rather than a rounded value of 1:

```
iValue = 3 / 2;
```

There is a shortcut method to these expressions, which we'll look at next.

A Handy Shortcut: Assignment with Operation

You can combine assignment and an arithmetic operation into one simple statement if the same variable appears on both sides of the operator, such as in the following:

```
nValue = nValue + 3.0;
```

The simplified statement is:

```
nValue += 3.0;
```

You can use all of the binary arithmetic operators in this type of shorthand technique, known as an *assignment with operation*:

```
nValue %= 3;
nValue -= 3;
nValue *= 4;
nvalue += 5;
nvalue /= 2;
```

You also can use the assignment with operation shortcut in combination with the four bitwise operators, which I'll briefly discuss in the next section.

The Bitwise Operators

This section covers JavaScript bitwise operators, and assumes that you have some experience with Boolean algebra. This functionality is not used extensively in Java-Script, and you can safely skip it during this first introduction to the language.

If you're not familiar with Boolean algebra and want to continue with this section, an excellent Boolean algebra reference, put together by the British Broadcasting Corporation (BBC), is available at *http://www.bbc .co.uk/dna/h2g2/A412642*.

Bitwise operators treat operands as 32-bit values made up of a sequence of zeros and ones. The operators then perform, literally, a bitwise manipulation of the result; the type of manipulation depends on the type of operator:

&

Bitwise AND operation, in which the resultant bit is 1 if and only if both values are 1.

|

Bitwise OR operation on bits, in which the result is 1 if and only if one of the operand bits is 1.

^

Bitwise XOR operation on bits, in which the combination of the two operand bits equals 1 if and only if both values are different. If the value of both is 1 or 0, the result is 0; otherwise, the result is 1.

~

Bitwise NOT operation on a bit, which returns the inverted value (complement) of the bit (i.e., 1 results in 0; 0 results in 1).

It might seem as though the bitwise operators don't have much use in JavaScript, except that they're a handy way of creating binary *flags* within a program. Binary flags are similar to variables except that they use much less memory (by a factor of 32). The Mozilla Core JavaScript 1.5 reference provides an example that uses binary flags (at *http://developer.mozilla.org/en/docs/Core_JavaScript_1.5_Reference/Operators/Bitwise _Operators*). In the example, the following variable represents four flags:

```
var flags = 0x5;
```

This is equivalent to the binary value of 0101 (disregarding leading zeros):

```
flag A: false
flag B: true
flag C: false
flag D: true
```

Each bit mask flag is then represented as follows:

```
var flag_A = 0x1; // 0001
var flag_B = 0x2; // 0010
var flag_C = 0x4; // 0100
var flag_D = 0x8; // 1000
```

To test whether flag_C is set in our flags variable, use the bitwise AND operator:

```
if (flags & flag_C) { // 0101 & 0100 => 0100 => true
    do stuff
}
```

You can use binary flags to conserve memory in your application. However, as even this small code example demonstrates, use of binary flags does compromise the code's readability, without providing any real gain in performance. Unless memory use is absolutely critical to your application, you may want to forgo the use of binary flags.

The Mozilla reference provides more information regarding the use of bitwise operators as a test of input; it's an interesting technique and an affirmation that although

JavaScript handles memory management behind the scenes, you can use tricks and techniques to get an edge when you need one.

Three additional bitwise operators are available: shift left (<<), shift right with sign (>>), and shift right with zero fill (>>>). These move the bits of the operand to the right or left by the number of places designated by the second operand (a value between 0 and 31):

```
newValue = oldValue >>> 3;
```

The statements we've covered to this point are simple assignment statements. We'll cover more complex control statements in the next few sections.

Conditional Statements and Program Flow

Normally in JavaScript, the program flow is linear: each statement is processed in turn, one right after another. It takes deliberate action to change this. You can put the code in a function that is only called based on some action or event. An alternative is to use some form of conditional test in which a block of code is processed only if the test results are true.

One of the more common approaches to changing the program flow in JavaScript is through just such a *conditional statement*. The typical conditional statement has the following format:

```
if (result of test is true) {
statements processed
}
```

The term *conditional* comes from the fact that a condition has to be met before the block associated with the statement is processed. The example equates to the statement "if some value (whether a result of an expression, a variable, or a literal) evaluates to true, process the following code; otherwise, jump to the end of the block and continue processing at the very next line."

The use of the if keyword signals the beginning of the conditional test, and the parenthetical expression encapsulates the test. The following code tests the tstValue variable to see whether it is equal to 3. If so, and only if so, it processes the code contained in curly braces following the conditional expression:

```
if (tstValue === 3) {
    alert("value is 3");
}
```

The use of curly braces isn't necessary in this example because only one line of JavaScript is processed if the condition evaluates to true. If more than one JavaScript statement needs to be processed, though, you must place all of the code within curly braces. These are commonly referred to as *JavaScript blocks* or *blocks of code*, and the curly braces let the processing application know that all of the JavaScript contained in the block is processed if the condition evaluates to true.

Because it's not unheard of that additional code is added at a later time, it's a good practice to use curly braces around a block of code processed through some flow-of-control event (such as a conditional statement), even if the block consists of only one line of code.

To make the JavaScript more readable, it's also considered good form to indent the code that's contained within the curly braces. If the contained code has another conditional statement, the statements associated with it are indented the same amount, but from the original position, and so on.

Example 3-1 demonstrates three nested conditional statements—each with a block of code, each indented. Each conditional statement tests a different variable. You can change the variable's initial value to test the different conditional expressions.

Example 3-1. Three nested conditional statements, indented for easier reading

```
<!DOCTYPE html PUBLIC "-//W3C//DTD XHTML 1.1//EN"
"http://www.w3.org/TR/xhtml11/DTD/xhtml11.dtd">
<html xmlns="http://www.w3.org/1999/xhtml" xml:lang="en">
<head>
<title>Nested Conditional Statements</title>
<meta http-equiv="Content-Type" content="text/html; charset=utf-8" />
<script type="text/javascript">
//<![CDATA[

function choices() {
   var prefChoice = 1;
   var stateChoice = 'OR';
   var genderChoice = 'F';

   if (prefChoice === 1) {
      alert("You've picked option 1. Here is what will happen...");

      if (stateChoice === 'OR') {
         alert ("You've picked 1 and you're from Oregon.");

         if (genderChoice === 'M') {
            alert("You've picked 1 and you're from Oregon and you're a man.");

         } // innermost block

      } // middle block

   } // outerblock
}

//]]>
</script>
</head>
<body onload="choices()">
<p>Imagine a form with five fields and a button here...</p>
</body>
</html>
```

Typically, JavaScript developers indent code by four spaces with each block, and line up the curly braces with the conditional statement. In addition, tabs can also be used to shorten the code length, though when using a *minify* tool to decrease the size of the JavaScript file, the use of tabs or spaces becomes moot. I use three spaces in the examples primarily because of space restrictions on the printed page (and it's an old habit I picked up when coding C years ago). There's no real rule about what to use for indentation, though, other than to try to be consistent in what you use.

 In addition, the closing curly bracket on each block is annotated with a comment. If the code is fairly long, complex, and full of nested blocks such as those in Example 3-1, using comments to document the ending curly bracket makes the code easier to read and maintain.

Example 3-1 also uses a conditional operator, the equality operator, to test the variable against a literal value. We'll cover this and other conditional operators later in the book. First, we'll take a look at a couple of other types of conditional statements.

The if...else Conditional Statement

In many applications, a conditional test is performed, a block of one or more statements is processed, and the flow of the program continues following the code block. However, not all logic can be expressed with just one test. Even within a spoken language, such as English, we have the concept of *if...then...else* to accommodate the listing of various options:

```
If the sun is out, we'll go to the park; otherwise, we'll go to the movies.
```

In JavaScript, the use of the keyword `else` performs the same functionality. It provides for processing an alternative set of statements if the condition being tested returns `false`:

```
if (expression) {
   ...
} else {
   ...
}
```

In the following code snippet, if the value in `stateCode` is MA for Massachusetts, the code sets the tax value to 3.5; otherwise, it sets the tax value to 4.5:

```
if (stateCode === 'MA') {
   taxPercentage = 3.5;
} else {
   taxPercentage = 4.5;
}
```

The state code is either MA or it isn't; the tax percentage is set regardless.

However, not all conditions are either/or. Some instances might have more than one possible conditional outcome of interest, and you'll need to capture a sequence of tests: if then...else if then...else if then... and so on. You can manage this in JavaScript by adding a conditional expression immediately following the else clause:

```
if (conditional expression) {
   block of code
} else if (other conditional expression) {
   block of code
}
```

You can chain these, one after the other, until all conditions have been tested.

In Example 3-2, the variable holding the state code is set in the code (purely for testing purposes—normally you don't know what the variable is). The example tests the three state codes and assigns a different tax percentage if any of the three matches.

Example 3-2. Testing a value with multiple conditional statements

```
<!DOCTYPE html PUBLIC "-//W3C//DTD XHTML 1.1//EN"
"http://www.w3.org/TR/xhtml11/DTD/xhtml11.dtd">
<html xmlns="http://www.w3.org/1999/xhtml" xml:lang="en">
<head>
<title>if...else</title>
<meta http-equiv="Content-Type" content="text/html; charset=utf-8" />
<script type="text/javascript">
//<![CDATA[

function choices() {
   var stateCode = 'MO';
   var taxPercentage = 0.0;

   if (stateCode === 'OR') {
      taxPercentage = 3.5;
   } else if (stateCode === 'CA') {
      taxPercentage = 5.0;
   } else if (stateCode === 'MO') {
      taxPercentage = 1.0;
   } else {
      taxPercentage = 2.0;
   }

   alert(taxPercentage);
}

//]]>
</script>

</head>
<body onload="choices()">
<p>Imagine a form with options to pick state code</p>
</body>
</html>
```

The program processes each conditional test in turn until it finds a condition that returns `true`. The code block associated with the test is processed, and the program continues on the first line after the conditional statement. If none of the conditional tests returns `true`, the block of code following the final `else` that doesn't have a condition is processed, and the tax percentage is set accordingly.

 I typically use single quotes when quoting simple values (`'OR'` or `'CA'`), and double quotes for phrases (`"this is a state"`). However, the type of quote you use makes no difference in how the code is processed. I'll use both types of quotes interchangeably in the book so that you get used to both.

You can continue adding additional `else if` statements testing the same variable, but after a time, the format becomes clumsy, hard to read, and inefficient. A better approach is to use the `switch` statement.

The switch Conditional Statement

The JavaScript `switch` statement is useful when several possible outcomes can result from a given expression. The JavaScript engine processes an expression which returns a value. Based on the resultant value, one or more blocks of code are processed:

```
switch (expression) {
    case firstlabel:
        statements;
         break;
    case secondlabel:
        statements;
         break;
    ...
    case lastlabel:
        statements;
        break;
    default:
        statements;
```

From the top, an expression that returns a value is given in the `switch` statement, and `case` statements are then evaluated, in sequence from top to bottom, to see whether any match. If a matching case is found, the statements contained within the particular `case` statement code block are processed. If the optional `break` statement is used at the end of the block, the program flow is transferred to the first line following the end of the `switch` statement. Otherwise, the program continues processing the code from the case following the one that was matched.

If none of the cases match, the JavaScript engine looks for an optional `default` statement; if it finds one, it processes its code block and the program continues with the first line following the switch. In the following code snippet, if the variable has a value of 3, the first case statement is processed; if it evaluates to 4, the second is processed; anything else triggers the default code block:

```
switch(someVariable) {
   case 3:
      block of code;
      break;
   case 4:
      block of code;
      break;
   default:
      block of code;
}
```

In the instance where the same set of statements is processed for two or more values, the case statements for the values can be listed, one after another, with the code block beneath the last case statement:

```
case labelone:
case labeltwo:
case labelthree:
   block of code;
   break;
```

In the preceding code, the code block is processed if any one of the three labels— labelone, labeltwo, or labelthree—is matched.

The switch statement is best explained with a demonstration. Example 3-3 accesses a state code, and if the value is OR, MA, or WI, it sets the tax percentage to 3.5 and the state percentage to 0.5; if the state code is MO, it sets the tax percentage to 1.0 and the state percentage to 1.5; if the state code is CA, NY, or VT, it sets the tax percentage to 4.5 and the state percentage to 2.6; if the state code is TX, it sets the tax percentage to 3.0 and leaves the state percentage at 0.0; otherwise, it sets the tax percentage to 2.0 and the state percentage to 2.3.

Example 3-3. Using a switch statement to test expression against multiple values

```
<!DOCTYPE html PUBLIC "-//W3C//DTD XHTML 1.1//EN"
"http://www.w3.org/TR/xhtml11/DTD/xhtml11.dtd">
<html xmlns="http://www.w3.org/1999/xhtml" xml:lang="en">
<head>
<title>switch</title>
<meta http-equiv="Content-Type" content="text/html; charset=utf-8" />
<script type="text/javascript">
//<![CDATA[

function choices() {
   var stateCode = 'MO';
   var statePercentage = 0.0;
   var taxPercentage = 0.0;

   switch (stateCode) {
      case 'OR':
      case 'MA':
```

```
            case 'WI' :
                statePercentage = 0.5;
                taxPercentage = 3.5;
                break;
            case 'MO' :
                taxPercentage = 1.0;
                statePercentage = 1.5;
            case 'CA' :
            case 'NY' :
            case 'VT' :
                statePercentage = 2.6;
                taxPercentage = 4.5;
                break;
            case 'TX' :
                taxPercentage = 3.0;
                break;
            default :
                taxPercentage = 2.0;
                statePercentage = 2.3;
    }

    alert("tax is " + taxPercentage + " and state is "
        + statePercentage);
}

//]]>
</script>
</head>
<body onload="choices()">
<p>Imagine a form with options to pick state code</p>
</body>
</html>
```

From the top, the content of the switch statement is just the state code variable,
stateCode. You also could have given the switch statement an expression using one of
the relational and/or logical operators, discussed in the next section.

The code then evaluates the case statements for a match to the value contained in the
stateCode. If the state code is OR, MA, or WI, the tax percentages are the same because
the case values are associated with the same code block. The same logic applies if the
state code is CA, NY, or VT.

If the state code is TX or MO, the code processes the individual case blocks. However,
if the state code of MO is used, the code sets the taxPercentage to 4.5 and the state
Percentage to 2.6, rather than the values in the code block associated with the MO state
code. This is because no break statement follows the code block associated with the
MO state code. Once the code block for the MO state code is processed, the program
continues to process statements until it reaches the end of the switch statement or a
break statement, whichever comes first. In the example, processing continues with the
next block and terminates at the end of the code block for the state codes of CA, NY,
and VT.

Finally, if none of the cases match, the `default` is processed and the program continues with the first statement after the `switch`.

Notice in the example that the only use of curly braces is around the `switch` control block itself. That's because with `switch`, program flow is controlled with the `break` statement, not with curly braces. However, indentation still applies, though it's not uncommon to place the processed statements on the same line as the case condition:

```
case 'OR' : taxPercentage = 3.5; statePercentage = 2.0; break;
```

Most of the expressions being tested in the conditional control statements have been fairly simple equality tests. You can use more complex conditional expressions, and even multiple expressions, with conditional operators, which we'll discuss next.

The Conditional Operators

You can use conditional operators to test for specific conditions: equality, identity, relational, and logical. Though the processes may differ, and they range from simple to complex, the result of using such operators is one of two values: `true` or `false`.

The Equality and Identity (String Equality) Operators

One of the most common operators used in a conditional expression is the equality operator, `==`. You use it when comparing one variable with another variable or literal value to see whether the two are the same:

```
// at some point in the application, assign 3 to variable nValue
var nValue = 3;
...
if (nValue == 3) ...
```

In this example, if the variable `nValue` is equal to 3, the conditional test evaluates to `true` and the code block following the `if` statement is processed. Otherwise, the flow of the program skips over the code block and goes to the first statement following that code block.

 Be careful not to leave off the second equals sign (=). If we do so, the expression becomes one of assignment, not of conditional testing. In the previous code snippet, if we left off the second equals sign, the variable `nValue` is assigned the value of 3, and because the assignment is successful, the conditional "test" returns `true`.

As with the addition operator, the equality operator converts the variable's data type if necessary to facilitate the evaluation of the expression. If one value is numeric and the other is a string, comparing both is successful if the value is "typographically" the same:

```
var nValue = 3.0;
var sValue = "3.0";
If (nValue == sValue) ...
```

This implicit type conversion or *casting* can lead to some interesting and unexpected side effects.

The equality operator is implicitly used in the `switch` statement, which means that both of the following cases are applicable if the `switch` expression evaluates to `"3.0"`:

```
case 3.0: ...
case "3.0": ...
```

Starting with JavaScript 1.3 (and ECMA-262, Edition 3) a new operator—the *identity*, or *strict equality* operator—was added specifically to test on both value and type. It's similar to the equality operator except that it uses three equals signs instead of two: ===. Unlike standard equality, the identity operator won't return success unless both operands are of the same value *and* have the same data type:

```
if (nValue === sValue)  // false
```

In addition to testing for both equality and strict equality, you can test for *not equals* and *strict not equals*. The not equals operator is !=:

```
if (sName != "Smith") ...
```

The strict not equals operator is !==:

```
if (sName !== "Smith")
```

Example 3-4 tests a numeric variable against a string literal, first with equality and then with strict equality. Following that, it tests a string variable against a numeric literal with not equals and strict not equals.

Example 3-4. Testing for precision between equals and strict equals

```
<!DOCTYPE html PUBLIC "-//W3C//DTD XHTML 1.1//EN"
"http://www.w3.org/TR/xhtml11/DTD/xhtml11.dtd">
<html xmlns="http://www.w3.org/1999/xhtml" xml:lang="en">
<head>
<title>Equality</title>
<meta http-equiv="Content-Type" content="text/html; charset=utf-8" />
<script type="text/javascript">
//<![CDATA[

function choices() {
    var sValue = "3.0";
    var nValue = 3.0;

    if (nValue == "3.0") alert("According to equality, value is 3.0");

    if (nValue === "3.0") alert("According to strict equality, value is 3.0");

    if (sValue != 3.0) alert ("According to equality, value is not 3.0");

    if (sValue !== 3.0) alert ("According to strict equality, value is not 3.0");
```

```
}

//]]>
</script>
</head>
<body onload="choices()">
<p>Some page content</p>
</body>
</html>
```

In the first case, the numeric variable containing a value of 3 is tested against the string-based "3.0" with the equality operator. The result is **true**, and the alert window opens. However, this comparison fails with strict equality, and the second alert window is not opened.

In the third case, the string variable with **"3.0"** is tested against the numeric literal, 3.0. The not equals test fails, because to this operator, both values are the same. However, with the strict not equals operator, the comparison does evaluate to **true** because the values are not the same (they have different data types) and the alert window opens.

 Example 3-4 also introduces a shortcut method of processing exactly one statement associated with a conditional statement. In this case, curly braces aren't necessary because the association is quite readable, and only one statement is being processed.

As you can see in Example 3-4, the strict equality operator is much more precise. If this is so, you might wonder why it's not more widely used.

The equality operator and its converse, not equals, have been around since the beginning of JavaScript, and all JavaScript engines support them. The strict equals/identity operator and its converse were added later, with JavaScript 1.3. In addition, with the first release of the ECMA-262 specification, the strict equals operator was dropped and was added back in with ECMA-262, Edition 3.0. As such, support for strict equals isn't guaranteed in older browsers. However, most modern browsers and even less modern browsers such as Internet Explorer 6 support strict equality, so you should be safe when using it over the regular equality operator.

 You should use strict equality and inequality in all situations where you can't guarantee that your variable types won't get mixed.

Testing for equality is helpful, but sometimes you need to test a range of values, not just for a specific value. Enter the greater than and less than relational operators.

Other Relational Operators

A *relational operator* is one in which one operand of an expression is compared to another in some way. The equality and strict equality operators are relational operators, which test whether the two operands are equal. At other times, we'll want relational operators to return true when one operand is either greater than or less than another operand.

The greater than operator (>) returns true if the left operand is a value greater than the operand on the right—*greater than* in this context being based on data type. For instance, a numeric value of 4 is greater than a value of 1, whereas the string "one" is alphabetically greater than the string "four":

```
var a = 1; var b = 4;
if (a > b) // false

var a2 = "one"; var b2 = "four";
if (a2 > b2) // true
```

The greater than or equals operator (>=) returns true if the left operand is of greater *or* equal value to the operand on the right:

```
var nValue = 1.0;
if (nValue > 3.0)  // false
...
if (nValue >= 1.0) // true
...
if (nValue >= 0.5) // true
...
```

The less than operator (<) returns true if the left operand is of less value than the operand on the right. The less than or equals operator (<=) returns true if the left operand is less than *or* equal to the value of the operand on the right, as demonstrated in the following test variations:

```
var nValue = 1.0

if (nValue < 3.0) // true
...
if (nValue <= 1.0) // true
...
if (nValue <= 0.5) // false
...
```

Like equality, type conversion occurs implicitly between numeric and string values with the less than/greater than operators. So, the following evaluates to false:

```
sValue = "1.0";
if (sValue >= 2.0) // false
```

String conversion occurs only when the format of the value is numeric. For instance, JavaScript does not convert "one" to "1" or "1.0" when doing implicit conversion.

For nonnumeric values, the greater than/less than operators compare two values typographically:

```
var strValue = "apple";
if (strValue < "banana") //true
if (strValue > "banana") //false
```

Testing to see whether a value is greater than or less than another is useful, but so is testing to see whether a variable or expression result is within a range of values. Example 3-5 tests a variable to see whether it falls within a given range, 0 to 100 inclusive, which means that the value could also be 0 or 100. It also tests the variable in the range between 0 and 100, excluding the values of 0 and 100. Final tests check whether the value is greater than 100 or less than zero (0). Appropriate message(s) are displayed based on the result of the different tests.

Example 3-5. Testing within a range of numbers

```
<!DOCTYPE html PUBLIC "-//W3C//DTD XHTML 1.1//EN"
"http://www.w3.org/TR/xhtml11/DTD/xhtml11.dtd">
<html xmlns="http://www.w3.org/1999/xhtml" xml:lang="en">
<head>
<title>Ranges of values</title>
<meta http-equiv="Content-Type" content="text/html; charset=utf-8" />
<script type="text/javascript">
//<![CDATA[

function values() {
   var nValue = 0;

   if (nValue >= 0 && nValue <= 100) {
      alert("value between 0 and 100 inclusive");
   }
   if (nValue > 0 && nValue < 100) {
      alert("value between 0 and 100 exclusive");
   }
   if (nValue > 100) {
     alert ("value over 100");
   }
   if (nValue < 0) {
     alert ("value is negative");
   }
}
//]]>
</script>
</head>
<body onload="values()">
<p>Some page content</p>
</body>
</html>
```

In this example, only one test succeeds, when testing whether the value is between 0 and 100 inclusive, as the test value is zero (0). Only one alert box is displayed.

The first two comparisons rely on an additional operator to establish the range: the logical AND operator, **&&**. We'll look at the logical operators in more detail later, but first, let's check out JavaScript's one and only ternary operator.

The One and Only JavaScript Ternary Operator

The operators we've looked at in this chapter have been unary (one operand) or binary (two operands). JavaScript also has one *ternary operator*, the conditional operator, which works with three operands. The following is an example of its use:

```
var nValue = 1.0;
var sResult = (nValue > 0.5) ? "value over 0.5" : "value not over 0.5";
```

In this example, sResult is set to **"value over 0.5"** because the condition evaluates to **true**, resulting in the second operand being returned. Here's the format of the conditional operator:

```
condition ? value if true : value if false;
```

The conditional operator becomes, in effect, a shortcut method for the fairly common "if (expression), do this; otherwise, do that", demonstrated in the following code:

```
var stateCode = 'OR';
var taxPercentage = 0.0;
if (stateCode == 'OR') {
    taxPercentage = 3.5;
} else {
    taxPercentage = 4.5;
}
```

Converting this code snippet into a statement using the conditional operator, the code becomes:

```
var stateCode = 'OR';
var taxPercentage = 0.0;
var taxPercentage = (stateCode == 'OR') ? 3.5 : 4.5;
```

It's a handy shortcut and a readable one, so its use is very common. In fact, I rarely use the longhand version of the code for any of my work. I demonstrate this operator again later in the book when I use it in code to resolve browser differences.

The Logical Operators

Most of the examples I've shown you so far in the book use a conditional expression that consists of one operator and two operands:

```
if (sValue == 'test')
```

However, many times a conditional expression depends on several different conditions being met. Each condition is represented by its own expression and the results of all expressions are combined and evaluated through the use of one of JavaScript's *logical operators*.

Three logical operators exist: two binary and one unary. The first is the logical AND, represented by two ampersand characters, &&. When you use it in a conditional statement, the AND operator requires that expressions on both sides of the operator evaluate to true for the entire expression to evaluate to true:

```
var nValue = 10;
if ((nValue > 10) && (nValue <=100)) // false because the value is not greater than
10
```

The result of using this expression joined by the AND operator is false because the variable, nValue, is equal to 10, which means the first expression is false. If the first expression evaluates to false, the JavaScript engine won't process the second expression because the entire statement is going to fail, regardless.

The second logical operator is the OR operator, represented by two vertical lines or bars, ||. When used in a conditional statement, the OR operator requires only one or the other of its expressions on either side to be true for the entire expression to evaluate to true:

```
var nValue = 10;
if ((nValue > 10) || (nValue <= 100)) // true because the value is less than 100
```

The result of this code is that the conditional statement is true because the variable is less than 100. Both sides of the logical OR operator must be evaluated because the operator requires a conditional test on one side to return true and the first conditional test returns false. When describing the logical operators, I mentioned how both conditional tests on either side of the operator may or may not be evaluated. The JavaScript engine does what is known as a *short-circuit evaluation* of the expression first. If the logical operator is AND (&&) and the first expression evaluates to false, the second isn't evaluated because the entire expression must evaluate to false. In using the logical OR operator, if the first expression evaluates to true, the second is not evaluated. An OR operator evaluates to true when one of its operands is true.

By understanding how short-circuit evaluation works, you can use first expressions that are less CPU/resource-intensive, thereby adding a little efficiency to your application. In particular, if you also need to check to ensure that the variable isn't null or undefined, do this check first, and then any further checking:

```
if ((nValue != null) && (nValue > 8))
```

This can prevent JavaScript errors if the variable hasn't been set or defined.

 Take advantage of short-circuit evaluation by placing the key expression or the less resource-intensive expression first when using logical AND/OR operators.

The final logical operator is the logical NOT, represented by the exclamation point, !. This operator returns the logical negation of the expression. If the expression is true, it returns false; if the expression is false, it returns true:

```
var nValue = 10;
if (!(nValue > 10)) // returns true
```

In the preceding code snippet, the result of the inner expression evaluates to false, as the variable is not greater than 10. However, logical negation converts the false to true.

Note that although the examples in this section use parentheses around the expressions, the use of parentheses isn't required; the relational operators have a higher precedence than do the logical operators, and therefore they are evaluated first. In Example 3-5, I didn't use the parentheses with the AND operator. However, I've found that they can make the entire expression more readable, as well as ensuring that the complex conditional expression evaluates in the order I want.

 For readability, and to ensure against unexpected results, surround the expressions on either side of the logical operator (&& or ||) with parentheses.

Advanced Statements: The Loops

The looping statements are similar to the conditional statements demonstrated earlier in that they depend on a conditional expression, regardless of whether their code blocks are processed. However, when the expression evaluates to true, the processor returns to the same condition again at the end of each loop, rather than continuing with the first statement following the loop.

The while Loop

The simplest JavaScript loop tests a condition at the start of each loop and continues if the expression evaluates to true. Some event in the code block controlled by the loop eventually changes the operands for the conditional test, forcing the expression to evaluate to false and the loop to terminate. You use the while keyword to designate this type of loop.

Example 3-6 tests a variable in a condition to see whether it is greater than 10. Within the loop code block, the variable is concatenated to a string and then incremented. When the variable is greater than 10, the loop terminates, and the string variable is printed in an alert window.

Example 3-6. Testing a value in a condition in a while loop

```
<!DOCTYPE html PUBLIC "-//W3C//DTD XHTML 1.1//EN"
"http://www.w3.org/TR/xhtml11/DTD/xhtml11.dtd">
<html xmlns="http://www.w3.org/1999/xhtml" xml:lang="en">
```

```
<head>
<title>while loop</title>
<meta http-equiv="Content-Type" content="text/html; charset=utf-8" />
<script type="text/javascript">
//<![CDATA[

function loops() {

    var strValue = "";
    var nValue = 1;

    while (nValue <= 10) {
        strValue+=nValue;
        nValue++;
    }
    alert(strValue);
}
//]]>
</script>
</head>
<body onload="loops()">
<p>Some page content</p>
</body>
</html>
```

The value displayed in the alert box is:

```
12345678910
```

This value represents the value of nValue as it is incremented with each loop. nValue is implicitly converted to a string when concatenated to a string.

The do...while Loop

In the preceding section, the while loop statement contains a conditional expression that is processed before the loop is executed. If the condition fails immediately, the loop's code block is never processed. Sometimes, though, you might want the code to be processed at least once, regardless of the condition and its success or failure. Enter the do...while loop.

Unlike the while loop, the do...while loop doesn't evaluate the conditional expression until after the end of the code block. As such, the block is always processed at least once. You can modify the loop in Example 3-6 as follows, if the code in the contained block is to be processed at least once:

```
do {
    strValue+=nValue;
    nValue++;
} while (nValue <= 10)
```

If the initial value of nValue had been 11, the loop's code block would still be processed at least once.

With both the `while` loop and the `do...while` loop, the conditional operation determines whether the loop is processed. Any condition can work, including complicated ones such as the following:

```
while (nValue >= 1 && nValue < 10) ...
```

In the preceding code snippet, the loop's code block is processed as long as `nValue` is greater than or equal to 1 but less than 10. This is an effective approach, but another loop—the `for` loop—is better at controlling loops processed a set number of times.

The for Loops

Rather than use an unknown expression, a `for` loop's code block is meant to be processed based on a fixed set of circumstances. There are a few different types of `for` loops, but only one is implemented in all browsers.

The most common `for` loop, and the one that is implemented in all browsers, initializes a variable to a beginning number, modifies the number with each loop, and then tests the value of the number against a condition—all in one statement. When the variable's value satisfies the condition, the loop is finished:

```
for (initial value; condition; update) {
...
}
```

The `for` loop actually consists of three different statements: an assignment (initial value), a conditional test, and then an update. In the following code snippet:

```
for (var i = 0; i < 10; i++) {
    document.writeln("hello");
}
```

a variable, `i`, is set to zero. With each iteration of the loop, the value is tested to see whether the condition is met—in this case, whether the variable's value is less than 10; if so, the loop code block is processed, and the conditional variable is incremented. With each iteration of the loop the value is incremented. The following list reiterates the steps:

- Assignment: `var i = 0;`
- Condition: `i < 10`
- Update: `i++`

A second variation of this type of `for` loop actually "counts" down the number:

```
for (var i = 10; i > 0; i--)
```

Example 3-7 demonstrates using a `for` loop to create the same numbered string as we created earlier, with the `while` loop. The application then resets the string variable back to an empty string (`""`), and this time traverses the number sequence "backward."

Example 3-7. Traversing a sequence of numbers forward and backward with the for loop

```
<!DOCTYPE html PUBLIC "-//W3C//DTD XHTML 1.1//EN"
"http://www.w3.org/TR/xhtml11/DTD/xhtml11.dtd">
<html xmlns="http://www.w3.org/1999/xhtml" xml:lang="en">
<head>
<title>for loop</title>
<meta http-equiv="Content-Type" content="text/html; charset=utf-8" />
<script type="text/javascript">
//<![CDATA[

function doFor() {

   var strValue = "";

   for (var i = 1; i <= 10; i++) {
      strValue+=i;
   }
   alert(strValue);

   strValue = "";
   for (var i = 10; i >= 0; i--) {
      strValue+=i;
   }
   alert(strValue);
}
//]]>
</script>
</head>
<body onload="doFor()">
<p>Some page content</p>
</body>
</html>
```

Because we want a countdown string starting with "1" in the first loop, we begin the for loop with a value of 1.

Which to use, count down or count up, with the for loop depends on whether you need to use the loop variable for something other than just the conditional test, such as accessing individual array elements. However, a second approach for accessing array elements leads to the next form of the for loop. But because it is associated with arrays, I'll demonstrate it in Chapter 4, when I cover arrays.

The third type of for loop is the for...in loop, which provides a way to iterate over an object's properties. Though we haven't covered creating custom objects yet, Example 3-8 creates a custom object named MyTest with three properties: one, two, and three. It assigns each one a value, and then uses a for...in loop to print the values to a web page.

Example 3-8. Using the for...in loop to access object properties

```
<!DOCTYPE html PUBLIC "-//W3C//DTD XHTML 1.1//EN"
"http://www.w3.org/TR/xhtml11/DTD/xhtml11.dtd">
<html xmlns="http://www.w3.org/1999/xhtml" xml:lang="en">
```

```
<head>
<title>for...in loop</title>
<meta http-equiv="Content-Type" content="text/html; charset=utf-8" />
<script type="text/javascript">
//<![CDATA[

function doFor() {

  var MyText = {
     one : "one",
     two : "two",
     three : "three"
  };

  for (var prop in MyText) {
     document.writeln(prop + "<br />");
  }

}
//]]>
</script>
</head>
<body onload="doFor()">
<p>Some page content</p>
</body>
</html>
```

Running this application results in the following:

```
one
two
three
```

You can also use `for...in` with an array, but the "property" value is really the index of each array element, and is not much different from the regular `for` loop:

```
var tsts = new Array('one','two','three');
for (indx in tsts) {
   alert(tsts[indx]);
}
```

Because the more traditional format is easier to read, you'll probably want to stick with it for array processing, and reserve `for...in` for processing object properties.

Test Your Knowledge: Quiz

1. In the following, add parentheses to the expression so that it evaluates to 8:

```
var valA = 37;
var valB = 3;
var valC = 18;
var resultOfComp = valA - valB % 3 / 2 * 4 + valC - 3;
```

2. Using a `switch` statement, test an expression for a value of `'one'`, `'two'`, or `'three'`, and set a variable to `'OK'` if the expression is `'one'` or `'two'`; `'OK2'` if the expression is `'three'`; and `'NONE'` if it doesn't match any of these.

3. You have three variables: `varOne`, `varTwo`, and `varThree`. How would you test all three such that a block of code is processed only if `varOne` is 33, `varTwo` is less than or equal to 100, but `varThree` is greater than 0?

4. In what three ways can you process a block of code exactly six times? In what conditions would you use one technique over another?

5. Would you alter the following conditional statement, and if so, why?

```
if (valTest1 == valTest2) ...
```

Test Your Knowledge: Answers

1. The solution is:

```
var resultOfComp = (valA - valB) % 3 / 2 * (4 + valC) - 3;
```

2. The solution is:

```
switch(val) {
    case 'one' :
    case 'two' :
        result = 'OK';
        break;
    case 'three' :
        result = 'OK2';
        break;
    default :
        result = 'NONE';
}
```

3. The solution is:

```
if ((varOne == 33) && (varTwo <= 100) && (varThree > 0))
```

4. The answer is:

```
for (var i = 0; i < 6; i++) {
    ...
}

i = 0;
while (i < 6) {
    ...
    i++;
}

i = 0;
do {
    i++;
    ...
```

```
    }
    while (i < 6)
```

Typically, you'll use the **do...while** loop when you want to execute a block of code at least once, regardless of condition. You'll use a **for** loop when you want to execute the block of code a set number of times. Finally, you'll probably want to use a **while** loop when the block of code impacts the condition.

5. If you're not sure of the variable's data type, you should consider using the strict equality operator:

```
    if (valTest1 === valTest2)
```

CHAPTER 4

The JavaScript Objects

The JavaScript objects are inherent components of the JavaScript language itself, and not the environment in which the JavaScript is processed. As such, they'll always be available regardless of environment.

Among the basic JavaScript objects are those that parallel our data types, which we discussed in Chapter 2: `String` for strings, `Boolean` for booleans, and of course, `Number` for numbers. They encapsulate the primitive types, providing additional functionality beyond the basic conversion functionality we discussed in that chapter.

Three additional built-in objects provide necessary functionality as well: `Math`, `Date`, and `RegExp`. `Math` and `Date` are relatively self-explanatory; they provide basic math and date functionality. If you haven't worked with regular expressions before, `RegExp` is the object that provides regular expression functionality. Regular expressions are powerful though extremely cryptic patterning capabilities that enable you to add very precise string matching to applications.

JavaScript also has one built-in aggregator object, the `Array`. All objects in JavaScript, in fact, are arrays, though we don't typically treat the objects as arrays. I'll discuss this in more detail later in the chapter. First, though, we'll revisit the basic data type objects introduced earlier, as we explore exactly what it means to be an "object" in JavaScript.

Primitive Data Types As Objects

I'll get into the details of JavaScript's object-oriented nature later in the book. For now, we'll look at the aspects of object-oriented functionality that are useful when working directly with the built-in JavaScript objects.

Objects in JavaScript have methods and other properties that you can access using the object property operator, represented by a period (.). For instance, to find the length of a string associated with a `String` object, you can access the object's `length` property:

```
var myName = "Shelley";
alert(myName.length);
```

You also access object functions, called *methods*, via the same property operator, because methods are also considered object properties. Here is an example of the `String` object's `strike` method, which encloses the string's text within HTML opening and closing string element tags:

```
var myName = "Shelley";
alert(myName.strike()); // returns <strike>Shelley</strike>
```

This example might be somewhat confusing because it looks like I'm creating a string primitive rather than a `String` object. In the code, the variable `myName` is a string primitive variable, `true`. However, when a `String` method is invoked on the variable, it's also an instance of a `String` object, with access to all of the `String` properties, including `length` and `strike`.

In Chapter 2, I mentioned how when an object method is invoked on a primitive data type, an object instance is created to wrap the primitive, the method call is processed, and then the object is discarded. The same principle applies to numbers and booleans as well.

However, instead of implicitly creating a `String`, `Boolean`, or `Number` object, you can explicitly create an object using the `new` keyword and the following syntax:

```
var myName = new String("Shelley");
```

The `new` keyword is important. If you omit it, you'll get a string primitive rather than a string object. In other words, both of the following lines of JavaScript create string primitives:

```
var strName = "Shelley";
var strName2 = String("Shelley");
```

Returning to the `String` object, once you create a `String` object instance, you can access the primitive value it *wraps* (encloses) using another method that all the objects share, `valueOf`:

```
var myName = new String("Shelley");
alert(myName.valueOf());
```

You can also access the primitive value directly, as though it were a primitive data type:

```
var myName = new String("Shelley");
alert(myName);
```

To repeat what I said earlier in Chapter 2, which technique to use—string primitive or `String` object instance—depends on how you're using the variable. If you're going to be accessing the object properties, such as the `String` object's `length` and `strike` methods, you'll want to create the variable as an object. If you create a string primitive and then access it like an object, JavaScript will convert the primitive to an object when you access a `String` property, but it does so by converting the primitive to a temporary `String` object, and then discarding the object when it's finished with the property. This isn't efficient.

```
var strName ="Shelley"; // string as primitive
alert(strName.length); // String object is implicitly created, its data value set
to strName, and length method processed
```

However, if you're using a string (or a number or boolean) as a primitive, you don't need the object properties, and it's more efficient just to use the string primitive technique of creating the variable:

```
var strName = "Shelley";
alert(strName);
```

Because we're exploring object properties in this chapter, the examples in the rest of this chapter create variables as object instances.

Boolean, Number, and String

Number and String object instances have their own unique properties, whereas Boolean does not. However, all three inherit certain properties and methods from a higher-level object, which I'll cover in detail in Chapter 13. For now, among the methods that all the objects inherit are toString and valueOf. As the Boolean object has only inherited properties, I'll use this object type to demonstrate each of these methods.

The Boolean Object

You actually can create an instance of a Boolean object in several different ways, depending on whether you want it to be set to an initial value of false or true. If you create the object using empty parentheses, the Boolean is created with a value of false:

```
var boolFlag = new Boolean();
```

You can also use a number to set the initial value, such as 0 for false:

```
var boolFlag = new Boolean(0);
```

Or 1 for true:

```
var boolFlag = new Boolean(1);
```

In addition, you can create and set the object using the literal true and false:

```
var boolFlag1 = new Boolean(false);
var boolFlag2 = new Boolean(true);
```

What's interesting is that if you create the Boolean instance with an empty string, the object is set to an initial value of false. However, if you create the Boolean instance with any nonempty string, the object is set to an initial value of true:

```
var boolFlag1 = new Boolean(""); // set to false
var boolFlag2 = new Boolean("false"); // set to true
```

Ignore what the string says in the second line in the code; the string isn't empty, so the object instance is set to an initial value of true. You can test this for yourself by using the valueOf method, as Example 4-1 demonstrates.

Example 4-1. Testing the value of a Boolean instance using the valueOf method

```
<!DOCTYPE html PUBLIC "-//W3C//DTD XHTML 1.1//EN"
"http://www.w3.org/TR/xhtml11/DTD/xhtml11.dtd">
<html xmlns="http://www.w3.org/1999/xhtml" xml:lang="en">
<head>
<title>Boolean valueOf</title>
<meta http-equiv="Content-Type" content="text/html; charset=utf-8" />
<script type="text/javascript">
//<![CDATA[

function newBool() {
   var boolFlag = new Boolean("false");
   alert(boolFlag.valueOf());
}

//]]>
</script>
</head>
<body onload="newBool()">
<p>Some page content</p>
</body>
</html>
```

Figure 4-1 shows the alert window and the Boolean instance value of true when the page is accessed in Opera. The valueOf method returns the value of the primitive that the Boolean (and Number and String) encapsulates.

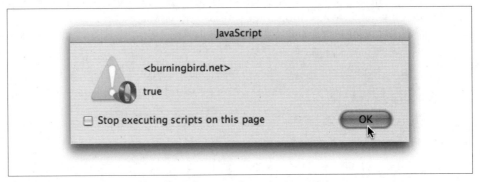

Figure 4-1. The result of calling valueOf on a Boolean instance

The method toString returns the same value as valueOf, except as a string, "true", rather than true:

```
var boolFlag = new Boolean("false");
var strFlag = boolFlag.toString(); // string containing "true"
```

The Number Object, Static Properties, and Instance Methods

Before getting into the `Number` object, a note about instance versus object properties.

The two methods we used with the `Boolean` object in the preceding section are known as *instance methods* because the methods are associated with the object instance, `boolFlag`, rather than the object class, `Boolean`. Neither the `toString` nor the `valueOf` method would be very useful without being attached to an instance, with its unique data to convert to a string or be returned as a value.

Another type of object method is known as a *static method*. Static methods don't operate on the instance data, but instead are called directly on the object class. All of the `Math` object's methods, which I'll cover later in the chapter, are static methods:

```
var newNum = Math.abs(oldNum);
```

The same *instance versus object* implementation also applies to properties that aren't methods. Specifically, five `Number` properties are accessible only via the `Number` object itself. These are:

`Number.MAX_VALUE`
> The maximum number representation in JavaScript

`Number.MIN_VALUE`
> The smallest positive number representation in JavaScript

`Number.NaN`
> Represents Not-a-Number

`Number.NEGATIVE_INFINITY`
> Represents negative infinity

`Number.POSITIVE_INFINITY`
> Represents infinity

Typically, you use the infinity properties only to test when an *overflow* condition has occurred. An overflow occurs when a number is created that is either too small or too large, and therefore exceeds the `MIN_VALUE` or `MAX_VALUE` property:

```
var someValue = -1 * Number.MAX_VALUE  * 2;
alert(someValue);

someValue = Number.MAX_VALUE * 2;
alert(someValue);
```

The alert would display the value of `-infinity` for `NEGATIVE_INFINITY` first, followed by `infinity` for `POSITIVE_INFINITY`.

I use the `Number` object in the listing of the four properties to highlight the importance of accessing these properties on the `Number` object itself, not on a `Number` instance. If you try to access these properties on a `Number` instance, a value of `undefined` will be returned:

```
var someNumber = new Number(3.0);
var maxValue = someNumber.MAX_VALUE; // undefined
```

The Number object's instance methods have to do with conversion—to a string, to a locale-specific string, to a given precision- or fixed-point representation, and to an exponential notation. The Number object has three instance methods:

toExponential
  Returns a string representing the number using exponential notation

toFixed
  Returns a string representing the number in fixed-point notation

toPrecision
  Returns a string representing the number using a specific precision

The global methods valueOf and toString are also supported for Number instances, as is an additional method, toLocaleString. The latter returns a locale-specific version of the number. Unlike with Boolean, the toString method for the Number object instance also takes one parameter, a base, which you can use to convert the number between decimal and hexadecimal, or between decimal and octal, and so on.

Example 4-2 demonstrates the various Number object instance methods.

Example 4-2. The Number object instance methods

```
<!DOCTYPE html PUBLIC "-//W3C//DTD XHTML 1.1//EN"
"http://www.w3.org/TR/xhtml11/DTD/xhtml11.dtd">
<html xmlns="http://www.w3.org/1999/xhtml" xml:lang="en">
<head>
<title>Number methods</title>
<meta http-equiv="Content-Type" content="text/html; charset=utf-8" />
<script type="text/javascript">
//<![CDATA[

function numbers() {

    // Number  methods
    var newNumber = new Number(34.8896);

    document.writeln(newNumber.toExponential(3) + "<br />");
    document.writeln(newNumber.toPrecision(3) + "<br />");
    document.writeln(newNumber.toFixed(6) + "<br />");

    var newValue = newNumber.valueOf();

    document.writeln(newValue.toString(2) + "<br />");
    document.writeln(newValue.toString(8) + "<br />");
    document.writeln(newValue.toString(10) + "<br />");
    document.writeln(newValue.toString(16) + "<br />");
}
//]]>
</script>
</head>
<body onload="numbers()">
<p>Some page content</p>
```

```
</body>
</html>
```

Figure 4-2 shows the results of running this JavaScript application in Safari.

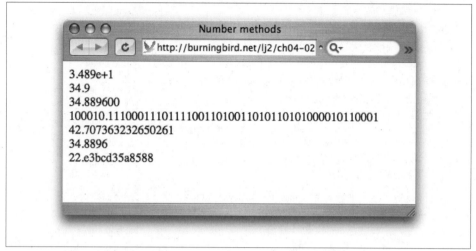

Figure 4-2. The Number object instance methods in Safari

The first method the code invokes is toExponential, which the number of digits appearing after the decimal point passed in as a parameter—in this case, 3. The second method is toPrecision, with a value of 3 also passed as a parameter, representing the number of significant digits to include in the string transformation. The third method the code called, toFixed, is the number of digits to print out after the decimal—rounded if applicable.

The code then obtains the value of the Number object using the valueOf method and assigns this value to a new variable before using the new variable with the toString method calls. It does this because toString uses the base parameter only if it's used with an actual number, not an object. The variable newNumber holds an object, not a number. Only after we get the actual number and assign it to a second variable can we use toString with different base representations.

The String Object

The String object is probably the most used of the built-in JavaScript objects. You can explicitly create a new String object using the new String constructor, passing the literal string as a parameter:

```
var sObject = new String("Sample string");
```

The String object has several methods, some associated with working with HTML and several not. Table 4-1 lists the properties and methods available via String object instances.

Table 4-1. String object methods

Method	Description	Arguments
valueOf	Returns the string literal that the String object is wrapping	None
length	The property, not the method, with the length of the string literal	Use without parentheses
anchor	Creates an HTML anchor	String with anchor title
big, blink, bold, italics, small, strike, sub, sup	Format and return the String object's literal value as HTML	None
charAt, charCodeAt	Return either a character (charAt) or character code (charCodeAt) at a given position	Integer representing position, starting at position zero (0)
indexOf	Returns the starting position of the first occurrence of a substring	Search substring
lastIndexOf	Returns the starting position of the last occurrence of a substring	Search substring
link	Returns HTML for the link	URL for the href attribute
concat	Concatenates strings together	Strings to concatenate onto the String's literal string
split	Splits the string into tokens based on some separator	Separator and maximum number of splits
slice	Returns a slice from the string	Beginning and ending positions of the slice
substring, substr	Return a substring	Beginning and ending locations of the string
match, replace, search	Regular expression match, replace, and search	String with regular expression
toLowerCase, toUpperCase	Convert case	None

One of the non-HTML-specific methods, concat, takes two strings and returns a result with the second string concatenated onto the first. Example 4-3 demonstrates how to create a String object and use the concat method.

Example 4-3. Creating a String object and calling the concat method

```
<!DOCTYPE html PUBLIC "-//W3C//DTD XHTML 1.1//EN"
"http://www.w3.org/TR/xhtml11/DTD/xhtml11.dtd">
<html xmlns="http://www.w3.org/1999/xhtml" xml:lang="en">
<head>
<title>String concatenation</title>
<meta http-equiv="Content-Type" content="text/html; charset=utf-8" />
<script type="text/javascript">
//<![CDATA[
```

```
function stringConcat() {

    var sObj = new String();
    var sTxt = sObj.concat("This is", " a ", "new string");
    alert(sTxt);
}
//]]>
</script>
</head>
<body onload="stringConcat()">
<p>Some page content</p>
</body>
</html>
```

There is no specified limit to the number of strings you can concatenate with the `String` `concat` method. However, I rarely use the `concat` method; if I'm going to be building a string, I prefer using string primitives and the string concatenation operator (+) simply because it is less cumbersome.

Of course, you're going to want to minimize concatenation as much as possible. Each time you concatenate one string to another, you're creating a new string object. Strings are *immutable* in JavaScript, which means you can't actually *change* a string once you've created it. When you assign a new string value or modify an old value, you're really just creating a new string which exists in memory, along with the old one, until the application goes out of scope (typically when the function is finished):

```
var newStr = "this is";
newStr+= " a new string"; // old string is discarded, new string is created
```

If you did a lot of concatenation, the performance of the application could suffer. However, most uses of string concatenation are simple variations of putting together a string with a few variable values, and you can use it without worrying much about performance.

The HTML formatting methods—`anchor`, `link`, `big`, `blink`, `bold`, `italics`, `sub`, `sup`, `small`, and `strike`—generate strings that enclose the `String` object instance's literal value within HTML element tags. Example 4-4 demonstrates how these formatting methods work, using one specific string with different methods.

Example 4-4. Working with the String object's formatting functions

```
<!DOCTYPE html PUBLIC "-//W3C//DTD XHTML 1.1//EN"
"http://www.w3.org/TR/xhtml11/DTD/xhtml11.dtd">
<html xmlns="http://www.w3.org/1999/xhtml" xml:lang="en">
<head>
<title>String HTML</title>
<meta http-equiv="Content-Type" content="text/html; charset=utf-8" />
<script type="text/javascript">
//<![CDATA[

function stringHTML() {
```

```
var someString = new String("This is the test string");

document.writeln(someString.big() + "<br />");
document.writeln(someString.blink() + "<br />");
document.writeln(someString.sup() + "<br />");
document.writeln(someString.strike() + "<br />");
document.writeln(someString.bold() + "<br />");
document.writeln(someString.italics() + "<br />");
document.writeln(someString.small() + "<br />");
document.writeln(someString.link('http://www.oreilly.com'));
}
//]]>
</script>
</head>
<body onload="stringHTML()">
<p>Some page content</p>
</body>
</html>
```

Figure 4-3 shows the derived page opened in Firefox. Note the HTML styling added to each variation of the string. What the image can't show is the blinking action of the string formatted with blink. blink is *deprecated* HTML, which means that more modern HTML and XHTML specifications have stopped supporting it, and eventually, browsers will stop supporting it as well. It definitely won't validate within a web page given a strict Document Type Declaration (DOCTYPE), such as in Example 4-4. However, if you use it with document.writeln, the page validates because the XHTML validators see the proper use of JavaScript, not the generated results. If you copy the generated results into a new document and run these with any XHTML validator, or try to serve the pages as XHTML rather than HTML, you'll receive an error for the use of blink.

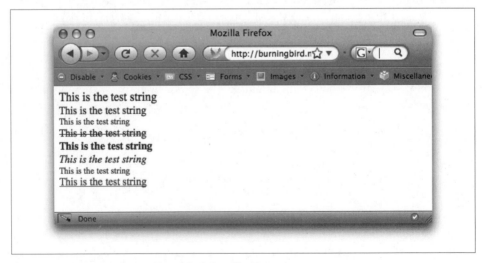

Figure 4-3. Page created using Example 4-4 application

Even if you don't receive an error directly, you should avoid using the HTML format methods (other than `anchor` and `link`) as much as possible, primarily because they don't use the more modern Cascading Style Sheets (CSS) styling. And whatever you do, avoid `blink`: it's an obnoxious behavior.

Returning to the `String` object's instance methods, the `charAt` and `charCodeAt` methods return the character and the Unicode character code, respectively, at a given location. The methods take one parameter—an index of the character to be returned:

```
var sObj = new String("This is a test string");
var sTxt = sObj.charAt(3);
document.writeln(sTxt);
```

The index values begin at zero; to return the character at the fourth position, pass in the value 3.

The `substr` and `substring` methods, as well as `slice`, return a substring given two parameters, though what's returned and the parameters differ among the three methods. The `substr` method takes a starting index and the length of the substring as parameters, whereas `substring` extracts the characters between two given indexes:

```
var sTxt = "This is a test string";
var ssTxt = sTxt.substr(5,8); // returns "is a tes"
var ssTxt2 = sTxt.substring(5,8); // returns "is "
```

If the stop index is less than the start for `substring`, the method swaps the two values. If you omit the end parameter for both, the rest of the string after the start index is returned. If the second index or length is longer than the string, the length of the string is used.

The `slice` method is similar to `substring` in that it takes two indexes, but unlike `substring`, if the stop index is less than the start index, the values aren't swapped, and an empty string is returned:

```
var ssTxt2 = sTxt.substring(4,1); // returns his
var ssTxt3 = sTxt.slice(4,1); // returns empty string
```

As the code examples in this section demonstrate, you can use the `String` methods with a string literal, as well as a `String` object. Just as a reminder: the application processing the JavaScript converts the variable to an object, calls the method, and then reconverts the object back to a primitive variable, discarding the object.

The `indexOf` and `lastIndexOf` methods return the index of a search string, with the former returning the first occurrence and the latter returning the last:

```
var sTxt = "This is a test string";
var iVal = sTxt.indexOf("t");
document.writeln(iVal);
```

Example 4-3 demonstrated concatenating strings together. If you want to do the reverse—split a string apart—use the split method. This method has two parameters: the first is the character that marks each break; the second, which is optional, is the number of splits to perform.

The JavaScript in Example 4-5 takes a string and splits it on the comma (,)—performing a break only on the first three commas. The resultant values are then split on the equals sign (=).

Example 4-5. Using the String split function to break a string into tokens

```
<!DOCTYPE html PUBLIC "-//W3C//DTD XHTML 1.1//EN"
"http://www.w3.org/TR/xhtml11/DTD/xhtml11.dtd">
<html xmlns="http://www.w3.org/1999/xhtml" xml:lang="en">
<head>
<title>Gotta Split</title>
<meta http-equiv="Content-Type" content="text/html; charset=utf-8" />
<script type="text/javascript">
//<![CDATA[

function splitString() {

   var inputString = new
String('firstName=Shelley,lastName=Powers,state=Missouri,statement="This is a test,
of split"');
   var arrayTokens = inputString.split(',',3);

   // process split on commas
   for (var i = 0; i < arrayTokens.length; i++) {
      document.writeln(arrayTokens[i] + "<br />");

      // now split on equals and write just value
      var newTokens = arrayTokens[i].split('=');
      document.writeln(newTokens[1] + "<br /><br />");
   }
}
//]]>
</script>
</head>
<body onload="splitString()">
<p>Some page content</p>
</body>
</html>
```

The result of running this JavaScript application is the following output to the web page:

```
firstName=Shelley
Shelley

lastName=Powers
Powers

state=Missouri
Missouri
```

This is a very handy way of processing form fields before they're submitted to the server, pulling in individual values from strings attached to the URL of the page, or a result returned from an Ajax call, which I demonstrate toward the end of the book.

Returning to the `String` object instance methods, `toUpperCase` and `toLowerCase`, convert the string to all upper- or lowercase characters, respectively, and return the converted result:

```
var someString = new String("Mix of upper and lower");
var newString = someString.toUpperCase(); // uppercases all of the letters
```

These are particularly useful functions if case is going to be an issue because you can convert the string to all upper- or lowercase before processing.

There is also one static method on the `String` object—`fromCharCode`:

```
var s = String.fromCharCode(345,99,99,76);
document.writeln(s);
```

The `fromCharCode` method takes Unicode values separated by commas and returns a string. However, as we discussed in Chapter 2, you can also embed Unicode characters directly into a string.

The last `String` methods depend on a concept known as *regular expressions*. Because regular expressions are associated with another built-in JavaScript object, `RegExp`, we'll look at all of the regular-expression-related `String` methods in the next section.

Regular Expressions and RegExp

Regular expressions are arrangements of characters that form a pattern that you can then use against strings to find matches, make replacements, or locate specific substrings. Most programming languages support some form of regular expression, and JavaScript is no exception.

You can create a regular expression explicitly using the `RegExp` object, although you can also create one using a literal. The following uses the explicit option:

```
var searchPattern = new RegExp('s+');
```

The next line of code demonstrates the literal `RegExp` option:

```
var searchPattern = /s+/;
```

In both cases, the plus sign (+) in the search pattern following the character s matches one or more consecutive uses of s in a string. The forward slashes with the literal (/s+/) mark that the object being created is a regular expression and not some other type of object.

The RegExp Methods: test and exec

The RegExp object has only two unique instance methods of interest: test and exec. The test method determines whether a string passed in as a parameter matches with the regular expression. The following example tests the pattern /JavaScript rules/ against the string to see whether a match exists:

```
var re = /JavaScript rules/;
var str = "JavaScript rules";
if (re.test(str)) document.writeln("I guess it does rule") ;
```

Matches are case-sensitive: if the pattern is /Javascript rules/, the result is false. To instruct the pattern-matching functions to ignore case, follow the second forward slash of the regular expression with the letter i:

```
var re =/Javascript rules/i;
```

The i option is a flag that modifies the pattern matching, forcing the matching process to disregard case. The other flags are g for a global match and m to match over many lines.

The global match instructs the pattern-matching process to find all occurrences of a pattern, regardless of where the pattern is in the line. Without the use of the global flag g, only the first match would either be replaced or returned. The multiline flag m enables the use of line-specific characters, such as ^ for the start of a line and $ for the end, to work across multiple lines.

If you're creating a RegExp object instance, the flags are passed as a second parameter:

```
var searchPattern = new RegExp('s+', 'g');
```

In the following snippet of code, the RegExp method exec searches for a specific pattern, /JS*/, across the entire string (g), ignoring case (i). A string with the matched pattern, available in the result array at the 0 index, is printed to the web page, as is the location where the next match will begin:

```
var re = new RegExp("JS*","ig");
var str = "cfdsJS *(&YJSjs 888JS";
var resultArray = re.exec(str);
while (resultArray) {
  document.writeln(resultArray[0]);
  document.writeln(" next match starts at " + re.lastIndex + "<br />");
      resultArray = re.exec(str);
}
```

The pattern described in the regular expression is the letter J, followed by any number of S's. Since the i flag is used, case is ignored, so the js substring is found. As the g flag is given, the RegExp lastIndex property is set to the location where the last pattern was found on each successive call, so each call to exec finds the next pattern. In all, the four items found are printed, and when no others are found, a null value is assigned to the array. Because the loop condition is just the array variable, setting the array to null results in the loop terminating. Running this code results in the following output:

```
JS next match starts at 6
JS next match starts at 13
js next match starts at 15
JS next match starts at 21
```

The **exec** method returns an array, but the array entries are not all matches, as you might have initially guessed, but rather are the current match and any parenthesized substrings. If you use parentheses to match substrings within the overall string, they are included in successive array entries in the resultant array following the overall matched string, contained in the 0 index for the array. If you altered the preceding code snippet to appear as in Example 4-6, other array entries would show the substring pattern matches.

Example 4-6. String and substring matching with RegExp

```
<!DOCTYPE html PUBLIC "-//W3C//DTD XHTML 1.1//EN"
"http://www.w3.org/TR/xhtml11/DTD/xhtml11.dtd">
<html xmlns="http://www.w3.org/1999/xhtml" xml:lang="en">
<head>
<title>RegExp string matching</title>
<meta http-equiv="Content-Type" content="text/html; charset=utf-8" />
<script type="text/javascript">
//<![CDATA[

window.onload=function() {
  var re = /(ds)+(j+s)/ig;
  var str = "cfdsJS *(&dsjjjsYJSjs 888dsdsJS";
  var resultArray = re.exec(str);
  while (resultArray) {
    document.writeln(resultArray[0]);
    document.writeln(" next match starts at " + re.lastIndex + "<br />");
    for (var i = 1; i < resultArray.length; i++) {
      document.writeln("substring of " + resultArray[i] + "<br />");
    }
    document.writeln("<br />");
    resultArray = re.exec(str);
  }
}
//]]>
</script>
</head>
<body>
<p></p>
</body>
</html>
```

The result from this example is:

```
dsJS next match starts at 6
substring of ds
substring of JS

dsjjjs next match starts at 16
substring of ds
```

```
substring of jjjs

dsdsJS next match starts at 31
substring of ds
substring of JS
```

These code samples demonstrated a couple of the special regular expression characters.
There are several regular expression characters, one of which is the plus sign (+) in
Example 4-6. Typically, books and articles throw all such characters into a table, and
then provide a couple of examples that use several together in a long and complicated
pattern, and that's the extent of the coverage. Because of this, many people have a lot
of trouble putting together regular expressions, and as a consequence, their applications don't work as they originally anticipated. I think regular expressions are important
enough to at least provide several examples, from simple to complex. If you have
worked with regular expressions before, you might want to skip this section—unless
you need the review.

Though you use `RegExp` methods in applications, you'll primarily use regular expressions and the `RegExp` object with the `String` object's `regex` methods: `replace`, `match`, and
`search`. The rest of the examples in this section demonstrate regular expressions using
these methods.

Working with Regular Expressions

You use the backslash character (\), usually called the *escape character*, to escape
whatever character follows it. In JavaScript regular expressions, the use of an escape
character results in two behaviors. If the character is usually treated literally, such as
the letter s, it's treated as a special character following the escape character—in this
case, a whitespace (space, tab, form feed, or line feed). Conversely, when you use the
backslash with a special character, such as the plus sign earlier, the character that follows the backslash is treated as a literal.

The JavaScript application in Example 4-7 searches a string for instances of a space
that's followed by an asterisk, and replaces the combination with a dash. Normally,
the asterisk is used to match zero or more of the preceding characters in a regular
expression, but in this case, we want to treat it as a literal.

Example 4-7. Escape character in regular expressions

```
<!DOCTYPE html PUBLIC "-//W3C//DTD XHTML 1.1//EN"
"http://www.w3.org/TR/xhtml11/DTD/xhtml11.dtd">
<html xmlns="http://www.w3.org/1999/xhtml" xml:lang="en">
<head>
<title>RegExp</title>
<meta http-equiv="Content-Type" content="text/html; charset=utf-8" />
<script type="text/javascript">
//<![CDATA[

function matchString() {
```

```
var regExp = /\s\*/g;
var str = "This *is *a *test *string";
var resultString = str.replace(regExp,'-');
alert(resultString);

}
//]]>
</script>
</head>
<body onload="matchString()">
<p>Some page content</p>
</body>
</html>
```

Applying the regular expression against the string results in the following line:

```
This-is-a-test-string
```

The regular expression pattern used in Example 4-7 is a very handy expression to keep in mind. If you want to replace all occurrences of spaces in a string with dashes, regardless of what's following the spaces, use the pattern /\s+\g in the replace method, passing in the hyphen as the replacement character.

Four of the regular expression characters are used to match specific occurrences of characters: the asterisk (*) matches the character preceding it zero or more times, the plus sign (+) matches the character preceding it one or more times, the question mark (?) matches zero or one of the preceding characters, and the period (.) matches exactly one character.

Two patterns of interest are the *greedy match* (.*) and the *lazy star* (.*?). In the first, because a period can represent any character, the asterisk matches until the last occurrence of a pattern, rather than the first. If you're looking for anything within quotes, you might think of using /".*"/. If you use regular expressions with a string, such as:

```
test='"one" or this is also a "test"'
```

the match begins with the first double quote and continues until the last one, not the second one:

```
"one" or this is also a "test"
```

The lazy star forces the match to end on the second occurrence of the double quote, rather than the last occurrence:

```
"one"
```

Example 4-8 contains a more complex regular expression. The application looks for a match on a date in the form of month name followed by space, day of month, and then year. The date begins after a colon.

Example 4-8. Patterns of repeating characters

```
<!DOCTYPE html PUBLIC "-//W3C//DTD XHTML 1.1//EN"
"http://www.w3.org/TR/xhtml11/DTD/xhtml11.dtd">
<html xmlns="http://www.w3.org/1999/xhtml" xml:lang="en">
<head>
<title>Find Date</title>
<meta http-equiv="Content-Type" content="text/html; charset=utf-8" />
<script type="text/javascript">
//<![CDATA[

function findDate() {

    var regExp = /:\D*\s\d+\s\d+/;
    var str = "This is a date: March 12 2009";
    var resultString = str.match(regExp);
    alert("Date" + resultString);

}
//]]>
</script>
</head>
<body onload="findDate()">
<p>Some page content</p>
</body>
</html>
```

Looking more closely at the regular expression, the first character in the pattern is the colon, followed by the backslash with a capital letter D: \D. This sequence is one way to look for any nonnumeric character; the asterisk following it means that any number of nonnumeric characters will match. The next part in the regular expression is a whitespace character, \s, followed by another new pattern, \d. Unlike the earlier sequence, \D, the lowercase letter means to match numbers only. The plus sign following this sequence means match one or more numbers. Another space follows \s in the pattern and then another sequence of numbers, \d+.

When matched against the string using `String match`, the date preceded by the colon is found, returned, and printed:

```
Date: March 12 2009
```

In the example, \D matches any nonnumeric character. Another way to create this particular match is to use the square brackets with a number range, preceded by the caret character (^). If you want to match any character except for numbers, use the following:

```
[^0-9]
```

The same holds true for \d, except now you want numbers, so leave off the caret:

```
[0-9]
```

If you wish to match on more than one character type, you can list each range of characters within the brackets. The following matches on any upper- or lowercase letters:

```
[A-Za-z]
```

Using this alternative set of patterns, you also could give the regular expression in Example 4-8 as follows:

```
var regExp = /:[^0-9]*\s[0-9]+\s[0-9]+/;
```

You can use the caret (^) in another pattern: you use it and the dollar sign ($) to capture specific patterns relative to the beginning and end of a line. When you use a caret outside the brackets, you match any sequence beginning a line; the dollar sign matches any sequence ending a line. In the following code snippet, the match is not successful because the character that was searched did not occur at the beginning of the line:

```
var regExp = /^The/i;
var str = "This is the JavaScript example";
```

However, the following would be successful:

```
var regExp = /^The/i;
var str = "The example";
```

If the multiline flag is given (m), the caret matches on the first character after the line break:

```
var regExp = /^The/im;
var str = "This is\nthe end";
```

The same positional pattern matching holds true for the end-of-line character. The following doesn't match:

```
var regExp = /end$/;
var str = "The end is near";
```

But this does:

```
var regExp = /end$/;
var str = "The end";
```

If the multiline flag is used, it matches at the end of the string and just before the line break:

```
var regExp = /The$/im;
var str = "This is really the\nend";
```

The use of parentheses is significant in regular expression pattern matching. Parentheses match and then remember the match. The remembered values are stored in the result array:

```
var rgExp = /(^\D*[0-9])/
var str = "This is fun 01 stuff";
var resultArray = str.match(rgExp);
document.writeln(resultArray);
```

In this code snippet, the array prints out This is fun 0 twice, separated by a comma, indicating two array entries. The first result is the match; the second, the stored value from the parentheses. If, instead of surrounding the entire pattern, you surround only a portion, such as /(^\D*)[0-9]/, this results in:

```
This is fun 0,This is fun
```

Only the surrounded matched string is stored.

Parentheses can also help you to switch material around in a string. RegExp recognizes special characters, labeled $1, $2, and so on, up to $9, that store substrings discovered through the use of the capturing parentheses. Example 4-9 finds pairs of strings separated by one or more dashes and switches the order of the strings.

Example 4-9. Swapping strings using regular expressions

```
<!DOCTYPE html PUBLIC "-//W3C//DTD XHTML 1.1//EN"
"http://www.w3.org/TR/xhtml11/DTD/xhtml11.dtd">
<html xmlns="http://www.w3.org/1999/xhtml" xml:lang="en">
<head>
<title>swap</title>
<meta http-equiv="Content-Type" content="text/html; charset=utf-8" />
<script type="text/javascript">
//<![CDATA[

function swapWords() {

    var rgExp = /(\w*)-*(\w*)/
    var str = "Java---Script";
    var resultStrng = str.replace(rgExp,"$2-$1");
    alert(resultStrng);
}
//]]>
</script>
</head>
<body onload="swapWords()">
<p>Some page content</p>
</body>
</html>
```

Here's the result of that JavaScript:

```
Script-Java
```

Notice that the number of dashes is also stripped down to just one dash. This example introduces another very popular pattern-matching character sequence, \w. This sequence matches any alphanumeric character, including the underscore (underline). It's equivalent to [A-Za-z0-9_]. Its converse is \W, which is equivalent to any nonalphanumeric character.

The last regular expression characters we'll examine in detail are the vertical bar (|) and the curly braces. The vertical bar indicates optional matches. For instance, the following matches to either the letter a or the letter b:

```
a|b
```

You can use more than one character with vertical bars to provide more options:

```
a|b|c
```

The curly braces indicate repetition of the preceding character a set number of times. The following searches for two **s** characters together:

```
s{2}
```

Regular expressions are extremely useful when processing data from Ajax applications, and when validating form contents, as I will demonstrate in Chapter 8.

The Date Object

In JavaScript, you use the `Date` object to create instances of dates. Once you have a date object instance, you can use several methods to access or modify the date (or components of the date) such as the year, day, and month.

Creating a date without passing in any parameters produces a date based on the client machine's date and time:

```
var dtNow = new Date();
```

Or, you can pass in optional parameters to the `Date` constructor to create a specific date. One option is to pass in the number of milliseconds since January 1, 1970 at 12:00:00:

```
var dtMilliseconds = new Date(5999000920);
```

The preceding code snippet results in the following date:

```
Wed, 11 Mar 1970 10:23:20 GMT
```

You can also use a string to create a date as long as you use the proper date format:

```
var newDate = new Date("March 12, 1980 12:20:25");
```

You can forgo the time in the string and just get a date with times set to zeros:

```
var newDate = new Date('March 12, 2008');
```

You can also pass in each value of the date as integers, in order of year, month (as 0 to 11), day, hour, minutes, seconds, and milliseconds:

```
var newDt = new Date(1977,11,23);
var newDt = new Date(1977,11,24,19,30,30,30);
```

The `Date` object instance methods feature several **get** and **set** methods for retrieving or setting specific components of the date. Each of the following gets specific values from the date according to local times:

getFullYear
: The four-digit year

getHours
: The hours component of the date/time

getMilliseconds
: The milliseconds component of the date/time

getMinutes
> The minutes component of the date/time

getMonth
> The month, as a number between 0 and 11 inclusive

getSeconds
> The seconds component of the date/time

getDay
> Returns the number representing the day of the week, starting with 0 for Sunday and ending with 6 for Saturday

getDate
> Returns the day of the month

Here are the Coordinated Universal Time (UTC) equivalents:

- getUTCFullYear
- getUTCHours
- getUTCMilliseconds
- getUTCMinutes
- getUTCMonth
- getUTCSeconds
- getUTCDay
- getUTCDate

Most of the get methods have equivalent set methods that set a component's value within a Date. An example would be setYear to set the year, setSeconds to set the seconds, or setUTCMonth to set a UTC month. The only method that doesn't have an equivalent set method is getDay. Also, two methods are deprecated, meaning they won't be available in the future. These are getYear and setYear.

Another method, getTimezoneOffset, returns the number of minutes (+ or −) of the offset of the local computer from UTC. Because I'm writing this in St. Louis, which is in UTC-5, I would get a value of 300 when calling this method against a local time date.

Six methods convert the date to a formatted string:

toString
> Outputs the string in local time

toGMTString
> Formats the string using GMT standards

toLocaleDateString *and* toLocaleTimeString
> Output the date and the time, respectively, using the locale

toLocaleString
> Converts the string using the current locale

toUTCString
    Formats the string using UTC standards

Also, three static methods are available directly on the `Date` object. `Date.now` returns the current date and time; `Date.parse` returns the number of milliseconds since January 1, 1970; and `Date.UTC` returns the number of milliseconds given the longest form of the constructor, described earlier:

```
var numMs = Date.UTC(1977,11,24,30,30,30);
```

Date.now is not standard. Creating a date primitive without using the `new` constructor also returns the current time:

```
var rightNow = Date();
```

Example 4-10 demonstrates several of the `Date` methods, including those that set date components, and methods to display the derived date.

Example 4-10. Several string setting and formatting Date methods

```
<!DOCTYPE html PUBLIC "-//W3C//DTD XHTML 1.1//EN"
"http://www.w3.org/TR/xhtml11/DTD/xhtml11.dtd">
<html xmlns="http://www.w3.org/1999/xhtml" xml:lang="en">
<head>
<title>Date</title>
<meta http-equiv="Content-Type" content="text/html; charset=utf-8" />
<script type="text/javascript">
//<![CDATA[

function testingDate() {

    // new date
    var dtNow = new Date();

    // set day, month, year
    dtNow.setDate(18);
    dtNow.setMonth(10);
    dtNow.setYear(1954);
    dtNow.setHours(7);
    dtNow.setMinutes(2);

    // output formatted
    document.writeln(dtNow.toString() + "<br />");
    document.writeln(dtNow.toLocaleString() + "<br />");
    document.writeln(dtNow.toLocaleDateString() + "<br />");
    document.writeln(dtNow.toLocaleTimeString() + "<br />");
    document.writeln(dtNow.toGMTString() + "<br />");
    document.writeln(dtNow.toUTCString());
}
//]]>
</script>
</head>
<body onload="testingDate()">
```

```
<p>Some page content</p>
</body>
</html>
```

The result of running Example 4-10 in Firefox 3.1 is:

```
Thu Nov 18 1954 07:02:19 GMT-0600 (CST)
Thu Nov 18 07:02:19 1954
11/18/1954
07:02:19
Thu, 18 Nov 1954 13:02:19 GMT
Thu, 18 Nov 1954 13:02:19 GMT
```

Given so many date options, it might be puzzling to figure out which specific locale to use in an application. I've found that a good rule of thumb is to reference everything in the web page reader's local time if her actions are isolated—such as when placing an order at an online store. However, if the person's actions are in relation to the actions of others, especially within an international audience (such as a weblog for comments), I recommend setting times to UTC to maintain a consistent framework for all of your readers.

The Math Object

Arithmetic isn't math, at least in JavaScript, where the operators for basic arithmetic described in Chapter 3 are not associated with the Math object. The Math object provides mathematical properties and methods, such as LN10, which is the logarithm of 10, and log(x), which returns the natural logarithm of x. It doesn't participate in simple arithmetic, such as addition and subtraction.

Unlike the other JavaScript objects, all of the Math object's properties and methods are static. This means you don't create a new instance of Math to get access to the functionality; you access the methods and properties directly on the shared object itself:

```
var newValue = Math.SQRT1;
```

The Math Properties

Several constant properties are associated with the Math object, including the familiar pi, as well as the square root of 2 and the national logarithm of 10. This following is a list of all of these properties:

E

    The value of e, the base of the natural logarithms

LN10

    The natural logarithm of 10

LN2

    The natural logarithm of 2

LOG2E
>   The approximate reciprocal of LN2—the base-2 logarithm of e

LOG10E
>   The approximate reciprocal of LN10—the base-10 logarithm of e

PI
>   The value of pi

SQRT1_2
>   The square root of 1/2

SQRT2
>   The square root of 2

Math in programming depends somewhat on the underlying architecture, and this includes how each browser that provides a JavaScript engine implements some of the math functions, as well as the operating system, machine, and so on. As such, the results of the trigonometric functions may vary somewhat, but hopefully not so much as to make the functions unusable within this context.

The Math Methods

The Math methods are relatively straightforward. Regardless of variable type, all arguments passed to the Math functions are converted to numbers first. You don't have to do any conversion in your code.

The abs function takes an argument representing a numeric value and returns the absolute value of that number. If the number is negative, the positive value is returned. The variable pVal is set to 3.4 in the following code snippet:

```
var nVal = -3.45;
var pVal = Math.abs(nVal);
```

Several trigonometric methods are also available: sin, cos, tan, acos, asin, atan, and atan2. These provide, respectively, the sine, cosine, tangent, arc cosine, arc sine, arc tangent, and computation of the angle between an *x*-point and the origin. Each takes a specific type of numeric argument and returns a result that is meaningful to the method:

Math.sin(x)
>   A specific angle, in radians

Math.cos(x)
>   A specific angle, in radians

Math.tan(x)
>   An angle, in radians

Math.acos(x)
>   A number between −1 and 1

```
Math.asin(x)
```
A number between −1 and 1

```
Math.atan(x)
```
Any number

```
Math.atan2(py,px)
```
The *y* and *x* coordinates of a point

The `Math.ceil` method rounds a number to the next highest whole number. The following two lines of JavaScript set the variable **pVal** to 4:

```
var nVal = 3.45;
var pVal = Math.ceil(nVal);
```

The following lines of JavaScript set **pVal** to −3:

```
var nVal = -3.45;
var pVal = Math.ceil(nVal);
```

The `Math.floor` method, on the other hand, rounds a number down—returning the next lowest whole number. The following JavaScript sets **pVal** to 3:

```
var nVal = 3.45;
var pVal = Math.floor(nVal);
```

The following lines of JavaScript sets **pVal** to −4:

```
var nVal = -3.45;
var pVal = Math.floor(nVal);
```

The `Math.round` method rounds to the nearest integer; whether this is higher or lower depends on the value. A value of 3.45 rounds to 3, whereas a value of 3.85 rounds to 4. A midway number, such as 3.5, would round up to 4. The result is the nearest integer regardless of whether the value is negative or positive.

`Math.exp(x)` calculates a number equivalent to e, the base of natural logarithms, raised to the value of the argument passed to the method:

```
var nVal = Math.exp(4) // equivalent to e⁴
```

`Math.pow` raises any number to a given power:

```
var nVal = Math.pow(3,2) // 3² or 9
```

`Math.min` and `Math.max` compare two or more numbers and return the minimum or the maximum:

```
var nVal = 1.45;
var nVal2 = 4.5;
var nVal3 = -3.33;
var nResult = Math.min(nVal, nVal2, nVal3) // set to -3.33
var nResult2 = Math.max(nVal, nVal2, nVal3) // set to 4.5
```

The last method, `Math.random`, generates a number between 0 (inclusive) and 1 (exclusive):

```
var nValue = Math.random();
```

You can multiply this value by 10 or 100 (or by any value) to generate random numbers beyond a value of 1. Unfortunately, you can't set limits to generate a random number within a range of values. You can emulate this behavior, though, as Example 4-11 demonstrates.

Example 4-11. A random-number generator

```
<!DOCTYPE html PUBLIC "-//W3C//DTD XHTML 1.1//EN"
"http://www.w3.org/TR/xhtml11/DTD/xhtml11.dtd">
<html xmlns="http://www.w3.org/1999/xhtml" xml:lang="en">
<head>
<title>Random Quote</title>
<meta http-equiv="Content-Type" content="text/html; charset=utf-8" />
<script type="text/javascript">
  //<![CDATA[

function getQuote() {

    var quoteArray = new Array(5);
    quoteArray[0] = "Quote one";
    quoteArray[1] = "Quote two";
    quoteArray[2] = "Quote three";
    quoteArray[3] = "Quote four";
    quoteArray[4] = "Quote five";

    iValue = Math.random(); // random number between 0 and 1
    iValue *= 5; // multiply by 5 to move the decimal
    iValue = Math.floor(iValue); // round to nearest integer
    alert(quoteArray[iValue]);
}

//]]>
</script>
</head>
<body onload="getQuote();">
  <p>some content</p>
</body>
</html>
```

An array is created with five quotes. A function is called when the page loads, which uses several `Number` and `Math` functions to generate an application number (between 0 and 4 inclusive). The number is used to access an array element, which is then output.

JavaScript Arrays

A JavaScript `Array` is an object, just like `String` or `Math`. As such, you create it with a constructor:

```
var newArray = new Array('one','two');
```

You also can create an array as a literal value, which doesn't require the explicit use of the `Array` object:

```
var newArray = ['one','two'];
```

Unlike `String` and `Number`, the JavaScript application immediately converts the literal to an object of type `Array`, assigning the result to the variable. `String`, `Number`, and `Boolean` literals are converted to objects only when object methods are called, and then discard the object instances immediately afterward.

Once the `Array` instance is created, you can access array elements by their index value—the number representing their location in the array:

```
alert(newArray[0]);
```

Array indexes start at 0 and go up to the number of elements, minus 1. So, an array of five elements would have indexes from 0 to 4.

Arrays don't have to be one-dimensional. It's not uncommon to have an array in which each element has multiple dimensions, and the way to manage this in JavaScript is to create an array where each element is an array itself. In the following code snippet, an array of three-dimensional values is created:

```
var threedPoints = new Array();
threedPoints[0] = new Array(1.2,3.33,2.0);
threedPoints[1] = new Array(5.3,5.5,5.5);
threedPoints[2] = new Array(6.4,2.2,1.9);
```

If the inner array contains the *x*, *y*, and *z* coordinates in order, you can access the *z* coordinate of the third point with the following code:

```
var newZPoint = threedPoints[2][2]; // remember, arrays start with 0
```

To add array dimensions, continue creating arrays in elements:

```
threedPoints[2][2] = new Array(4.4,4.6,44) // and so on
var newthreedZPoint = threedPoints[2][2][1];
```

You do not have to know the number of elements for an array ahead of time. As the examples demonstrate, you can create an array with a fixed number of elements in the array declaration, or just add elements as you go along. You can also set the size of an array by adding its *nth* or last element first:

```
var testArray = new Array();
testArray[99] = 'some value'; // testArray is now an array with 100 elements
```

To find the length of an array (the number of elements), use the `Array` property called `length`:

```
alert(testArray.length); // outputs 100
```

If you access the length of a multiple-dimension array, you'll get the number of elements for only a particular dimension:

```
alert(threedPoints[2][2].length); // outputs 3
alert(threedPoints[2].length); // outputs 3
alert(threedPoints.length); // outputs 3
```

In addition to `length`, the `Array` object also has a few other properties of interest, and several methods. One such method is `splice`, which allows you to insert and/or remove elements from an array—a rather handy method to have. In the following code snippet, `splice` adds two elements and removes two, starting at index 2 (the third element):

```
var fruitArray = new Array('apple','peach','orange','lemon','lime','cherry');
var removed = fruitArray.splice(2,2,'melon','banana');
document.writeln(removed + "<br />");
document.writeln(fruitArray);
```

The preceding code generates the following two lines:

```
orange,lemon
apple,peach,melon,banana,lime,cherry
```

The removed elements are returned as an array from the `splice` method call.

The `slice` method slices an array and returns the result:

```
var newFruit = fruitArray.slice(2,4); // returns an array of 3 elements: melon,
banana, and lime
```

The `concat` method concatenates one array onto the end of the other, returning an array with entries of apple, peach, melon, banana, lime, cherry, orange, and lemon:

```
var newFruit = fruitArray.concat(removed);
```

Neither `concat` nor `slice` alters the original array. Instead, they return a new array containing the results of the operation.

In the examples, I've been printing out the arrays directly. The JavaScript engine converts the arrays to a string, using a default separator of a comma (,) between array elements. If you want to designate a different separator, use the `join` method to generate a string, passing in what you want used as the separator, such as a space:

```
var strng = fruitArray.join(" ")
```

You can also reverse the order of the elements in an array using the `reverse` method:

```
fruitArray.reverse();
```

In many cases, the exact order of the elements in an array is unimportant. Sometimes, though, you want to have the order preserved, such as when the array serves as a queue. Several methods are useful for maintaining arrays as queues or lists, which we'll look at next.

FIFO Queues

You can use arrays to track a queue of items, where each is added *FIFO* (first-in, first-out). Four handy `Array` methods can maintain queues, lists, and the like: `push`, `pop`, `shift`, and `unshift`.

The push method adds elements to the end of an array, whereas the unshift method adds elements to the beginning of the array. Both return the new length of the array.

The pop method removes the last element of the array, and the shift method removes the first element. Both return the element retrieved from the array.

All four methods modify the array—either adding or removing elements permanently from the array. Example 4-12 demonstrates how you can maintain a FIFO queue in JavaScript.

Example 4-12. FIFO queue using Array methods

```
<!DOCTYPE html PUBLIC "-//W3C//DTD XHTML 1.1//EN"
"http://www.w3.org/TR/xhtml11/DTD/xhtml11.dtd">
<html xmlns="http://www.w3.org/1999/xhtml" xml:lang="en">
<head>
<title>FIFO</title>
<meta http-equiv="Content-Type" content="text/html; charset=utf-8" />
<script type="text/javascript">
    //<![CDATA[

function pushPop() {

    // create FIFO queue and add items using push
    var fifoArray = new Array();
    fifoArray.push("Apple");
    fifoArray.push("Banana");

    var ln = fifoArray.push("Cherry");

    // print out length and array
    document.writeln("length is " + ln + " and array is " + fifoArray + "<br />");

    // use shift to shift the items off the array
    for (var i = 0; i < ln; i++) {
       document.writeln(fifoArray.shift() + "<br />");
    }

    // print out length
    document.writeln("length now is " + fifoArray.length + "<br /><br />");

    // now, same with unshift
    var fifoNewArray = new Array();

    fifoNewArray.unshift("Learning");
    fifoNewArray.unshift("Java");
    ln = fifoNewArray.unshift("Script");

    document.writeln("length is " + ln + " and array is " + fifoNewArray + "<br
/>");

    // unshift
    for (var i = 0; i < ln; i++) {
      document.writeln(fifoNewArray.pop() + "<br />");
    }
```

```
    document.writeln("new length is " + fifoNewArray.length );
}

//]]>
</script>
</head>
<body onload="pushPop();">
</body>
</html>
```

The first thing to notice in this example is that I've paired `shift` and `push`, and `unshift` and `pop`. The reason for this is the order in which these methods work. The `push` method adds an element to the end of an array, and as each new element is added, it pushes the first elements to the front of the array. The `pop` method removes the items from the end of the array first, creating a LIFO list (last-in, first-out)—a perfectly legitimate queue, but not what we're after with the program. We want the first element added to be the first element retrieved. The `shift` method removes elements from the top of the array, which does suit our needs.

The same applies to `unshift` and `pop`. The `unshift` method adds items to the top of an array, each new item pushing the older ones farther down the list, while `pop` removes them from the bottom of the queue first. This again maintains the order of items, and this is what we're after—not the order of the array elements themselves, but the order in which they're added.

The result of running this JavaScript in our target browsers (all except for current versions of Internet Explorer, which don't return a length when using `unshift`) is the following:

```
length is 3 and array is Apple,Banana,Cherry
Apple
Banana
Cherry
length now is 0

length is 3 and array is Script,Java,Learning
Learning
Java
Script
new length is 0
```

Example 4-12 also demonstrated how `for` loops can traverse an array. Rather than have to individually write out each `shift` or `pop` method call, the application iterated through the same call the same number of times as elements in the array. This example is small, but you can imagine how much of a time-saver this can be with a larger array.

Typically, when traversing an array with a `for` loop, the variable that's adjusted with each loop is incremented (or decremented when counting down) and is used as an array index:

```
for (var i = 0; i < someArray.length; i++) {
    alert(someArray[i]);
}
```

However, you do not have to use the index; it's there if you need it. And as implied, you count down with a for loop as well as count up:

```
for (var i = someArray.length-1; i >= 0; i--) ...
```

As an alternative, you can use the for...in loop to access each array element:

```
var programLanguages = new Array
('C++','Pascal','FORTRAN','BASIC','C#','Java','Perl','JavaScript');
for (var itemIndex in programLanguages) {
    document.writeln(programLanguages[itemIndex] + "<br />");
}
```

Other methods are associated with the array that require the use of a callback function, which we will cover in Chapter 5.

Test Your Knowledge: Quiz

1. Comma-separated strings are a common data format. How would you create an array of elements when given a comma-separated string? Write the code for the following string, and then access the third element: "cats,dogs,birds,horses".

2. The \b special character can define a word boundary, and \B matches on a nonword boundary. Define a regular expression that will find all occurrences of the word *fun* in the following string and replace them with *power*:

    ```
    "The fun of functions is that they are functional."
    ```

3. Create code to get today's date, modify it by a week, and print out the new date.

4. Given a number of 34.44, write code that would round the number down. Do the same to round the number up.

5. Given a string such as the following, use pattern matching and replace all existing punctuation with commas, and then load it as an array and print out each value:

    ```
    var str = "apple.orange-strawberry,lemon-.lime";
    ```

Test Your Knowledge: Answers

1. Use the String.split method, passing in a comma as the delimiter. Solution is:

    ```
    var animalString = "cats,dogs,birds,horses";
    var animalArray = String.split(animalString,",");
    alert(animalArray[2]); // alert box displays birds
    ```

2. The solution is:

```
var funPattern = /\bfun\b/;
var strToSearch = "The fun of functions is that they are functional";
var afterMatch = strToSearch.replace(funPattern,"power");
```

3. There is no Date function that manipulates weeks, but we know that a week is seven days at 24 hours a day, for a total of 168 hours. Use the getHours method to get the current date's hours, add 168 to it, reset the hours, and then print out the date:

```
var dtNow = new Date();
var hours = dtNow.getHours();
hours+=168;
dtNow.setHours(hours);
document.writeln(dtNow.toString());
```

4. Math.floor can round the number down, and Math.ceil can round the number up. The solutions are:

```
var baseNum = 34.44;
var numFloor = Math.floor(baseNum); // returns 34
var numCeil = Math.ceil(baseNum); // returns 35
```

5. The solution is:

```
var strToAlter = "apple.orange-strawberry,lemon-.lime";
var puncPattern = /[\.|-]/g;
var afterMatch = strToAlter.replace(puncPattern,",");
var fruits = afterMatch.split(',');
for (var i = 0; i < fruits.length; i++)
    document.writeln(fruits[i]);
```

Functions

JavaScript functions are a key part of the language, but they're not quite what they seem. They look like they would belong in the family of statements, but actually they're objects just like all the others we covered in the preceding chapter. You can define a function, create a new one, and even print one out.

Thanks to this functionality, you can assign a function to a variable or to an array element, or even pass one as an argument to another function call. This makes a function a very flexible and useful object, but also a confusing one for new JavaScript developers.

There are three approaches to creating functions in JavaScript: declarative/static, dynamic/anonymous, and literal. It's important to understand the impact of each type of declaration before you use it.

Declarative Functions

The most common type of function uses the declarative/static format. This approach begins with the `function` keyword, followed by the function name, parentheses containing zero or more arguments, and then the function body:

```
function functionname (param1, param2, ..., paramn) {
   function statements
}
```

The curly braces around the function's statements are a requirement, even if the function body consists of only one statement.

Unless I'm creating a new library with new objects, or defining functions on the fly based on events, this is the syntax I use most often, and the syntax I've been using for chapter examples in the book to this point.

The declarative function is parsed once, when the page is loaded, and the parsed result is used each time the function is called. It's easy to spot the function definition in the code, it's simple to read and understand, and it has limited negative consequences, such as memory leaks. It's also more familiar to developers who have worked with other programming languages.

The following snippet of code creates a function that uses this function format, which is called immediately after it's declared:

```
function sayHi(toWhom) {
    alert("Hi " + toWhom);
}
sayHi("World!");
```

In the preceding code, calling the function results in an alert window that displays "Hi World!" Barring JavaScript errors, no matter what string is passed to the function or how many times the function is called, the same function object is used and the result is the same: an alert window opens with a message.

Function Naming Conventions and Size

Functions perform actions. As such, you'll want to incorporate into the function name a verb that summarizes the activity of the function as much as possible. The following are good examples of function names:

- runQuote
- printDate
- processName
- addNumbers

The verb typically begins the function name, followed by one or more nouns, with the first letter of each noun capitalized. This naming practice isn't a requirement for JavaScript, and it's not always the approach that developers prefer. However, it does have the advantage of being easy to read and somewhat self-documenting.

If you have a hard time naming the function because it's performing more than one task, you may want to consider splitting the function into smaller units, which also encourages reusability. Instead of a function that parses a form for values, validates the entries, and then uses the values in an Ajax server call, you could create a function that validates email addresses or zip code entries and then use these in other functions. The advantage is that when you package the validation functions in separate files, you can use them in many JavaScript applications.

In fact, the rule should be to keep functions small, specific to a task, and as general as possible.

Function Returns and Arguments

Functions communicate with the calling program through the arguments passed to the function and the values returned from it.

Variables based on primitives, such as a string, boolean, or number, are passed to a function by value. This means that if you change the actual argument in the function, the change is not reflected in the calling program.

Objects passed to a function, on the other hand, are passed by reference. Changes in the function to the object are reflected in the calling program.

Example 5-1 passes two arguments to a function: one is a string variable and the other is an array. The code modifies both arguments in the function and then outputs their contents in the calling program. The string remains unchanged because it's a primitive value, but the array object's second member has a different value, and a third array member has been added.

Example 5-1. Function arguments, passed as value and by reference

```
<!DOCTYPE html PUBLIC "-//W3C//DTD XHTML 1.1//EN"
"http://www.w3.org/TR/xhtml11/DTD/xhtml11.dtd">
<html xmlns="http://www.w3.org/1999/xhtml" xml:lang="en">
<head>
<title>Pass Me</title>
<meta http-equiv="Content-Type" content="text/html; charset=utf-8" />
<script type="text/javascript">
//<![CDATA[

function alterArgs(strLiteral, aryObject) {

    // overwrite original string
    strLiteral = "Override";
    aryObject[1] = "2";
    aryObject[aryObject.length] = "three";
}

function testParams() {
    var str = "Original Literal";
    var ary = new Array("one","two");

    document.writeln("string literal is " + str + "<br />");
    document.writeln("Array object is " + ary + "<br /><br />");

    alterArgs(str,ary);

    document.writeln("string literal is " + str + "<br /> ");
    document.writeln("Array object is " + ary);
}

//]]>
</script>
</head>
<body onload="testParams();">
<p>Some page content</p>
</body>
</html>
```

Figure 5-1 shows the Example 5-1 application loaded in Firefox. The first two lines are the string literal and array object before the function call; the second two are the same values after the function call.

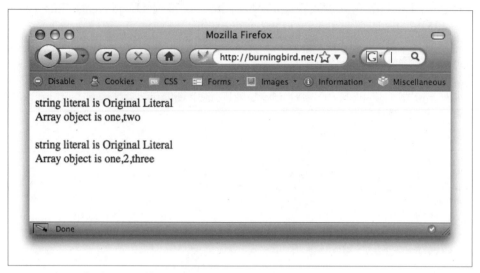

Figure 5-1. Result of running the Example 5-1 application in Firefox

A function may or may not return a value. If it does, the `return` statement can occur anywhere in the function code, and there could even be more than one `return` statement. When the JavaScript processing application encounters a `return` statement, it stops processing the function code at that point and returns control to the calling statement.

One reason you might have more than one `return` statement is if you want to terminate and exit the function when a condition is met. In the following snippet of code, if a condition isn't met in the function, the function terminates immediately; otherwise, processing continues:

```
function testValues(numValue) {
    if (isNaN(numValue)) {
        return "error -- not a number";
    }
    ...
    return ...
}
```

Functions don't require return values, though they may be useful in error handling—returning a value of `false` if the function isn't successful, for example. (I cover more sophisticated methods of error handling in Chapter 13.)

Opposite in behavior to the declarative function is the dynamic/anonymous function, discussed in the next section.

Anonymous Functions

Functions are objects. As such, you can create them—just like a `String` or `Array` or other type—by using a constructor and assigning the function to a variable. In the following code, a new function is created using the `Function` constructor, with the function body and argument passed in as arguments:

```
var sayHi = new Function("toWhom","alert('Hi ' + toWhom);");
sayHi("World!");
```

This type of function is often referred to as an *anonymous function* because the function itself isn't directly declared or named.

The JavaScript processing application, unlike with the declarative function, creates the anonymous function dynamically; each time it's *invoked* or called, the function is dynamically reconstructed. If the function is used in a loop, this means it's created with each iteration of the loop, whereas a declarative/static function would be created only once. As such, you might think anonymous functions aren't too useful. However, a dynamic function is a great way to define the functionality necessary to meet a need that's determined only at runtime.

Here's the syntax of an anonymous function using a constructor:

```
var variable = new Function ("param1", "param2", ... , "paramn", "function body");
```

The first parameters are the arguments to the function as you would define them in a declarative function. The last parameter is the function body. The whole function is assigned to a variable:

```
var func = new Function("x", "y", "return x * y")
```

This is equivalent to the following using a declarative/static function:

```
function func (x, y) {
    return x * y;
}
```

Example 5-2 takes the dynamic nature of an anonymous function to its extreme. The user provides the function body and the value of the two parameters defined for the function, via a prompt dialog window. The whole function is invoked, and the result is printed to the page.

Example 5-2. A dynamic/anonymous function

```
<!DOCTYPE html PUBLIC "-//W3C//DTD XHTML 1.1//EN"
"http://www.w3.org/TR/xhtml11/DTD/xhtml11.dtd">
<html xmlns="http://www.w3.org/1999/xhtml" xml:lang="en">
<head>
<title>Build a Function</title>
<meta http-equiv="Content-Type" content="text/html; charset=utf-8" />
<script type="text/javascript">
//<![CDATA[
```

```
function buildFunction() {

    // prompt for function and args
    var func= prompt("Enter function body:");
    var x = prompt("Enter value of x:");
    var y = prompt("Enter value of y:");

    // invoke anonymous function
    var op = new Function("x", "y", func);
    var theAnswer = op(x, y);

    // print out results
    alert("Function is: " + func);
    alert( "x is: " + x +
                " y is: " + y);
    alert("The answer is: " + theAnswer);
}

//]]>
</script>
</head>
<body onload="buildFunction();">
<p>Some content</p>
</body>
</html>
```

Because JavaScript is loosely typed, the function can work with number values:

```
Function is: return x * y
x is: 33 y is: 11
The answer is: 363
```

It can also work with strings:

```
Function is: return x + y
x is: This is y is: the string
The answer is: This is the string
```

The only requirement is that the operation has to be meaningful for the data type. Even then, a JavaScript error won't occur because the browser doesn't see the error; it occurs at runtime. You'll end up with something like the following:

```
Function is: return x * y
x is: this is y is: the answers
The answer is: NaN
```

You can also get unexpected results. If you use the plus sign (+) with two numbers, you'll get the following (rather than a numeric result) because JavaScript interprets the arguments within the context as strings and performs concatenation:

```
Function is: return x + y;
x is: 2 y is: 3
The answer is: 23
```

To ensure expected results, you can use explicit conversion:

```
Function is: return parseInt(x) + parseInt(y);
x is: 2 y is: 3
The answer is: 5
```

Needless to say, you should use anonymous functions with caution. I don't recommend allowing your web page readers to define the functions used within your pages. However, dynamic functions can be an interesting way to deal with user input, as long as you strip out anything in that input that can cause problems: embedded links, messing around with cookies, calling server-side functionality, creating new functions, and so forth.

 If you run into problems with Example 5-2 with IE8, you may need to set security parameters to work with window prompts.

Another hybrid approach to creating functions combines the static capabilities of the declarative function with some of the anonymity of the anonymous functions: the function literal, discussed next.

Function Literals

Before introducing the next—and potentially confusing—type of function, a little refresher on objects and literals might be helpful. As I demonstrated in earlier chapters, JavaScript objects can have a literal form. Rather than use a constructor and the object, you can use a representation. You can construct a string using the `String` constructor, and access the `String` methods:

```
var str = new String("Learning Java");
document.writeln(str.replace(/Java/,"JavaScript"));
```

You can also use a variable based on the primitive string type and still access the `String` object's methods, as the JavaScript engine implicitly wraps the literal in an object when the `String` method is invoked:

```
var str2 = "Learning Java";
document.writeln(str2.replace(/Java/,"JavaScript"));
```

In fact, you don't even need a variable:

```
document.writeln("Learning Java".replace(/Java/,"JavaScript"));
```

What works for strings also works for functions, which means you don't have to use a function constructor to create a function and assign it to a variable; it literally becomes a *function literal*:

```
var func = function (params) {
statements;
}
```

Function literals are also known as *function expressions* because the function is created as part of an expression, rather than as a distinct statement type. They resemble anonymous functions in that they don't have a specific function name. However, unlike anonymous functions, function literals are parsed only once. In fact, other than the fact that the function is assigned to a variable, function literals resemble declarative functions:

```
var func = function (x, y) {
    return x * y;
}
alert(func(3,3));
```

The function literal's uniqueness is apparent when you extend the concept to do something such as pass a function as a parameter to a function. Example 5-3 demonstrates this interesting property. The example defines a function, `funcObject`, with three parameters, the third of which is a function processing the first two parameters.

Example 5-3. Passing a function to a function

```
<!DOCTYPE html PUBLIC "-//W3C//DTD XHTML 1.1//EN"
"http://www.w3.org/TR/xhtml11/DTD/xhtml11.dtd">
<html xmlns="http://www.w3.org/1999/xhtml" xml:lang="en">
<head>
<title>Function Literal</title>
<meta http-equiv="Content-Type" content="text/html; charset=utf-8" />
<script type="text/javascript">
//<![CDATA[

// invoking third argument as function
function funcObject(x,y,z) {
    alert(z(x,y));
}

function testFunction() {

// third parameter is function
funcObject(3,4,function(x,y) { return x * y})
}

//]]>
</script>
</head>
<body onload="testFunction();">
<p>some content</p>
</body>
</html>
```

The result of this application is an alert window with the value **"12"**. Another variation of the function call could be:

```
funcObject(4,2,function(x,y) { return x - y})
```

The result of this function call is that parameter y would be subtracted from parameter x, with a value of **2** printed to the alert window.

A second form of the function literal isn't anonymous, in that the function is given a name:

```
var func = function multiply(x,y) {
    return x * y;
}
```

However, *the name is accessible only from within the function itself.* This isn't all that handy, unless you're implementing a recursive function.

Functions and Recursion

A function that invokes itself is called a *recursive* function. Typically, you use a recursive function when a process must be performed more than once, with each new iteration of the process performed on the previously processed result. The use of recursion isn't common in JavaScript, but it can be useful when dealing with data that's in a tree-line structure, such as the Document Object Model (DOM). However, it can also be memory- and resource-intensive, as well as complicated to implement and maintain. As such, use recursion sparingly, and make sure you test thoroughly.

In the preceding section, I wrote about named function literals, in which the function is given a name but only the function itself can access that name. This is an ideal setup for recursion.

Example 5-4 uses a recursive function to traverse a numeric array, add the numbers in the array, and add the numbers to a string.

Example 5-4. JavaScript function recursion

```
<!DOCTYPE html PUBLIC "-//W3C//DTD XHTML 1.1//EN"
"http://www.w3.org/TR/xhtml11/DTD/xhtml11.dtd">
<html xmlns="http://www.w3.org/1999/xhtml" xml:lang="en">
<head>
<title>Recursion</title>
<meta http-equiv="Content-Type" content="text/html; charset=utf-8" />
<script type="text/javascript">
//<![CDATA[

function runRecursion() {

    var addNumbers = function sumNumbers(numArray,indexVal,resultArray) {

        // recursion test
        if (indexVal == numArray.length)
            return resultArray;

        // perform numeric addition
        resultArray[0] += Number(numArray[indexVal]);

        // perform string concatenation
        if (resultArray[1].length > 0) {
            resultArray[1] += " and ";
```

```
            }
            resultArray[1] += numArray[indexVal].toString();

            // increment index
            indexVal++;

            // call function again, return results
            return sumNumbers(numArray,indexVal,resultArray);
        }

        // create numeric array, and the result array
        var numArray = ['1','35.4','-14','44','0.5'];
        var resultArray = new Array(0,''); // necessary for the initial case

        // call function
        var result = addNumbers(numArray,0, resultArray);

        // output
        document.writeln(result[0] + "<br />");
        document.writeln(result[1]);
    }
//]]>
</script>
</head>
<body onload="runRecursion();">
<p>some content</p>
</body>
</html>
```

The result of running Example 5-4 is a page output of:

```
66.9
1 and 35.4 and -14 and 44 and 0.5
```

In this JavaScript application, the sumNumbers literal function tests to see whether the index value passed as a parameter is equal to the length of an array of numbers, also passed as a parameter. If it is not, the function then adds the next member number value to the sum total, as well as concatenates the number to a string, both of which are members of a two-element array passed as a parameter.

When the index value is equal to the number array length, the function returns the resultArray. Because the function was called recursively, the result is passed up from each iteration of sumNumbers until the last iteration, when the value is returned to the application that first invoked the function through the variable to which it was assigned.

Of course, with this example, you could use a while loop to achieve the same results. However, as I mentioned earlier, when you're working with tree-structured data such as the DOM, recursion is extremely valuable, as is the function literal used to implement this process. However, not all uses of function literals in all browsers are without potential negative side effects. One area of risk associated with nested functions is possible memory leaks from a concept called *closure*.

Nested Functions, Function Closure, and Memory Leaks

Another interesting aspect of function literals in JavaScript is their use as nested functions. Consider the following:

```
function outer (args) {
    function inner (args) {
        inner statements;
    }
}
```

With a nested function, the inner function operates within the scope of the outer function, including having access to the outer function's variables and arguments. The outer function, though, does not have access to the inner function's variables, nor does the calling application have access to the inner function. (Well, not unless it is created as a function literal and is returned to the calling application, which then adds its own complication.)

Example 5-5 demonstrates creating a nested, inner-function literal, which is then returned to the calling application (shown in bold in the example). The inner function has access to the outer function's parameter and variable. It also has a parameter of its own, to which the outer function has no access.

When the inner function is passed to the application via the outer function and is invoked directly, it concatenates the string passed as a parameter to the original outer function call, to the string passed to the inner function as a parameter, and returns the result. Changing the parameter to the inner function changes the string, as does calling the outer function again with a different parameter, and getting another instance of the inner function.

Example 5-5. Nested functions and closure

```
<!DOCTYPE html PUBLIC "-//W3C//DTD XHTML 1.1//EN"
"http://www.w3.org/TR/xhtml11/DTD/xhtml11.dtd">
<html xmlns="http://www.w3.org/1999/xhtml" xml:lang="en">
<head>
<title>Nested</title>
<meta http-equiv="Content-Type" content="text/html; charset=utf-8" />
<script type="text/javascript">
//<![CDATA[

// outer function
function outerFunc(base) {

    var punc = "!";

    // return inner function
    return function (ext) {
        return base + ext + punc;
    }

}
```

```
function processNested() {

    // create access to inner function
    var baseString = outerFunc("Hello ");

    // inner function still has access to outer function argument
    var newString = baseString("World!");
    alert(newString);

    // and still
    var notherString = baseString("Reader!");
    alert(notherString);

    // create another instance of inner function
    var anotherBase = outerFunc("Hiya, Hey ");

    // another local string
    var lastString = anotherBase("you!");
    alert(lastString);
}
//]]>
</script>
</head>
<body onload="processNested();">
<p>Some content</p>
</body>
</html>
```

The result of this application is three alert boxes popping up with "Hello World!", "Hello Reader!", and "Hiya, Hey you!", consecutively.

How does this work? Isn't this in violation of scoping rules, which state that when a function terminates, all of the memory for its local variables gets released via automatic garbage collection?

Not quite.

Each time a new scope is created in a JavaScript application, an associated *scoping bubble*, if you will, is created to enclose it. This applies to functions, which operate in their own scope.

Normally, when the function terminates, the scope is released because it's no longer necessary. However, in the case of an inner function that's returned to the outer application and assigned to an external variable, the scope of the inner function is attached to the outer function, which in turn is attached to the calling application—just enough to maintain the integrity of the inner function and the outer function argument and variable. Returning a function literal created as an internal object within another function, and assigning it to a variable in the calling application, is known as *closure* in JavaScript. This concept of *scope chaining* ensures that the data necessary for the application to work is in place.

This is an important concept in JavaScript libraries, and we'll explore closures later in the book; however, there's a problem associated with closures—you can create closures accidentally. In Example 5-5, if a new reference to the inner function is created for each string created, rather than reusing the variable referencing the inner function, there will be a lot of instances of that object over time.

Accidental closure can also occur when a circular reference is created, such as the following from the Mozilla documentation site:

```
function leakMemory() {
    var el = document.getElementById('el');
    var newObj = { 'el': el };
    el.newObj = newObj;
}
```

We'll get into the DOM in Chapter 11, and we'll use the `getElementById` method extensively in the second half of this book, but in this code example, the DOM is accessed to get an element identified by `el`. The element is then used to create a new object reference (`newObj`) using a format I'll also introduce later in the book. The new function literal creates an unnamed object that assigns the retrieved DOM object to a property named `el`.

Then comes the kicker: we assign `newObj` to a newly added property on the original element retrieved from the DOM (perfectly acceptable behavior in JavaScript), which literally means we've assigned the object as a property of itself. This is not something I want to encourage, but most browsers can manage to terminate the closure and reclaim the memory—except earlier versions of Internet Explorer.

Older (but still popular) versions of IE (6.x and 7.x) provide their own memory management for DOM objects, in addition to memory management for JavaScript objects. In the case of accidental closures caused from such circular references as this and the crossover between JavaScript and DOM objects, the memory is allocated and is never freed—not even when the page is closed. In fact, the only time the memory is freed is *when the browser is closed*.

The memory leak that results is usually small, unless you put all of this into a loop, in which case the memory loss could build quickly. Because of the problem with memory leaks, and the prevalence of older versions of IE, you should use caution when using closure, as demonstrated in this section. Thankfully, this memory leakage was fixed with IE8.

 For an excellent overview of closures, see the paper by Jim Ley on the topic, at *http://jibbering.com/faq/faq_notes/closures.html*.

Callback Functions

In "JavaScript Arrays" in Chapter 4, I wrote that some methods depend on functions that are invoked automatically based on some event. The `Array` methods are `filter`, `forEach`, `every`, `map`, and `some`, and the functions used are function literals, though when used in this manner, they're usually referred to as *callback functions*.

 The `Array` object callback functions are not standard ECMAScript. Though the example in this section works with Safari, Opera, and Firefox, it does not work with Internet Explorer, including the newer IE8.

Returning to the `Array` methods, the `filter` method ensures that elements are not added to any element unless they pass certain criteria. Rather than have to test a value and then add it individually to an array if the element passed whatever filter you're applying, you can just toss everything at the array and let `filter` take care of the work for you.

The `forEach` method takes a function that's processed against each element. Unlike `filter`, the array is not impacted by the function. The `map` method runs the callback function against all the array elements and creates a new array from the results. It's similar to `forEach`, in that the callback is run against every array element. However, you use `forEach` primarily to process a function against each array element; you use `map` to create a new array with the results of running the function against each array element.

The `every` method runs the callback function against every element in the array until one element returns a `false` value. Finally, the `some` method is the opposite of `every`, in that it runs the callback function against every element until one returns a `true` value.

Each callback function has three parameters: `element`, `index`, and `array`. Some return a value, others don't. None impact the original array.

Example 5-6 demonstrates how to use a callback function with an `Array`. In this example, the original array contains elements that are themselves an array containing color values, but several of the "colors" have values beyond the allowed range of 0 to 255. After the array is built, one function is attached, `checkColor`, which checks each array element for the proper color range and filters out those that don't fit within that range.

This leads to a second problem in that several of the color arrays no longer have the necessary three elements for the red-green-blue settings. A second callback function is then applied to the array to ensure that the three RGB values are present.

Example 5-6. Using callback functions with the Array filter method

```
<!DOCTYPE html PUBLIC "-//W3C//DTD XHTML 1.1//EN"
"http://www.w3.org/TR/xhtml11/DTD/xhtml11.dtd">
<html xmlns="http://www.w3.org/1999/xhtml" xml:lang="en">
<head>
<title>Callbacks</title>
<meta http-equiv="Content-Type" content="text/html; charset=utf-8" />
```

```
<script type="text/javascript">
//<![CDATA[

// check color range callback function
function checkColor(element,index,array) {
  return (element >= 0 && element < 256);
}

// check to ensure three RGB colors
function checkCount(element,index,array) {
  return (element.length == 3);
}

function testingCallbacks() {

   // color array
   var colors = new Array();
   colors[0] = [0,262,255];
   colors[1] = [255,255,255];
   colors[2] = [255,0,0];
   colors[3] = [0,255,0];
   colors[4] = [0,0,255];
   colors[5] = [-5,999,255];
   colors[6] = [255,255,1204556];

   // filter on color range
   var testedColors = new Array();
   for (var i in colors) {
      testedColors[i] = colors[i].filter(checkColor);
   }

   // print results of first round
   document.writeln("<h3>First check</h3>");
   for (i in testedColors) {
      document.writeln(testedColors[i] + "<br />");
   }
   // filter fewer than three values
   var newTested = testedColors.filter(checkCount);

   document.writeln("<br /><h3>Second</h3>");
   // print survivors
   for (i in newTested) {
      document.writeln(newTested[i] + "<br />");
   }
}
//]]>
</script>
</head>
<body onload="testingCallbacks();">
<p>Some content</p>
</body>
</html>
```

In the end, only four of the color points survive both checks—the second through the fifth array elements, as the printout demonstrates:

```
First check
0,255
255,255,255
255,0,0
0,255,0
0,0,255
255
255,255

Second
255,255,255
255,0,0
0,255,0
0,0,255
```

Though callback functions simplify application JavaScript, they are optional. You can use control loops to test the members of an array. If you need to support IE, you'll have to use control loops.

Function Type Summary

To summarize, there are three different function types:

Declarative function
   A function in a statement of its own, beginning with the keyword `function`. Declarative functions are parsed once, are static, and are given a name for access.

Anonymous function
   A function created using a constructor. It's parsed each time it's accessed and is not given a name specifically.

Function literal or function expression
   A function created within another statement as part of an expression. It is parsed once, is static, and may or may not be given a specific name. If it is named, the name is accessible only from within the function itself.

Declarative functions are available in all forms of JavaScript in all browsers. Anonymous functions based on the function constructors are dynamic, memory-intensive, and based on later versions of JavaScript; as such, they may not be available with older browsers. Function literals are later innovations, based on JavaScript 1.5. Only the most modern browsers support these, including the most common ones: Mozilla, Firefox, IE, and Safari. However, how each of these works with function literals can lead to interesting complications in memory usage, as we examined earlier in this chapter, in the section "Nested Functions, Function Closure, and Memory Leaks."

Function literals also form the basis for most advanced Ajax libraries, as you'll see when we take a closer look at Ajax and advanced uses of JavaScript in the last few chapters of the book. In addition, function literals are what you use with object event handlers that require callback functions, such as those associated with the `Array` object.

Speaking of objects, as mentioned earlier, functions in JavaScript are also objects in addition to being sequences of statements. In the last section of this chapter, I'll cover this concept more fully. First, though, let's take a quick look at function scope and its impact on global versus local variables.

Function Scope

In Chapter 2, I mentioned global and local variables and the concept of variable *scope*. Scope is really related to whether a variable is accessible beyond the scope of a function.

The use of the **var** keyword with a variable in a function tells the JavaScript processing application that the variable is declared with local scope, which means it's available only within the function's block of code. Outside the function, the variable is undefined:

```
function test () {
   var myTest = "test";
   ...
   alert(myTest); // prints out "test"
}
alert(myTest); // undefined
```

You can use the **var** keyword with a variable outside a function, but whether you use the keyword or not, the variable has global scope because it's not contained within any function.

In addition, if you forget to use the **var** keyword for a variable within a function, the JavaScript processing application considers it to be a global variable and treats it accordingly:

```
function test() {
   myTest = "test";
   ...
   alert(myTest); // prints out "test"
}
alert(myTest); // prints out "test"
```

Now, with a smaller application, a global variable may not cause any harm. However, with larger applications, other global variables could be using the same name, in which case, your use of the global variable may overwrite important application information. Conversely, your important information may also be overwritten.

Performance is also an issue. When a variable is declared locally and the function terminates, the resources used for that variable are freed up via a process known as *garbage collection*, and are made available for other application uses. Global variables, however, are not freed up until the entire application is terminated.

The short version of all of this is to remember to use **var** with variables in functions, and to avoid global variables. If you do need globally accessible data, you might want to create a custom object for your application and then assign all the global values you need to it. This, at least, provides some control over how many globals you have floating around your application. I'll cover custom objects in detail in Chapter 13.

Newer and future versions of JavaScript will even allow us to define a variable within the scope of a control block, such as a `while` loop. Instead of using the `var` keyword, though, you'd use the `let` keyword, as follows:

```
function myTest() {
    var someVar = 1;
    while(someTest) {
        let someVar = 2; // different variable
    }
}
```

However, the use of `let` and block-level scoping is very new and is not widely implemented, so I wouldn't depend on it just yet.

Function As Object

Whatever you can create using a constructor has properties and methods above and beyond the obvious, and functions are no exception.

The `Function` object seems to be the JavaScript object that's had the most changes over time. Originally, the `arity` property provided the number of arguments. This has been replaced by calling the `length` method off of the function name—or by accessing `length` on the arguments array. This itself used to be accessible via the function name, but then it was changed to being accessible as `arguments` within the function call.

The only standard properties and methods allowed for the `Function` object, other than those that are standard for all objects, such as `toSource` and `toString`, is `length` for number of arguments, and a couple of methods, `apply` and `call`, which I'll cover in more detail in Chapter 13.

In addition, as you'll also see in Chapter 13, when building custom objects, it's the function's ability to reference its own scope through a specialized keyword, `this`, that's important for building classes of new objects.

Test Your Knowledge: Quiz

1. A factorial is a number, n, that is the product of all numbers from 1 to n, usually written as 3! (1 × 2 × 3 or 6). Write a JavaScript function that uses recursion to figure out the factorial of a number given the number.

2. How can a function modify variables outside its scope? Write a function that takes an array of numbers from 1 to 5 and replaces the entries with string representations of the numbers (i.e., "one", "two", etc.).

3. Create a function that takes a data object and a function as parameters and invokes the function using the data object.

Test Your Knowledge: Answers

1. One solution is:

```
function findFactorial(n) {

    if (n == 0) return 1;

    return (n * findFactorial(n-1));
}

var num = findFactorial(4); // returns 24
```

2. If an object, such as an array, is passed as a function parameter, modifications to the array are generally reflected outside the function. One solution to the coding question is as follows:

```
function makeArray() {

    var arr = [1,5,3];
    alert(arr);
    alterArray(arr);
    alert(arr);
}

function alterArray(arrOfNumbers) {
  for (var i = 0; i < arrOfNumbers.length; i++) {
    switch(arrOfNumbers[i]) {
      case 1 : arrOfNumbers[i] = "one"; break;
      case 2 : arrOfNumbers[i] = "two"; break;
      case 3 : arrOfNumbers[i] = "three"; break;
      case 4 : arrOfNumbers[i] = "four"; break;
      case 5 : arrOfNumbers[i] = "five"; break;
    }
  }
}
```

3. An anonymous function suits these requirements:

```
function invokeFunction(dataObject, functionToCall) {
    functionToCall(dataObject);
}
var funcCall = new Function('x','alert(x)');
invokeFunction ('hello', funcCall);
```

CHAPTER 6

Troubleshooting, Debugging, and Cross-Browser Issues

Up to this point, most of what I've shown you regarding JavaScript has been fairly simple to create and debug because the examples were contained within the same page as the HTML. For the rest of the book, though, the examples will become more complex, and they'll start to introduce the built-in object models, including the Document Object Model (DOM). The increasing complexity and use of object model will require a debugger that allows you to minutely control JavaScript execution as well as more closely examine the objects your code is accessing.

In addition, beginning with Chapter 7, differences in browser JavaScript support will become more apparent. Though support for JavaScript has improved vastly since I first began using it 12 years ago, not all browsers support all of the functionality available in JavaScript. In addition, browser vendors are always testing new and future JavaScript enhancements, and it's important to know when to use (and when not to use) a new feature.

Simple Ways to Debug

Long-time programmers may sneer at the approach, but one of the simplest debugging methods is to use some form of output functionality to check the values of variables after processing. Though more sophisticated debugging tools are available, this still is a simple way to check out the state and value of a variable during application processing.

With JavaScript, the simplest way to output information is with an alert window, as we've been using in previous chapters:

```
alert(someVariable);
```

If you're interested in a quick check of data and you don't want to open a debugger, add the alert box, check the values you need to check, and then immediately remove the alert box.

The next section discusses more sophisticated methods for debugging JavaScript applications, using tools specific to each browser.

Development and Debugging Tools by Browser

I'm not sure what has been better for JavaScript developers in the past few years: the fact that most of the mainstream browsers support most of the same JavaScript functionality, or that most provide decent tools for developers to debug JavaScript applications, as well as check out how they're performing and what they're doing.

Firefox and Firebug

Firefox is currently the second most popular web browser in use today, but it's probably the most popular when it comes to more complex Ajax development. One reason for its popularity among JavaScript developers is the Firefox extension, Firebug.

 Download Firebug from *http://getfirebug.com/*.

Firebug offers a tabbed interface that provides access to the JavaScript console and any messages, and the ability to inspect the HTML or CSS, peruse the DOM objects accessible on any page, examine any network calls made in a specific page, and, most importantly for our purposes, open a JavaScript debugging window, as shown in Figure 6-1.

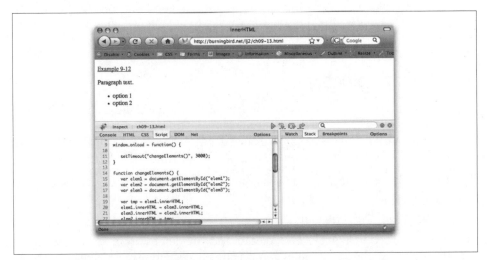

Figure 6-1. A web page with the script opened in the Firebug extension for Firefox

Within Firebug's scripting window, you can select which JavaScript file you're interested in debugging from a drop-down list of all of those available for the web page. Once the script is opened, you can review the script, and add stop points within the code, called *breakpoints*. You use a breakpoint to tell the scripting engine to stop processing the script at that point in time so that you can check out local and global variables, as well as DOM objects, to see what's happening in the application and where a problem might be occurring.

In Firebug, you set a breakpoint by right-mouse-clicking the line where you want the breakpoint to happen. Figure 6-2 shows Firebug with two breakpoints added to a page's scripting block.

Figure 6-2. Two breakpoints in Firebug

When you load the page or take a particular action to process the script, Firebug stops script execution at the location of the breakpoint and won't continue until it's instructed to continue. At that point, information regarding the scripting process and the state of local and global variables as well as the DOM appears in the rightmost Firebug panel, as shown in Figure 6-3.

A lot of information is available for the local variables in the application I've opened in the figures (see Example 9-13 in Chapter 9), because each variable is assigned an element from the web page. In Figure 6-3, you can see that variable `elem1` has been assigned a reference to a `div` element within the page with an identifier of `"elem1"`. You can also

Figure 6-3. After a breakpoint is reached in Firebug

see all available properties and methods applicable to this object. It's rather surprising the number of properties and methods that are built into every page element object.

Along the top of the right frame are arrow options that tell the script debugger to continue processing the program until the end or until the next breakpoint is reached, to step over the next statement, to step into the next statement (helpful if the statement is a function call), or to step out of a statement (if within a function).

Of course, this is a simple scripting example. Figure 6-4 shows Firebug in action on a complex JavaScript application I have in use at one of my websites—the Lightbox photo expansion software. Some of these JavaScript libraries and applications can be several hundred or even thousands of lines long.

You can access the Lightbox library, used to view photo shows inline in a page, at *http://www.lokeshdhakar.com/projects/lightbox2/*.

The two other right-frame window-tabbed options display the current programming stack and the existing breakpoints (rather essential with larger applications and lots of breakpoints).

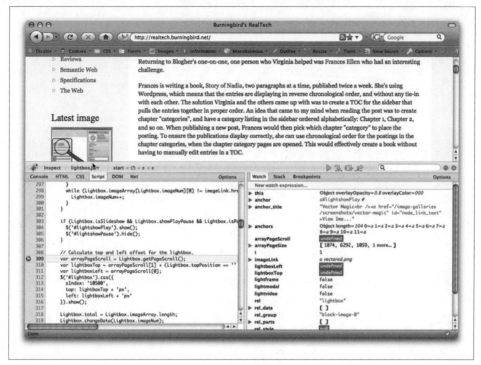

Figure 6-4. Firebug with a complex JavaScript application

The stack shows the nesting of the script at the point a breakpoint is reached. In Figure 6-5, the breakpoint has stopped within an object method named `changeData`, which is derived from an object encapsulated by another popular JavaScript library, jQuery, and after a specific event (managed by jQuery) has been triggered.

Firebug also has a JavaScript console where you not only can view status and errors, but also can type in JavaScript and have it processed, and then copy the script into your own web pages or applications.

In addition to debugging, you can also use Firebug as a replacement for the `document.writeln` and alerts we're using in this book to communicate the results of JavaScript actions. Instead of writing the values to the page, you can write them to the Firebug console.

Using console.log

To write to the Firebug console, use the following in your code:

```
console.log("Here is the result: %s", theVariable);
```

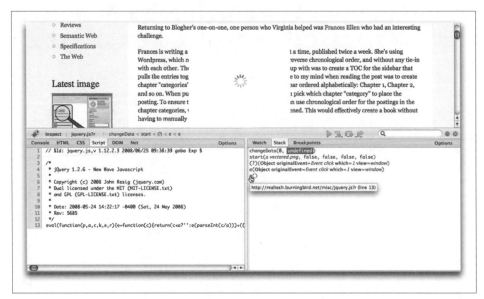

Figure 6-5. The programming stack in Firebug

The string used to write out to the console can accept variable input, used to replace the placeholders, such as %s for a string and %d for a number:

```
console.log("My name is %s and I'm %d years old", myName,myAge);
```

Example 6-1 demonstrates the use of the Firebug console with our original "Hello, World!" example.

Example 6-1. Using the Firebug console to communicate a JavaScript result

```
<!DOCTYPE html PUBLIC "-//W3C//DTD XHTML 1.1//EN"
"http://www.w3.org/TR/xhtml11/DTD/xhtml11.dtd">
<html xmlns="http://www.w3.org/1999/xhtml" xml:lang="en">
<head>
<title>Hello, World!</title>
<meta http-equiv="Content-Type" content="text/html; charset=utf-8" />

<script type="text/javascript">
function hello() {

   // say hello to the world
   var msg = "Hello, World!";
   console.log("%s",msg);
}
</script>
</head>
<body onload="hello()">
<p>Hi</p>
</body>
</html>
```

Figure 6-6 shows the Firebug console in action with Example 6-1.

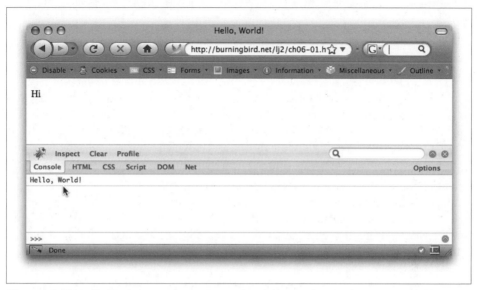

Figure 6-6. Using the Firebug console to print out JavaScript results

Of course, the Firebug console is available only with Firebug. However, talk among browser developers has it that most debuggers, including those covered later in this chapter, will support `console.log` to write to a debugger console. If so, this approach will soon replace `document.write` and `alert` as a way to communicate JavaScript results. This is good because `document.write` modifies the web page, and the `alert` box isn't the best way to view results.

Until then, though, we'll have to stick with our old tried-and-true approaches.

 I'll cover how to incorporate external JavaScript libraries, such as jQuery, in Chapter 14.

Firefox, the Web Developer Toolkit, and NoScript

Firebug is the most used of the Firefox development tools, but I've found a couple of other Firefox extensions to be invaluable for JavaScript and other web development.

One of the oldest and most popular web tools for Firefox is the Web Developer toolkit (available at *https://addons.mozilla.org/en-US/firefox/addon/60*). This toolkit adds several drop-down menu items in a separate toolbar, featuring one-click options to validate the page's HTML and CSS, check for accessibility, view the CSS and cookies, check out the images, and view the source—including the dynamic source—after JavaScript has modified the page. The latter is especially important, as not a lot of tools provide a really good look at a page after JavaScript has mucked around with it.

The toolkit also provides a way to disable standard page functionality, including the cache, as well as JavaScript. It's important that your JavaScript applications *degrade gracefully* if scripting is disabled. Using the feature from the Web Developer toolkit makes it easy to test how your web pages perform when scripting is disabled.

The Web Developer toolkit "Disable JavaScript" option is not the only way to test how your website does with scripting disabled. Another popular Firefox extension is NoScript (at *https://addons.mozilla.org/en-US/firefox/addon/722*), which allows you to control in which sites you'll enable scripting and in which sites you'll disable scripting.

In fact, numerous other JavaScript-specific extensions are available for Firefox, including multiple variations of consoles in addition to the console provided by Firebug, the popular Greasemonkey extension that allows you to actually modify Firefox behaviors, and even JavaScript editors. Many of these extensions can help you not only debug your JavaScript, but also ensure that your JavaScript is validated before you publish the page.

Of course, too many extensions can make Firefox a dull browser. When I'm not actively developing a web application, I disable most of the developer extensions I've loaded into Firefox, including (and especially) Firebug. However, I keep the Web Developer toolkit active, as I like to use it to snoop through other developers' work.

Opera and Dragonfly

With the release of Opera 9.5, Opera also released a development tool with a whimsical name: Dragonfly. It resembles Firebug in that you can load scripts, set breakpoints, and investigate variables. However, it was in alpha state as of this writing, so much of the functionality was incomplete and buggy.

Download Dragonfly at *http://www.opera.com/products/dragonfly/*.

Let's focus specifically on the script debugging component of Dragonfly. Once you've installed Dragonfly, you use the application by selecting Tools→Advanced→Developer Tools from the Opera main menu. Dragonfly opens as a multiframe debugging window along the bottom, just as Firebug does. You'll see multiple tabbed windows, but you'll want to select the Scripts window to pick a site or script, as shown in Figure 6-7.

Once the script is loaded, you can inspect the source, and set breakpoints by clicking the Source tab, as shown in Figure 6-8.

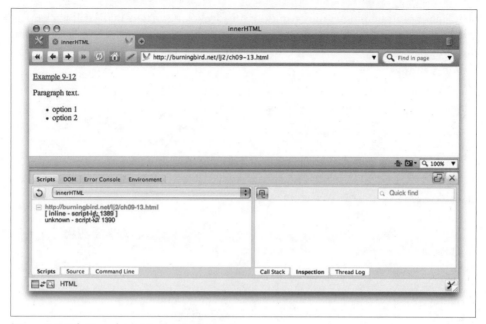

Figure 6-7. Selecting a script in Dragonfly

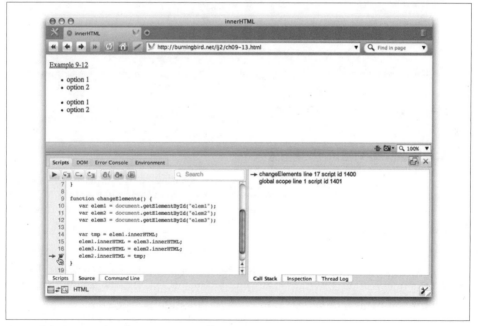

Figure 6-8. Setting a breakpoint in Dragonfly

The rightmost frame shows the execution thread; clicking an item in the call stack opens the Inspection frame, displaying the program variables (see Figure 6-9). It's interesting to compare what Opera shows for the property values of the page elements with what Firebug shows.

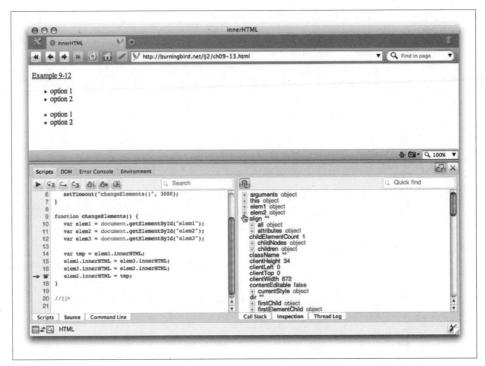

Figure 6-9. Inspecting local variables after a breakpoint is reached

Safari/WebKit and the Web Inspector

Safari, which is based on the open source WebKit, has built-in developer tools available on the menu. Included among these is the Error console, which will display any scripting errors, and the Web Inspector, which lets you examine the HTML, CSS, and JavaScript.

With the newer builds of WebKit, which will be incorporated into the next version of Safari, the web developer's capability has been expanded to provide a built-in script debugger, as shown in Figure 6-10. At the time of this writing, the functionality was very limited, including the ability to set program stops in the script. However, once the new functionality is incorporated into Safari, it should be a full-featured debugger.

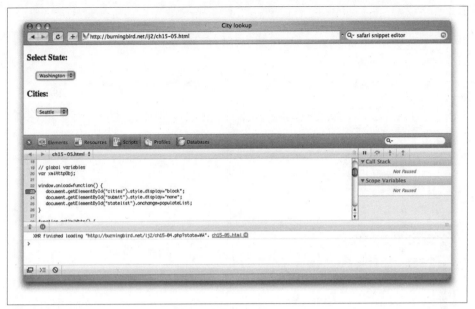

Figure 6-10. New debugger in the WebKit Web Inspector

In the meantime, Safari and WebKit have other debugging options available from the Develop menu, including the following options that could be useful when developing with JavaScript:

- Turn caching on or off
- Disable JavaScript
- Disable a runaway JavaScript timer (this is handy when you're working with timers)
- Disable styles
- Disable images
- Disable site-specific hacks

Internet Explorer

With the release of IE8, Microsoft also released a decent debugging tool, which you can access by clicking the Development Tools toolbar item. A separate window opens with three panels labeled HTML, CSS, and Script. All three are interesting, but I'm going to focus on just the Script panel.

When you click the Script tab, you'll see a two-panel window, with the script source on the left and an information window on the right, as shown in Figure 6-11.

To begin script debugging, click the Start Debugging button and then add as many breakpoints into the code as you wish. Just as with Firebug and Dragonfly, all you need to do to create a breakpoint is click the line where you want the processing to pause.

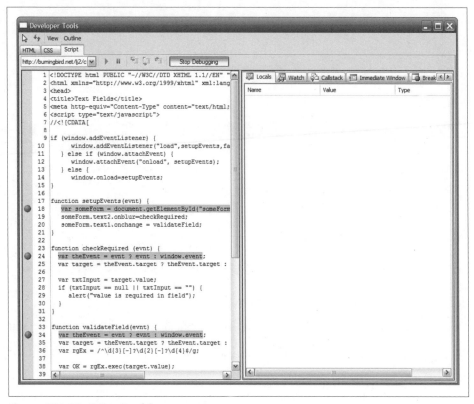

Figure 6-11. The IE8 script debugger

Also, as with Fircbug and Dragonfly, when you reach a breakpoint, you have options to step into the code, step over the code, or continue processing. When the processing stops, you can then explore local and global variables, as shown in Figure 6-12.

Dealing with Cross-Browser Differences

Ten years ago, dealing with cross-browser differences between the two dominant browsers at the time—Internet Explorer and Netscape's Navigator—was a heroic and painful process because standardization of JavaScript and the DOM was either relatively new or nonexistent at the time. Now we have many more browsers, but our job is much easier as most of our browsers support most of the same specifications—most, but not all.

Differences still exist, and all of the differences aren't just between Firefox-Opera-Safari and Internet Explorer: there are differences among all of our target browsers.

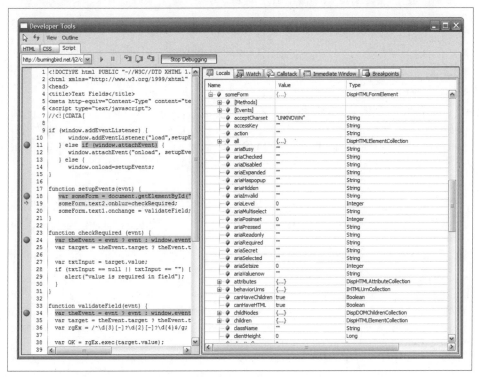

Figure 6-12. After reaching a breakpoint and examining a web page element assigned to a local variable

Object Detection

Traditionally, we checked the user agent string from the navigator object to determine not only the browser type, but also the version. The following is an example (from an old *NetscapeWorld* article, now available at the Wayback Machine, at *http://web.archive .org/web/19981205085025/http://developer.netscape.com/docs/examples/javascript/ browser_type.html*):

```
// *** BROWSER VERSION ***
this.major = parseInt(navigator.appVersion)
this.minor = parseFloat(navigator.appVersion)

this.nav  = ((agt.indexOf('mozilla')!=-1) && ((agt.indexOf('spoofer')==-1)
            && (agt.indexOf('compatible') == -1)))
this.nav2 = (this.nav && (this.major == 2))
this.nav3 = (this.nav && (this.major == 3))
this.nav4 = (this.nav && (this.major == 4))
this.nav4up = this.nav && (this.major >= 4)
this.navonly     = (this.nav && (agt.indexOf(";nav") != -1))

this.ie   = (agt.indexOf("msie") != -1)
```

```
this.ie3  = (this.ie && (this.major == 2))
this.ie4  = (this.ie && (this.major == 4))
this.ie4up = this.ie  && (this.major >= 4)

this.opera = (agt.indexOf("opera") != -1)
```

As you can imagine, the process became painful and quickly lost favor to the use of *object detection*.

With object detection, the JavaScript application accesses the object being detected in a conditional statement. If the object doesn't exist, the condition evaluates to `false`. As an example, the following checks to ensure that the most basic level of object model support is provided in the browser or other user agent:

```
if (document.getElementById)...
```

If this condition returns `false`, most dynamic web page effects are out. Luckily, all modern browsers support a fairly consistent model. All of our target browsers support `document.getElementById`, which is critical for accessing specific elements. All support the `style` property, which allows you to change the CSS style properties of an element.

Still, even now, differences exist. For instance, starting in Chapter 7, we'll look at event handling in JavaScript. Most browsers supportDOM Level 2 event handling, but Microsoft's Internet Explorer, including the recent IE8, does not. Based on this, any event handling will require object detection. As an example, if you want to discover which element received a click event in a web page, you have to do something similar to the following in JavaScript, which is from Example 12-9 in Chapter 12:

```
function showBlock(evnt) {

    var theEvent = evnt ? evnt : window.event;
    var theSrc = theEvent.target ? theEvent.target : theEvent.srcElement;
    var itemId = "elements" + theSrc.id.substr(5,1);
    var item = document.getElementById(itemId);
    if (item.style.display=='none') {
        item.style.display='block';
    } else {
        item.style.display='none';
    }
}
```

Focus your attention on the two lines of highlighted code. In DOM Level 2, the `event` object should be passed as a parameter to the event handler function. However, IE8 does not automatically pass the `event` object. Instead, you have to access the `event` object directly from the `window` object.

You use object detection with a ternary operator (described in Chapter 3) to test whether the parameter, `evnt`, is actually a nonnull, defined object. If it is, it's assigned to a local variable, `theEvent`. If it isn't, the `window.event` property is assigned to the local variable:

```
var theElement = evnt ? evnt : window.event;
```

We're not finished yet; we're after the actual object that was clicked. And again, we have browser differences.

With most browsers, the `target` property holds a reference to the element that actually received the event. However, with IE, you access this element through `srcElement`:

```
var theSrc = theEvent.target ? theEvent.target : theEvent.srcElement;
```

Example 6-2 shows a page that uses this approach to print out the target of the click event.

Example 6-2. Using object detection to find an event target

```
<!DOCTYPE html PUBLIC "-//W3C//DTD XHTML 1.1//EN"
"http://www.w3.org/TR/xhtml11/DTD/xhtml11.dtd">
<html xmlns="http://www.w3.org/1999/xhtml" xml:lang="en">
<head>
<title>object detection</title>
<meta http-equiv="Content-Type" content="text/html; charset=utf-8" />
<style type="text/css">
div {
        position: absolute;
        top: 30px;
        left: 50px;
    }
#div1 img {
filter:
progid:DXImageTransform.Microsoft.AlphaImageLoader(src=fig0902.png,
sizingMethod='scale');
}

</style>
<script type="text/javascript">
//<![CDATA[

window.onload=function() {
  document.getElementById("div1").onclick=getSrc;
}

function getSrc(evnt) {

    var theEvent = evnt ? evnt : window.event;
    var theSrc = theEvent.target ? theEvent.target : theEvent.srcElement;
    alert(theSrc.src);
}

//]]>
</script>
</head>
<body>
<div id="div1">
<img src="fig0902.png" alt="" />
</div>
</body>
</html>
```

Object detection has proven effective over the years. Even if one browser doesn't support an object at one point, chances are it will sometime in the future, and when it doesn't, the functionality is already in place for the application to work.

 The unusual CSS setting beginning with "filter" shown in Example 6-2 is a way of enabling PNG transparency for older Internet Explorer versions, which don't support alpha transparency. It's not important to the JavaScript example, other than to demonstrate that differences among browsers extend beyond JavaScript.

However, as effective as object detection is, it's not foolproof.

Where Object Detection Fails

Object detection requires two things from the object being tested: that it be defined and that it not be null. Both examples in the preceding section apply to the event object, as it is guaranteed to be defined and set within browsers that support DOM Level 2 event handling.

However, object detection has problems in cases where an object may be defined but has not yet been assigned a value. In other words, the object is part of the browser's supported object model, but it hasn't been assigned a value. If the object is defined but not set, a conditional statement such as the following will still fail:

```
if (someobject) {...}
```

A good example of this type of problem occurs when you're testing to see what form of opacity a browser supports.

The modern versions of Opera, Firefox, and Safari support the CSS2 `opacity` attribute on the `style` object. To set the opacity of an element to 50%, use the following syntax:

```
document.getElementById("div1").style.opacity=0.5;
```

Opacity varies from 0 (transparent) to 1 (fully opaque).

In the past, however, Internet Explorer has implemented opacity only within a special filter:

```
document.getElementById("div1").style.filter='alpha(opacity=' + 50 + ')';
```

Rather than assign the opacity value to an `opacity` property, it assigns the value to a filter, with a given format (alpha opacity in an assignment statement). In addition, opacity ranges from 0% to 100%.

How do you test for browser differences to know which assignment to use? You could always test to see whether the filter property is supported:

```
if (div1.style.filter) { ... }
```

However, what happens if the `filter` property is supported, but hasn't been set yet? As we'll see in Chapter 12, style properties accessible via JavaScript aren't set even if the `style` attribute is set in a stylesheet. First, you must set the properties within the script—or within an inline style attribute—to be accessible on the style object.

In this instance, if the opacity filter hasn't been set previously in code, the `filter` object is defined but is null. The condition fails, even for Internet Explorer, which supports the `filter` object.

Another variation of object detection, especially if there's a chance the object hasn't been set first, is to test to see whether it's defined, regardless of whether it's null:

```
if (div1.style.filter != undefined) { ... }
```

This works with Firefox and IE, but not with Opera or Safari. The reason is that neither Opera nor Safari returns an undefined value when accessing the `undefined` property directly.

OK then, so how about testing the object's type, using the `typeof` function, to see whether the object is undefined:

```
if (typeof(div1.style.filter) != "undefined") { ... }
```

This code works for Firefox, IE, and Safari...but not for Opera because Opera does have a `filter` property, but unlike IE, it doesn't seem to be used for setting opacity. With Opera, you'll get a false positive on the object, which means opacity doesn't work with the browser.

The problem at this point is that we're not necessarily testing the right object. We should be testing support for `style.opacity`. Example 6-3 uses variations of testing for `style.opacity` as well as `style.filter`. The only true test that works for all browsers is the last, which tests to see whether the opacity object is defined. This test succeeds for Opera, Firefox, and Safari, and fails, as we would expect, for IE.

Example 6-3. Testing object existence for style.filter and style.opacity

```
<!DOCTYPE html PUBLIC "-//W3C//DTD XHTML 1.1//EN"
"http://www.w3.org/TR/xhtml11/DTD/xhtml11.dtd">
<html xmlns="http://www.w3.org/1999/xhtml" xml:lang="en">
<head>
<title>object detection</title>
<meta http-equiv="Content-Type" content="text/html; charset=utf-8" />
<meta http-equiv="X-UA-Compatible" content="IE=EmulateIE7" />
<style type="text/css">
div {
        position: absolute;
        top: 30px;
        left: 50px;
    }
#div1 img {
filter:
progid:DXImageTransform.Microsoft.AlphaImageLoader(src=fig0902.png,
sizingMethod='scale');
```

```
}

</style>
<script type="text/javascript">
//<![CDATA[

window.onload=function() {

    var divElement = document.getElementById("div1");

    // testing existence of filter
    var tst1 = (divElement.style.filter) ? "filter exists" : "filter does not exist";
    alert(tst1);

    // testing existence of filter
    var tst2 = (typeof(divElement.style.filter) !== "undefined") ? "filter exists" :
"filter does not exist";
    alert(tst2);

    // testing existence of filter
    var tst3 = (divElement.style.filter !== undefined) ? "filter exists" : "filter
does not exist";
    alert(tst3);

    // testing existence of opacity
    var tst4 = (divElement.style.opacity) ? "opacity exists" : "opacity does not
exist";
    alert(tst4);
    // testing existence of opacity
    var tst5 = (typeof(divElement.style.opacity) !== "undefined") ? "opacity exists"
: "opacity does not exist";
    alert(tst5);
}

//]]>
</script>
</head>
<body>
<div id="div1">
<img src="fig0902.png" alt="" />
</div>
</body>
</html>
```

The trick with object detection is to know which object to detect, and to know how to "phrase" the object detection (to ensure that you're testing for object definition, not necessarily existence).

Of course, as you'll see when we continue this example in Chapter 13, sometimes whether an object exists first is moot when it comes to creating cross-browser objects. However, what isn't moot is what happens when a browser that normally supports one property no longer does.

DOCTYPE, X-UA-Compatible, and Quirks Mode

In Example 1-2 in Chapter 1, the first line of the web page contains a Document Type Declaration (DOCTYPE) of XHTML 1.1 strict. Though all of the examples in the book have an *.html* extension, specifying the XHTML DOCTYPE can impact how the JavaScript is processed. It's all based on a concept called *quirks mode*.

As some browsers improved their support for markup and CSS standards, browser developers also wanted to maintain backward compatibility with pages created for older versions of their browser. One way to do this is to render a page in such a way that it supports the browser's earlier, nonstandard, "quirky" behavior, in a mode called (appropriately enough) "quirks mode." Depending on the DOCTYPE, a browser will render the page contents in quirks mode or strict or standards mode.

The mode is important because support for JavaScript is one of the "standards," along with Cascading Style Sheets (CSS) and the actual page markup that is interpreted differently when the page is processed in standards mode over quirks mode. In particular, Internet Explorer is the browser most impacted by quirks mode over standards mode. In quirks mode, IE presumes that the markup, CSS, and JavaScript are based on older implementations, such as those for IE 5.x or even earlier.

The XHTML transitional and strict DOCTYPEs trigger standards mode for most browsers, depending on whether the page is served up as XHTML with an optional XML prolog:

```
<?xml version="1.0" encoding="UTF-8" ?>
```

Firefox, Safari, and Opera interpret the XML prolog as standards mode, whereas Internet Explorer interprets the page with the prolog as quirks mode.

The HTML 4.01 strict DOCTYPE can also trigger standards mode for most browsers, as well as the newer HTML5 DOCTYPE, but for the examples in this book, I'll stick with XHTML Strict 1.1.

The DOCTYPE isn't the only nonscript element of the page that can trigger how a browser processes the JavaScript. Beginning with the first beta release of IE8, a new meta tag, X-UA-Compatible, is used specifically with IE8 to trigger quirks mode, IE7 standards mode, or the newer standards support in IE8.

Breaking Backward Compatibility: The IE8 http-equiv Meta Tag

With object detection, and focusing our code on functionality that is based on some standard or industry specification, we should guarantee that our code will work in future as well as past browsers. However, in one browser, such guarantees aren't in operation: Internet Explorer, specifically, the new IE8.

Microsoft has been endeavoring to update its browser support to the standards, but in the process, backward compatibility with functions created specifically for IE may break. Previously, to turn on standards mode as compared to quirks mode, you added standard DOCTYPE declarations, as I described in the preceding section. However, once you've used these declarations, you can't use them again.

Instead, Microsoft introduced new values for the HTTP meta tag, `http-equiv`, which can let IE8 know whether to process a web page as IE8 or as equivalent to IE7:

```
<meta http-equiv="X-UA-Compatible" content="IE=IE7" />
```

The problem with this tag, though, is that it instructs IE8 to behave in IE7 standards mode, which the browser already does (more or less). Beginning with the second beta release of IE8, Microsoft introduced a second value for the meta tag, `EmulateIE7`, which emulates IE7's behavior in conjunction with the DOCTYPE:

```
<meta http-equiv="X-UA-Compatible" content="IE=EmulateIE7" />
```

You'll see in Chapter 13 how essential this meta tag is, because although most of the examples in this book work with IE7 and IE8, opacity does not. With IE8 (at least with the first beta release) Microsoft eliminated its own proprietary opacity filter, but it didn't implement the CSS2 opacity style. This means no opacity is supported in IE8 (beta 1 release). The only way to implement opacity is to add this meta tag to the header.

Microsoft supports standards mode by default with IE8, but only for external web pages. Intranet pages are set to the older IE7 standards mode by default, unless the *compatibility mode*, as Microsoft terms it, is turned off among the browser options. This functionality is particularly fluid, and what Microsoft will eventually support in the final release of IE8 is a bit of a mystery.

Test Your Knowledge: Quiz

1. Write the code to check to see what the value of a variable is, without recourse to browser-specific debugger.

2. The CSS attribute `text-shadow` has an interesting history. It was added to CSS2, but no browser implemented it, and it was removed in CSS 2.1. However, then browsers implemented it, and now it's being added into CSS3. At the time of this writing, this attribute was implemented in two of our four target browsers. Can you use object detection to successfully test for this style attribute? Write cross-browser code that sets this CSS attribute for an existing header element.

Test Your Knowledge: Answers

1. The quickest approach to testing a variable is to use the alert box:

```
// test some variable
alert(firstName); // value will either be set, null, or undefined
```

2. At first, you would think you could test to see whether `textShadow`, the script-enabled name for the CSS attribute, is implemented in the style object, but as the opacity/alpha example demonstrated earlier, this isn't always an approach you can depend on.

The simplest approach is to set the `textShadow` value regardless of browser support, in which case the `text-shadow` for the element will change for those browsers that support it, and the value will be dynamically set (and ignored) for browsers that don't:

```
var headerElement = document.getElementById("pageHeader");
headerElement.style.textShadow="#ff0000 2px 2px 3px";
```

CHAPTER 7

Catching Events

Events are fired when certain activity occurs within a web page, including when the page is finished loading. In JavaScript, you can capture these events via "hooks" known as *event handlers*, which you can then use to call a function or to process some other JavaScript.

Events in JavaScript are also associated with page elements and are not intrinsic to the language itself. In previous chapters, the applications used the `onload` event handler to call a function when the page was finished loading. The actual event is the `load` event, which is associated with the browser `window` object. The `onload` event handler is triggered when the page is finished loading into the browser window.

To make working with events more challenging, event handling is one aspect of JavaScript that has changed significantly over the years, and is still one area where differences exist among browsers. Luckily, these differences are fairly easy to overcome. Before we discuss cross-browser event handling, though, we'll take a quick look at the events and when they're typically activated.

The Events

The events themselves are relatively intuitive to understand. The World Wide Web Consortium (W3C) categorizes events into three distinct areas: user interface (mouse, keyboard), logical (result of a process), and mutation (action that modifies a document). Table 7-1 lists some basic events, their descriptions, and the affected objects.

Table 7-1. Events and affected objects

Event	Description	Affected object(s)
abort	When the image is prevented from loading	An image element
blur, focus	When an object loses or receives focus	Applicable to window and form elements
change	When a selection changes	Applicable to form elements where the value changes and after the element loses focus

Event	Description	Affected object(s)
click, double click (dblclick)	Clicking or double-clicking (two clicks in rapid succession) with the mouse	Most page elements
contextmenu	Clicking with the right mouse button (bringing up the context menu)	A web page document
error	When the page or image can't load	A web page document and image
keydown, keyup, keypress	Pressing a key or releasing it, and the act of doing both	A web page document and certain form elements
load, unload	When the image or page is finished loading, or the page loses focus	A web page document and image (load only)
mousedown, mouseup	Pressing down on the mouse button, releasing the mouse button	Most page elements
mouseover, mouseout	Moving the mouse over an element, moving the mouse away from an element	Most page elements
mousemove	The mouse moves	Most page elements
reset	A form is reset	The form
resize	A window or frame is resized	A window or frame
select	Selecting text	A form text area or input
scroll	When an object is scrolled	A window, frame, or element with overflow set to auto (presence of the scroll bar)
submit	A form is submitted	A form

Some proprietary events don't appear in Table 7-1, and we'll cover them in the text.

Event handlers are named the same as the event, with the addition of the prefix "on", as in onload, onblur, onsubmit, and so on. Older applications use the CamelCase style of naming convention with events, capitalizing the first letter of the event (onLoad, onSubmit, etc.). However, because many of these event handlers are also attributes within page elements, and XHTML doesn't support element attributes with uppercase characters, the older style of event handler is no longer used.

Level 0 Event Handling

To reiterate, an *event handler* has the following syntax:

    onload

where the event handler starts with "on", followed by the event type: load, click, and so forth.

Events are associated with page elements, and you can add them to the elements as attributes. Adding events as an attribute to an HTML element is sometimes known as an *inline model* or *inline registration model*.

You can implement the JavaScript to process directly in the handler:

```
<body onload="var i = 23; i *= 3; alert(i);">
```

More frequently, though, you'd call a function:

```
<body onload="calcNumber();">
```

Notice in both cases that the JavaScript is surrounded by quotes. Even if you're using HTML and are not enclosing other attributes, you will want to make sure the JavaScript is enclosed.

You also can access an event handler directly as a property on each object. The following assigns a function to the `onload` event property of the `window` object:

```
window.onload=calcNumber;
```

To disable the event handling, assign the event handler to `null`. This approach of assigning a function to an event handler that is an object property is sometimes called the *traditional model* or *traditional registration model*.

Example 7-1 demonstrates both the traditional and inline event models based on the window load. As these are the same events, using the same event handler, you might expect the alert window with the message to show twice.

Example 7-1. Capturing a load event with both traditional and inline event handlers

```
<!DOCTYPE html PUBLIC "-//W3C//DTD XHTML 1.1//EN"
"http://www.w3.org/TR/xhtml11/DTD/xhtml11.dtd">
<html xmlns="http://www.w3.org/1999/xhtml" xml:lang="en">
<head>
<title>Event Handling</title>
<meta http-equiv="Content-Type" content="text/html; charset=utf-8" />
<script type="text/javascript">
//<![CDATA[

function helloMsg() {
   var helloString = "hello there";
   alert(helloString);
}

function helloTwice() {
   var helloString = "hi again";
   alert(helloString);
}

window.onload=helloTwice;
//]]>
</script>
</head>
<body onload="helloMsg();">
```

```
<p>Some content</p>
</body>
</html>
```

The alert window with the message "hello there" pops up for the first event handler, assigned using the traditional model. However, the second message for the event handler assigned using the inline model does not display.

Only one alert window opens because only one event handler is allowed for any given event and object in the Document Object Model (DOM) Level 0 event model; the function assignments are not cumulative. If you want more than one function to be processed based on an event for a specific object, you need to list them in the event handler code, either inline:

```
<body onload="helloMsg(); helloTwice()">
```

or using the traditional method:

```
function helloMsg() {
var helloString = "hello there";
alert(helloString);
helloTwice();}
```

The inline events work with all browsers, but you should restrict their use. If you add events to HTML elements and change the function name or the behavior of the JavaScript, but you've assigned the function to event handlers in objects in several different pages, you have to go into each page, and each page element, and manually make the change. For anything but the simplest sites, this is prohibitive. A better approach would be to use the traditional method, which works with all modern browsers.

 The best approach is to use the newer event handling procedures, for reasons I'll detail later in this chapter.

With some events, such as a form **submit**, you might not want the default behavior based on the event to continue after your event handler function is processed. For instance, if the values entered into form fields do not validate, you're not going to want the form to continue being submitted to the server. For this type of event handler behavior, you can return a value of **false** from the event handler function:

```
function doSomething() {
    // does some code
    return false;
}
```

Returning **false** from the event handler JavaScript signals the browser to terminate the event at that point. You'll see this in action later in the chapter when we move into form processing.

For many events, knowing that an event happened is enough, but for others, such as click or mousedown, you might want additional information about the event, including the location of the mouse when the event occurred. The question is, how is this information accessed? That's the bit of cross-browser event irregularity—albeit fixable—that we'll look at next.

The Event Object

Traditional event handling is also referred to as DOM Level 0 event handling because it's based on the earliest implementations of the browser DOM, known as Level 0. You can split DOM Level 0 events into two camps: the old Netscape camp, which is now Mozilla/Firefox and also includes Opera and Safari, and Internet Explorer. For the most part, you can get an interactive page to work with both types of event handling, but you might have to use a few tricks. One trick concerns how to get access to the Event object.

An Event object is associated with all events. It has properties that provide information about the event, such as the location of a mouse click in the web page. The Event object in Firefox is quite similar to that in IE, though a couple of methods differ. However, the way in which you access the object is drastically different.

IE attaches Event as a property of the window object. When your code accesses the window object as part of event processing, the data it contains is populated accordingly. In Example 7-2, the IE Event object is accessed from Windows when the mouse button is pressed, and the screen x and y locations appear in a pop-up window.

Example 7-2. Accessing the IE Event object

```
<!DOCTYPE html PUBLIC "-//W3C//DTD XHTML 1.0 Transitional//EN"
"http://www.w3.org/TR/xhtml1/DTD/xhtml1-transitional.dtd">
<html>
<head>
<title>X/Y Marks the Spot</title>
<meta http-equiv="Content-Type" content="text/html; charset=utf-8" />
<script type="text/javascript">
//<![CDATA[

function mouseDown() {
  var locString = "X = " + window.event.screenX + " Y = " + window.event.screenY;
  alert(locString);
}

document.onmousedown=mouseDown;
//]]>
</script>

</head>
<body>
</body>
</html>
```

This method of capturing the `Event` object persists into Internet Explorer 8, as well as older IE versions. However, if you access the page with Firefox, Opera, or Safari, the application fails. The Netscape-based browsers—such as Firefox and Mozilla, Opera, and Safari—obtain the `Event` object differently: it's passed as part of the function. In this case, the function to work with a browser such as Firefox looks like this:

```
function mouseDown (theEvent) {
  var locString = "X = " + theEvent.screenX + " Y = " + theEvent.screenY;
  alert(locString);
}
```

One way to handle these cross-browser differences is to test whether the `Event` object passed into the function is instantiated. If it is, assign the `Event` to a local variable; otherwise, assume that the `window.event` is the event, and assign it to the variable. Example 7-3 shows a cross-browser-compatible version of Example 7-2.

Example 7-3. A cross-browser-compatible version of the Event object in Example 7-2

```
<!DOCTYPE html PUBLIC "-//W3C//DTD XHTML 1.1//EN"
"http://www.w3.org/TR/xhtml11/DTD/xhtml11.dtd">
<html xmlns="http://www.w3.org/1999/xhtml" xml:lang="en">
<head>
<title>Event Handling</title>
<meta http-equiv="Content-Type" content="text/html; charset=utf-8" />
<script type="text/javascript">
//<![CDATA[

function mouseDown(nsEvent) {
  var theEvent = nsEvent ? nsEvent : window.event;
  var locString = "X = " + theEvent.screenX + " Y = " + theEvent.screenY;
  alert(locString);
}

document.onmousedown=mouseDown;
//]]>
</script>
</head>
<body>
<p>Some content</p>
</body>
</html>
```

Example 7-3 also demonstrates the usefulness of the ternary operator, which we covered in Chapter 2. In this example, the operator is used to test whether the `nsEvent` object is defined. If it is, it's assigned to the application variable; otherwise, the `event` property of the `window` object is assigned to the application variable.

Once you have the `Event` object, you'll want to do something with it. The following `Event` properties are compatible across browsers:

altKey
> Boolean if the Alt key is pressed at the time of the event

clientX
> The client *x* coordinate of the event

clientY
> The client *y* coordinate of the event

ctrlKey
> **Boolean** if the Ctrl key is pressed at the time of the event

keyCode
> The code (number) of the key pressed

screenX
> The screen *x* coordinate of the event

screenY
> The screen *y* coordinate of the event

shiftKey
> **Boolean** if the Shift key is pressed at the time of the event

type
> The type of event

I'll cover the client and screen system in more detail later in the book, when we start to create dynamic pages.

Testing the Ctrl keys is a good way to determine whether a certain sequence of keys are pressed—each perhaps leading to a different set of actions. In addition, accessing the key code (number) is handy if you're creating something such as a slide show, where you might want to intercept the N or P key for the next or previous slide.

Among the properties that aren't compatible across browsers are `fromElement`, which is IE-specific, and `relatedTarget`, which is the equivalent for the Mozilla/Firefox event handling path. These properties capture the object the mouse moved away from with mouse events. Comparable properties are `toElement` and `currentTarget` (IE and Mozilla, respectively), which designate the element to which the mouse moved. These sets of properties are useful when doing drag-and-drop.

To work around the cross-browser differences related to event target, make an additional use of the ternary operator:

```
var oldElement = theEvent.fromElement ? theEvent.fromElement :
theEvent.relatedTarget;
```

The IE `srcElement` and Mozilla et al. `target` are properties that represent the object receiving the event:

```
var theSrc = theEvent.target ? theEvent.target : theEvent.srcElement;
```

Three additional properties that aren't cross-browser-compatible are `cancelBubble`, `preventDefault`, and `stopPropagation`. These have to do with event bubbling, which we'll cover next.

I demonstrate `preventDefault` in Chapter 8.

Event Bubbling

When you click a web page, you're not just clicking the document, you're also clicking a link, or perhaps a `div` element. In most cases, you don't have to worry about the container including the link because you've most likely set an event handler for only one element. What happens, though, if you set the same event handler for multiple nested elements? In what order do they fire, and how do you keep the event from triggering the event handler if you want only one element to be impacted at a time?

One approach to managing events in a stack of elements is known as *event bubbling*. In event bubbling, the innermost element would fire its event, followed by the next in the stack, and so on, until it reached the outermost element. If event handlers were assigned to all of these elements, all of their events would fire in turn.

In Example 7-4, the web page has two `div` elements, one inside the other. They, and the `document` object, are assigned event handler functionality for the `mousedown` event.

Example 7-4. Bubble-up behavior with multiple elements

```
<!DOCTYPE html PUBLIC "-//W3C//DTD XHTML 1.1//EN"
"http://www.w3.org/TR/xhtml11/DTD/xhtml11.dtd">
<html xmlns="http://www.w3.org/1999/xhtml" xml:lang="en">
<head>
<title>Event Handling</title>
<meta http-equiv="Content-Type" content="text/html; charset=utf-8" />
<script type="text/javascript">
//<![CDATA[

// set up event handlers for div elements
window.onload=setupEvents;

function setupEvents() {

  document.getElementById("first").onmousedown=function() {
    alert("first element event");
  }

  // second element event handler functionality
  document.getElementById("second").onmousedown=function () {
      alert("second element event");
  }

  document.onmousedown=function() {
    alert("document event");
  }
}
```

```
//]]>
</script>
</head>
<body>
<div id="first" style="padding: 20px; background-color: #ff0; width: 150px; ">
  <div id="second" style="background-color: #f00; width: 100px; height: 100px;
border: 1px dashed #000">
  </div>
</div>
</body>
</html>
```

Clicking on the innermost `div` element in the page, in any of our target browsers, will result in three alert windows popping up, with the following sequence of messages:

1. Select element event

2. First element event

3. Document event

These messages reflect the innermost `div` element, outermost `div` element, and document, in stack order. The event moves down the stack and then bubbles up, firing event handler events along the way. Figure 7-1 shows how this process works.

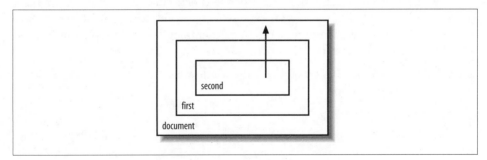

Figure 7-1. An event bubbling up between page elements

If you have a stack of elements and want the event handlers for only one element to fire, you can cancel event bubbling. To cancel an event within IE, use the IE event's `cancelBubble` property; for the Mozilla model, use the event's `stopPropagation` method. You can determine which to use by testing for the existence of the `stopPropagation` method and, based on the result, using one or the other:

```
function stopEvent(evnt) {
    if (evnt.stopPropagation) {
      evnt.stopPropagation();
    } else {
      evnt.cancelBubble = true;
    }
}
```

Note that I test whether the `stopPropagation` function exists rather than the `cancelBubble` function because `cancelBubble` will return `false` if the value is false *or* if the property doesn't exist.

If you added a call to this function to the end of the mouse click event handler for the first `div` element shown in Example 7-4, the first two alerts would still show, but not the last for the document event handler because the event would be canceled before reaching that high in the stack:

```
document.getElementById("first").onmousedown=function(evnt) {
   var theEvent = evnt ? evnt : window.event;
   alert("first element event");
   stopEvent(theEvent);
}
```

We've been accessing the `event` object, but what about the target of the event—how can we access this consistently? The item of interest here is `this`.

Event Handlers and this

Within an event handler function or object method, one way to access the properties of the containing element in JavaScript is to use the special `this` keyword.

The `this` keyword represents the owner of the function or method currently being processed. For a global function, `this` represents the window. For an object method, `this` represents the object instance. And in an event handler, `this` represents the element that received the event.

The following event handler function for the window `onload` event uses `this` to access the window's `status` property:

```
window.onload=setupEvents;

function setupEvents() {
   alert(this.status);
}
```

From Example 7-4, `this` in the function attached to the first `div` element's `onclick` event handler refers to the `div` element itself:

```
document.getElementById("first").onmousedown=function() {
   alert(this); // in Firefox outputs "[object HTMLDivElement]"
   alert("first element event");
}
```

Using `this` is a handy way of accessing form values after events, without having to follow the path of `document`, to form name, to field name, and so on. In Example 7-5, the `blur` event for a `form` element is assigned to an `onblur` event handler, which then uses `this` to access the `form` element's `value` property.

Example 7-5. Use of this with event handlers

```
<!DOCTYPE html PUBLIC "-//W3C//DTD XHTML 1.1//EN"
"http://www.w3.org/TR/xhtml11/DTD/xhtml11.dtd">
<html xmlns="http://www.w3.org/1999/xhtml" xml:lang="en">
<head>
<title>this</title>
<meta http-equiv="Content-Type" content="text/html; charset=utf-8" />
<script type="text/javascript">
//<![CDATA[

window.onload=setObjects;

function setObjects() {
    document.getElementById("personData").firstName.onblur=testValue;
}

function testValue() {
    alert("Hi " + this.value); // form field value
}
//]]>
</script>
</head>
<body>
<form id="personData" action="">
<p>
First Name: <input type="text" id="firstName" /><br /><br />
Second Name: <input type="text" id="secondName" />
</p>
</form>
</body>
</html>
```

After you type in a first name and then tab to or click the second field, an alert window opens and displays the first form field's value.

> The use of this is an integral part of working with the DOM as well as custom objects, and I will cover it more fully in later chapters.

The event model we've covered to this point has focused on events bubbling up, from inner elements to outer elements. A variation on how events are processed for elements in a stack is known as *event capturing* or *cascade-down* event handling. With our three-element example, the events would fire from the outside in: the document event handler would fire first, then the first div element, and then the second.

The W3C event model, which we'll cover in the next section, actually allows for both types of event handling: event capturing and bubbling up.

The DOM Level 2 Event Model

The event handling to this point has demonstrated an older, pre-DOM event handling model. Many major browsers still support this older model, but JavaScript developers are encouraged to move to a newer, specification-based event model known as the DOM Level 2 event model.

Two major differences between the older model and the newer DOM Level 2 event model is that 1) the newer model isn't as dependent on a specific event handler property, and 2) you can register multiple event handler functions for any one event on any one object. Instead of the event handler property, each object has three methods: `add EventListener`, `removeEventListener`, and `dispatchEvent`. You use the first to add an event listener, the second to remove an existing listener, and the third to dispatch a new event.

The syntax of `addEventListener` is:

```
object.addEventListener('event',eventFunction,boolean);
```

The event, such as `click` or `load`, is the first parameter; the event handler function is the second; and whether the event is treated as a cascade-down or bubble-up event is the third. If the third parameter is `false`, the event listener is treated as a bubble-up event, as demonstrated in the older event model examples; otherwise, `true` turns the event listener into an event-capturing model.

In Example 7-6, a form with one element, a submit button, is added to the page, and the `click` event is captured for it and the form, as well as for `document`. Handlers are attached to the event for both cascade-down (`cascadeDown`) and bubble-up (`bubbleUp`) event handling. In the handler functions, `this` is passed into an alert to print out what object is currently receiving the event. When the page is unloaded, the event handling is cleaned up.

Example 7-6. Trapping events with DOM Level 2 event handlers

```
<!DOCTYPE html PUBLIC "-//W3C//DTD XHTML 1.1//EN"
"http://www.w3.org/TR/xhtml11/DTD/xhtml11.dtd">
<html xmlns="http://www.w3.org/1999/xhtml" xml:lang="en">
<head>
<title>Capture/Bubble</title>
<meta http-equiv="Content-Type" content="text/html; charset=utf-8" />
<script type="text/javascript">
//<![CDATA[

function cascadeDown(evnt) {
   alert("Capturing: " + this);
}

function bubbleUp(evnt) {
   alert("Bubbling: " + this);
}
```

```
window.onload=setup;

function setup(evnt) {

   // capturing
  document.addEventListener('click',cascadeDown,true);
   document.forms[0].addEventListener('click',cascadeDown,true);
   document.forms[0].elements[0].addEventListener('click',cascadeDown,true);

   // bubble up events
   document.addEventListener("click",bubbleUp,false);
   document.forms[0].addEventListener("click",bubbleUp,false);
   document.forms[0].elements[0].addEventListener("click",bubbleUp,false);
}

//]]>
</script>
</head>
<body>
<form style="background-color: #f00; width: 100px; height: 100px; padding: 10px"
action="">
<p>
   <input type="submit" value="Submit" /><br />
</p>
</form>
</body>
</html>
```

Clicking the button generates six alert messages. In Firefox, these are the values that
output, in order:

```
Capturing: [object HTMLDocument]
Capturing: [object HTMLFormElement]
Capturing: [object HTMLInputElement]
Bubbling: [object HTMLInputElement]
Bubbling: [object HTMLFormElement]
Bubbling: [object HTMLDocument]
```

What's happening with the application is that the capturing event is processed first,
and the handlers for the document, the form, and the submit button are processed, in
that order. This makes sense when you consider that *cascade* means the outermost
element in the stack of elements is processed first, then the next, and so on, until the
innermost target element is reached.

Next, the bubbling phase occurs, and the order of processing this time is from submit
button, to form, to document—from the bottom up. Again, the event order makes
sense when you think of events firing from the innermost element and "bubbling" up
to the outermost element.

What happens if you want to stop the propagation of the event in the stack? Use the
stopPropagation method on the event in the function where you want the event propagation to end:

```
function cascadeDown(evnt) {
    ...
    evnt.stopPropagation();
}
```

To permanently remove an event listener, use the `removeEventListener` method:

```
document.forms[0].elements[0].removeEventListener("click",cascadeDown,true);
```

The method won't work while an event is being processed, but the next time the submit button is clicked, the capture event handler function is not invoked for the form element. The capture event handler function is still invoked for the form and the document, though.

The concept and execution of `addEventListener` and `removeEventListener` are terrific, except for one thing: Microsoft supports only its own event handler model. Even within the new IE8, the company supports only what it has created itself.

Because it took several years for Microsoft to release IE7, and close to three years for it to release IE8, it's unlikely that a Microsoft product will support the W3C event model anytime soon. In fact, I doubt the company ever will, so we'll need to look at a workaround.

The comparable IE methods for `addEventListener` and `removeEventListener` are `attachEvent` and `detachEvent`, respectively. The syntax for `attachEvent` is:

```
object.attachEvent("eventhandler", function);
```

The syntax for `detachEvent` is the same as for `attachEvent`: the first parameter is the event handler, and the second is the function.

Though the methods to attach the events differ between Firefox et al. and IE, it's relatively easy to compensate for this difference. Example 7-7 provides an example of cross-browser functionality that handles the `click` event for a specific document element.

Example 7-7. Cross-browser event handling

```
<!DOCTYPE html PUBLIC "-//W3C//DTD XHTML 1.1//EN"
"http://www.w3.org/TR/xhtml11/DTD/xhtml11.dtd">
<html xmlns="http://www.w3.org/1999/xhtml" xml:lang="en">
<head>
<title>Capture/Bubble</title>
<meta http-equiv="Content-Type" content="text/html; charset=utf-8" />
<script type="text/javascript">
//<![CDATA[

function clickMe(evnt) {
    var eventTarget = evnt.target ? evnt.target : evnt.srcElement;
    alert(eventTarget + " " + evnt.type);
    var canBeCanceled = evnt.cancelable ? evnt.cancelable : "NA";
    alert("Can be canceled? " + canBeCanceled);
    var bubbleEvent = evnt.bubbles ? evnt.bubbles : "NA";
    alert("Bubbling? " + bubbleEvent);
    var theTime = evnt.timeStamp ? evnt.timeStamp : "NA";
```

```
      alert(theTime);
}

window.onload=setup;
window.onunload=cleanup;

function setup(evnt) {
    var evtObject = document.getElementById("clickme");

    // test for object model
    if (evtObject.addEventListener) {
       document.addEventListener("click",clickMe,false);
    } else if (evtObject.attachEvent) {
       evtObject.attachEvent("onclick", clickMe);
    } else if (evtObject.onclick) {
       evtObject.onclick=clickMe;
    }
}

// cleanup
function cleanup() {
    var evtObject = document.getElementById("clickme");
    if (evtObject.detachEvent) {
        evtObject.detachEvent("onclick",clickMe);
    }
}

//]]>
</script>
</head>
<body>
<div id="clickme" style="background-color: #ff0; width: 200px; height: 200px;
padding: 20px">
<p>Click Me</p>
</div>
</body>
</html>
```

The code tests to see whether addEventListener is supported. If it is, it's used to attach the event. If it isn't, attachEvent is used, if it's supported. If both of these fail, the old Level 0 event handler is used.

Unlike with the older traditional event handling, an Event object is passed with the attachEvent method, as it is passed with addEventListener. However, which properties are supported on the Event object differs among browsers.

In the event handler function, the properties cancelable (whether the event can be canceled), timestamp, bubbles (if this a bubbling event), and event target are accessed and output. However, most of these properties are not supported with IE, so a ternary operator is used to test each, and to define a string with "NA" (for not applicable) for those that don't apply. The properties do work with Firefox and Safari/WebKit, and most work with Opera, except for timestamp. IE's srcElement property is also accessed in place of `target` for the IE model. The example demonstrates that although the differences among the browsers are significant, they can be resolved.

Unfortunately, though, not all differences are as easily resolved. In IE, the contextual object, `this`, is associated with the `window` object regardless of object and event. With DOM Level 2 event handling, `this` is associated with the object that received the event.

Another concern with the Microsoft model is that memory is set aside for each event handler, and if you reload the page, additional memory continues to be set aside for each successive page load—leading to significant memory usage after awhile. To avoid excessive memory use, you can trap the window `unload` event and detach each event with `detachEvent`. This kick-starts the memory management system to unload that memory when the page is unloaded. In Example 7-7, the `cleanup` function was assigned to the `window.onunload` event handler and manages this activity. It's not necessary to clean up the use of `addEventListener` in the window `unonload` event.

 The memory problems with IE may be solved with IE8. However, because the memory problems still exist with older versions of IE, it's best to leave the cleanup code in.

As for the `Event` object that gets passed, this isn't the same among event model implementations, either. Differences also exist in properties on the `Event` object and the events supported.

The following is a list of properties on the `Event`; whether they are set depends on the type of event. Not all browsers support all `Event` properties; where a property is not supported, an undefined value is returned when the property is accessed:

altKey
:   The state of the Alt key (pressed or not)

bubbles
:   If the event bubbles through the DOM (not IE)

button
:   The mouse key

cancelBubble
:   Whether bubbling has been canceled

cancelable
:   Whether the event can be canceled

charCode
:   The Unicode value of the character key pressed (for IE, use `keyCode`)

clientX
:   The horizontal position of the event

clientY
> The vertical position of the event

ctrlKey
> The state of the Ctrl key (pressed or not)

currentTarget
> A reference to the currently registered target (for IE, use `srcElement`)

detail
> Detail regarding the event

eventPhase
> Which phase event is being evaluated

isChar
> Whether an event produces a character

keyCode
> The Unicode value of the noncharacter key pressed

layerX
> The x position relative to the current layer (element) if the element is absolutely positioned

layerY
> The y position relative to the current layer (element) if the element is absolutely positioned

metaKey
> Whether the Meta key was pressed

pageX
> The x position relative to the page

pageY
> The y position relative to the page

screenX
> The x position relative to the screen

screenY
> The y position relative to the screen

shiftKey
> The state of the Shift key

target
> The original object to receive the event

timeStamp
> The time when the event was created

view
> The `AbstractView` from which the event was generated (the `window` object, based on an effort to standardize the `window` object across implementations)

`which`

> The Unicode value of the key pressed, regardless of whether it was a character

The easiest way to discover which properties are supported on each event is to use a script debugger and examine the `Event` object. I covered the various script debugging tools for the different browsers in Chapter 6.

The events I discussed earlier in this section are supported in the newer event system, as are additional ones relative to the DOM. These include `keypress`, `click`, the mouse events, window loading, and events specific to working with forms and form elements.

Generating Events

Events usually start when someone does something in the web page. He pushes a button, clicks a link, makes a selection, and so on. Sometimes, though, you might want to trigger an event.

To trigger an event on a web page or page element, the event must be associated with the type of element. For instance, you can trigger a click on a form button, but not a form text-input field. To generate the click event for the form button, use the `click` event, and call the `click` object on the method:

```
<input type="button" id="someButton" value="Some Button" />
...
document.getElementById("someButton").click();
```

One reason for directly invoking an event is to use the `focus` event on an input field to move the cursor to the field. In Example 7-8, when the page is loaded, the focus is set to the last-name field rather than the first-name field, which is the first field and would normally receive the focus first.

Example 7-8. Using focus to move the cursor to a field

```
<!DOCTYPE html PUBLIC "-//W3C//DTD XHTML 1.1//EN"
"http://www.w3.org/TR/xhtml11/DTD/xhtml11.dtd">
<html xmlns="http://www.w3.org/1999/xhtml" xml:lang="en">
<head>
<title>Focus</title>
<meta http-equiv="Content-Type" content="text/html; charset=utf-8" />
<script type="text/javascript">
//<![CDATA[

window.onload=setObjects;

function setObjects() {
   document.getElementById("personData").lastName.focus();
}

//]]>
</script>
</head>
<body>
```

```
  <form id="personData" action="">
     <p>
First Name: <input type="text" name="firstName" /><br /><br />
Last Name: <input type="text" name="lastName" />
</p>
</form>
</body>
</html>
```

In the next chapter, we'll use focus and a few other tricks to create dynamic forms validation—moving the cursor to a field that's invalid and highlighting the errors directly in the page.

Test Your Knowledge: Quiz

1. Create code to assign an event handler function to the document's click event using the DOM Level 0 approach.
2. Now, attach the click event handler for the document using the more modern DOM Level 2 event handling functionality (don't worry about cross-browser issues).
3. How would you make the code in question 2 safe for all browsers?
4. Given an onclick event handler on the document object, how can you find the screen location for the click?
5. Using the DOM Level 2 event system, how would you stop an event from bubbling to other elements?
6. Convert the following DOM Level 0 event handler to a cross-browser DOM Level 2 approach:

   ```
   <body onload="functionCall();">
   ```
7. Write JavaScript to capture the keydown event on the document and print out the key pressed using a document.writeln function call.

Test Your Knowledge: Answers

1. The solution is:

   ```
   document.onclick=clickMe;
   ```
2. The solution is:

   ```
   document.addEventListener("click",clickMe,false);
   ```
3. The solution is:

   ```
   if (document.addEventListener) {
       document.addEventListener("click",clickMe,false);
   } else if (document.attachEvent) {
   ```

```
            document.attachEvent("onclick", clickMe);
    }
```

4. If you're using the DOM Level 0 event handling system, you either access the event object on the `window` object or pass it in as a function parameter. For DOM Level 2, the event object is always passed into the event handling function. From the event object, access the `screenX` and `screenY` properties.

5. The IE approach differs from that which most browsers support; as such, you have to support both IE and the other browsers. Test whether the `stopPropagation` method is supported on the event object. If so, invoke it; otherwise, set the `cancelBubble` property to `true`.

6. The solution is:

```
if (window.addEventListener) {
    window.addEventListener("load",functioncall,false);
} else if (window.attachEvent) {
    window.attachEvent("onload", functioncall);
}
```

7. Though we haven't covered capturing keyboard events, you typically capture the `keydown` event and then access the Unicode key code from the `which` property on the event:

```
window.onload=function() {
    if (document.addEventListener) {
      document.addEventListener("keydown",getKey,false);
    } else if (document.attachEvent) {
      document.attachEvent("keydown", getKey);
    }
}

function getKey(evnt) {
  var theEvent = evnt ? evnt : window.event;
  alert(theEvent.which);
}
```

CHAPTER 8

Forms, Form Events, and Validation

In JavaScript, you access forms through the Document Object Model (DOM) via the `document` object using a couple of different approaches. The first approach is to use the `forms` property on the `document` object. Forms are just one of the many page elements that are collected in arrays and are attached to the document. Where the form appears in the forms array is dependent on where the form appears in the page, minus 1, as arrays in JavaScript are zero-based. If the page has two forms, you would access the first using the zero (0) index:

```
var theForm = document.forms[0];
```

The problem with accessing the form using the array index is that if you change the page—if you add or remove a form—your JavaScript no longer works because the array access is positionally dependent. A better approach is to give the form an identifier, and then to access it using the document's `getElementById` method:

```
<form id="someform" ...>
...
var theForm = document.getElementById("someform");
```

I used `document.getElementById` in a couple of examples in Chapter 7, and I'll use it again in this chapter. I'll cover the method in more depth in Chapter 9; for now, all you need to know is that the method provides access to a web page element given the element's identifier. In the preceding code snippet, the method returns access to the form element identified by `"someform"`.

Also, as discussed in Chapter 7, you can intercept a form before submitting it to the server in three ways: you can capture the `submit` event using an inline event handler; capture the event using a traditional event handler; or use the more modern `add EventListener/attachEvent` option. The important aspect of whatever you use is that once you've validated the form contents, you need to be able to cancel the event if the contents fail.

Attaching Events to Forms: Different Approaches

The primary event associated with a form is submit, and the event handler is onsubmit. Here's how to attach the event handler to the form using the traditional method:

```
document.getElementById("someform").onsubmit=formHandler;
```

When you attach an event handler inline to the form, incorporate it into a return statement:

```
<form name="someForm" onsubmit="return formHandler();">
```

With either method, to cancel the submission, just return false from the event handler function; returning true or using no explicit return value allows the form submission to continue.

These approaches work, but they're not easy to maintain; I'm covering them here to be thorough and because you'll see both in existing JavaScript applications. The better approach to event handling uses the more modern DOM Level 2 event listener. However, the event handling approaches I covered in Chapter 7 can quickly become a pain when you have to type the same code for each event you want to capture, especially when you're working with forms. This is why reusable cross-browser event listening functions are some of the most forms of common JavaScript you'll see.

Cross-Browser Event Handling

In Example 7-7 in Chapter 7, I demonstrated a cross-browser function for capturing an event and attaching an event handler function:

```
// test for object model
if (evtObject.addEventListener) {
    document.addEventListener("click",clickMe,false);
} else if (evtObject.attachEvent) {
    evtObject.attachEvent("onclick", clickMe);
} else if (evtObject.onclick) {
    evtObject.onclick=clickMe;
}
```

For today's JavaScript applications, you'll want to use attachEvent and add EventListener for cross-browser compatibility, but you're not going to always want to have to type this code for each event—especially when you're validating forms, which could have dozens of events.

A better approach is to create a reusable event handling function, such as the following:

```
function catchEvent(eventObj, event, eventHandler) {
    if (eventObj.addEventListener) {
        eventObj.addEventListener(event, eventHandler,false);
    } else if (eventObj.attachEvent) {
        event = "on" + event;
        eventObj.attachEvent(event, eventHandler);
```

```
        }
    }
```

In this function, a page element, a specific type of event, and a reference to an event handler function are passed into the function. A test first checks to see whether the addEventListener property is accessible on the event object. If so, it's used to attach the event handler to the event. If not, the attachEvent property is checked next, and it's used if it's available. First, though, the event has to be modified to include the "on" prefix because attachEvent expects events passed in as "onclick" rather than just "click".

Lastly, if neither attachEvent nor addEventListener is available—which is unlikely to happen with most browsers in use today—the traditional DOM Level 0 event handling method is used to attach the event handler directly to the event handler property on the object.

 I'll still use the traditional event handling approach with many examples in the book, primarily because this simpler (though less robust) approach keeps the code samples smaller.

Of course, when validating forms, if a form field fails validation, you need to cancel the event, which means you need a second generic event handling function.

Canceling an Event

For form validation, within the submit event handler function, you'll want to either set cancelBubble to true (for Microsoft) and the returnValue property to false on the event object accessed via window, or use the preventDefault method call (other browsers) in combination with stopPropagation on the event object passed into the event handler to stop the form submission:

```
function formFunction(evnt) {
    var event = evnt ? evnt : window.event;
    ...
        if (event.preventDefault) {
            event.preventDefault();
            event.stopPropagation();
    } else {
            event.returnValue = false;
            event.cancelBubble = true;
    }
}
```

I introduced cancelBubble and stopPropagation in Chapter 7, but returnValue and preventDefault are new. As a reminder, cancelBubble prevents the event from bubbling up to other elements that also capture the event in IE, and stopPropagation does the same for other browsers that follow DOM Level 2 event handling. Part of the prevention of default behavior is to also stop the event from moving on to other elements.

The `returnValue` property is equivalent to returning `false` explicitly in the function, and `preventDefault` prevents the default behavior based on the object and the event. For instance, with a click event on a submit button, calling `stopPropagate` and setting `returnValue` to `false` prevents the default form submission behavior.

Just as with the event handler function in the preceding section, canceling an event handling process also is a great candidate for a reusable function:

```
function cancelEvent(event) {
    if (event.preventDefault) {
        event.preventDefault();
        event.stopPropagation();
    } else {
        event.returnValue = false;
        event.cancelBubble = true;
    }
}
```

The example applications use both `cancelEvent` and `catchEvent` throughout this chapter.

A typical validation procedure is to capture the `submit` event, access the individual form elements and check the data, and then provide a message to the web page reader about what's missing or invalid. If the form is rather large, though, several fields could have bad data, and listing all of them isn't a friendly response.

More efficient approaches exist, especially with larger forms. For instance, you can validate each field as the user enters the data or makes a selection. Each section that follows covers the different types of form input elements, how to get data from each, and other tweaks you can perform using JavaScript.

Selection

The `select` element and its associated options provide a way to choose one or more items from a list. You define the `select` element using the following syntax:

```
<select name="theSelection" multiple="multiple">
<option value="Opt1">Option 1</option>
<option value="Opt2">Option 2</option>
...
<option value="Optn">Option n</option>
</select>
```

The `select` element has the following properties that are accessible from JavaScript:

`disabled`
    Whether the element is disabled

`form`
    The containing form

length
> The number of options in the `options` array

options
> The array of options

selectedIndex
> For a single select element, the number of items selected; for a multiple select element, the first item selected

type
> The type of element

The `select` options are included in the `options` array. Each is an object with several properties. However, for forms validation, the properties of interest are `selected`, `value`, and `text`. The `selected` property is set to `true` if the option is selected; the option value is given in `value`; the text that's visible to the web page reader is given in `text`.

You can get the `selected` options from a selection in two ways, depending on whether the user can select multiple options or only one. If the user can select only one option at a time, using the `select` property of `selectedIndex` on the `options` array returns the selected object:

```
var slIdx= document.getElementById("formname").theSelection.selectedIndex;
var opt = document.getElementById("formname").theSelection.options[slIdx];
```

If the user can select multiple options, the code needs to iterate through the entire `options` array and check which options are selected. Example 8-1 creates a multiple-selection list with three options. When the form is submitted, the option `text` and `value` for each selected option are displayed in the pop-up window.

Because two events need to be captured—the window `load` event and the form `submit`—the JavaScript also uses the reusable `catchEvent` (described earlier) with the object, event, and function passed in as parameters.

Example 8-1. Processing the results of a multiple-selection list

```
<!DOCTYPE html PUBLIC "-//W3C//DTD XHTML 1.1//EN"
"http://www.w3.org/TR/xhtml11/DTD/xhtml11.dtd">
<html xmlns="http://www.w3.org/1999/xhtml" xml:lang="en">
<head>
<title>Select</title>
<meta http-equiv="Content-Type" content="text/html; charset=utf-8" />
<script type="text/javascript">
//<![CDATA[

function catchEvent(eventObj, event, eventHandler) {
   if (eventObj.addEventListener) {
      eventObj.addEventListener(event, eventHandler,false);
   } else if (eventObj.attachEvent) {
      event = "on" + event;
      eventObj.attachEvent(event, eventHandler);
   }
```

```
}

catchEvent(window,"load",setupEvents);

function setupEvents(evnt) {
   catchEvent(document.getElementById("someForm"), "submit", checkForm);
}

function checkForm(evnt) {

   var opts = document.getElementById("someForm").selectOpts.options;

   for (var i = 0; i < opts.length; i++) {
      if (opts[i].selected) {
         alert(opts[i].text + " " + opts[i].value);
      }
   }
   // no server side-processing, cancel submit event
   return false;
}


//]]>
</script>
</head>
<body>
<form id="someForm" action="">
<p>
<select id="selectOpts" multiple="multiple">
<option value="Opt1">Option One</option>
<option value="Opt2">Option Two</option>
<option value="Opt3">Option Three</option>
</select>
<input type="submit" value="Submit" />
</p>
</form>
</body>
</html>
```

Because the values are just printed out rather than validated, the form submission is allowed to continue, so the custom cancelEvent function, described in the preceding section, isn't used.

You normally use selection lists when you have a larger number of options—such as a list of states in the United States or cities in China. Because of possible performance issues, you'll most likely want to limit your selection to one entry so that you can specifically access the option using selectedIndex, rather than have to iterate over a larger array. Still, the time to run through an array is short; the number of options picked is up to you.

You can also dynamically build a selection list based on real-time events.

Dynamically Modifying the Selection

Using JavaScript, you can create and remove selection list items on the fly, perhaps based on some other user input. To add a new option to the application shown in Example 8-1, create a new `option` element and add it to the `options` array:

```
opts[opts.length] = new Option("Option Four", "Opt4");
```

Because arrays are zero-based, you can always add a new `array` element at the end by using the array's `length` property as the index.

To remove an option, just set the `option` entry in the array to `null`. This resets the array so that there is no gap in the numbering.

```
opts[2] = null;
```

To remove all options, set the array length to zero (0):

```
opts.length = 0;
```

I modified Example 8-1 slightly to remove an option once it's selected. The changes appear in bold in Example 8-2.

Example 8-2. Removing the selected option

```
<!DOCTYPE html PUBLIC "-//W3C//DTD XHTML 1.1//EN"
"http://www.w3.org/TR/xhtml11/DTD/xhtml11.dtd">
<html xmlns="http://www.w3.org/1999/xhtml" xml:lang="en">
<head>
<title>Select</title>
<meta http-equiv="Content-Type" content="text/html; charset=utf-8" />
<script type="text/javascript">
//<![CDATA[

function catchEvent(eventObj, event, eventHandler) {
    if (eventObj.addEventListener) {
        eventObj.addEventListener(event, eventHandler,false);
    } else if (eventObj.attachEvent) {
        event = "on" + event;
        eventObj.attachEvent(event, eventHandler);
    }
}

function cancelEvent(event) {
    if (event.preventDefault) {
        event.preventDefault();
        event.stopPropagation();
    } else {
        event.returnValue = false;
        event.cancelBubble = true;
    }
}

catchEvent(window,"load",setupEvents);

function setupEvents(evnt) {
```

```
            catchEvent(document.getElementById("someForm"), "submit", checkForm);
    }

    function checkForm(evnt) {
        var theEvent = evnt ? evnt : window.event;

        var opts = document.getElementById("someForm").selectOpts.options;

        for (var i = 0; i < opts.length; i++) {
            if (opts[i].selected) {
                opts[i] = null;
            }
        }

        cancelEvent(theEvent);
    }

//]]>
</script>
</head>
<body>
<form id="someForm" action="">
<p>
<select id="selectOpts" multiple="multiple">
<option value="Opt1">Option One</option>
<option value="Opt2">Option Two</option>
<option value="Opt3">Option Three</option>
</select>
<input type="submit" value="Submit" />
</p>
</form>
</body>
</html>
```

I canceled the form submission using cancelEvent, because when a form is submitted,
the page is reloaded, and this will repopulate the list with all the options—completely
wiping out the change we just made with JavaScript.

It's not unusual to modify a selection list based on the answers given in other form
elements—especially if you're using a drop-down listbox, in which the options don't
show until the user clicks the arrow to open the list. Note, though, that the box may
resize horizontally depending on the length of each option. One way around this
resizing is to set the width of the box dynamically, also using JavaScript. I cover setting
the display attributes of page elements in Chapter 12.

Selection and Auto-Selection

In addition to processing the array elements during a form submit, you can capture
when a change is made to the selection and perform additional automated selections.
Automated selection is a form of validation, in that it ensures that options that should
be selected together are selected together. You can accomplish this type of activity by

capturing a change event for the form field, testing whether it should have an associated option, and then selecting it. This can be a lot less frustrating for the people filling out the forms; they won't have to wait until they've filled in all the fields to validate the whole form, only to find out they didn't select all the grouped options.

I made another modification to Example 8-1 to demonstrate automated selection. In Example 8-3, two options are nested with two others so that if you select the parent option, you'll automatically get the nested option; however, the converse is not true—selecting the nested option does not give you the parent option.

Example 8-3. Using just-in-time validation with a selection

```
<!DOCTYPE html PUBLIC "-//W3C//DTD XHTML 1.1//EN"
"http://www.w3.org/TR/xhtml11/DTD/xhtml11.dtd">
<html xmlns="http://www.w3.org/1999/xhtml" xml:lang="en">
<head>
<title>Select</title>
<meta http-equiv="Content-Type" content="text/html; charset=utf-8" />
<script type="text/javascript">
//<![CDATA[

function catchEvent(eventObj, event, eventHandler) {
    if (eventObj.addEventListener) {
        eventObj.addEventListener(event, eventHandler,false);
    } else if (eventObj.attachEvent) {
        event = "on" + event;
        eventObj.attachEvent(event, eventHandler);
    }
}

function cancelEvent(event) {
    if (event.preventDefault) {
        event.preventDefault();
        event.stopPropagation();
    } else {
        event.returnValue = false;
        event.cancelBubble = true;
    }
}

catchEvent(window,"load",setupEvents);

function setupEvents(evnt) {
    catchEvent(document.getElementById("selectOpts"),"change",checkSelect);
}

function checkSelect(evnt) {

    var theEvent = evnt ? evnt : window.event;

    var opts = document.getElementById("someForm").selectOpts.options;
    for (var i = 0; i < opts.length; i++) {
        if (opts[i].selected) {
            switch(opts[i].value) {
```

```
                    case "Opt1" : opts[i + 1].selected = true;
                                  break;
                    case "Opt3" : opts[i + 1].selected = true;
                                  break;
                    case "Opt4" : opts[i + 1].selected = true;
                                  break;
                }
            }
        }
        // no server-side processing, cancel submit event
        cancelEvent(theEvent);
}

//]]>
</script>
</head>
<body>
<form id="someForm" action="">
<p>
<select id="selectOpts" multiple="multiple">
<option value="Opt1">Option One</option>
<option value="Opt1a"> -- Option OneA</option>
<option value="Opt2">Option Two</option>
<option value="Opt3">Option Three</option>
<option value="Opt3a"> -- Option ThreeA</option>
<option value="Opt4">Option Four</option>
<option value="Opt4a"> -- Option FourA</option>
<option value="Opt5">Option Five</option>
</select>
<input type="submit" value="Submit" />
</p>
</form>
</body>
</html>
```

Having some options automatically selected can ensure the accuracy of the data. It's also rather impressive-looking without requiring a lot of effort.

Automated selection is a form of *just-in-time validation*, though most of the time we think of validation as checking to see whether an input field has the correct data. I'll demonstrate this latter form of just-in-time validation later in the chapter, but for now, know that selecting logically grouped options and disabling inappropriate options are also useful variations particularly suited to the use of JavaScript.

How often you use just-in-time validation depends on the form's complexity and purpose. Using this approach for every form element could irritate users rather than help them, but waiting to validate after the form is submitted to the server, and providing a long list of needed changes, could overwhelm users. As always, the code can do only so much; you'll need to use your own judgment as to how and when to use it.

Radio Buttons and Checkboxes

Radio buttons and checkboxes provide one-click option choosing, usually with a smaller number of options than a selection. They differ in that radio buttons allow only one choice, but you can select as many checkboxes as you like.

Here is the syntax for a radio button:

```
<form id="someForm" action="">
<p>
<input type="radio" value="Opt 1" name="radiogroup" />Option 1<br />
<input type="radio" value="Opt 2" name="radiogroup" />Option 2<br />
</p>
</form>
```

Notice that the name is the same for both options. That's how the buttons are grouped. To access the radio button group, use the `document.getElementById` function, passing in the radio button group name:

```
var buttons = document.getElementById("radioGroup");

for (var i = 0; i < buttons.length; i++) {
   if (buttons[i].checked) {
      alert(buttons[i].value);
   }
}
```

As noted earlier, checkboxes differ from radio buttons in that you can select more than one checkbox; in addition, the `type` of the `input` element is set to `checkbox`, and you have to iterate through all the `checkbox` elements to see which one has been checked.

You define checkboxes as follows:

```
<form id="someForm" action="">
   <p>
      Option 1: <input type="checkbox" name="checkbox1" value="Opt1" /><br />
      Option 2: <input type="checkbox" name="checkbox2" value="Opt2" /><br />
   </p>
</form>
```

To see which checkbox has been selected, you have to iterate through all of the checkbox items. One approach to doing this is to create an array of elements based on the checkbox names, and iterate through the bunch, checking to see whether the checkbox has been checked.

A different approach provides another sneak peek into the DOM functionality we'll cover in Chapter 11. It requires the use of a `document` method called `getElementsByTagName`.

The `getElementsByTagName` method returns all items of a specific element type. You can get all elements of a specific type for the whole page, or you can access one element using `getElementById` and then pull together a collection of the elements it contains that match the element type.

The application in Example 8-4 comprises a form with four checkboxes. Which ones are checked is irrelevant, as is the number of checkboxes checked. However, at least one must be checked, and the JavaScript validates that one checkbox has indeed been checked.

Example 8-4. Checking the checkboxes

```
<!DOCTYPE html PUBLIC "-//W3C//DTD XHTML 1.1//EN"
"http://www.w3.org/TR/xhtml11/DTD/xhtml11.dtd">
<html xmlns="http://www.w3.org/1999/xhtml" xml:lang="en">
<head>
<title>Checkbox</title>
<meta http-equiv="Content-Type" content="text/html; charset=utf-8" />
<script type="text/javascript">
//<![CDATA[

function catchEvent(eventObj, event, eventHandler) {
    if (eventObj.addEventListener) {
        eventObj.addEventListener(event, eventHandler,false);
    } else if (eventObj.attachEvent) {
        event = "on" + event;
        eventObj.attachEvent(event, eventHandler);
    }
}

function cancelEvent(event) {
    if (event.preventDefault) {
        event.preventDefault();
        event.stopPropagation();
    } else {
        event.returnValue = false;
        event.cancelBubble = true;
    }
}

catchEvent(window,"load",setupEvents);

function setupEvents(evnt) {
  catchEvent(document.getElementById("someForm"), "submit",checkColors);
}
function checkColors(evnt) {

    var theEvent = evnt ? evnt : window.event;
    var colorOpts =
document.getElementById("someForm").getElementsByTagName("input");

    // check through input elements for checkbox and checked
    var isChecked = false;
    for (var i = 0; i < colorOpts.length; i++) {
      if ((colorOpts[i].type == "checkbox") && (colorOpts[i].checked)) {
        isChecked=true;
        break;
      }
    }
```

```
      // none were checked
      if (!isChecked) {
         alert("You must check one of the four color checkboxes");
         cancelEvent(theEvent);
      }
   }
}

//]]>
</script>
</head>
<body>
<form id="someForm" action="">
   <p>
   <input type="checkbox" name="color1" value="red" /> : red<br />
   <input type="checkbox" name="color2" value="blue" /> : blue<br />
   <input type="checkbox" name="color3" value="green" /> : green<br />
   <input type="checkbox" name="color4" value="yellow" /> : yellow<br /><br />

   <input type="submit" value="Submit" />
</p>
</form>
</body>
</html>
```

There are two things to note in Example 8-4: the first is that the elements being accessed are identified by "input" and not "checkbox"; there is no "checkbox" element. The code accesses the `input` element's `type` attribute to find out what type of element is triggering the event. Second, we have to see whether the `input` element is a `checkbox` *and* that it's checked before setting the flag that signals that at least one checkbox item has been checked. And because all we care about is that one checkbox is checked, we break out of the `for` loop when we find the first checked checkbox, as we don't need to go through the rest of the items.

Other than ensuring that a checkbox item is selected, it's difficult for your users to screw up with checkboxes or radio buttons. You could match the behavior of the buttons with other form options, but if you need to restrict one or more radio buttons or checkboxes, a better option is to disable the option rather than validating it post-event. You can disable an option using the following JavaScript:

```
document.getElementById("someForm").radiogroup[1].disabled=true;
```

You can capture the `click` event for the group if you want to modify other form elements based on a radio button or checkbox selection. To attach an event handler, you attach it to the group:

```
document.getElementById("someForm").radiogroup.onclick=handleClick;
```

As with options, you can create new checkbox or radio button elements, except that you'll need to ensure that the option you create is an input element and that you set the type accordingly. You'll also attach the new element to the form:

```
var newCheckbox = document.createElement("input");
newCheckbox.type="checkbox";
```

```
newCheckbox.name="colors1";
newCheckbox.checked=true;
someForm.appendChild(newCheckbox);
```

You can also use dynamic web effects (covered in Chapter 12) to hide or expose checkboxes and other form elements, but you're better off setting the `disabled` property in JavaScript to manage the dynamic nature of the control. Once a form element is disabled, it is no longer capable of receiving events or of being set.

Though these past few sections demonstrate how you can use just-in-time validation with all form element types, we mainly use validation for freeform text fields, covered next.

The text, textarea, password, and hidden Input Elements

The `text`, `textarea`, and `password` fields are probably the most used, as well as the `input` elements most likely to need validation. The `hidden` field usually doesn't have a problem with validation, but it is a text-based field, so I've thrown it in with the group to keep like controls together.

You define the single-row text-based input elements in HTML as follows:

```
<input type="text|hidden|password" name="fieldName" value="Some value" />
```

Setting the `type` attribute defines the type of field. The `text` field is regular text, the `hidden` field isn't visible to the user filling in the form, and the `password` field hides the text with bullets—just in case someone is looking over the user's shoulder.

The `textarea` field is similar, except that unlike the other input fields, it has an opening and closing tag, and you can set both column and row widths. In addition, the `textarea` form element is its own element; it's not a form of `input`:

```
<textarea name="fieldName" rows="10" cols="10">Initial text</textarea>
```

In JavaScript, you can access the values of fields for all text input types via the form element `value` property. To demonstrate this property, Example 8-5 defines a form with all four text form element types. When the form is submitted, it uses JavaScript to access all three input text fields to build a string from their content, which it then adds to the `textarea` input element.

Example 8-5. Accessing text-based input fields from JavaScript

```
<!DOCTYPE html PUBLIC "-//W3C//DTD XHTML 1.1//EN"
"http://www.w3.org/TR/xhtml11/DTD/xhtml11.dtd">
<html xmlns="http://www.w3.org/1999/xhtml" xml:lang="en">
<head>
<title>Text Fields</title>
<meta http-equiv="Content-Type" content="text/html; charset=utf-8" />
<script type="text/javascript">
//<![CDATA[

function catchEvent(eventObj, event, eventHandler) {
```

```
    if (eventObj.addEventListener) {
        eventObj.addEventListener(event, eventHandler,false);
    } else if (eventObj.attachEvent) {
        event = "on" + event;
        eventObj.attachEvent(event, eventHandler);
    }
}

function cancelEvent(event) {
    if (event.preventDefault) {
        event.preventDefault();
        event.stopPropagation();
    } else {
        event.returnValue = false;
        event.cancelBubble = true;
    }
}

catchEvent(window,"load",setupEvents);

function setupEvents(evnt) {
    catchEvent(document.getElementById("someForm"), "submit",validateForm);
}

function validateForm(evnt) {

    var theEvent = evnt ? evnt : window.event;

    var strResults = "";
    var textInputs =
document.getElementById("someForm").getElementsByTagName("input");
    for (var i = 0; i < textInputs.length; i++) {
        if (textInputs[i].type != "submit") {
            strResults += textInputs[i].value;
        }
    }
    document.getElementById("text4").value=strResults;

    // don't wipe out results
    cancelEvent(theEvent);
}


//]]>
</script>
</head>
<body>
<form id="someForm" action="">
<p>
<input type="text" name="text1" /><br />
<input type="password" name="text2" /><br />
<input type="hidden" name="text3" value="hidden value" />
<textarea name="text4" cols="50" rows="10">The text area</textarea>
<input type="submit" value="Submit" />
</p>
```

```
</form>
</body>
</html>
```

In the example, because the submit button is also an input form element, the code checks to ensure that the element currently being processed is not of type "submit". Also, notice in the code that the form submission is canceled regardless of the values in the text fields. If you didn't cancel the submittal, the form fields would be reset, and you'd lose the string you just created. Figure 8-1 shows this application opened in the Google Chrome browser.

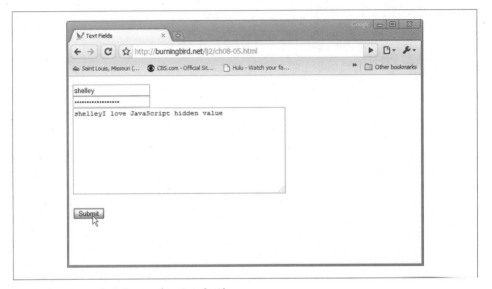

Figure 8-1. Example 8-5 opened in Google Chrome

Text Validation

Text fields are the form elements most likely to have bad data resulting from a misunderstanding of what's required or from typographical errors. As such, these are the fields you'll most likely want to validate.

The events of interest when performing immediate (or just-in-time) validation are change, focus, and blur. When the cursor moves into a text input field, a focus event is fired; when the cursor leaves, the blur event is fired. A change event happens when the contents of the field are changed *and* the cursor moves out of the field. You'll most likely want to capture the change event to validate contents, and the blur event to make sure the field has some value—if it's a required field, of course.

By modifying the application in Example 8-5, the application in Example 8-6 captures the blur event for the password field, and tests the field's value to ensure that there is some value. In addition, when the first text field is changed, the value is validated against a regular expression pattern, nnn-nn-nnnn, for a Social Security number (SSN).

Example 8-6. Applying just-in-time validation with text-based input fields

```
<!DOCTYPE html PUBLIC "-//W3C//DTD XHTML 1.0 Transitional//EN"
"http://www.w3.org/TR/xhtml1/DTD/xhtml1-transitional.dtd">
<html>
<head>
<title>JiT RegEx</title>
<meta http-equiv="Content-Type" content="text/html; charset=utf-8" />
<script type="text/javascript">
//<![CDATA[

function catchEvent(eventObj, event, eventHandler) {
   if (eventObj.addEventListener) {
      eventObj.addEventListener(event, eventHandler,false);
   } else if (eventObj.attachEvent) {
      event = "on" + event;
      eventObj.attachEvent(event, eventHandler);
   }
}

catchEvent(window,"load",setupEvents);

function setupEvents(evnt) {
  catchEvent(document.getElementById("text2"), "blur",checkRequired);
  catchEvent(document.getElementById("text1"), "change", validateField);
}

function checkRequired (evnt) {
  var theEvent = evnt ? evnt : window.event;
  var target = theEvent.target ? theEvent.target : theEvent.srcElement;

  var txtInput = target.value;
  if (txtInput == null || txtInput == "") {
    alert("value is required in field");
  }
}

function validateField(evnt) {
  var theEvent = evnt ? evnt : window.event;
  var target = theEvent.target ? theEvent.target : theEvent.srcElement;
  var rgEx = /^\d{3}[-]?\d{2}[-]?\d{4}$/g;

  var OK = rgEx.exec(target.value);
  if (!OK) {
    alert("not an ssn");
  }

}
//]]>
</script>
</head>
<body>
```

```
<form name="someForm">
<input type="text" name="text1" id="text1" /><br />
<input type="password" name="text2" id="text2" /><br />
<input type="hidden" name="text3" value="hidden value" />
<textarea name="text4" cols=50 rows=10>The text area</textarea><br /><br />
<input type="submit" value="Submit" />
</form>
</body>
</html>
```

Now, if the SSN doesn't have the proper format, the user will be notified as soon as she leaves the field. In addition, if she doesn't provide a password, another alert window opens. Of course, alert windows become irritating over time, and later in the book we'll look at better ways to provide feedback.

Use extreme care if you decide to enforce a required field using the focus method to return the cursor to the field—especially in combination with a pop-up window giving an error. In some browsers, such as Opera, this can trigger a never-ending loop. It can also irritate your users considerably. The bottom line is that you should not enforce a required field through the use of focus.

This example also demonstrates how important regular expressions are with any form of user input. The next section looks more closely at applying regular expressions to form text fields.

Input Fields and Regular Expression Validation

Most form fields just require some text without giving any concern to the format. However, certain types of fields may require a specific format. Rather than sending the data across to the server to see whether the data is valid, we'll use regular expressions to validate the format of the data first.

Some of the more common validations using regular expressions against text input fields occur with the following scenarios:

- Warranty or purchase certificates
- Email addresses
- Phone numbers
- SSNs or other forms of identification
- Dates
- State abbreviations
- Credit card numbers
- Web page URLs or other forms of Uniform Resource Identifiers (URIs)

Rather than try out various regular expressions directly in code, Example 8-7 contains a little application, the JiT RegEx Machine, that takes a regular expression typed in one field and a string in another and then does a pattern match when the form is submitted. The results are output to a third field.

Example 8-7. The JiT RegEx Machine application

```
<!DOCTYPE html PUBLIC "-//W3C//DTD XHTML 1.0 Transitional//EN"
"http://www.w3.org/TR/xhtml1/DTD/xhtml1-transitional.dtd">
<html>
<head>
<title>The JiT RegEx Machine</title>
<meta http-equiv="Content-Type" content="text/html; charset=utf-8" />
<script type="text/javascript">
//<![CDATA[

if (window.addEventListener) {
    window.addEventListener("load",setupEvents,false);
  } else if (window.attachEvent) {
    window.attachEvent("onload", setupEvents);
  } else {
    window.onload=setupEvents;
}

function setupEvents(evnt) {
   document.someForm.onsubmit=validateField;
}

function validateField(evnt) {

  var rgEx = new RegExp(document.someForm.text1.value);
  var OK = rgEx.exec(document.someForm.text2.value);

  // result and print out
  if (!OK) {
     document.someForm.text3.value = "Not a match";
  } else {
     document.someForm.text3.value = "The Pattern matched!";
  }

  return false;

}
//]]>
</script>
</head>
<body>
<form name="someForm" style="padding: 10px">
Regular Expression: <input type="text" name="text1" /><br /><br />
<textarea name="text2" cols=50 rows=10></textarea><br />
Result: <input type="text" name="text3" /><br /><br />
<input type="submit" value="Check RegExp" />
</form>
</body>
</html>
```

Certificates of purchase and warranty numbers may have a pattern that requires certain letters and/or numbers to appear in certain positions. As an example, if you have a certificate identifier that is 13 characters long, with the characters *BUS* in the sixth through eighth positions and alphanumeric characters in the remaining spots, you might try the following regular expression:

```
^\w{5}BUS\w{5}
```

If you're validating an email address, which requires an "at" symbol (@), some form of domain, and few additional restrictions, then the following should work:

```
^.+@[^\.].*\.[a-z]{2,}
```

As for date, the following could work if you want a date in the format mm/dd/yyyy:

```
^\d{2}\/\d{2}\/\d{4}
```

Are these examples too simple? Well, check out the following for SSNs:

```
^(?!000)([0-6]\d{2}|7([0-6]\d|7[012]))([ -]?)(?!00)\d\d\3(?!0000)\d{4}$
```

The preceding regular expression comes courtesy of the Regular Expression Library, an invaluable resource located at *http://regexlib.com/*. This regular expression pattern validates not only against the format, but also what is known about SSNs—the number groupings and so on. Other regular expression patterns that are at least as complex can differentiate between a Visa credit card and a MasterCard.

 If you want to become an expert at regular expressions, spend some time at the Regular Expression Library. Or, you can buy a copy of *Mastering Regular Expressions* by Jeffrey E.F. Friedl (O'Reilly). This is the definitive guide on regular expressions.

On the other hand, do you need to differentiate between Visa and MasterCard? The important point to remember about regular expressions is that you can get carried away trying to find the perfect validation pattern, spending more time than the validation is worth. You have to weigh your time against how important it is to validate the entry before submitting it to the server.

Forms, the Sandbox, and XSS

When JavaScript was first released, there was understandable concern about opening a web page that would execute a bit of code directly in your machine. What if the JavaScript included something harmful, such as code to delete all Word documents, or worse, to copy them for the script originator?

To prevent such occurrences and to reassure browser users, JavaScript was built to operate in a *sandbox*: a protected environment in which the script can't access the resources of the browser's computer. Additionally, browsers implement security conditions above and beyond those established as a minimum for the JavaScript language. These are defined in a browser-specific *security policy*, which determines what the script can and cannot do.

One such security policy dictates that a script may not communicate with pages other than those from the same domain where the script originated. Most browsers provide the means to customize this policy even further, making the environment in which the script operates more, or less, restrictive.

Unfortunately, even with the JavaScript sandbox and browser security policies, JavaScript has had a rough time, and hackers have discovered and exploited several JavaScript errors—some browser-dependent, some not. One of the more serious is known as *cross-site scripting* (XSS). This is actually a class of security breaks (some coming through JavaScript, others through holes in the browsers, and still others through the server) that can lead to cookie theft and exposure of client or site data and a host of other serious problems. They can also lead to destructive actions on your server and database, and put your site visitors at risk.

An example of an XSS vulnerability is known as the *SQL injection attack*. This type of attack happens when users attach actual SQL at the end of text within an input field. An example (from my book, *Adding Ajax*, also from O'Reilly) is the following, typed as is into a field accessing something similar to a post title:

```
x' where ID = '1'; DROP TABLE wp_users; update wp_posts set post_title='x
```

If this input field text is not "scrubbed" and is attached directly into a SQL command in something such as PHP, you could end up with the following:

```
update wp_posts set post_title = 'x' where ID = '1'; DROP TABLE wp_users; update
wp_posts set post_title = 'x' where ID = '$post';
```

The part that's patched in is made in such a way that the update is meant to succeed, including accounting for strings that will be attached to the SQL on either side of the input field.

To prevent XSS attacks such as SQL injection from occurring, text input is tested to ensure that all it contains is acceptable data, and that no SQL is attached to the text. Where this action should occur, though, is open for debate.

I believe all such security cleanup and validation should occur in the server application, not the least of which applications now have multiple entry points: through frontend applications, such as our JavaScript clients, and through direct server-to-server application calls. In addition, I feel that exposing your cleanup criteria within your JavaScript makes it easier to discover where you may still have vulnerabilities in your system.

However, others believe that frontend developers should be just as worried about security issues as backend developers. In particular, if we have no control over the backend, it might be better to be safe rather than sorry with our input.

Additionally, other XSS vulnerabilities go beyond SQL, including those that might embed unsafe URLs into text that will end up being published (such as comment fields). One way around these types of problems is to encode HTML (convert HTML elements into harmless text), or filter out any HTML. Again, though, most of this filtering and encoding is likely to occur at the server, rather than through JavaScript on the client.

Regardless of where cleanup and prevention filtering occur, it's important to be aware of how vulnerable your form input fields are and to ensure that nothing comes through from these fields except for safe, valid text.

 The CERT site is the authority on security issues, and you can find the page discussing XSS at *http://www.cert.org/advisories/CA-2000-02 .html*. The CGISecurity.com site has an in-depth FAQ on XSS; you can find it at *http://www.cgisecurity.com/articles/xss-faq.shtml*.

Test Your Knowledge: Quiz

1. How do you stop a form submittal if the form data is incomplete or invalid?

2. What event(s) do you want to capture on text input fields to validate the contents before the form is submitted?

3. What code would you use to ensure that a field has only letters and whitespace?

4. Create the JavaScript that captures an event when a radio button is checked, then disables a text input field if one button is clicked, and enables it if another button is clicked.

Test Your Knowledge: Answers

1. If you're using DOM Level 0 events, returning `false` from the event handler and the event handler script cancels the submittal. If you're using DOM Level 2, set `cancelBubble` to `true` for IE, and call the `preventDefault` method for other browsers, both based on the `event` object.

2. The `blur` event is triggered when the field loses focus. This is a good time to check the text field to make sure it has valid data.

3. Here's one approach:

```
var fieldPattern = /^[A-Za-z\s]*$/g;
var OK = fieldPattern.exec(document.forms[0].text1.value);
```

4. First, the code must assign an event handler function to each radio button's `onclick` event handler:

```
document.forms[0].radiogroup[0].onclick=handleClick;
document.forms[0].radiogroup[1].onclick=handleClick;
```

If there are several buttons, you can accomplish this process more easily in a `for` loop. In the `handleClick` function, test the check status of the button and disable the form element accordingly. As an example, to disable the submit button:

```
function handleClick() {
    if (document.forms[0].radiogroup[1].checked) {
        document.forms[0].submit.disabled=true;
    } else {
        document.forms[0].submit.disabled=false;
    }
}
```

CHAPTER 9

Browser As Puzzle Box

The Browser Object Model (BOM) is a set of objects inherited from the browser context in which most JavaScript applications function. Sometimes referred to as the Document Object Model (DOM) Level 0, or even as the DOM, the BOM is a finite set of common web objects that have been accessible via JavaScript since earlier versions of Netscape Navigator and Microsoft's Internet Explorer.

Previous chapters demonstrated some of the objects, such as `window`, `document`, and `form`. This chapter looks at these objects more closely, as well as the other objects that complete the BOM.

The Structure of the Browser at a Glance

The BOM forms a hierarchy of objects, with objects at each level accessible via parent objects above them. You can access all of the elements of the BOM via `window`, which is the topmost element. The next level below features `document`, the object used most often in previous examples. The level also contains the `navigator`, `frames`, `location`, `history`, and `screen` objects. From the `document`, several collections of objects are accessible: `forms`, `anchors`, `links`, `cookies`, and `images`. As I demonstrated in Chapter 8, the `form` object also has collections of elements as children.

Figure 9-1 shows the BOM at a glance, and how all of these elements relate to each other.

An object property can be a single object that may or may not have its own properties (including methods), or it can reference a *collection* of objects, each with its own properties. In Figure 9-1, the properties that are collections are shaded.

Within collections, you can access individual items in one of two ways. The first way is to use an array index, such as `document.images[0]` and `document.images[1]` to access the first two images that occur in the page as the page is loaded. The second approach is to access the element by its `name` attribute:

```
var img = document.images("somename");
```

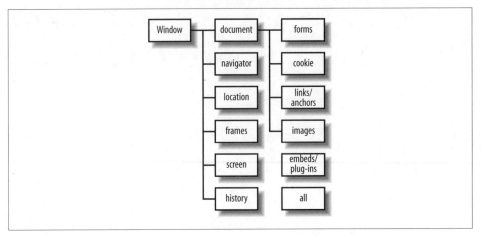

Figure 9-1. Hierarchy of the BOM

Note that you access an element by its name using a function call (with parentheses) rather than an array with square brackets. Additionally, a limitation to using the name approach and assigning names to elements via the `name` attribute occurs if you're using an XHTML strict Document Type Declaration (DOCTYPE), as we are for the examples in this book. Assigning the `name` attribute to most page elements, including `img` and `form` elements, results in a validation error. This occurs because within XML, which forms the basis of XHTML, only the `id` attribute is allowed for element identification.

A third approach to accessing these elements, which has little dependence on them being part of a collection, is to use the element's `id` attribute. Instead of a name, give the element a unique identifier and use the `getElementById` syntax I demonstrated in earlier chapter examples:

```
var theImage = document.getElementById("someimageid");
```

The `name` attribute is still allowed with the XHTML transitional DOCTYPE and with form elements (but not forms) for XHTML transitional and strict. You can use the following technique to access specific form elements in HTML and XHTML:

```
var theElement = document.forms[0].elements("someelement").value;
```

Returning to the BOM, as you can see in Figure 9-1, `window` is the top dog in this bunch. We'll look at that object first.

The window Object

The browser window encompasses the entire browser environment, including the window "chrome" (the part of the browser that surrounds the document), the actual web page, and the page events.

Chrome in this instance means the general components that make up a browser window, not Chrome, the Google browser.

The window object is global and is always present, even if its presence is implicitly (rather than explicitly) stated. In previous chapters, you used a global function, alert, and though this function may seem "independent" of any object, it is implicitly a part of the window object—as is the document and other second-level objects, as well as all global variables and other objects not specifically associated with any other object within an object model.

The window object is interesting beyond being just a parent to all other elements. Through it you can manually set the status in the browser status bar, open a new window, resize one that's already open, and then close it again. This ability to open a new window is handy if you're providing separate windows for help or additional information, though with the growing popularity of dynamic web effects and Ajax, as well as the growing disfavor of using pop-up windows, much of this type of communication now occurs *within* a document rather than within a separate window.

Different security constraints across browsers may inhibit the use of some of this functionality.

The window object's methods and properties fall into four categories:

- Creating new windows and manipulating the behavior of existing windows
- Creating compartmentalized documents (frames and iframes) within the window
- Creating and controlling timers
- Properties for controlling specific elements of the browser window, such as document, navigator, screen, and so on

Creating and Controlling Windows

For the first window category, creating new windows, three methods provide quick pop-up windows (each for a specific purpose), and a fourth can create a window with as much or as little window infrastructure included as you wish.

The Dialogs: alert, confirm, and prompt

Three simple pop-up window object methods create a window with minimal window chrome, each serving a specific purpose. These are usually referred to as the *dialog windows*.

You should be familiar with the `alert` box or window, which is a quick way to provide a message to the person accessing the page. The only parameter it takes is a message string, and it returns no value:

```
alert("This is the message");
```

The `confirm` method creates a dialog with one question and two buttons: Cancel and OK. The message is passed as a parameter, and, depending on which button is clicked, a `true` (OK) or `false` (Cancel) value is returned:

```
var result = confirm("Do you want fries with that?");
```

The `prompt` method opens a window with a field for entering text, as well as the Cancel and OK buttons. It takes two parameters: a message providing the prompt for the response, and a default string which is used to fill in the text field:

```
var response = prompt("What's your name?", "Wouldn't you like to know...");
```

If you don't have a specific string for the second parameter, you'll probably want to pass in an empty string anyway. Otherwise, some browsers, such as IE, will fill the field with `"undefined"`.

Some browsers may also restrict the use of `prompt` for security reasons. You may have to have your JavaScript application users enable support for the `prompt` dialog for it to display. A better choice is to use a form.

 None of these methods are preceded by a reference to the `window` object, which is global, with an assumed presence.

I refer to these types of windows as *pop ups* because that's basically what they do: pop up. However, this term is normally reserved for those windows that seem to take over your desktop every time you visit a web page. Yes, you know the type: the ones you instruct your browser to prevent. However, not all windows that open are full of moving bunnies with an invitation to shoot one and win a Big Prize. Opening a separate window can be an effective way to provide additional information, without taking the person away from the current page.

Creating Custom Windows

There are many reasons to open a new window: to access a help system, provide additional information, review a shopping cart or other information, and yes, even display animated bunnies with roving bulls-eyes.

To open a window and control its contents, size, position, and so on, use the `window` `open` method. This method takes several parameters, all of which are optional:

- The first parameter is the URL of the document to open, if any.
- The second parameter is the name given to the window, and you can use it for communication between the parent and child windows, or among siblings if many windows are opened.
- The third parameter is a set of window options, all contained in one string and separated by commas, and all of which control the appearance and behavior of the new window.

In the following line of code, a window is created and is named "test". It contains a link to the main O'Reilly website, is 600×400 pixels, and doesn't have a location or toolbar:

```
window.open("http://oreilly.com","test","width=600,height=400,toolbar=no,
location=no");
```

You cannot set all options in all circumstances. Those that impact certain components of the window frame and window layering position you can modify from the default only if the script has a `UniversalBrowserWrite` privilege, usually granted with script signing. Because support for script signing isn't very widespread, it's best to avoid any dependency on these options.

Table 9-1 lists the common options that most browsers support, their purpose, and their default values.

Table 9-1. Cross-browser-compatible window.open options

Option	Purpose	Default value
alwaysLowered	Referred to as a "pop-under" window; puts the window under the parent window unless the parent window is minimized	Default is no; defined to work only with UniversalBrowserWrite
alwaysRaised	Opens the window on top of the parent window	Default is no; defined to work only with UniversalBrowserWrite
dependent	Opens a window that is dependent on the parent window; when the parent closes, all dependent windows close	Default is no
directories	Displays personal bookmarks or the links bar in the browser, depending on the browser type	Default is yes; the user can override this in some browsers
height	Height of the content area, in pixels	Minimum of 100 pixels
width	Width of the content area, in pixels	Minimum of 100 pixels
outerHeight	Height of the entire browser window, in pixels	Minimum of 100 pixels
outerWidth	Width of the entire browser window, in pixels	Minimum of 100 pixels
top	Position of the topmost edge of the browser window	Must be positioned on-screen
left	Position of the leftmost edge of the browser window	Must be positioned on-screen

Option	Purpose	Default value
menubar	If yes, renders the menu bar	The user can override this in some browsers
toolbar	If yes, renders the toolbar	The user can override this in some browsers
location	If yes, renders the location on the address bar	IE7 forces the location to always display
status	If yes, renders the status bar at the bottom of the browser window	Defaults to yes for some browsers
resizable	If yes, the window is resizable	The user can override this in some browsers
scrollbars	If yes, the window has scroll bars (if the loaded document doesn't fit)	The user can override this in some browsers
modal	Opens a window that must be closed before returning to the main window	Dialog windows are modal windows; in some browsers, this requires UniversalBrowserWrite
dialog	Opens a dialog window similar in appearance and behavior to the alert window	
minimizable	Only when the dialog is set to yes; inserts buttons to minimize the window	
titlebar	Renders or removes the title bar	On by default; requires UniversalBrowser Write; the user can override this in some browsers
close	Renders or removes the close button (icon)	On by default; requires UniversalBrowser Write; the user can override this in some browsers

As you can see, security is a primary concern when it comes to pop-up windows.

Example 9-1 is an application that uses a **prompt** method to get a string to open a new window. Try out variations of the **option** string, and see the differences. An example of one **option** string is the following:

```
menubar=yes,location=yes,resizable=yes
```

Note that you will most likely have to alter your browser's security settings for the **prompt** dialog to display. In addition, you'll have to unblock pop ups for the page to get the new window to display.

Example 9-1. Using a prompt dialog to get window.open options

```
<!DOCTYPE html PUBLIC "-//W3C//DTD XHTML 1.1//EN"
"http://www.w3.org/TR/xhtml11/DTD/xhtml11.dtd">
<html xmlns="http://www.w3.org/1999/xhtml" xml:lang="en">
<head>
<title>Windows</title>
<meta http-equiv="Content-Type" content="text/html; charset=utf-8" />
<script type="text/javascript">
//<![CDATA[

window.onload = function() {
   var optionString = prompt("Enter your option string", "");
   optionString = optionString ? optionString : "";
```

```
    window.open("http://burningbird.net","test",optionString);
}

//]]>
</script>
</head>
<body>
<p>some content</p>
</body>
</html>
```

Your code can check whether the window was blocked by testing the return value. If it's `null`, the window was blocked. How each browser controls pop ups differs, but each will give you some noticeable clue that a pop up has been blocked, as well as give web page readers an option to unblock it.

If no `option` string is given in Example 9-1, the newly opened window will either in a tab, which is the default behavior for most browsers, or resemble the parent window. When certain options are specified, others—such as `toolbar`, `location`, and `menubar`— may be off by default, or may be dependent on the browser you're using. Other options exist when opening a window, but many violate accessibility standards. An example of this is `fullscreen`. This option opens a browser to fill the screen, an option which you should use with caution.

Once you have a `window` object, you can adjust it from the parent window or have a window adjust itself. I'll cover the methods for managing window modification next.

Modifying a Window

Among the methods that can manipulate a window are those that affect its size, focus, and position. You can manipulate newly opened windows using a reference to the window; manipulate parent windows through the keyword `opener`; and manipulate the window that contains the running script by using the keyword `self`.

In the following code, the window containing the JavaScript being run is moved to a position of `0,0` for top and left:

```
self.moveTo(0,0);
```

If instead you want to reference a window you open from code, you'll need to capture a reference to the window, which is returned from the `window.open` call:

```
var newWindow = window.open("http://somecompany.com","NewWindow", "...options...");
newWindow.moveTo(0,0);
```

The opening window can reference any window it creates. The newly created window can also reference the window that opened it using the **opener** keyword:

```
opener.moveTo(0,0);
```

Each window can invoke the other window's methods, including getting access to the window objects, document, frames, location, and so on. There are few limitations to this cross-window communication, other than that most browsers do not let the opened window close the original window.

 Closing the original window could lose the user's back-button history, opened tabs, half-filled fields, and so on. Browsers that allow a new window to close the previously opened window pop up a dialog asking permission from the user first.

Once you have a reference to a window (through an open window reference, through **self**, or through **opener**), you can set the focus to that window, or reset it back to the opening window through the **focus** method. Another method, **blur**, sets the focus to whatever window would normally get the focus next:

```
newWindow.focus();
...
newWindow.blur();
```

You can resize windows using the **resizeBy** and **resizeTo** methods. The **resizeBy** method relatively adjusts the current dimensions by a given width and height, in pixels:

```
newWindow.resizeBy(50,50);
```

The **resizeTo** method resizes the window to an absolute width and height, again in pixels:

```
opener.resizeTo(100,100);
```

One of the more helpful methods is **moveTo**, which moves a window's upper-left corner to a given **x,y** dimension:

```
self.moveTo(x,y);
```

You can use the **moveTo** method to open context-sensitive help windows that are positioned exactly where an event occurs. In Example 9-2, a page with a single form element is opened; a red-colored block underneath has the words "Click for Help." In the **script** element, an event listener is attached to this block to capture the **click** event. When the page opens, the focus is set to the form element for a person to type in his name. However, there's no submit button, so it's not surprising that the user would then click the "Click for Help" button to get help.

Example 9-2. Opening a help window

```
<!DOCTYPE html PUBLIC "-//W3C//DTD XHTML 1.1//EN"
"http://www.w3.org/TR/xhtml11/DTD/xhtml11.dtd">
<html xmlns="http://www.w3.org/1999/xhtml" xml:lang="en">
```

```
<head>
<title>Windows</title>
<meta http-equiv="Content-Type" content="text/html; charset=utf-8" />
<script type="text/javascript">
//<![CDATA[

function catchEvent(eventObj, event, eventHandler) {
  if (eventObj.addEventListener) {
      eventObj.addEventListener(event, eventHandler,false);
    } else if (eventObj.attachEvent) {
      event = "on" + event;
      eventObj.attachEvent(event, eventHandler);
    }
}

catchEvent(window,"load",setupEvents);

function setupEvents(evnt) {

    document.forms[0].elements[0].focus();

    var evtObject = document.getElementById("panicbutton");
    catchEvent(evtObject,"click",openHelp);

}

function openHelp(x) {

    var optionString =
"width=200,height=150,menubar=no,toolbar=no,scrollbars=no,location=no,resizeable=no
";
    var helpWindow = window.open("help.html","test",optionString);
    helpWindow.focus();
    helpWindow.moveTo(x.screenX,x.screenY);
    return false;
}

//]]>
</script>
</head>
<body>
<form id="currentForm" action="">
<p>
Your name: <input type="text" size="50" />
</p>
</form>
<div id="panicbutton" style="width:100px;height:40px;background-color:#f00;
padding: 5px; margin-left: 50px">
<p>Click for Help</p>
</div>
</body>
</html>
```

A small window opens with minimal chrome, located just below and to the right of where the click has occurred, as shown in Figure 9-2. It's positioned based on the `click` event because when the window is opened, it's moved to the screen location of the `click` event. Once the window is opened, the focus is set to this window.

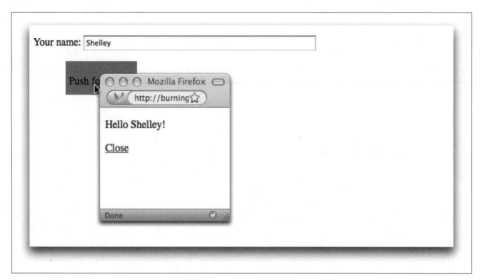

Figure 9-2. Small, newly opened and positioned help window

Example 9-3 contains the contents of the window that opens. It actually accesses the opener window, finds the form element, and copies whatever value it has. This provides a message in the window, which also has a link to close the window.

Example 9-3. Opened window

```
<!DOCTYPE html PUBLIC "-//W3C//DTD XHTML 1.1//EN"
"http://www.w3.org/TR/xhtml11/DTD/xhtml11.dtd">
<html xmlns="http://www.w3.org/1999/xhtml" xml:lang="en">
<head>
<title>Windows</title>
<meta http-equiv="Content-Type" content="text/html; charset=utf-8" />
<script type="text/javascript">
//<![CDATA[

window.onload=function() {

  var nmStr = opener.document.forms[0].elements[0].value;
  document.writeln("<p>Hello " + nmStr + "!</p>");
  document.writeln("<p><a href='' onclick='self.close(); return
false'>Close</a></p>");
}

//]]>
</script>
```

```
</head>
<body>
<p>some content</p>
</body>
</html>
```

Pop ups that try to sell site visitors something aren't especially well liked. Opening a help window, positioning it to where an event occurs, and communicating information between the windows can be very helpful. Later, in Chapter 12, we'll create the same effect with hidden page elements, but for now, you have a way to provide context-sensitive help.

Up to this point, you've been working with one window. However, through the use of *frames*, you can segment the browser window and give each segment a different URL and purpose.

Frames

The `frame` object has the following properties: `parent`, `length`, and `name`. The `name` and `parent` properties are particularly important for cross-frame communication. A `parent` *frameset* (the window containing the frames) can access each *child* frame through its name (or through the `frames` array using the number of the object as an index); each frame can access the `frameset` through the generic term, `parent`. Siblings can access each other by accessing `parent` and then the name of the sibling.

In Example 9-4, a `frameset` with two frames is loaded. The two frames are known as `framea` and `frameb`.

Example 9-4. Frameset loading two frames

```
<!DOCTYPE html PUBLIC "-//W3C//DTD XHTML 1.0 Frameset//EN"
"http://www.w3.org/TR/xhtml1/DTD/xhtml1-frameset.dtd">
<html xmlns="http://www.w3.org/1999/xhtml" xml:lang="en">
<head>
<title>Frames</title>
<meta http-equiv="Content-Type" content="text/html; charset=utf-8" />
</head>
<frameset cols="50%,*">
<frame name="framea" src="framea.html" />
<frame name="frameb" src="frameb.html" />
</frameset>
</html>
```

A document named *framea.html* is loaded into `framea`. It has one link that, when clicked, accesses its sibling through its parent and changes the frame location to itself, as shown in Example 9-5. The second frame document, *frameb.html*, has a different header and page title, but the exact same functionality, except that it steals `framea`'s spot for itself.

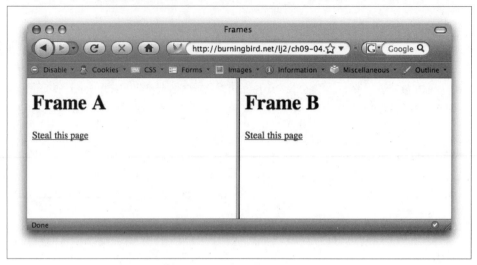

Figure 9-3. The Frames application page when first loaded

Example 9-5. Each frame loading itself

```
<!DOCTYPE html PUBLIC "-//W3C//DTD XHTML 1.1//EN"
"http://www.w3.org/TR/xhtml11/DTD/xhtml11.dtd">
<html xmlns="http://www.w3.org/1999/xhtml" xml:lang="en">
<head>
<title>Frame A</title>
<meta http-equiv="Content-Type" content="text/html; charset=utf-8" />
<script type="text/javascript">
//<![CDATA[

window.onload=function() {
  var theFrame = document.getElementById("thelink");
  theFrame.onclick = function () {
      parent.frameb.location.replace("framea.html");
  }
}

//]]>
</script>
</head>
<body>
<h1>Frame A</h1>
<p><a href="" id="thelink">Steal this page</a></p>
</body>
</html>
```

The individual frame pages load themselves using the location's **replace** method. Figure 9-3 shows the page when loaded; Figure 9-4 shows the page after clicking on the link in Frame B, which wins the tug-o-war over who owns the page.

I'm not fond of frames. Yes, they are extremely useful, and they're still a terrific way to manage applications in which an action in the left window (or top window) can trigger

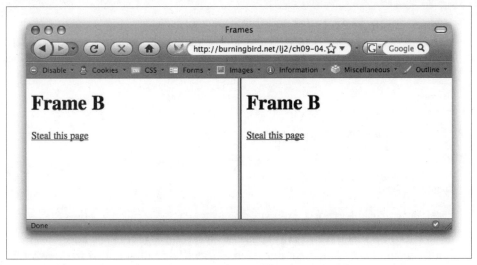

Figure 9-4. The Frames application page after Frame B's link is clicked

a change in the right (or bottom) window. Each frame can then scroll separately from the other, without any effort on our part.

However, too many companies had (or still have) a habit of opening other websites into frames, which basically wraps the other site's content in their own environment. Most of us didn't care for this. Luckily, thanks to JavaScript, we can defeat this technique using a second window object, `location`.

The location Object

The `location` object's properties are related to the page location. You've seen one of its functions, `replace`, being used to replace the page for one of the frames. Another is `reload`, which instructs the browser to refresh the document. It also has properties associated with the page location, including the `host`, `port`, and `protocol` properties, as listed in Table 9-2.

Table 9-2. Location object properties

Property	Purpose
hash	For URLs of the format http://<some.com>/<somepage>#<somehash>, this property contains "somehash"—the value after the hash mark
host	The hostname (domain) and port of the URL
hostname	The hostname (domain) only
href	The entire URL (read and write)
pathname	The pathname that follows the domain
port	The URL port

Property	Purpose
protocol	The protocol used with the URL, such as "http:"
search	The query string, if one exists, that derives the page; this includes anything following the first question mark of the URL
target	If given, the URL's target name

A URL such as the following:

http://learningjavascript.info/ch09-01.htm?a=1

breaks down into the following discrete `location` property values:

```
host/hostname: learningjavascript.info
protocol: http:
search: ?a=1
href: http://learningjavascript.info/ch09-01.htm?a=1
```

Returning to the initial issue regarding frames, and your pages being loaded into them without your permission, use the `location` object—in conjunction with a few other odds and ends—to defeat this technique.

Modify the *frameb.html* file in the example in the preceding section to add a link to another file, the contents of which are shown in Example 9-6. In the page, a script block tests whether the document is opened within the topmost window, or whether it is opened within `frameset`. In the JavaScript, if the window is not the top window (if it is loaded into a frame), it sets the top-window location to itself—effectively bumping the `frameset` out of the way. Different browsers use different functionality to replace the page, and the code tests first to see whether the `replace` method is available, and if not, it uses an alternative approach (setting the `href` property).

Example 9-6. Preventing a window from opening within frameset

```
<!DOCTYPE html PUBLIC "-//W3C//DTD XHTML 1.1//EN"
"http://www.w3.org/TR/xhtml11/DTD/xhtml11.dtd">
<html xmlns="http://www.w3.org/1999/xhtml" xml:lang="en">
<head>
<title>Destroy all frames</title>
<meta http-equiv="Content-Type" content="text/html; charset=utf-8" />
<script type="text/javascript">
//<![CDATA[

window.onload = function() {
if (self != top) {
  if (top.location.replace)
      top.location.replace(self.location.href);
   else
      top.location.href=self.document.href;
  }
}

//]]>
```

```
</script>
</head>
<body>
<p>Frames, no way</p>
</body>
</html>
```

Simple and clean. However, you'll find few pages that frame-protect themselves nowadays. Frames just aren't as popular as they once were, and most people don't want to add unnecessary functionality to their pages.

Not all frames require a `frameset` parent. For instance, you can embed the `iframe` in a page, rather than a `frameset`, which I'll cover next.

Remote Scripting with the iframe

Unlike regular frames, an `iframe` is embedded within a page. You can give it height and width, or you can hide it by setting both the height and width to zero. The `iframe` considers the page in which it's embedded to be its parent, and that's how it communicates with the higher-level page. Normally, you can access it by using the document's `getElementById` method; you can also load content into it using the `target` attribute.

An `iframe` also has a strategic place within the world of client/server development because of the `iframe`'s participation in a process called *remote scripting*. With remote scripting, a client page can access remote services on the server and have those services return data to the client, without having to reload the client. Today, this functionality is typically called *Ajax*, and most remote scripting is managed through a specialized object, as you'll see in Chapter 14. However, you also can accomplish remote scripting through the `iframe`.

 The concept of using the `iframe` for remote scripting was introduced at the Apple Developer Network in an article written by Eric Costello; it is available at *http://developer.apple.com/internet/webcontent/iframe .html*.

Example 9-7 contains an `iframe` that is hidden from view by making its `width` and `height` properties equal to zero. The page also contains a form with two radio buttons, each given a specific color. Clicking on either button will display a text string associated with the color: "Apple" for red, "Sky" for blue.

Example 9-7. Communicating with an embedded iframe

```
<!DOCTYPE html PUBLIC "-//W3C//DTD XHTML 1.0 Transitional//EN"
"http://www.w3.org/TR/xhtml1/DTD/xhtml1-transitional.dtd">
<html xmlns="http://www.w3.org/1999/xhtml" xml:lang="en" lang="en">
<head>
<title>Windows</title>
<meta http-equiv="Content-Type" content="text/html; charset=utf-8" />
```

```
<script type="text/javascript">
//<![CDATA[

function catchEvent(eventObj, event, eventHandler) {
  if (eventObj.addEventListener) {
      eventObj.addEventListener(event, eventHandler,false);
  } else if (eventObj.attachEvent) {
      event = "on" + event;
      eventObj.attachEvent(event, eventHandler);
  }
}

catchEvent (window, "load", function() {
   catchEvent(document.forms[0],"click",colorChange);
   });

// remote scripting using iframe
function colorChange() {
   var colors = document.forms[0].color;
   var result = document.getElementById('result');
   for (var i = 0; i < colors.length; i++) {
     if (colors[i].checked) {
        var myFrame = document.getElementById("myFrame");
        myFrame.contentWindow.location.href="service.php?color=" + colors[i].value;
        myFrame.onload=function () {
           result.innerHTML =
myFrame.contentWindow.document.getElementById("val2").innerHTML;
        }
     }
   }
}

//]]>
</script>
</head>
<body>
<div>
  <form action="">
    <p>
      <input type="radio" name="color" value="red"/>Red<br />
      <input type="radio" name="color" value="blue" />Blue
    </p>
  </form>
</div>
<iframe
  name="myFrame"
  id="myFrame"
  style="width:0; height:0; border: 0"
  src="service.php"></iframe>
<div id="result">
</div>
</body>
</html>
```

When the page is loaded, the iframe source is set to a PHP page, *service.php*, shown in Example 9-8. Clicking on either of the radio buttons will cause the JavaScript to reload the *service.php* page into the iframe, but will pass the value of the checked radio button as part of the query string for the application. This value is used to return a new document with the following values if the color picked is red:

```
<div id='val1'><p>Rose</p></div>
<div id='val2'><p>Apple</p></div>
```

Or the following, if blue is picked:

```
<div id='val1'><p>Berry</p></div>
<div id='val2'><p>Sky</p></div>
```

To access the window object associated with the iframe, a new property is introduced, contentWindow, which represents the window object of the iframe. You have to use contentWindow to capture the onload event handler for the iframe.

When the frame window is finished loading, another function accesses an element in the newly loaded window with a given identifier of 'val2', and then assigns the HTML for this element to a result div element within the parent page.

Example 9-8. PHP application page to process color request

```
<!DOCTYPE html PUBLIC "-//W3C//DTD XHTML 1.0 Transitional//EN"
"http://www.w3.org/TR/xhtml1/DTD/xhtml1-transitional.dtd">
<html>
<head>
<meta http-equiv="Content-Type" content="text/html; charset=utf-8" />
</head>
<body>
<?php

$color = $_GET['color'];
if ($color == 'red') {
   printf("<div id='val1'>Rose</div>");
   printf("<div id='val2'>Apple</div>");
} else if ($color == 'blue') {
   printf("<div id='val1'>Berry</div>");
   printf("<div id='val2'>Sky</div>");
}

?>
</body>
</html>
```

This seems like a lot of work for such a minor result, but the example not only demonstrates an older remote scripting technique, but also indirectly demonstrates a modern technique used with Ajax applications interested in maintaining an association between the dynamic page effect and the back button. In addition, this application demonstrates some issues facing current JavaScript developers as we move among versions of HTML and XHTML.

First, the DOCTYPE for the example is for XHTML transitional, because the `iframe` element is deprecated in XHTML 1.0 strict. So, why use the element? If you load the page, and click the blue button and then the red button, although the parent page isn't reloading, you'll notice that the browser is getting a load event for the `iframe`. If you click the back and forward buttons, the page will reflect the "history" of your actions, even though the document with the `iframe` hasn't been reloaded. You can see this more clearly if you use Firefox and open the Net communication window in Firebug, as shown in Figure 9-5. Clicking the back and forward buttons several times will show how each generates a Net call, as well as history for the back button.

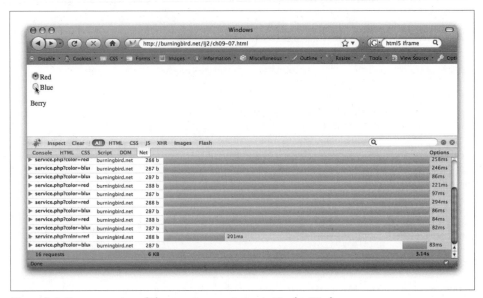

Figure 9-5. Demonstration of iframe remote scripting in Firefox/Firebug

Loading a new `iframe` document adds an entry to the browser back-button history. Modern Ajax applications take advantage of this by actually storing the state of an Ajax application at a specific point in time, and then updating the `iframe`, passing in a value, typically a number, similar to what Example 9-7 did, except the value in this case represents the state. You can pull the state value from the `iframe`, just as we did in Example 9-7 with the color-related values, and then use it to retrieve the cached state to restore the page accordingly.

Though the actual implementation of how you can use the `iframe` to maintain page state in Ajax applications is beyond the scope of this book, this example does demonstrate why the `iframe` is still used in today's applications, even while being deprecated in XHTML. In addition, though the element is deprecated in XHTML 1.0 and 1.1, the `iframe` is included as part of X/HTML5. Of course, other modifications in HTML5 mean the `iframe` is no longer necessary for tracking history, but I'll leave this discussion for *Learning JavaScript*, Third Edition.

For now, we'll return to the present, and the next set of objects: timers.

Adding and Controlling Timers

There property (location object) are two types of timers: one that's set once, and one that reoccurs over an interval. You can cancel both, though the one-time timer method fires just once.

To create a nonrepeating timer, use the `setTimeout` method. It takes a minimum of two parameters: the function literal or function name to run when the timer delay ends, and the length of the timer delay in milliseconds. If there are any parameters to send to the function, they are listed at the end of the call, separated by commas. The method returns the identifier of the timeout:

```
var tmOut = setTimeout(func, 5000,"param1",param2,...,paramn);
```

To clear the timeout, use the `clearTimeout` method:

```
clearTimeout(tmOut);
```

If you want the timer delay to repeat over an interval, use the `setInterval` method. This takes a minimum of two parameters: the function name and the timer interval. As with `setTimeout`, it returns an identifier:

```
Var tmOut = setInterval("functionName", 5000);
```

Again, to stop or cancel the interval timer, use the `clearInterval` method. If you want to have a repeating delay, but still use a function literal or pass in parameters, you can use `setTimeout` and reset the timer when the previously set timer expires.

 Internet Explorer does not support the parameters appended at the end of `setInterval` and `setTimeout`. Example 9-9 demonstrates how to get around this limitation and be able to send parameters to functions.

Example 9-9 uses a timer to trigger a function, which changes the background color of a `div` element, going gradually but quickly from white to yellow. This is similar to other yellow "flashes" you may have seen in Ajax applications to signal where a change has occurred or to draw attention to something. I'll get into the mechanics of the dynamic web effects in the next chapter. For now, let's just focus on the timer.

Example 9-9. Using timer to "flash" a div element

```
<!DOCTYPE html PUBLIC "-//W3C//DTD XHTML 1.1//EN"
"http://www.w3.org/TR/xhtml11/DTD/xhtml11.dtd">
<html xmlns="http://www.w3.org/1999/xhtml" xml:lang="en">
<head>
<title>Timers</title>
<meta http-equiv="Content-Type" content="text/html; charset=utf-8" />
<style type="text/css">
#block
```

```
{
    width: 400px;
}
</style>
<script type="text/javascript">
//<![CDATA[

window.onload=function () {
    document.getElementById("block").style.backgroundColor="#ffffff";
    setTimeout("colorFlash(255)",300);
}

function colorFlash(newColor) {
    var hexVal = newColor.toString(16);

    // make sure length is 2
    if (hexVal.length < 2) {
      hexVal= "0" + hexVal;
    }

    var colorString = "#ffff" + hexVal;
    var blockDiv = document.getElementById("block");
    blockDiv.style.backgroundColor=colorString;
    if (newColor > 0) {
       newColor-=5;
       setTimeout("colorFlash(" + newColor + ")", 50);
    }
}

//]]>
</script>
</head>
<body>
<div id="block">
<h1>Hello</h1>
</div>
</body>
</html>
```

A color fade or flash usually occurs when you change only one parameter of the red-green-blue spectrum that makes up a color. In this case, the red and green channels are left at 255 each (hexadecimal of ff), but the blue channel is changed, from 255 all the way to zero.

 The length of the converted hexadecimal is checked to see whether it's longer than two characters. If not, "0" is prepended because hexadecimal colors can't be five characters in length.

The first call to setTimeout passes in a value of 255 for the blue channel to the timer function, colorFlash. The background color of the div element is modified, the blue channel number is decremented, and its value is concatenated to the function and passed to `setTimeout`. This is a way of updating the timer value with each iteration, without having to use a global variable to store the current value of the blue channel.

 IE8 beta 2 demonstrated erratic behavior with this example, and I had to turn on Compatibility View mode to get reliable results.

The application does have a termination point: when the blue channel value is less than 0. At that point, the timer is no longer invoked because the terminating color has been reached. Another approach is to use `setInterval` and then clear it once the end color has been reached.

 You'll want to avoid any type of timer operation that could generate a `document.write` or other method that alters the makeup of the document object. This leaves the page in an unstable state. Instead, modify components of the document rather than the entire document itself.

The history, screen, and navigator Objects

I'm saving the most important BOM object, the `document`, for last. First, though, let's take a quick look at `history`, `screen`, and `navigator`.

The history Object

The `history` object maintains a history of pages loaded into the browser. As such, its methods and properties have to do with navigation through web pages using the browser's Back and Forward buttons.

You can traverse through `history` using properties, such as `next` and `previous`, or using the methods `back` and `forward`. You can find the current page with `current`, and get the length of `history` (the number of pages stored in the history cache). You can also go to a specific page using the `go` method and passing in a page number—a negative number to go backward that many pages:

```
history.go(-3);
```

and a positive number to go forward:

```
history.go(3);
```

The `history` object, as they say, takes care of itself; you, as the page developer, don't have to worry much about it. About the only time when `history` becomes a concern is when you're using Ajax page effects, which work outside the normal patterns of page loading, as I mentioned in "Remote Scripting with the iframe" earlier in this chapter.

The screen Object

The screen object contains information about the display screen, including its width and height, as well as its color or pixel depth. Though not used very often, it is a good reference for any functionality that might change the size of the browser window or create colorful objects requiring a certain palette.

The exact properties supported can change from browser to browser and version to version. At a minimum, the screen object supports most of the following:

availTop *(or* top*)*
> The topmost pixel position where a window can be positioned

availLeft *(or* left*)*
> The leftmost pixel position where a window can be positioned

availWidth *(or* width*)*
> The width of the screen in pixels

availHeight *(or* height*)*
> The height of the screen in pixels

colorDepth
> The color depth of the screen

pixelDepth
> The bit depth of the screen

The reason for the discrepancy between actual and available height and/or width is to accommodate the toolbar residing at the top, bottom, or side of many display screens.

In earlier dynamic page implementations, developers would test the color depth of the screen and change it to lower-resolution images more appropriate to the configuration. However, even today's less expensive monitors now support color depths greater than the older 8 pixels, and most support true color. As such, the extra overhead to process the screen and return the images no longer has the payback it once had. Still, the color depth could alter your use of colors with style settings, so it's helpful information—as are the available width and height if you're working with a page layout.

The navigator Object

The navigator object provides information regarding the browser or other agent that accesses the page. This includes being able to check the operating system, browser or browser family, security policy, language, and whether cookies are enabled. Some browsers also provide an array of installed plug-ins and other properties applicable to the specific user agent.

The navigator object usually supports the following:

appCodeName
> The name of the browser code base

appName
: The name of the browser

appMinorVersion
: The minor version number (e.g., 52 for version 1.52) of the browser

appVersion
: The major version number (e.g., 1.00 for version 1.52) of the browser

cookieEnabled
: Whether cookies are enabled

mimeTypes
: The array of Multipurpose Internet Mail Extension (MIME) types supported

onLine
: Whether the user is online

platform
: The platform on which the browser is operating

plugins
: The array of plug-ins supported in the browser

userAgent
: The full agent description for the browser (or other user agent)

userLanguage
: The language supported in the browser

The `mimeTypes` collection consists of `mimeType` objects, which have properties of `description`, `type`, and `plugin`. The `plugins` collection consists of plug-in objects with properties of a `mimeType` array of its own: `description`, `filename`, length of `mimeType` array, and plug-in name.

Several browsers also support the following methods: `javaEnabled`, to test for Java enabling in the browser; `preference`, to get and set browser preferences; and `taintEnabled`, to check whether data taint checking (a security feature) is enabled.

Chances are you'll never need any of these collections. In fact, about the only time you'll need to access the `navigator` object is to check whether cookies are enabled, or perhaps to see which browser is accessing the page.

The history, screen, and navigator Properties in Action

Example 9-10 is a page that accesses the three `window` properties just covered—`history`, `screen`, and `navigator`—printing out property values and providing a couple of options for testing history. Try it out in various browsers, in as many operating systems as you can, to see what's supported and what's not.

Example 9-10. Exploring the history, screen, and navigator objects

```
<!DOCTYPE html PUBLIC "-//W3C//DTD XHTML 1.1//EN"
"http://www.w3.org/TR/xhtml11/DTD/xhtml11.dtd">
<html xmlns="http://www.w3.org/1999/xhtml" xml:lang="en">
<head>
<title>Timers</title>
<meta http-equiv="Content-Type" content="text/html; charset=utf-8" />
<script type="text/javascript">
//<![CDATA[

window.onload=function () {
document.writeln("<h1>screen object</h1><p>");
document.writeln("screen.availTop: " + screen.availTop + "<br />");
document.writeln("screen.availLeft: " + screen.availLeft + "<br />");
document.writeln("screen.availWidth: " + screen.availWidth + "<br />");
document.writeln("screen.availHeight: " + screen.availHeight + "<br />");
document.writeln("screen.colorDepth: " + screen.colorDepth + "<br />");
document.writeln("screen.pixelDepth: " + screen.pixelDepth + "<br /></p>");

document.writeln("<h1>navigator object</h1><p>");

document.writeln("navigator.userAgent: " + navigator.userAgent + "<br />");
document.writeln("navigator.appName: " + navigator.appName + "<br />");
document.writeln("navigator.appCodeName: " + navigator.appCodeName + "<br />");
document.writeln("navigator.appVersion: " + navigator.appVersion + "<br />");
document.writeln("navigator.appMinorVersion: " + navigator.appMinorVersion + "<br
/>");
document.writeln("navigator.platform: " + navigator.platform + "<br />");
document.writeln("navigator.cookieEnabled: " + navigator.cookieEnabled + "<br />");
document.writeln("navigator.onLine: " + navigator.onLine + "<br />");
document.writeln("navigator.userLanguage: " + navigator.userLanguage + "<br />");

if (navigator.mimeTypes) {
   document.writeln("navigator.mimeTypes[1].description: " +
navigator.mimeTypes[1].description + "<br />");
   document.writeln("navigator.mimeTypes[1].type: " + navigator.mimeTypes[1].type +
"<br />");
}

if (navigator.plugins) {
   for (var i = 0; i < navigator.plugins.length; i++) {
      document.writeln("navigator.plugins[i].description: " +
navigator.plugins[i].description + "<br />");
   }
}

document.writeln("</p>");
document.onclick=function () {
   history.back();
   return false;
}
}

//]]>
</script>
```

```
</head>
<body>
<h1>Hello</h1>
</body>
</html>
```

You might be surprised at what shows up in some of the collections, such as the
`plugins`, as shown in Figure 9-6. I know I was surprised to see one that provided digital
rights management, when I don't remember having installed a plug-in of this nature.

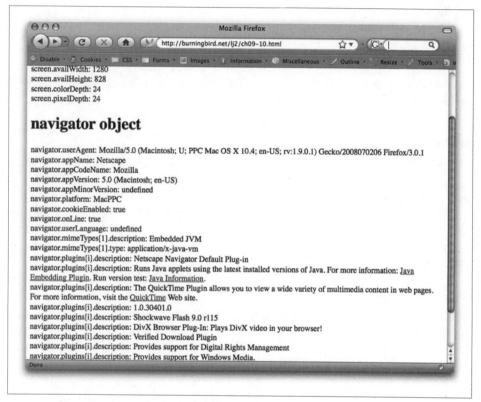

Figure 9-6. Display from application in Example 9-10

As for the `mimeType` object, some browsers also support a suffix property on the object,
such as `*.html` and so on.

These three objects just demonstrated are the last of the objects directly accessible via
the `window` object, save one. The last object I'll cover in this chapter is an old friend by
now: the `document`. In a way, most of the rest of the book focuses on the `document` object.
However, we'll take a little time to look at it from a BOM perspective before I cover its
role in the more modern DOM Levels 1 and up.

The Document Object

Returning to Figure 9-1 at the beginning of the chapter, you can see that the `document` object is what provides access to any element contained within the browser page. This includes forms and form elements, covered earlier. This also includes the collection of page images, links, and embedded objects; in fact, all elements contained within the page boundaries have `document` as their parent. Older variations of `document` had another collection, called `layers`, and the newer browser versions all share a `style` property, but the figure gives you an idea of how important the `document` is to dynamic page development.

Previous chapters covered the `document` object methods of `getElementById` and `getElementsByTagName`, as well as `writeln`; Chapter 10 provides information on accessing all page elements using generic methods. For now, I want to pull back to the older method of accessing page elements through the various document collections, focusing on links, images, and the all-purpose `all` collection.

Links

The difference between a link and an anchor is the type of anchor attributes used. Both are based on the anchor tag (`<a></a>`). However, if an `href` attribute is provided, it's a link; if the `name` attribute is provided, it acts as an anchor, which can provide a focus to a specific point in the page. If you've ever accessed a web page URL that looks like the following:

> *http://<someco.com>/index.html#one*

The value of the hash (#) and of "one" is a page fragment. Accessing this URL loads the web page, and the browser scrolls the page to a link given a name of "one".

The `links` collection of the `document` object consists of all hypertext links in the page, accessible as an array, starting with the first link in the page and moving down and to the right. However, you can also add an identifier for each hypertext link and access the link in the array through this identifier.

Each item in the collection is a `link` object, which has properties of its own. Some properties are similar to those found with `location`: `host`, `protocol`, `port`, `search`, and `hash`, each of which returns that specific piece of the hypertext link. You can also access the complete link through the `href` property, and the associated linked object (`text`) through `text`. This can be handy if you're pulling links from a document in a web page into a handy sidebar reference. Just make sure you don't write the links out to the same page as the `document` because you'll confuse the browser by adding new links at the same time you're trying to process existing links.

In Example 9-11, the page contains text with three links. The `links` collection is accessed through the `document` object, and the `href` property of each link is extracted and output through an `alert`.

Example 9-11. Pulling links from a page

```
<!DOCTYPE html PUBLIC "-//W3C//DTD XHTML 1.1//EN"
"http://www.w3.org/TR/xhtml11/DTD/xhtml11.dtd">
<html xmlns="http://www.w3.org/1999/xhtml" xml:lang="en">
<head>
<title>Links</title>
<meta http-equiv="Content-Type" content="text/html; charset=utf-8" />
<script type="text/javascript">
//<![CDATA[

window.onload=function () {
    var links = "";
    for (var i = 0; i < document.links.length; i++) {
      links = links + document.links[i].href + "\n\n";
    }
    alert(links);
}

//]]>
</script>
</head>
<body>
<p>The <a
href="http://msdn.microsoft.com/workshop/author/dhtml/reference/objects/link.asp">links</a>
collection off of the document
<a href="http://www.w3.org/TR/html4/struct/objects.html">object</a> consists of all
hypertext links in the page, accessible as an array, starting with the first link in
the page and moving down and to the right. However, you can also add an identifier
for each hypertext link and access it in the array through this identifier.</p>
<p>Each item in the collection is a
<a href="http://www.devguru.com/Technologies/ecmascript/quickref/link.html">link</a>
object, which has properties of its own. Among these are those similar to what we found
with location: host, protocol, port, search, and hash, each of which returns that
specific piece of the hypertext link. You can also access the complete link through
the href property, and the associated linked object (text) through text. This can be
handy if you're pulling links from a document in a web page, into a handy sidebar
reference or other functionality such as this.
</p>
</body>
</html>
```

When the page is opened in a browser, an alert pops up with the links.

Images

One of the earliest dynamic page-development techniques was to alter images within the document. This is still a popular technique for simple photo slide show types of applications, enabled through the document `images` collection.

As with links, images are objects in their own right, and you can set their attributes—such as `src`, the source URL for the image—directly. You can also create new instances of an `image` using the `new` constructor:

```
    var newImage = new Image();
    newImage.src="someimage.png";
```

In Example 9-12, a slide show is created of book figures—Figures 9-1 through 9-5, to be precise—and two div elements to act as "next" and "previous" buttons to traverse the images. The images are pre-loaded into an array, and clicking on either div element will replace the src attribute of the current img element, with whichever image is next (or previous) in the array. Modifying the img element's src attribute causes the new image to display in the web page.

Example 9-12. Creating a slide show using the images collection

```
<!DOCTYPE html PUBLIC "-//W3C//DTD XHTML 1.1//EN"
"http://www.w3.org/TR/xhtml11/DTD/xhtml11.dtd">
<html xmlns="http://www.w3.org/1999/xhtml" xml:lang="en">
<head>
<title>Slideshow</title>
<meta http-equiv="Content-Type" content="text/html; charset=utf-8" />
<script type="text/javascript">
//<![CDATA[

var currentPhoto = 0;
var pics = new Array();

window.onload=function() {
    for (var i = 0; i < 5; i++) {
        pics[i] = new Image();
    }
    pics[0].src = "fig0901.png";
    pics[1].src = "fig0902.png";
    pics[2].src = "fig0903.png";
    pics[3].src = "fig0904.png";
    pics[4].src = "fig0905.png";

    document.getElementById("next").onclick=nextPic;
    document.getElementById("prev").onclick=prevPic;
}

function changePhoto(photo) {
    document.images[0].src = pics[photo].src;
}

function nextPic() {
  currentPhoto++;
  if (currentPhoto < pics.length) {
    changePhoto(currentPhoto);
  } else {
    alert("at the end of the photo list");
  }
}

function prevPic() {
  if (currentPhoto > 0) {
    currentPhoto--;
```

```
      changePhoto(currentPhoto);
    } else {
      alert("at the beginning of the photo list");
    }
  }

//]]>
</script>
</head>
<body>
<div id="next"><span>Next</span></div>
<div id="prev"><span>Previous</span></div>
<img src="fig0901.png" />
</body>
</html>
```

Again, as with the previous example with links, this example tends to blur the line between DOM Levels 0 and 1. However, it also works in all of the most popular web browsers, which is what's important for our purposes.

Also, notice in Example 9-12 that, along with the images, you can change the src attribute. This differs from Example 9-11, which just outputs the link attributes. The image source is an attribute that can be read or written, whereas the link attributes can only be read. There are ways, though, to adjust all page elements, and we'll look at them in the next section.

innerHTML

Over the years, various browsers supported a variety of properties and objects to allow script modification of a web page. The DOM has replaced most of them. However, modern browsers still support one document property: innerHTML.

You can use the innerHTML property to change whatever HTML is contained within a page element. It's still popular because you don't have to build up the contents to modify a page element. Instead, you can just create a string with HTML and use innerHTML to attach it to the web page. However, using innerHTML means that whatever is added to the web page isn't incorporated into the page document tree, which can play havoc if you mix innerHTML with newer DOM methods.

To demonstrate innerHTML, in Example 9-13, the web page contains three div elements, each containing further markup. The first div contains a paragraph; the second, an unordered list; and the third, a hypertext link. When the page loads, these are accessed using the getElementsById document method, and their content is interchanged using innerHTML. The process is triggered by a timer event, so you can see the page before and after the change.

Example 9-13. Accessing named elements and changing their inner HTML

```
<!DOCTYPE html PUBLIC "-//W3C//DTD XHTML 1.1//EN"
"http://www.w3.org/TR/xhtml11/DTD/xhtml11.dtd">
<html xmlns="http://www.w3.org/1999/xhtml" xml:lang="en">
<head>
<title>innerHTML</title>
<meta http-equiv="Content-Type" content="text/html; charset=utf-8" />
<script type="text/javascript">
//<![CDATA[

window.onload = function() {

    setTimeout("changeElements()", 3000);
}

function changeElements() {
    var elem1 = document.getElementById("elem1");
    var elem2 = document.getElementById("elem2");
    var elem3 = document.getElementById("elem3");

    var tmp = elem1.innerHTML;
    elem1.innerHTML = elem3.innerHTML;
    elem3.innerHTML = elem2.innerHTML;
    elem2.innerHTML = tmp;
}

//]]>
</script>
</head>
<body>
<div id="elem1">
<p>Paragraph text.</p>
</div>
<div id="elem2">
<ul>
<li>option 1</li>
<li>option 2</li>
</ul>
</div>
<div id="elem3">
<p><a href="ch09-12.html">Example 9-12</a></p>
</div>
</body>
</html>
```

The innerHTML property is all of the HTML that's contained within the identified element. It's a read/write property, which means it can be accessed, modified, or completely replaced. What's fascinating, though, is that this isn't reflected in the document
source. If you look at the view source, the HTML elements reflect the web page before
the dynamic modification. However, if you're using the Web Developer toolkit in Firefox, one option is View Generated Source, which displays the source of the page after
the change.

All the major browsers support innerHTML, though each may have its own minor quirks in implementation (which is why you need to test your effects before putting them into production). The World Wide Web Consortium (W3C) has deprecated the use of innerHTML, but browsers support it because of its widespread use and because it's so easy to use compared to the DOM methods that accomplish the same task. In addition, as of this writing, innerHTML is supported with HTML5.

One document collection I didn't cover in this chapter is the cookies collection, which we'll look at in detail in Chapter 10, where we'll focus on various client-side storage techniques.

Test Your Knowledge: Quiz

1. What kind of dialog do you open if you want a text response? Use this dialog in code to ask for the user's first name.

2. Define a timer that invokes a function, callFunction, every 3,000 milliseconds, passing in two parameters: paramA and paramB.

   What code would you use to check to see whether cookies are enabled?

3. Create a new window that is sized to 200×200 pixels, has no toolbar or status bar, and opens the Google search page.

4. What two techniques can you use to access a form element within a web page?

Test Your Knowledge: Answers

1. Use the prompt dialog box if you want a text response. The solution is:

   ```
   var firstName = prompt("Enter your first name", "");
   ```

2. Here's the timer:

   ```
   setTimeout(callFunction, 3000, paramA, paramB);
   ```

3. You can use the navigator object to test whether cookies are enabled:

   ```
   if (navigator.cookieEnabled) ...
   ```

4. Here's the solution:

   ```
   var newWindow =
   window.open("http://www.google.com","","width=200,height=200,toolbar=no,status=no
   ");
   ```

   If the form is given an identifier, you can use document.getElementById. You can also access a form element from the document's forms collection.

CHAPTER 10

Cookies and Other Client-Side Storage Techniques

Originally, JavaScript was not intended to be used to create large and complex applications, or to communicate independently with the server. The primary way to store any information on the client was through an object known as a *cookie*.

Cookies are bits of data storage on the client based on key information, provided by the server, that allows JavaScript developers to persist information either during a session (until a browser is closed) or between sessions (web accesses). The original concept was that only those requests to get or write cookies associated with the web page's domain would be given access, and therefore the information would be secure. Based on this premise, JavaScript was used to persist everything from a person's login name and password to her shopping cart contents. It's rare for a commercial website nowadays to not have some form of cookie implemented—whether you want it or not.

Over time, breaks in the security of cookies, as well as concerns regarding privacy, have tarnished the reputation of JavaScript cookies. Concerns about privacy in particular have led to more people turning off cookie support in their browsers. Still, cookies are very popular and, if they're not abused, are very helpful.

However, cookies have also shown themselves to be limited, and not just for security reasons. The amount of storage and the ease of access for cookies have not stood the test of time for larger Ajax applications. In the past few years, new methods for storing data on the client have been developed, and I'll briefly touch on these toward the end of the chapter.

First, though, let's return to that issue of cookies and security.

The JavaScript Sandbox and Cookie Security

Some browser-specific security options are available, such as the use of signed scripts, but JavaScript developers prefer security policies inherent to all uses of JavaScript. One is the *JavaScript sandbox*, which, among other things, includes no file-access functionality: that is, you cannot open, create, or delete a file from the operating system directly from within JavaScript. In addition, it provides only low-level networking capabilities, such as the ability to load a web page. Lastly, with the JavaScript sandbox, JavaScript applications are restricted from initiating a connection to another site, and transmit data silently—a concept known as the *same-origin security policy*.

The Same-Origin Security Policy

The same-origin security policy ensures that there is no communication via script between pages that have different domains, protocols, or ports. The same-origin security policy applies to communication between separate pages, or from a parent window to an embedded window, such as frames or iframes.

Why is this restriction so important? If a website pops open a small window that ends up behind your main page, and you continue on to other sites, such as the website of your bank, JavaScript in that pop-up window could listen in on your activities in that separate page. The same-origin security policy prevents this type of snooping by preventing JavaScript in a page opened in one domain from having any access to a page, and to a page's Document Object Model (DOM) or resources, opened in another domain.

An example of same-origin restriction is a page opened from a domain such as *http:// www.somecompany.com* trying to access information from a page accessed from any of the following domains:

http://othercompany.com
> This would fail because the domain is different: *somecompany.com* is not the same as *othercompany.com*.

https://www.somecompany.com
> This would fail because the protocol is different: *https* is not the same protocol as *http*.

http://www.somecompany.com:8080
> This would fail because the port is different: the original request did not specify any port in the URL (falling back on the default port, usually 80).

http://other.somecompany.com
> This would fail because the host is different; the use of the other hostname (subdomain) changes the host. If instead you used *http://somecompany.com*, without any specific subdomain, accessing all subdomains including *www.somecompany .com* and *other.somecompany.com* would succeed.

Using document.domain

Unfortunately, the issue of same origin can work against a site developer's efforts. The use of alternative hostnames with the same domain, known as *subdomains*, such as *about.somecompany.com* and *help.somecompany.com*, is becoming increasingly popular, and the same-origin restriction can become prohibitive. To work around this restriction, there's a property on the `document` object, `domain`, which when set allows subdomain pages to communicate with each other—but *only* subdomain pages, and *only* if the document property and the original host domain match.

If the page containing the JavaScript is accessed through the URL *http://admin.some company.com*, you can set `document.domain` to *somecompany.com*, which is the domain of the original access. You cannot set it to *othercompany.com*, which is a different domain.

The following will work:

```
document.domain = "somecompany.com";
```

This will not:

```
document.domain = "othercompany.com";
```

When set, JavaScript in a page at *admin.somecompany.com* could then communicate with a page opened at *help.somecompany.com*.

Luckily, the same-origin policy does not apply when linking scripts in from other domains. You can link scripts from anywhere, and they'll be treated as though the JavaScript originates within the page—including the same domain for all further communication. Without this ability to link scripts in from other domains, you would be unable to implement functionality such as that used with Google Maps:

```
<script src="http://maps.google.com/maps?file=api&v=2&key=yourkey"
        type="text/javascript"></script>
```

The policy of same origin does apply, however, to the implementation of cookies.

All About Cookies

Why *cookie*? The original name for a cookie came from the term *magic cookie*—a token passed between two programs. Though accessible from JavaScript, cookies aren't really script-based: they're a mechanism of the HTTP server. As such, they're accessible by the client and server.

Whatever the name, cookies are small key/value pairs associated with an expiration date and a domain/path, both of which are meant to ensure that the right cookies are read by the right servers. The information they contain is transmitted as part of the web page request, and thus the data is available to the server and to the browser.

Storing and Reading Cookies

Cookies are accessible, like most other browser elements, through the `document` object. To create a cookie, you'll need to provide a cookie name, or *key*, an associated value, a date when it expires, and a path associated with the cookie. To access a cookie, you access the `document.cookie` value and then parse the cookie out.

To create a cookie, just assign the `document.cookie` value a string with the following format:

```
document.cookie="cookieName=cookieValue; expires=date; path=path";
```

The cookie name and value are whatever you want and need, as long as the value is a simple value. I've used cookie names starting with a dollar sign (`$cookieName`), with an underscore (`_cookieName`), and with other characters.

I've also experimented with different cookie values, and depending on the browser, what gets attached to the cookie is the string conversion of whatever the object is— `Number`, `Array`, or some other object. However, this varies significantly among browsers. To ensure consistent results, I recommend that you use only primitive types (`string`, `boolean`, and `number`) that convert cleanly to strings.

 You can also use JavaScript Object Notation (JSON) conversion to set and retrieve complex objects in cookies, as per the O'Reilly article at *http://www.oreillynet.com/onlamp/blog/2008/05/dojo_goodness_part_8 _jsonified.html*. I'll discuss JSON in more detail in Chapter 15.

As for the rest of the document cookie-setting string, the expiration date must be in a specific GMT (UTC) format. Creating a `date` object and then using the `toGMTString` is sufficient to ensure that the date works. If no date is provided, the cookie is considered session-only and is eliminated as soon as the browser session ends.

The cookie path is especially important. The domain and path are compared with the page request, and if they don't sync up, the cookie can't be accessed or set. This prevents other sites from accessing any and all cookies set on your browser, though this security has been circumvented in the past.

A path setting of `path=/` sets the cookie's allowable path to the top-level directory at your domain. If you access the page at *http://somedomain.com*, this means the cookie is accessible by any subdirectory off of *http://somedomain.com*. If you specify a subdirectory, such as *path=/images*, the cookie is accessible only from web pages in this subdirectory. Conversely, if you have many subdomains at your website, such as *sub1 .somedomain.com*, *sub2.somedomain.com*, and so on, you can make a cookie accessible at all of them by specifically giving the higher-level domain: `path=somedomain.com`.

 It's important to be selective about where your cookies are accessible. Be restrictive by setting your path to the topmost level essential for your application.

The following code snippet shows an example of a JavaScript function that sets a cookie to a specific key and value, with an expiration date in 2010 and setting the path to the top-level subdirectory:

```
function setCookie(key,value) {
    var cookieDate = new Date(2010,11,10,19,30,30);
    document.cookie=key + "=" + encodeURI(value) + "; expires=" +
cookieDate.toGMTString() + "; path=/";
}
```

You use the `encodeURI` function to escape any special characters that might be part of the cookie value. This makes your cookie more secure, as it scrubs out actual HTML, including script elements. In addition, `encodeURI` enables the use of characters specific to the cookie format, including the equals (=) and semicolon (;) characters.

Other approaches to coding a cookie function adjust the date and the path, as well as the key and value. Note that there is one space following the semicolons in the string.

 A fourth parameter for a cookie is a flag on whether the cookie is secure or not. You can request a secure cookie only by using SSL (HTTPS rather than HTTP).

Getting the cookie is not as easy because all cookies get concatenated into one string, separated by semicolons on the `cookie` object. The following is an example of a cookie string:

```
var1=somevalue; var2=3.55; var3=true
```

I've seen several approaches used to get the keys. One uses the `String` split method to split on the semicolon; others use a variety of searches on substrings. The example function I've created uses a mix of both techniques:

```
function readCookie(key) {
  var cookie = document.cookie;

  var first = cookie.indexOf(key+"=");

  // cookie exists
  if (first >= 0) {
    var str = cookie.substring(first,cookie.length);
    var last = str.indexOf(";");

    // if last cookie
    if (last < 0) last = str.length;

    // get cookie value
    str = str.substring(0,last).split("=");
    return decodeURI(str[1]);
  } else {
    return null;
```

```
        }
    }
```

In the preceding code, the key is concatenated to the equals sign, and the resultant combination is searched in the string. When it's found, its first position gets a substring of the rest of the string. Within this new string, the semicolon is searched, and if it's found, the string is either parsed to the semicolon (if more than one cookie remains) or accessed as a whole (there is only one cookie). Finally, the string is split on the equals sign to get the key and the value, separately. The return value is *unescaped* using the decodeURI function to return the original value.

To erase the cookie, eliminate its value or set the date to a past date, or do both, as the following JavaScript function demonstrates:

```
function eraseCookie (key) {

    var cookieDate = new Date(2000,11,10,19,30,30);
    document.cookie=key + "=; expires=" + cookieDate.toGMTString() + "; path=/";
}
```

The next time the document cookie string is accessed, the cookie will no longer exist.

Before you use any cookie functionality, it's best to first test to make sure cookies are implemented and enabled for the browser. It's not unusual for people to turn cookies off, and you'll want to account for this in your code. To check whether cookies are enabled, use another built-in browser object, navigator, and the cookieEnabled property:

```
if (navigator.cookieEnabled) ...
```

Note that not all browsers return the correct value when testing the cookieEnabled property. For instance, IE 6.x does not set this property correctly. In these cases, there's little you can do other than set the cookie and see whether you can find it.

Taking all of this together, Example 10-1 demonstrates an application that sets a value as a cookie that's accessed and incremented each time the page is loaded. When the value exceeds 5, the cookie gets erased, and in the next iteration (page load) the cookie gets re-created.

Example 10-1. Setting, reading, and erasing cookies

```
<!DOCTYPE html PUBLIC "-//W3C//DTD XHTML 1.1//EN"
"http://www.w3.org/TR/xhtml11/DTD/xhtml11.dtd">
<html xmlns="http://www.w3.org/1999/xhtml" xml:lang="en">
<head>
<title>innerHTML</title>
<meta http-equiv="Content-Type" content="text/html; charset=utf-8" />
<script type="text/javascript">
//<![CDATA[

// if cookie enabled
window.onload=function() {
```

```
    if (navigator.cookieEnabled) {

        var sum = readCookie("sum");
        if (sum) {
            var iSum = parseInt(sum) + 1;
            alert("cookie count is " + iSum);
            if (iSum > 5) {
                eraseCookie("sum");
            } else {
                setCookie("sum",iSum);
            }
        } else {
            alert("no cookie, setting now");
            setCookie("sum", 0);
        }
    }

}
// set cookie expiration date in year 2010
function setCookie(key,value) {

    var cookieDate = new Date(2010,11,10,19,30,30);
    document.cookie=key + "=" + encodeURI(value) + "; expires=" +
cookieDate.toGMTString() + "; path=/";
}
// each cookie separated by semicolon;
function readCookie(key) {
  var cookie = document.cookie;
  var first = cookie.indexOf(key+"=");

  // cookie exists
  if (first >= 0) {
    var str = cookie.substring(first,cookie.length);
    var last = str.indexOf(";");

    // if last cookie
    if (last < 0) last = str.length;

    // get cookie value
    str = str.substring(0,last).split("=");
    return decodeURI(str[1]);
  } else {
    return null;
  }
}
// set cookie date to the past to erase
function eraseCookie (key) {

    var cookieDate = new Date(2000,11,10,19,30,30);
    document.cookie=key + "= ; expires="+cookieDate.toGMTString()+"; path=/";
}
//]]>
</script>
</head>
<body>
```

```
<p>Paragraph text.</p>
</body>
</html>
```

Cookies are handy little buggers, but one of their limitations is that you can store only 20 cookies, up to 4 KB in total size, for a given domain. For most cases, this is more than satisfactory; in fact, you should use even this smaller client-side storage sparingly. Still, sometimes you might want to store larger amounts of data.

Flash Shared Objects, Google Gears, and HTML5 DOM Storage

To store larger cookies or more complex objects, previous applications have used a variety of hacks, including a LiveConnect interface between JavaScript and Java applets, or ActiveX controls. Another approach is to use hidden elements in forms to persist the data from a form submission to the resultant web page.

In the past few years, though, a host of new approaches have arisen, inspired by the popularity of Ajax and interest in rich Internet applications (RIAs). These approaches range from using a proprietary object, the Flash Shared Object, to putting hope in the future of HTML5 and its local storage capability. The only difficulty with all the approaches is that they're not implemented across all browsers.

In May 2008, Paul Duncan identified the different approaches to client-side storage. Paraphrasing his list, the approaches are as follows:

- Flash 9 persistent storage
- Gears (from Google)
- HTML5 `localstorage` and `whatwg_db`
- IE's `userdata` behavior
- The cookie

You can install Gears as a plug-in; it is also built in by default in Google's Chrome web browser. Once Gears is available, local storage can be set using the `localServer` object:

```
<script type="text/javascript" src="gears_init.js"></script>
<script type="text/javascript">
  var localServer = google.gears.factory.create('beta.localserver');
  var store = localServer.createManagedStore('test-store');
  store.manifestUrl = 'site-manifest.txt';
  store.checkForUpdate();
</script>
```

Alternatively, you can use a fully featured relational database, if your system supports the underlying SQLite database implementation:

```
<script type="text/javascript" src="gears_init.js"></script>
<script type="text/javascript">
  var db = google.gears.factory.create('beta.database');
  db.open('database-test');
```

```
    db.execute('create table if not exists Test' +
               ' (Phrase text, Timestamp int)');
    db.execute('insert into Test values (?, ?)', ['Monkey!', new Date().getTime()]);
    var rs = db.execute('select * from Test order by Timestamp desc');

    while (rs.isValidRow()) {
      alert(rs.field(0) + '@' + rs.field(1));
      rs.next();
    }
    rs.close();
</script>
```

The Gears functionality is really quite powerful, but that power is dependent on your users either using Chrome or having the Gears plug-in installed. This could be prohibitive in an open web environment.

You can see examples of Gears pulled from the Gears API at *http://code .google.com/apis/gears/design.html*. You can download the Gears plug-in from *http://gears.google.com/*.

Flash Shared Objects (SO) operate in a manner similar to HTTP cookies. They're stored and accessible based on domain, and pages served from one domain cannot access SOs created from another domain. Adobe incorporated this sandbox protection as part of the design of SOs from Flash version 7 onward.

Unlike the HTTP cookie, with its 4 KB limit, SO storage is unlimited—but only silently up to the first 100 KB. This means that if a web page or web application from one domain tries to set an SO that's larger than 100 KB, a message box opens asking for permission to use the space. The client then has to provide explicit permission for the SO to be set.

The Flash 9 SO is described at *http://livedocs.adobe.com/flash/9.0/Ac tionScriptLangRefV3/flash/net/SharedObject.html*.

Firefox, WebKit, and IE8 have implemented variations of HTML5's `localStorage` and `sessionStorage` objects—popularly known as DOM storage—and Opera has committed to implementing these more advanced client-side storage approaches in a future release. From a future perspective, DOM storage will be the only cross-browser solution built into browsers, other than cookies.

Here is an example of using `localStorage`, pulled from Microsoft documentation:

```
<p>
  You have viewed this page
  <span id="count">an untold number of</span>
  time(s).
```

```
    </p>
    <script>
      var storage = localStorage[location.hostname];
      if (!storage.pageLoadCount) storage.pageLoadCount = 0;
      storage.pageLoadCount = parseInt(storage.pageLoadCount, 10) + 1;
      document.getElementById('count').innerHTML = storage.pageLoadCount;
    </script>
```

Here is an example pulled from Mozilla of its DOM storage implementation of sessionStorage:

```
// Get the text field that we're going to track
var field = document.getElementById("field");

// See if we have an autosave value
// (this will only happen if the page is accidentally refreshed)
if ( sessionStorage.autosave ) {
    // Restore the contents of the text field
    field.value = sessionStorage.autosave;
}

// Check the contents of the text field every second
setInterval(function(){
    // And save the results into the session storage object
    sessionStorage.autosave = field.value;
}, 1000);
```

Of course, the data stored in these examples could also be stored in a cookie, but HTML5 storage has advantages over cookies in the amount of data you can store, as well as the complexity of the data and data access—including, as demonstrated in the preceding example, session-based recovery.

The real limitation of HTML5 storage is that implementations do differ among browsers, and no browser has a fully working implementation of DOM storage because the specification is currently under development.

 You can find the HTML5 specification, including a description of DOM storage, at *http://www.w3.org/html/wg/html5/*. You can find the IE8 documentation at *http://msdn.microsoft.com/en-us/library/ cc197062(VS.85).aspx*. And you can find the Mozilla documentation at *http://developer.mozilla.org/en/DOM/Storage*.

A couple of the approaches I've outlined are dependent on plug-ins (Flash and Gears), or on the browser used (IE's userdata), or on a specification that is still undergoing change (the HTML5 DOM Storage specification). However, one open source library, Dojo Storage, has sought to provide a cross-browser solution via a library you can include in your applications. At the time of this writing, though, the library didn't support all browsers in all circumstances; however, this will probably have changed by the time you read this book. What's left that's cross-browser-compatible are standard cookies, or a cross-browser library which Paul Duncan released, called PersistJS.

You can find Paul Duncan's article and announcement of PersistJS at *http://pablotron.org/?cid=1557*. The Dojo Offline Toolkit is available at *http://dojotoolkit.org/offline*.

As interesting as all of these approaches are, though, cookies are still the only client-side storage technique known to have support by default across all browsers. Unless you need the enhanced storage capabilities defined in the other approaches, you'll probably want to stay with cookies, at least for the next year or so.

Test Your Knowledge: Quiz

1. Name some ways to store material on the client machine.
2. What are the components of a script cookie?
3. How should you define a cookie to be destroyed when the browser closes?
4. What type of data should be scrubbed on user input?
5. Think of a website you have created or might create in the future. Now, think of five different uses for script cookies. In all of these uses, could you see needing more space than is provided for cookies?

Test Your Knowledge: Answers

1. There are several ways to save data or other material on a client machine:
   - Use cookies
   - Use a third-party plug-in, such as Flash or Google Gears
   - Ask the user to right-click a linked-in resource and save it to her computer
   - Insert a downloadable file as a link
   - Create a browser extension to save data
   - Use HTML5's `localStorage`
2. A script cookie consists of a cookie name, a value, an expiration date for the cookie, and a path associated with the cookie.
3. Do not provide any expiration date, and/or set the value to nothing.
4. Any data that can be invoked in the browser, or can be used to snoop around a client's cookies, or can run a server-side process, should be scrubbed on user input. In particular, the phrase "javascript:" or script tags should be scrubbed from input.

   However, scrubbing input is not as cleanly defined as you think. For content-management tools, it may be feasible for a person to enter script into a specific posting or page. But in a multiuser environment, an individual could use script to find out information about the other users of the system.

5. There is no right or wrong answer to this question. Following are some uses of cookies:

   - To maintain a person's name, URL, and email for a comment system
   - To provide live feedback on data entries
   - To enable a spellchecker
   - To store login information
   - To maintain a shopping cart

   None of these uses would need more than 4 KB of space.

CHAPTER 11

The DOM, or Web Page As Tree

The first release of the World Wide Web Consortium Document Object Model (W3C DOM) was DOM Level 1, issued as a recommendation in 1998. This release helped to define the infrastructure for the DOM—the schema and Application Programming Interface (API) that future versions of the DOM could use as a base of functionality. It also helped to establish a core component of each recommendation that is required for a DOM-compliant user agent (such as a browser); all other specifications are issued as separate, but related, optional modules. This module approach helped to encourage early adoption, and maintain consistency with critical elements.

DOM Level 2 followed in 2000, and expanded on the earlier Level 1 release, while still maintaining consistency with the earlier release. You were already exposed to one aspect of this release in our discussion of Level 2 event handling in Chapter 7. DOM Level 2 added increased support for Cascading Style Sheets (CSS), improved access for document elements, and namespace support in the XML recommendation.

DOM Level 3 was released in 2004. In addition to extensions and improvements to the previous releases, this version adds modules to extend support for web services, as well as increased support for XML, including XPath support. DOM Level 3 is the last of the W3C levels—at least, the last planned W3C level release.

This chapter doesn't provide a complete reference for all of the objects in the DOM APIs. Instead, I focus on representative objects, how they interact with one another, and their impact within the browser page.

A Tale of Two Interfaces

When the W3C released the first version of the DOM, the organization also released two different APIs: the Core API and the HTML API.

The DOM Core is a language- and model-neutral API that you can implement in any language, not just JavaScript, and for any XML-based model, not just XHTML. As such, it is literally the core of the DOM, and it provides all the functionality you need to modify, remove, or create web page content.

Prior to the release of the DOM specification, however, browsers had already implemented the Browser Object Model (BOM) in various forms, some proprietary and some not. To maintain backward compatibility with previous work, the W3C also released a custom subset of the DOM API: the DOM HTML API.

The DOM HTML API is an object-oriented, hierarchical view of the web page, with objects mapped to HTML elements: `HTMLDocumentElement` for the `document`, `HTMLBodyElement` for the `body`, and so on. Using it is very similar to how you used the BOM in Chapter 9. The primary difference between the BOM API and the DOM HTML API is that the latter is an attempt to formalize a subset of all previous effort into one API that works with all browsers. The W3C also extended the DOM HTML API to make it more compatible with the underlying Core API.

The Core API is a generic API that, as I mentioned, can work with any form of standard XML. This includes the XHTML of the web page, but it also includes the XML returned with Ajax calls, which I cover in Chapter 15. The API consists of objects such as `Node` and `NodeList`, `Attr`, `Element`, and the all-important `Document`. The Core API also provides a basic set of data types and expected behaviors that browsers must support, though much of this support is not obvious when working with JavaScript.

The HTML API is covered in the first two W3C releases, but not the third. This is because the additions and modifications documented in the W3C DOM Level 3 are specific to the Core API, and the HTML API isn't directly impacted.

Because of the need for backward compatibility, redundancy has been built into the DOM. You can implement the same functionality, such as creating a new HTML table row, using the DOM Core API and the DOM HTML API. Which one you use depends on your preferences as much as anything else, though it is important to be as consistent as possible. The DOM HTML API is more self-documenting because of its specialized object names. However, if you're creating your own libraries of reusable objects, you might want to use the more generic DOM Core API. With most JavaScript applications, you'll most likely need to use functionality from both APIs, as I'll demonstrate in the remainder of this chapter.

 A good source for an overview of the different DOM specifications is the OASIS Cover Pages article at *http://xml.coverpages.org/dom.html*. In addition, *JavaScript: The Definitive Guide* by David Flanagan (O'Reilly) includes an extended reference of DOM objects.

The DOM HTML API

This section introduces DOM (HTML) Level 1 and DOM (HTML) Level 2. I say "introduces" because the DOM (HTML or Core or both) is too large to cover in one chapter. However, in this section, I'll introduce the basic concepts behind the DOM (HTML) in enough detail, I hope, so that you'll be able to extrapolate from the objects

I do cover to all of the objects documented in the specification. Speaking of which, you can find the DOM (HTML) Level 1 specification at *http://www.w3.org/TR/REC-DOM -Level-1/* and associated ECMAScript binding at *http://www.w3.org/TR/REC-DOM -Level-1/ecma-script-language-binding.html*. You can find the DOM (HTML) Level 2 specification at *http://www.w3.org/TR/DOM-Level-2-HTML/*, with associated ECMA-Script binding at *http://www.w3.org/TR/DOM-Level-2-HTML/ecma-script-binding .html*.

> The ECMAScript *binding* is a mapping of JavaScript objects and their equivalent DOM specification objects. If you use the specifications as reference, the DOM specification explains what each object is, and the ECMAScript binding provides details regarding how the objects are implemented in ECMAScript (JavaScript).

The DOM HTML Objects and Their Properties

The DOM HTML API is a set of object *interfaces* rather than actual object classes. These interfaces can access existing or newly created page objects, and each is associated with a specific type of page object.

> I've introduced a new term, *interface*. For our purposes, an interface is an object representing the specific page element. It differs from a class in that there is no constructor; objects are created through other functions rather than directly.

Earlier, I mentioned the necessity of redundancy in the models because of backward compatibility. In addition to being partially redundant, the two models—Core and HTML—also overlap, with the HTML API objects incorporating methods and properties from both models. As such, HTML API objects inherit properties and methods of a basic HTML `Element`, as well as the core `Node` object (discussed later in this chapter). Most of the DOM (HTML) objects also inherit from `HTMLElement`, which has the following properties, based on the allowable element attributes:

`id`
> The element identifier

`title`
> A descriptive title for the element's contents

`lang`
> The language of the element and its contents

`dir`
> The directionality of the text (left to right, right to left)

className
  Equivalent to the `class` attribute

Each HTML object takes its name from the HTML formal element name, which is not necessarily the element's tag name. `HTMLFormElement` is the HTML form element's interface object, but `HTMLParagraphElement` is the object for the paragraph (p) element. The objects provide access to all valid attributes for the elements, such as `align` for `HTMLDivElement` and `src` for `HTMLImageElement`.

Most of the DOM (HTML) properties are read and write, which means you can alter them as well as access them from JavaScript. To demonstrate, Example 11-1 accesses an image using the `document.images` collection. Within the HTML DOM Level 1, the image element has the attributes listed for `HTMLElement`, but also those for `HTMLImageElement`, including several that have been deprecated for HTML 4.0. Among those still valid within HTML 4.0 and later are `height`, `width`, and `src`.

In the example, valid image attributes are concatenated to a string which is output via an alert window. Following the message, several of the attributes on the image element are modified.

Example 11-1. Reading and modifying an image element's properties

```
<!DOCTYPE html PUBLIC "-//W3C//DTD XHTML 1.1//EN"
"http://www.w3.org/TR/xhtml11/DTD/xhtml11.dtd">
<html xmlns="http://www.w3.org/1999/xhtml" xml:lang="en">
<head>
<title>Modifying HTML Elements</title>
<meta http-equiv="Content-Type" content="texl/html; charset=utf-8" />
<script type="text/javascript">
//<![CDATA[

window.onload=function() {

    var img = document.images[0];

    // get existing image attributes
    var imgAttr = img.id + " " + img.alt + " " + img.className;
    alert(imgAttr);

    // modify
    img.src="osprey.jpg";
    img.width="800";
    img.height="498";
    img.alt="Alternative";
    img.align="left";
    img.title="Osprey";
}
//]]>
</script>
</head>
<body>
<p><img src="ospreythumb.jpg" alt="test image" class="testimage" id="original"
/></p>
```

```
</body>
</html>
```

Note that the img attribute class is accessed through the DOM as className. The other attributes are named the same in XHTML and in the DOM.

This technique of modifying elements via JavaScript is also a way to "work around" the stringent requirements for XHTML. In the example, the width and height of the image were modified in JavaScript, but these attributes are not allowed in the img element when the page has a Document Type Declaration (DOCTYPE) of XHTML strict. Using JavaScript allows you to add deprecated or custom attributes to page elements and still have the document validate. Although this is a trivial example of this technique, as you can add width and height using the style attribute, this trick is a way of adding custom attributes to page elements for more sophisticated Ajax applications.

 The reason for the strict DOCTYPE is to ensure the page works the same in all browsers. Practice caution when using JavaScript to "override" the DOCTYPE by modifying the page elements dynamically.

Several of the DOM HTML interface objects also provide methods to create, remove, or otherwise modify associated page elements. The table elements, in particular, have a set of specialized methods and specific objects. However, the process is somewhat code-intensive, made more so because, as I mentioned earlier, the API objects have no constructor and cannot be created independent of other objects. To create these interface objects, you'll need to use one of the *factory methods*. Factory methods are what they sound like: methods that act as factories, turning out objects on demand. Instead of cars and iPods, though, these factories produce objects such as table cells and rows.

In Example 11-2, an image and an HTML table with just table column headers are added to the document. When the document loads, a function is called that accesses the table and image using document.getElementById (another object/method supported in both the BOM and the DOM [HTML] Level 1). The purpose of the application is to retrieve the image src attribute and output its value using the table.

To add to the table, the application uses the table element's factory method, insertRow, passing in a value of –1, which appends the row to the end of the table. To insert a row in a specific position among existing rows, pass in the position where the row is added instead.

The insertRow method returns an object that implements the HTMLTableRowElement interface. Another factory method on the HTMLTableRowElement interface object, insertCell, in turn creates an object, HTMLTableCellElement, representing a specific table row cell. Two such cells are created through insertCell: one for each table data (td) element in the table.

To add text to the newly created table cells, a factory method on the document object, createTextNode, is used to create a text object of the string passed to the method. The text object is appended to the table `cell` object using an `HTMLElement` method, `appendChild`, on each table cell object.

Example 11-2. Outputting image properties to a table using DOM HTML interfaces

```
<!DOCTYPE html PUBLIC "-//W3C//DTD XHTML 1.1//EN"
"http://www.w3.org/TR/xhtml11/DTD/xhtml11.dtd">
<html xmlns="http://www.w3.org/1999/xhtml" xml:lang="en">
<head>
<title>Modifying HTML Elements</title>
<meta http-equiv="Content-Type" content="text/html; charset=utf-8" />
<script type="text/javascript">
//<![CDATA[

window.onload=function() {

    // get table and image
    var tbl = document.getElementById('table1');
    tbl.border="5px";
    tbl.cellPadding="5px";

    var img = document.getElementById("img1");
    img.vspace="10";

    // for each attribute, add table row
    var row1 = tbl.insertRow(-1);

    // create two table cells
    var cell1 = row1.insertCell(0);
    var cell2 = row1.insertCell(1);

    // create text values
    var txtAttr1 = document.createTextNode("src");
    var txtAttr1Val = document.createTextNode(img.src);

    // append to text values to cells
    cell1.appendChild(txtAttr1);
    cell2.appendChild(txtAttr1Val);

}
//]]>
</script>
</head>
<body>
<p><img src="ospreythumb.jpg" alt="test image" class="testimage" id="img1"  /></p>
<table id="table1">
<tr><th>Attribute</th><th>Value</th></tr>
</table>
</body>
</html>
```

It's just as easy to remove elements, in this case, removing cells and rows using the methods `removeCell` and `removeRow`, respectively. As you can see, adding elements to the web page using the DOM HTML API isn't complicated, but it can be tedious.

Example 11-2 also demonstrated the overlap between the DOM Core and HTML Level 1 objects, using HTML-specific methods such as `insertRow` in addition to the more XML-generic `document.createTextNode` and `object.appendChild` methods.

Figure 11-1 shows the web page with the dynamically created HTML table.

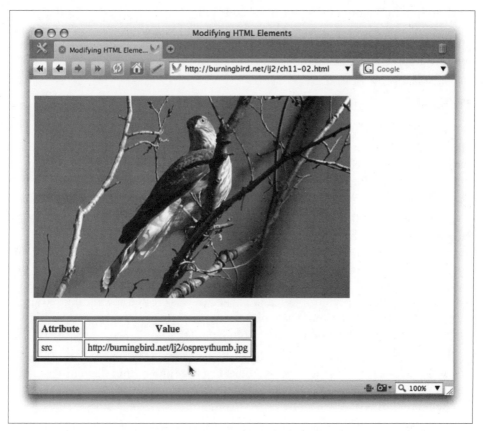

Figure 11-1. Web page with image and dynamically created HTML table

DOM (HTML) Collections

Other DOM HTML interfaces don't directly represent specific HTML elements because they represent collections of objects instead.

The collections of objects that you can access through the parent element, such as `document` or `form`, are represented by the `HTMLCollection` interface, introduced in the DOM (HTML) Level 1 specification. The `HTMLCollection` interface has one property, `length`, and two methods: `item`, which takes a number index, and `namedItem`, which takes a string. Both methods return specific objects in the collection.

The `images` collection for the `document` object was accessed as an array in Example 11-2. This is typically how you access images using the BOM. Using the DOM, instead of accessing an image using an array index, you can use the `item` method, passing in the same index number:

```
var img = document.images.item(0);
```

The result of this code is the same as the code in Example 11-2: the individual image object (`HTMLImageElement`) is set to a local variable. The main difference in the two types of code is that you're using a method call rather than an array index. You could also find the number of images in the page using `length`:

```
var numImages = document.images.length;
```

The `namedItem` also works if you want to access the element given a name or identifier:

```
var img = document.images.namedItem("original");
```

However, a more common and simpler approach to getting an element by an identifier is to use `document.getElementById`, primarily because the use of the `id` attribute is more universal, whereas the use of `name` is heavily restricted, based on DOCTYPE.

The DOM (HTML) Level 2 specification expanded on `HTMLCollection` by introducing a specific type of collection object, `HTMLOptionsCollection`, within the ECMAScript language binding. The `HTMLOptionsCollection` represents the list of options for a `select` element, itself represented by `HTMLSelectElement`. Accessing the `options` property on the latter interface returns the `HTMLOptionsCollection` object, from which you can access individual items with `item` and `namedItem`. No other collection has its own specialized language-specific object, and I believe it was created specifically because of browser implementation. Since the object has the same methods and property as `HTMLCollection`, you can treat the two as the same.

Collections can be handy ways of dealing with a group of like items. For instance, if you want to look for all of the hypertext links in a page and output them in a list at the end of the page for easier referral, you could create an application such as that shown in Example 11-3.

In the application, the links are accessed as individual elements (`HTMLLinkElement`) from the `document.links` collection. Among the properties applicable to `HTMLLinkElement` is `href`, which contains the Uniform Resource Identifier (URI, of which URLs are one specific type) for the link. This value is printed out within a `paragraph` element, which is then appended to a `div` element at the end of the page.

Example 11-3. Using the links collection to print out a list of URLs in a page

```
<!DOCTYPE html PUBLIC "-//W3C//DTD XHTML 1.1//EN"
"http://www.w3.org/TR/xhtml11/DTD/xhtml11.dtd">
<html xmlns="http://www.w3.org/1999/xhtml" xml:lang="en">
<head>
<title>Modifying HTML Elements</title>
<meta http-equiv="Content-Type" content="text/html; charset=utf-8" />
```

```
<script type="text/javascript">
//<![CDATA[

window.onload=function() {

    // get the links and the div element
    var theLinks = document.links;
    var theHrefs = document.getElementById("hrefs");

    // for each link
    for (var i = 0; i < theLinks.length; i++) {

        // get href
        var href = theLinks.item(i).href;

        // create text node from href, append to new paragraph element
        var p = document.createElement("p");
        var txt = document.createTextNode(href);
        p.appendChild(txt);

        // append new paragraph to div element
        theHrefs.appendChild(p);
    }
}
//]]>
</script>
</head>
<body>
<p>A good reference for the DOM is the <a
href="http://xml.coverpages.org/dom.html">OASIS Technology Report
on the DOM</a>. In addition, the primary DOM location at the W3C is the <a
href="http://www.w3.org/DOM/">W3C Document Object Model page</a>, from which you
can then access each DOM level. A handy interactive guide to
test your user agent (browser) and its compliance to the DOM can be found at
<a href="http://www.w3.org/2003/02/06-dom-support.html">the W3C</a>, though I'm not
sure how up-to-date it is
since it's not showing the DOM Level 3 support browsers have implemented.</p>
<div id="hrefs">
<h3>The links</h3>
</div>
</body>
</html>
```

Figure 11-2 shows the page in Opera.

Example 11-3 again demonstrated the mix between the DOM (HTML) API and the DOM (Core) API. Accessing the individual links collection and getting each link element's href value comes from the HTML API, and creating a new paragraph element and text node and appending both comes directly from the Core API.

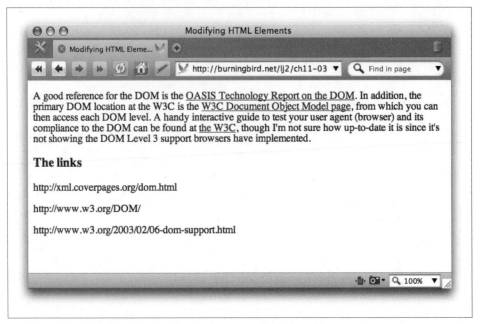

A good reference for the DOM is the OASIS Technology Report on the DOM. In addition, the primary DOM location at the W3C is the W3C Document Object Model page, from which you can then access each DOM level. A handy interactive guide to test your user agent (browser) and its compliance to the DOM can be found at the W3C, though I'm not sure how up-to-date it is since it's not showing the DOM Level 3 support browsers have implemented.

The links

http://xml.coverpages.org/dom.html

http://www.w3.org/DOM/

http://www.w3.org/2003/02/06-dom-support.html

Figure 11-2. Page with Example 11-3, demonstrating the links collection

Understanding the DOM: The Core API

The DOM (HTML) API was created specifically to bring in the many implementations of the BOM that existed across browsers. However, over the past several years, the industry has moved away from using HTML (with all the proprietary extensions) and toward the XML-based XHTML. The DOM HTML API is still valid for XHTML, but another set of interfaces—the DOM Core API—has gained popularity among current JavaScript developers.

 What goes around comes around. A new movement is underway to create HTML5, the next generation of HTML. Pieces of HTML5 have already been implemented in most browsers.

The W3C specifications for the DOM describe a document's elements as a collection of *nodes*, connected in a hierarchical tree-like structure. If you're using Firefox 3.x as a browser and have installed the DOM Inspector add-on, you can open the DOM Inspector to look at the page objects and you'll see that the page contents strongly resemble a tree. A web page has head and body tags, the body has a header (h1) as well as div elements, which contain paragraphs, which contain text, and so on. The page would have a structure somewhat like the following, also shown in Figure 11-3.

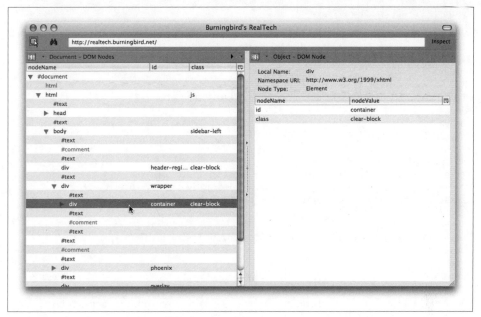

Figure 11-3. Screenshot of the DOM Inspector for my site, realtech.burningbird.net

```
#document
html
    head
    body
        h1
        div
            p
                #text
            p
                #text
```

The DOM (Core) provides a specification that allows you to access the nodes of this content tree using one of two different techniques: looking for all of the tags of a certain type, or traversing the different levels—walking the tree and exploring each node at each level. Not only can you read the nodes in the tree, but you can also remove them, or create entirely new nodes.

The DOM Tree

To better understand the document tree, consider a web page, shown in Example 11-4, which has a head and body section, a page title, and a div element that itself contains an h1 header and two paragraphs. One of the paragraphs contains italicized text; the other has an image—in other words, it's a typical web page.

Example 11-4. A typical web page

```
<!DOCTYPE html PUBLIC "-//W3C//DTD XHTML 1.1//EN"
"http://www.w3.org/TR/xhtml11/DTD/xhtml11.dtd">
<html xmlns="http://www.w3.org/1999/xhtml" xml:lang="en">
<head>
<title>Page as Tree</title>
<meta http-equiv="Content-Type" content="text/html; charset=utf-8" />
</head>
<body>
<div id="div1">
<h1>Header</h1>
<!-- paragraph one -->
<p>To better understand the document tree, consider a web page that has a head and
body section, a page title, and the body contains a div element that itself
contains a header and two paragraphs. One of the paragraphs contains <i>italicized
text</i>; the other has an image--not an uncommon web page.</p>
<!-- paragraph two -->
<p>Second paragraph with image. <img src="osprey.jpg" alt="bird" /></p>
</div>
</body>
</html>
```

Within the DOM tree structure, an element contained within another element is considered a *child node*. In Example 11-4, the text is a child node of a paragraph or header; paragraphs are child nodes of the `div` element, which is itself a child node of the document body. The element that is the container for the children nodes is known as the *parent node*; in this case, the `div` is the parent to the `paragraph` elements. Other contained elements at the same level (sharing the same parent) are considered *sibling nodes*. The `paragraph` elements are siblings to each other, and to the header (`h1`) element. Figure 11-4 shows a graphical representation of the page, diagrammed as a tree.

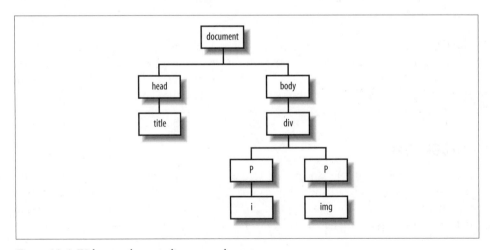

Figure 11-4. Web page elements diagrammed as a tree

Information, such as the relationship among the nodes, is accessible via each node's shared properties and methods, covered next.

Node Properties and Methods

Regardless of its type, each node in the document tree has one thing in common with all the others: each has all of the basic set of properties and methods of the DOM (Core) `Node` object. The `Node` object's properties record the relationships associated with the DOM content tree, including those of sibling elements, children, and the parent. It also has properties that provide other information about the node, such as `type`, `name`, and, if applicable, `value`. The following is a list of `Node` properties:

nodeName
> The object name, such as `HEAD` for the head element.

nodeValue
> If not an element, the value of the object.

nodeType
> The numeric type of the node.

parentNode
> The node that is the parent to the current node.

childNodes
> The `NodeList` of children nodes, if any.

firstChild
> The first node in the `NodeList` children.

lastChild
> The last node in the `NodeList` children.

previousSibling
> If a node is a child in `NodeList`, it's the previous node in the list.

nextSibling
> If a node is a child in `NodeList`, it's the next node in the list.

attributes
> A `NamedNodeMap`, which is a list of key/value pairs of attributes of the element (not applicable to other objects).

ownerDocument
> The owning `document` object, helpful in environments with more than one document.

namespaceURI
> The namespace URI, if any, for the node.

prefix
> The namespace prefix, if any, for the node.

`localName`
> The local name for the node if the `namespaceURI` is present.

You can see the XML influence in the `Node` properties, especially with regard to namespaces. However, when accessing HTML elements as nodes within a browser, the `namespace` properties are typically `null`. Also, note that some properties are valid for elements, such as those wrapping page elements like `html` and `div`; others are valid only for `Node` objects that are not elements, such as the `text` objects associated with paragraphs.

To get a better feel for this element/not element dichotomy, Example 11-5 is an application that accesses each `Node` object within a web page `document.body` element and pops up a dialog listing the node properties. The `nodeType` property provides the type of node as a numeric, and the `nodeName` is the actual object name currently being processed. If the node is not an element, its `nodeValue` property value is printed; otherwise, `null` is printed.

In addition, if the `Node` object is an element, it will have a `style` property. The application sets the background color of the object currently being processed (using a random color generator) so that you can get visual feedback as the page processing progresses. (It also outputs this background color information to the message, as a secondary feedback method.)

Example 11-5. Accessing Node properties

```
<!DOCTYPE html PUBLIC "-//W3C//DTD XHTML 1.1//EN"
"http://www.w3.org/TR/xhtml11/DTD/xhtml11.dtd">
<html xmlns="http://www.w3.org/1999/xhtml" xml:lang="en">
<head>
<title>Page as Tree</title>
<meta http-equiv="Content-Type" content="text/html; charset=utf-8" />
<script type="text/javascript">
//<![CDATA[

// random color generator
function randomColor() {
        var r=Math.floor(Math.random() * 255).toString(16);
        r = (r.length < 2) ? "0" + r : r;
        var g=Math.floor(Math.random() * 255).toString(16);
        g = (g.length < 2) ? "0" + g : g;
        var b=Math.floor(Math.random() * 255).toString(16);
        b = (b.length < 2) ? "0" + b : b;

        return "#"+r+g+b;
}

// output some node properties
function outputNodeProps(nd) {

    var strNode = "Node Type: " + nd.nodeType;
    strNode += "\nNode Name: " + nd.nodeName;
    strNode += "\nNode Value: " + nd.nodeValue;
```

```
    // if style set (property of Element)
    if (nd.style) {
        var clr = randomColor();
        nd.style.backgroundColor=clr;
        strNode += "\nbackgroundColor: " + clr;
    }

    // print out the node's properties
    alert(strNode);

    // now process node's children
    var children = nd.childNodes;
    for(var i=0; i < children.length; i++) {
        outputNodeProps(children[i]);
    }
}

window.onload=function() {
    outputNodeProps(document.body);
}
//]]>
</script>
</head>
<body>
<div id="div1">
<h1>Header</h1>
<!-- paragraph one -->
<p>To better understand the document tree, consider a web page that has a head and
body section, a page title, and the body contains a div element that itself
contains a header and two paragraphs. One of the paragraphs contains
<i>italicized text</i>; the other has an image--not an uncommon web
page.</p>
<!-- paragraph two -->
<p>Second paragraph with image. <img src="ospreythumb.jpg" alt="bird" /></p>
</div>
</body>
</html>
```

In the application, when the nodeValue property is not null, the style property is set.
However, when the nodeValue property has a value (even if it's only a blank), the
style property is not set. Figure 11-5 shows the page opened in Safari, and in mid-run.

Also, note that elements containing text, such as a paragraph, actually contain a reference to a text node, which is what contains the text. In fact, you might be surprised at
how many individual nodes this rather simple web page has.

Not all browsers have the same printouts. For instance, IE does not create text objects
for whitespace outside a tag, whereas other browsers do. This is important to understand and remember if you're going to be creating JavaScript applications that make
extensive changes to the structure of the web page.

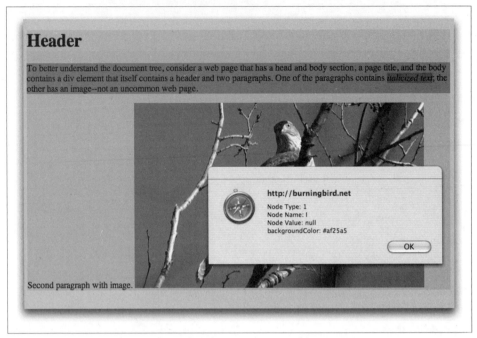

Header

To better understand the document tree, consider a web page that has a head and body section, a page title, and the body contains a div element that itself contains a header and two paragraphs. One of the paragraphs contains *italicized text*, the other has an image--not an uncommon web page.

http://burningbird.net

Node Type: 1
Node Name: l
Node Value: null
backgroundColor: #af25a5

OK

Second paragraph with image.

Figure 11-5. Traversing the page tree

Another approach to traversing a document tree is to use the W3C's optional Level 2 Traversal and Range Specification at *http://www.w3 .org/TR/DOM-Level-2-Traversal-Range/*. This specification provides an API for objects that allow more sophisticated tree traversal, as well as the capability to deal with ranges of objects.

One property of node, nodeType, is a numeric. Rather than search for a specific node type using value of 3 or 8, the DOM specifies a group of constants you can access on the node representing each type. Here are the constants:

ELEMENT_NODE
> Value of 1

ATTRIBUTE_NODE
> Value of 2

TEXT_NODE
> Value of 3

CDATA_SECTION_NODE
> Value of 4

ENTITY_REFERENCE_NODE
> Value of 5

ENTITY_NODE
> Value of 6

PROCESSING_INSTRUCTION_NODE
> Value of 7

COMMENT_NODE
> Value of 8

DOCUMENT_NODE
> Value of 9

DOCUMENT_TYPE_NODE
> Value of 10

DOCUMENT_FRAGMENT_NODE
> Value of 11

NOTATION_NODE
> Value of 12

These constants are helpful in maintaining more readable code, not to mention not having to memorize the individual values. For Example 11-5, you could add the following to display a message rather than just the numeric nodeType:

```
switch(nd.nodeType) {
  case Node.ELEMENT_NODE : strNode += "\nNode type is Element"; break;
  case Node.TEXT_NODE : strNode += "\nNode type is text"; break;
  case Node.COMMENT_NODE : strNode += "\nNode type is comment"; break;
  default : strNode += "\nNode type isn't specified"; break;
}
```

Unfortunately, the constant implementation is not universal. Internet Explorer doesn't implement these constants, and there's no indication when they will be implemented in IE. There is a workaround, however, which is to extend the Node object to include these constants, as in the following, which uses my own special constant:

```
Node.SHELLEY_TYPE = 23;
if (23 == Node.SHELLEY_TYPE) alert("I'm cool, I'm a nodeType constant");
```

However, rather than extend the object, you could also just create a global custom object that has these values as an array property. I discuss custom objects in more detail in Chapter 13.

Other than its self-identification and navigation capabilities, the Node also has several methods that you can use to replace nodes or insert new nodes. You use these in conjunction with the document object.

The DOM Core Document Object

As you'd expect, the document object is the Core interface to the web page document. It provides methods to create and remove page elements, as well as control where they occur in the page. It also provides two methods for accessing page elements, both of which you saw in earlier chapters: getElementById and getElementsByTagName.

The getElementsByTagName method returns a list of nodes (NodeList) representing all page elements of a specific tag:

```
var list = document.getElementsByTagName("div");
```

You can then traverse the list and process each node for whatever reason.

 If the document has a DOCTYPE of HTML 4.01, all element references are in uppercase. If the document is XHTML 1.0 or later, the element tags are in lowercase. However, I've found that most browsers accept uppercase element tags, even with the XHTML DOCTYPEs.

To demonstrate getElementsByTagName, Example 11-6 also uses a frameset to load a source document in one pane and the script document in another.

Example 11-6. A frameset opening a sample page and an active page with script

```
<!DOCTYPE html PUBLIC "-//W3C//DTD XHTML 1.0 Frameset//EN"
"http://www.w3.org/TR/xhtml1/DTD/xhtml1-frameset.dtd">
<html xmlns="http://www.w3.org/1999/xhtml" xml:lang="en">
<head>
<title>Highlighting</title>
<meta http-equiv="Content-Type" content="text/html; charset=utf-8" />
</head>
<frameset cols="80%,*">
<frame name="docin" src="ch11-04.html" />
<frame name="docout" src="ch11-07.html" />
</frameset>
</html>
```

One of the frame pages, *ch11-07.html*, shown in Example 11-7, has three page "buttons" (div elements) that, when clicked, open prompts for three values: the highlight color, the source window to open, and the element tag for which to search.

Example 11-7. Script page opening another document in a frame and highlighting all elements of a given type

```
<!DOCTYPE html PUBLIC "-//W3C//DTD XHTML 1.1//EN"
"http://www.w3.org/TR/xhtml11/DTD/xhtml11.dtd">
<html xmlns="http://www.w3.org/1999/xhtml" xml:lang="en">
<head>
<title>Page as Tree</title>
<meta http-equiv="Content-Type" content="text/html; charset=utf-8" />
<style type="text/css">
div {
    border: 1px solid #000;
    padding: 5px;
}
</style>
```

```
<script type="text/javascript">
//<![CDATA[

var highlightColor = "#ffff00";
function changeColor() {
  highlightColor=prompt("Enter highlight color (hexidecimal format)",highlightColor);
}

function loadPage() {
    var pageURL = prompt("Enter page in this domain","");
    top.docin.location.href=pageURL;
}

function highlightElements() {
    var elemTag = prompt("Enter tag element name to highlight:","p");
    var nodes = top.docin.document.getElementsByTagName(elemTag);

    // highlight each
    for (var i = 0; i < nodes.length; i++) {
        var mynode = nodes[i];
        mynode.style.backgroundColor=highlightColor;
    }
}

//]]>
</script>
</head>
<body>
<div onclick="changeColor()">
<p>Click to change highlight color</p>
</div>
<div onclick="loadPage()">
<p>Click to load source page</p>
</div>
<div onclick="highlightElements()">
<p>Click to search for, and highlight, a specific tag</p>
</div>
</body>
</html>
```

The application opens the source document in the first pane and then finds all elements of a type and highlights them with the given color—in this case, several elements, including list items, paragraphs, as well as a Scalable Vector Graphics (SVG) element in my main website page, as shown in Figure 11-6.

I can't load just any document with Example 11-7, though. The JavaScript sandbox prevents me from calling getElementsByTagName for a document that's outside the domain of the application page making this call. In other words, the application works with any page from the same domain as the script page, but no other.

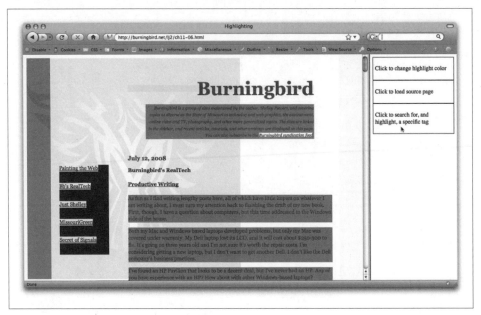

Figure 11-6. Highlighting same-tagged elements

The script can also work within the same document, which makes it effective if you want to highlight all like elements in a page based on some event—for example, all text input form elements or thumbnail images.

 Because of an open bug on setting the style for the element, Example 11-7 does not work with IE8 beta 2, unless you set the Compatibility View or use the compatibility meta tag.

Another way to access elements is via the newly implemented `getElementsByClassName`. This method returns a `nodeList` consisting of elements with a given class name, such as the following `div` element:

```
<div class="test">...</div>
```

To access this `div` element use:

```
var nds = document.getElementsByClassName("test");
```

Another variation is to list class names separated by a space to make a list of all elements with class names equal to all entries:

```
var nds = document.getElementsByClassName("test test2");
```

This is a very handy method. Unfortunately, though, it is implemented in Safari 3.1, Opera 9.5, and Firefox 3.x and later; it's not implemented in Internet Explorer, including IE8.

In addition to getElementsByTagName and getElementsByClassName, the document object has several methods that can create new objects. I demonstrate these in "Modifying the Tree" later in this chapter. First, though, we'll look at the Element object and the concept of elements in context.

 A newer query method, querySelector, is even better than getElements ByClassName, and I demonstrate its use in Chapter 12.

Element and Access in Context

Another important element in the DOM Core is, appropriately enough, Element. All page elements within a document inherit an API and properties from Element. The majority of the functionality has to do with getting and setting the attributes, or checking for the existence of attributes:

- getAttribute(*name*)
- setAttribute(*name,value*)
- removeAttribute(*name*)
- getAttributeNode(*name*)
- setAttributeNode(*attr*)
- removeAttributeNode(*attr*)
- hasAttribute(*name*)

Other methods—most having to do with the namespaces associated with the attributes—exist as well, but these aren't methods you'll typically use with a web page.

Element attributes are not always accessible as object properties. Properties are a component of the object *class*, rather than instances of the class. So, properties would be associated with the document object, Element, Node, or even HTML elements such as HTMLDocumentElement. However, if you want to work with an element's attributes, and they're not exposed as a property on the object class, you can use the Element methods.

Here's an image embedded in a web page:

```
<img src="dotty.gif" width="100" alt="an image" align="left" />
```

The following code accesses the image's attributes using the Element.getAttribute method, concatenating them into a string, which is then printed in an alert:

```
var img = document.images[0];
var imgStr = img.getAttribute("src") + " " +
             img.getAttribute("width") + " " +
             img.getAttribute("alt") + " " +
             img.getAttribute("align");
alert(imgStr);
```

The following changes the value for the `width` and the `alt` using the complementary `Element.setAttribute` method:

```
img.setAttribute("width","200");
img.setAttribute("alt","This was an image");
```

`Element` also shares a method with the `document`: `getElementsByTagName`. Rather than work on all elements within the `document`, it operates on elements within the context of the `document`.

In fact, all the examples so far in the book have operated within the context of the `document` object, more or less. For the most part, this is sufficient. However, sometimes you'll want to work only with those elements nested within another element. Through the functionality inherited by the DOM Core, especially the `Node` and `Element` objects, any object in the page that you can access through a discrete access method such as `getElementById` can form a new context for working with content.

In the following HTML, two `div` blocks contain paragraphs: the first contains two; the second, one.

```
<div id="div1">
<p>one</p>
<p>two</p>
</div>
<div id="div2">
<p>three</p>
</div>
```

The paragraphs don't have identifiers, so you can't access each individually using `getElementById`. You can instead use `getElementsByTagName` by passing in the paragraph tag:

```
var ps = document.getElementsByTagName("p");
```

However, in doing so, you'll get all paragraphs in the document. This might be what you want, but what if you want just the paragraphs within the first `div` block?

To access the paragraphs within the context of just the `div` element, you'll access the `div` using `getElementById`:

```
var div = document.getElementById("div1");
```

Then, because the `div` element inherits from the `Element` object, you can use `getEle mentsByTagName` to get all paragraphs:

```
var ps = div.getElementsByTagName("p");
```

The only paragraphs in the node list returned are those nested within the first `div` block, identified by `div1`.

As more web pages are designed using CSS and are built in layers with elements nested within other layers, working with elements *in context* is a way to maintain some level of control over which components of the page are impacted by the JavaScript application. This is never more noticeable than when you use this approach to modify the document.

Modifying the Tree

Earlier, you saw how you could use the `Element` object's methods to modify a specific element object. You'll need three different objects to modify the overall document tree.

The `document` is the owner/parent of all page elements. Because of this ownership, most factory methods for creating instances of new elements are methods on the Core `document` object. The `Node`, however, maintains the navigation within the Core API; supporting the hierarchical structure of the document tree, in which each node has a relationship to other nodes and navigation follows this natural structure: parent/child, sibling/sibling. Finally, the `Element` provides a way to access elements within context to apply changes to nested elements. All three are essential objects when it comes to modifying the document tree.

Table 11-1 lists the `document` factory methods and the types of Core objects they create. The table also provides a brief introduction to several of the Core objects.

Table 11-1. Factory methods of the document object

Method	Object created	Description
`createElement(tagname)`	Element	Creates a specific type of element
`createDocumentFragment`	DocumentFragment	The `DocumentFragment` is a lightweight document, used when extracting a section of the document tree
`createTextNode(data)`	Text	Holds any text in the page
`createComment(data)`	Comment	XML comment
`createCDATASection(data)`	CDATASection	CDATA section
`createProcessingInstructions(target,data)`	ProcessingInstruction	XML processing instruction
`createAttribute(name)`	Attr	Element attribute
`createEntityReference(name)`	EntityReference	Creates an element to be placed later
`createElementNS(namespaceURI,qualifiedName)`	Element	Creates a namespaced element
`createAttributeNS(namespaceURI,qualifiedName)`	Attr	Creates a namespaced attribute

It's simple to create a new node, such as a text node. All you need to do is call the appropriate factory method on the document, and the node is returned:

```
var txtNode = document.createTextNode("This is a new text node");
```

Just to refresh your memory, factory methods are ways of creating objects that don't have their own constructor.

Once you have a new node, you can manipulate it as you would manipulate an existing page element of the same type. To add a new paragraph and text to the new div element, use the following:

```
var newDiv = document.createElement("div");
var newP = document.createElement('p');
var newText = document.createTextNode('New paragraph');
newP.appendChild(newText);
newDiv.appendChild(newP);
```

Once you've created the new node, you can add it directly into an existing document tree, using the following Node methods:

insertBefore(newChild,refChild)
:   Inserts a new node before the existing node, given as refChild

replaceChild(newChild,oldChild)
:   Replaces the existing node

removeChild(oldChild)
:   Removes the existing child

appendChild(newChild)
:   Appends a child node to the document

Remember, though, that you must use these methods within context to be effective. In other words, they have to operate on the element that contains the nodes that are being replaced or removed (or where the new node is being placed).

If the web page has a div element with a nested header, and the header is what's being replaced, you'll need to access the div element to modify its structure:

```
var div = document.getElementById("div1");
var hdr = document.getElementById("hdr1");
div.removeChild(hdr);
...
<div id="div1">
<h1 id="hdr1">Header</h1>
</div>
```

Demonstrating this more comprehensively, Example 11-8 is a variation of the static page used in previous examples in this chapter. It contains paragraphs, div blocks, an image, and a header. The script consists of a function, changeDoc, that's accessed when the page is clicked (not loaded). This script manipulates the page document tree by removing the header, replacing the image with text, and adding a new header to the end of the document.

Example 11-8. Modifying a document

```
<!DOCTYPE html PUBLIC "-//W3C//DTD XHTML 1.0 Transitional//EN"
"http://www.w3.org/TR/xhtml1/DTD/xhtml1-transitional.dtd">
<html>
<head>
<title>Modifying Document</title>
<meta http-equiv="Content-Type" content="text/html; charset=utf-8" />
<script type="text/javascript">
//<![CDATA[

document.onclick=changeDoc;

function changeDoc() {

    // first, remove header
    var hdr = document.getElementById("hdr1");
    var div = document.getElementById("div1");
    div.removeChild(hdr);

    // replace the image with text
    var img = document.getElementById("img1");
    var p = document.getElementById("p2");
    var txt = document.createTextNode("New text node");
    p.replaceChild(txt,img);

    // add new element
    var div2= document.createElement("div");
    div2.innerHTML="<h1>The End</h1>";
    document.body.appendChild(div2);
}
//]]>
</script>

</head>
<body>
<div id="div1">
<h1 id="hdr1">Header</h1>
<!-- paragraph one -->
<p id="p1">To better understand the document tree, consider a web page that has a
head and body section, has a page title, and contains a DIV element that itself
contains an H1 header and two paragraphs. One of the paragraphs contains
<i>italicized text</i>; the other has an image--not an uncommon web page.</p>
</div>
<!-- paragraph two -->
<p id="p2">Second paragraph with image. <img id="img1" src="dotty.gif" alt="dotty" /></p>
</body>
</html>
```

Figure 11-7 shows the page before modification, and Figure 11-8 shows the page after modification.

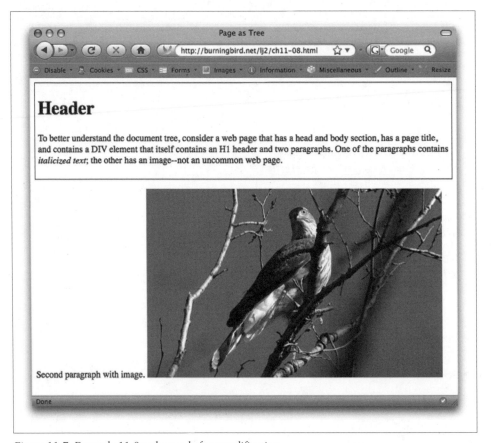

Figure 11-7. Example 11-8 web page before modification

The first modification to the document is to remove the header from the `div` block. Both the `div` and its contained header element are accessed using `getElementById`. Once the application has both the `div` and its contained header element, the header element is passed to the `removeChild` method on the `div` block, removing the element from the `div` and the page.

 If you're adding a lot of nodes to the DOM tree, one performance enhancement you can implement is to create a `documentFragment` using `createDocumentFragment`, append the nodes to it, and then append the `documentFragment` to the tree. Read more on the use of `documentFragment` for performance improvement at John Resig's weblog, at *http://ejohn.org/blog/dom-documentfragments/*.

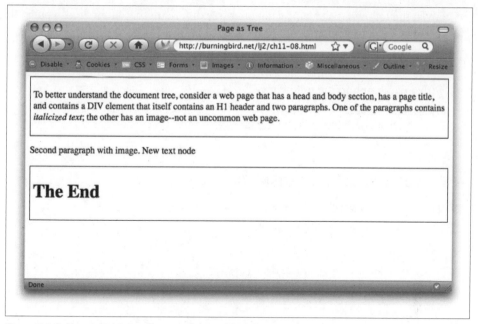

To better understand the document tree, consider a web page that has a head and body section, has a page title, and contains a DIV element that itself contains an H1 header and two paragraphs. One of the paragraphs contains *italicized text*; the other has an image--not an uncommon web page.

Second paragraph with image. New text node

The End

Figure 11-8. Example 11-8 web page after modification

The next modification replaces the image contained in the last paragraph with text created using a text node. Both the image and the paragraph are loaded into JavaScript variables using `getElementById`. A new text node is then created and it and the image node are passed to the `replaceChild` method on the paragraph node.

The last modification creates a new `div` element and uses the `innerHTML` property to generate a new header within the new `div` element, demonstrating a mix of the old BOM functionality with the newer DOM. The new `div` element is appended to the `body` element, which results in a new header with the words "The End" printed at the end of the document.

And it is the end—of this chapter, that is. There's plenty more still to come.

Test Your Knowledge: Quiz

1. What attributes are supported for all HTML elements?
2. Using the HTML DOM when given a named element, how would you find its element type?
3. Given a node in the Core DOM, how would you print out the element types of each of its children?
4. How would you find out the IDs (identifiers) given all `div` elements in a page?

5. Given the following element, what are three different types of methods you could use to access this element?

```
<div id="elem1" class="thediv">...</div>
```

6. Rather than use innerHTML, how would you go about replacing the header element with a paragraph in the following div:

```
<div id="elem1">
<h1>This is a header</h1>
</div>
```

Test Your Knowledge: Answers

1. The attributes are id, title, lang, dir, and className.

2. Access the element's tagName attribute.

3. The solution is:

```
var children = targetNode.childNodes;
for (var i = 0; i < children.length; i++) {
    alert(children[i].nodeType);
}
```

4. The solution is:

```
var divs = document.getElementsByTagName('div');
for (var i = 0; i < divs.length; i++) {
    alert(divs[i].id);
}
```

5. The three approaches are:

```
var theDiv = document.getElementById('elem1');

var theDivs = document.getElementsByTagName('div');
var theDiv = theDivs[0];

var theDivs = document.getElementsByClassName('thediv');
var theDiv = theDivs[0];
```

6. The solution is:

```
var targetElement = document.getElementById('elem1');
var specChild = targetElement.getElementsByTagName('h1')[0];
var newPara = document.createElement('p');
var paraTxt = document.createTextNode('hello');
newPara.appendChild(paraTxt);

targetElement.replaceChild(newPara,specChild);
```

CHAPTER 12

Dynamic Pages

Dynamic web pages created through the use of JavaScript, previously called *DHTML* or *Dynamic HTML* and now typically called *Ajax*, have been around for close to 12 years. The key element to the concept was the introduction of Cascading Style Sheets (CSS) in addition to the Document Object Model (DOM), though there was no universal object model in the early years.

It's through CSS that we can define the appearance of page elements without having to rely on external applications, plug-ins, or excessive use of images. It's also through CSS and stylesheets that we can separate the presentation of page elements from their organization.

However, it was through the DOM that we could access stylesheet properties from JavaScript, changing individual element properties even after the page had finished loading. Combined with CSS, this was a powerful means to make web pages far more interactive than ever before.

JavaScript, CSS, and the DOM

This chapter assumes that you're familiar with CSS and how to add stylesheets to a web page. If you're unfamiliar with CSS, you may want to read a good tutorial or book on CSS before reading the rest of this chapter. I recommend Eric A. Meyer's *CSS: The Definitive Guide* (O'Reilly).

The Style Property/Attributes

Typically, you retrieve and set CSS style properties via the `style` property. The concept of `style` as a property originated with Microsoft, but the World Wide Web Consortium (W3C) adopted and included it in the DOM Level 2 CSS module. Through the W3C DOM, all nodes have an associated `style` object as a property, which means you can change any page element's style properties with JavaScript.

To change any style setting using JavaScript, you must first use one of the DOM access methods I outlined in earlier chapters to get a handle on the individual element (or elements):

```
var tstElem = document.getElementById("testelement");
```

To change the style attribute, use straight assignment:

```
tstElem.style.color="#fff";
```

This works with any valid CSS2 property and on any valid X/HTML object, as long as the attribute has meaning for the element. For instance, a span element is usually not displayed as a block (with a line break before and after), so setting a top and bottom margin doesn't have a lot of meaning.

Example 12-1 shows how to modify several CSS attributes, using the by now very familiar getElementById method to access a div element, and the style object to set various CSS properties.

Example 12-1. Applying several style property changes to a div element

```
<!DOCTYPE html PUBLIC "-//W3C//DTD XHTML 1.1//EN"
"http://www.w3.org/TR/xhtml11/DTD/xhtml11.dtd">
<html xmlns="http://www.w3.org/1999/xhtml" xml:lang="en">
<head>
<title>DHTML</title>
<meta http-equiv="Content-Type" content="text/html; charset=utf-8" />
<script type="text/javascript">
//<![CDATA[

window.onload=function() {

  setTimeout("changeCSS()",3000);
}

function changeCSS() {
  var div = document.getElementById("div1");
  div.style.backgroundColor="#f00";
  div.style.width="500px";
  div.style.color="#fff";
  div.style.height="200px";
  div.style.paddingLeft="50px";
  div.style.paddingTop="50px";
  div.style.fontFamily="Verdana";
  div.style.borderColor="#000";
}
//]]>
</script>
</head>
<body>
<div id="div1">
<p>Hello CSS</p>
</div>
</body>
</html>
```

Notice in the example the naming convention used with the CSS properties. If the CSS attribute has a hyphen, such as `border-color`, the hyphen is removed and the first letter of the second term is capitalized: `border-color` in CSS becomes `borderColor` in JavaScript. Other than that, the names of the CSS properties used in JavaScript are the same as the names of the properties used in a stylesheet.

> The exception is for the CSS `float` property. IE uses `styleFloat`, and everyone else uses `cssFloat`.

If modifying the `style` attribute is simple, reading it is less so. If you do not set the `style` property through JavaScript or by using the `style` attribute inline in the element, even if you set the value with a stylesheet the property value will be either blank or undefined. This is important to remember because it will trip you up more than anything else when you're dynamically changing the CSS properties of elements. The style settings used to render the object initially are internal to the browser and are based on a combination of stylesheet settings, as well as element inheritance.

> Unless you set the `style` property via JavaScript or directly inline using the `style` attribute on the element, the value is blank or undefined when you access it via script, even if you set the value through a stylesheet.

To access the style, you need to use other properties, each specific to different types of browsers. Microsoft and Opera support a `currentStyle` property on the element, whereas Mozilla and Safari/WebKit support `window.getComputedStyle`. Unfortunately, these don't work consistently across browsers.

For the `getComputedStyle` method, you must pass in the CSS attribute using the same syntax you use when setting the style in the stylesheet. However, for the `currentStyle` method, you use the JavaScript notation.

Example 12-2 demonstrates a variation of a function that gets the style settings for an object and a specific CSS property. First, it tests whether `currentStyle` is supported, and if not, it tests for `getComputedStyle`. An appropriate message, including the actual style setting, is printed to an alert window. The background color is then set in the script, and the `style` property directly displayed after setting, to show how the value is now available directly on the `style` property once it is set in JavaScript.

Example 12-2. Attempting to get CSS style information

```
<!DOCTYPE html PUBLIC "-//W3C//DTD XHTML 1.1//EN"
"http://www.w3.org/TR/xhtml11/DTD/xhtml11.dtd">
<html xmlns="http://www.w3.org/1999/xhtml" xml:lang="en">
<head>
<title>DHTML</title>
<meta http-equiv="Content-Type" content="text/html; charset=utf-8" />
```

```
<style type="text/css">
   #div1 { background-color: #ffff00 }
</style>
<script type="text/javascript">
//<![CDATA[

function getStyle(obj,jsprop,cssprop) {
    if (obj.currentStyle) {
        alert('currentStyle ' + obj.currentStyle[jsprop]);
    } else if (window.getComputedStyle) {
        alert('getComputed ' +
document.defaultView.getComputedStyle(obj,null).getPropertyValue(cssprop));
    } else {
      alert("neither currentStyle nor getComputed supported");
    }
}

function changeElement() {
    var obj = document.getElementById("div1");
    alert(obj.style.backgroundColor);
    getStyle(obj,"backgroundColor","background-color");
    obj.style.backgroundColor="#ff0000";
    alert(obj.style.backgroundColor);
}

document.onclick=changeElement;

//]]>
</script>
</head>
<body>
<div id="div1">
<p>Hello CSS</p>
</div>
</body>
</html>
```

Opening and clicking the page in Firefox and Safari returns alert boxes that have no value—getComputed rgb(255,255,0) and rgb(255,0,0), respectively. The same page returns no value—currentStyle #ffff00 and #ff0000 for Opera and IE, though IE returns currentStyle #ffff00 for the second alert message.

Notice in the script that the syntax to get the computed value is document.default View.getComputedStyle rather than window.getComputedStyle. The document.default View property is a DOM AbstractView object, which is the base interface from which all views derive. You could use window.getComputedStyle, but there's no guarantee that the defaultView (current viewport) is actually set to the window element, and the results could be unreliable across browsers.

Even when the style property is accessible, what is returned also varies among browsers; for instance, accessing something simple, such as font color.

Opera returns the hexadecimal format for the color:

```
#ff0000
```

IE also returns the hexadecimal format, but the computed value uses the shortcut version of `#ff0`, whereas Firefox and Safari return the RGB setting:

```
RGB(255,0,0)
```

You need to convert between the two formats, RGB and hexadecimal, if you want a consistent result, and then you'll need to convert between shortcut and long hexadecimal formats.

What would be returned if the background color for the `div` element wasn't set? Let's say that the `body` element was given the background color, rather than the `div` element. What would you get?

In Firefox, IE, and Opera, the default background color for the `div` element is `"transparent"`. However, in Safari, the default background color is also transparent, but Safari doesn't return `"transparent"`, it returns the RGBA (Red-Green-Blue-Alpha) equivalent, `rgba(0,0,0,0)`, where the last value is the alpha transparency setting—in this case, zero.

Retrieving style settings from the page is fraught with interesting challenges, perhaps more so than are fun, entertaining, or even useful. When a property isn't set directly, its derived value is based on computed as well as cascading CSS rules, which not only *can* differ among browsers, but also will probably *always* differ among browsers. One of the reasons JavaScript libraries such as Prototype, Dojo, and jQuery are so popular is that these libraries work through all the computed style differences so that you don't have to.

A good rule of thumb when working with dynamic effects with CSS is to try to avoid retrieving information directly from the page style settings. Instead, whenever possible, use program variables to hold values and use `style` only to set attributes.

The CSS `style` properties tend to fall into families of like properties: fonts, borders, the container for elements, positioning, display, and so on. In the rest of this chapter, I'll cover several attributes, demonstrating how to work with each using JavaScript. As you read through the chapter, don't hesitate to take some time along the way to stop and improvise on all of the examples.

Fonts and Text

One of the first presentation-specific HTML elements was `font`, and it's also one of the older HTML elements you still find, all too frequently, in web pages. It's not surprising that `font` and `text` properties were of such interest in building web pages. Few changes you can make to an element's `style` attributes can have such an effect as changing the `text` or `font` properties.

Notice that I said "text or font properties." The font properties have to do with the characters themselves: their family, size, type, and other elements of the characters' appearance. The text attributes, though, have more to do with decoration attached to the text and include text decoration, alignment, and so on.

Font Style Properties

Fonts have several style attributes. The following is a list of their CSS names and their associated JavaScript-accessible style attributes:

font-family

Access it as fontFamily in JavaScript. This adjusts the font family (such as serif, Arial, or Verdana) for the font. When specifying a multiword font family, type the family name exactly, including spaces.

font-size

Access it as fontSize in JavaScript. This sets the size of the font. You can use different units when setting the font size. If you use em or pt with the size (such as 12pt or 2.5em), the font is resized according to the web page reader's personal settings. If you use px (pixel), the font is maintained at that size regardless of user settings. You can also use one of the predefined font sizes of xx-small, x-small, small, medium, large, x-large, or xx-large, or use the relative sizing, smaller or larger, in addition to using a percentage based on the parent element.

font-size-adjust

Access it as fontSizeAdjust. This is the ratio between the height of the letter x and the height specified in font-size. This setting preserves this ratio, though it's rarely given.

font-stretch

Access it as fontStretch. This expands or contracts the font. You can use one of the following: normal, wider, narrower, ultra-condensed, extra-condensed, condensed, semi-condensed, semi-expanded, expanded, ultra-expanded, or extra-expanded.

font-style

Access it as fontStyle. You can use normal (default), italic, or oblique.

font-variant

Access it as fontVariant. Use small-caps as a value if you want to use the small-cap variant of the font.

font-weight

Access it as fontWeight. Use this to set the font's weight (boldness). Use normal, bold, bolder, lighter, or a numeric of 100, 200, 300, 400, 500, 600, 700, 800, or 900.

You can change many of the font attributes all at once using just font itself. In the following code:

```
div1.style.font="italic small-caps 400 14px verdana";
```

a single string is used to change the `style`, `variant`, `weight`, `size`, and `font-family`. Many of the CSS properties have shortcut methods such as this. You assign them in JavaScript just as you would in CSS. In CSS, all the settings are to the right of the colon; in JavaScript, everything that's to the right of the colon is included in the quotes on the right side of the assignment statement.

Text Properties

For this chapter, I decided to group several attributes that affect the appearance of text, though unlike `font`, they're not part of the same family. Here are the CSS text attributes I most often set:

`color`
> Access it as `color`. This is the color of the text.

`line-height`
> Access it as `lineHeight`. This is the space from the top of one line to the bottom of the line below it. You specify a value in a manner similar to specifying the font size, or you can use `normal`.

`text-decoration`
> Access it as `textDecoration`. Use `none`, `underline`, `overline`, or `line-through`. Please don't use `blink`.

`text-indent`
> Access it as `textIndent`. This specifies how much to indent the first line of text.

`text-transform`
> Access it as `textTransform`. Use `none`, `capitalize` (to capitalize every word), `uppercase`, or `lowercase`.

`white-space`
> Access it as `whiteSpace`. Use `normal`, `pre`, or `nowrap`.

`direction`
> Access it as `direction`. Use `ltr` (left to right) or `rtl` (right to left).

`text-align`
> Access it as `textAlign`. This specifies how the text contents are aligned. Use `left`, `right`, `center`, or `justify`.

`word-spacing`
> Access it as `wordSpacing`. This is the amount of space between words. Use `normal`, or specify a length.

What are typical uses for modifying font and/or text properties? One useful modification is to provide a way to expand the size of a block of text to make it more legible, or to highlight the data for some reason. In Example 12-3, clicking one of two links will either make a text block very large as well as justified, or return it to what it was previously. Note that a stylesheet is used to set the text originally so that when the text is "returned" to the smaller size, the font and text settings are identical, regardless of default settings per browser.

Example 12-3. Modifying a text block

```
<!DOCTYPE html PUBLIC "-//W3C//DTD XHTML 1.1//EN"
"http://www.w3.org/TR/xhtml11/DTD/xhtml11.dtd">
<html xmlns="http://www.w3.org/1999/xhtml" xml:lang="en">
<head>
<title>readThis</title>
<meta http-equiv="Content-Type" content="text/html; charset=utf-8" />
<style type="text/css">
div
{
    width: 600px;
}
#smaller
{
    background-color: #00f;
    cursor: pointer;
}
#larger
{
    background-color: #0f0;
    cursor: pointer;
}
#div1
{
    font-size: 15px;
    letter-spacing: normal;
    text-align: left;
    text-transform: none;
    line-height: 18px;
    font-weight: normal;
}
</style>
<script type="text/javascript">
//<![CDATA[
function makeMore() {
    var div = document.getElementById("div1");
    div.style.letterSpacing="5px";
    div.style.textAlign="justify";
    div.style.textTransform="uppercase";
    div.style.fontSize="25px";
    div.style.fontWeight="900";
    div.style.lineHeight="30px";
}

function makeLess() {
    var div = document.getElementById("div1");
    div.style.fontSize="15px";
    div.style.letterSpacing="normal";
    div.style.textAlign="left";
    div.style.textTransform="none";
    div.style.fontWeight="normal";
```

```
        div.style.lineHeight="18px";
}

window.onload=function() {
        document.getElementById('smaller').onclick=makeLess;
        document.getElementById('larger').onclick=makeMore;
}
//]]>
</script>
</head>
<body>
<div id="smaller">
<p>Make smaller</p>
</div>
<div id="larger">
<p>Make larger</p>
</div>
<div id="div1">
<p>
Lorem ipsum dolor sit amet, consectetuer adipiscing elit. Praesent rutrum erat a
orci. Ut quis nisi. Curabitur eu nulla. Nullam vulputate tortor. Proin scelerisque.
Mauris eleifend odio non enim. Nunc tortor tortor, viverra at, tempor eu, tincidunt
in, risus. Duis libero. Aliquam a sapien et justo vehicula volutpat. In at nibh in
eros lacinia blandit. Donec nec ligula id nisl convallis convallis. Suspendisse
condimentum lacinia ante. Ut et ligula quis magna pharetra rhoncus. Morbi ornare
lobortis augue. Nunc convallis semper massa.
</p>
</div>
</body>
</html>
```

Chances are you wouldn't increase the text to the size shown in this example, or use this type of justification, but this example does show what kind of transformation you can create using JavaScript and CSS. Another typical use is to change the font color of a text field associated with a form element or block of text to show that it doesn't apply, to literally "gray out" the font.

Position and Movement

Before CSS, if you wanted to control the layout of the page with any consistency, you had to use an HTML table. As for any form of animation, you had to use either something such as an animated GIF, or a plug-in such as Flash.

Netscape and Microsoft together helped bring an end to all of this with the co-introduction of a specification called CSS-P, or CSS Positioning. Consider the page as a graph, with both x and y coordinates. With CSS-P, you can set an element's position within this coordinate system. Add JavaScript, and you can move elements around the page.

Dynamic Positioning

The proposed CSS-P attributes were eventually incorporated into the CSS2 specification. The positioning properties in CSS2 include the following:

position
> The `position` property takes one of five values: `relative`, `absolute`, `static`, `inherit`, or `fixed`. `static` positioning is the default setting for most elements. This means they're part of the page flow, and other elements in the page impact the element's position, and it impacts all elements that follow. `relative` positioning is similar except that the element is offset from its normal position. A position set to `absolute` takes the element out of the page flow, allowing you to set its position absolutely in the page. This also allows you to layer elements, one on top of another, just by positioning them in the same location. A `fixed` position is similar to `absolute` positioning, except the element is positioned relative to some viewport.

top
> Setting an element's `top` property sets its position relative to the top of the container.

left
> Setting an element's `left` property sets its position relative to the left side of the container.

bottom
> The `bottom` property has as its zero value the bottom of the page. Higher values move the element up the page.

right
> The `right` property has as its zero value the right side of the page. Higher values move the element toward the left.

z-index
> You may want to add the `z-index`. If you draw a line perpendicular to the page, this is the `z-index`. As I mentioned earlier, with `absolute` positioning, elements can be layered on top of one another. Their position within the stack is controlled by one of two things. The first is its position in the page. Elements defined later in the web page are located higher in the stack; earlier elements are located lower in the stack. The second factor influencing the position of the element in the stack is the `z-index`. You can use both negative and positive integers, with a value of 0 being the normal rendering layer (relative positioning), `negative` pushing an element lower than this, and `positive` pushing an element higher.

The `display` attribute also influences both positioning and layout, but I cover it in "Display, Visibility, and Opacity" later in this chapter. The attribute `float` is also involved in positioning, but it doesn't play well with dynamic page effects, so I won't cover it.

The top, right, bottom, and left properties, as well as z-index, work only if you set position to something other than static, the default position value. You can set elements outside the visible page by setting any of the properties to a negative value. You also can move elements based on events, such as mouse clicks.

One dynamic web page effect is a *fly-in*, where elements seem to literally "fly in" from the sides of the document. This is a good approach for tutorials or other efforts in which you want to introduce one topic after another, based on a mouse click or keyboard entry from the web page reader.

Example 12-4 demonstrates a fly-in with three elements coming from the top left. It uses a timer to create the movement and to reset it after each "slide" until the x, the top value, is greater than value (100 + value * the number of the element, to create an overlap). The elements are "hidden" when they are originally positioned off the page, to the left and top, because setting elements beyond the page to the right or bottom results in a scroll bar being added to the page.

Example 12-4. Element positioning and movement with fly-ins

```
<!DOCTYPE html PUBLIC "-//W3C//DTD XHTML 1.1//EN"
"http://www.w3.org/TR/xhtml11/DTD/xhtml11.dtd">
<html xmlns="http://www.w3.org/1999/xhtml" xml:lang="en">
<head>
<title>Fly-Ins</title>
<meta http-equiv="Content-Type" content="text/html; charset=utf-8" />
<style type="text/css">
div
{
        padding: 0 5px;
}
#nav
{
        background-color: #ccc;
        width: 100px;
        cursor: pointer;
}
#div1
{
        background-color: #00f;
        color: #fff;
        font-size: larger;
        position: absolute;
        width: 400px;
        height: 200px;
        left: -410px;
        top: -400px;
        }
#div2 {
        background-color: #ff0;
        color: #;
        font-size: larger;
        position: relative;
        width: 400px;
```

```
              height: 200px;
              left: -410px;
              top: -400px;
              z-index: 4;
              }
      #div3 {
              background-color: #f00;
              color: #fff;
              font-size: larger;
              position: fixed;
              width: 400px;
              height: 200px;
              left: -410px;
              top: -400px;
              }
      </style>
      <script type="text/javascript">
      //<![CDATA[

      // global placeholders
      var slides = ["div1","div2","div3"];
      var x = 0;
      var y = 0;
      var currentSlide = 0;

      window.onload=function () {
          document.getElementById("nav").onclick=nextSlide;
      }

      function nextSlide() {
          setTimeout("moveBlock()",1000);
      }

      function moveBlock() {
          x+=20;
          y+=20;
          var obj = document.getElementById(slides[currentSlide]);
          obj.style.top = x + "px";
          obj.style.left = y + "px";
          if (x < (100 + currentSlide * 60)) {
              setTimeout("moveBlock()", 100);
          } else {
              currentSlide++;
              x = 0; y = 0;
          }

          if (currentSlide >= slides.length) {
              document.getElementById("nav").onclick=null;
          }
      }

      //]]>
      </script>
      </head>
      <body>
```

```
<div id="nav">
<p>Next slide</p>
</div>
<div id="div1">
<p>Blue block that is absolutely positioned.</p>
</div>
<div id="div2">
<p>Yellow block that is relatively positioned, and given a z-index of 4.</p>
</div>
<div id="div3">
<p>Red block that has fixed positioning.</p>s
</div>
</body>
</html>
```

Figure 12-1 shows the page opened in Safari, after all three blocks are displayed. Note that the second yellow block seems displaced farther down the page because it's moved relative to the first blue block. Also notice that it overlays the red block, though the red block comes later in the document. This is because of the `z-index` positioning of the yellow block. Both the red and blue blocks have a default `z-index` of 0.

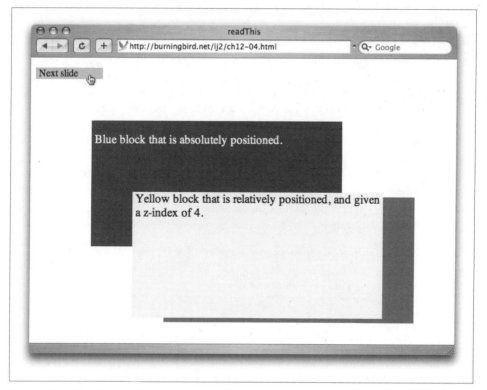

Figure 12-1. Three blocks, dynamically moved into the page

To make the page more accessible, you could add a hypertext link to the `div` element that acts as the navigation button. This link could change the navigation to open pages with the fly-in information. Alternatively, you could position all three information blocks in the page (in such a way that all of them are visible), and use `script` to hide them only if JavaScript is enabled.

Another common use of dynamic page effects associated with movement has as much to do with tracking the movement of the web page reader as it does elements in the page. The technique is called *drag-and-drop*, and I discuss it next.

Drag-and-Drop

One dynamic web page item that generated considerable interest when it was first introduced was *drag-and-drop*. Shopping-cart examples featuring drag-and-drop popped up all over, until sanity prevailed.

Reawakening the interest in drag-and-drop was Google Maps' use of the technique to allow you to move a map within a constrained space. This was the first time I'd seen a really effective use of drag-and-drop. We'll take a look at Google Maps and its associated Application Programming Interface (API) in a later chapter, but for now, let's look at implementing our own, very tiny emulation of drag-and-drop technology.

 What makes the Google Maps approach really exciting is that as you scroll through a map, the application actually pulls up the next pieces of the map from the server—a process sometimes called *tiling*—and integrates them into the page using a caching mechanism. With this, you seem to never reach the end of the map. It's really well done.

Example 12-5 creates a `div` element and embeds a screenshot from the book within the element. The image can be moved around its container using drag-and-drop. In addition to demonstrating the drag-and-drop behavior, this small application also uses the `overflow` attribute, to *clip* the part of the image that is too big for its container. This functionality prevents any overlap of the image outside the defined space.

Example 12-5. The Google Maps effect: drag-and-drop of an object in a container

```
<!DOCTYPE html PUBLIC "-//W3C//DTD XHTML 1.1//EN"
"http://www.w3.org/TR/xhtml11/DTD/xhtml11.dtd">
<html xmlns="http://www.w3.org/1999/xhtml" xml:lang="en">
<head>
<title>Google Maps Effect</title>
<meta http-equiv="Content-Type" content="text/html; charset=utf-8" />
<style type="text/css">
#div1 {
    overflow: hidden;
    position: relative;
    top: 100px;
    left: 100px;
```

```
        border: 5px solid #000;
        width: 400px;
        height: 200px;
}
img {
      border: 1px solid #000;
      }
</style>
<script type="text/javascript">
//<![CDATA[

// global variables
var dragObject  = null;
var mouseOffset = null;

// capture mouse events
document.onmousemove = mouseMove;
document.onmouseup   = mouseUp;

// create a mouse point
function MousePoint(x,y) {
   this.x = x;
   this.y = y;
}

// find mouse position
function mousePosition(evnt){
  var x = parseInt(evnt.clientX);
  var y = parseInt(evnt.clientY);
  return new MousePoint(x,y);
}

// get element's offset position within page
function getMouseOffset(target, evnt){
   var theEvent = evnt ? evnt : window.event;
   var mousePos  = mousePosition(theEvent);

   var x = mousePos.x - target.offsetLeft;
   var y = mousePos.y - target.offsetTop;
   return new MousePoint(x,y);
}

// turn off dragging
function mouseUp(evnt){
   dragObject = null;
}
// capture mouse move, only if dragging
function mouseMove(evnt){
   if (!dragObject) return;
   var theEvent = evnt ? evnt : window.event;
   var mousePos = mousePosition(theEvent);

   // if draggable, set new absolute position
   if(dragObject){
      dragObject.style.position = 'relative';
```

```
            dragObject.style.top      = mousePos.y - mouseOffset.y + "px";
            dragObject.style.left     = mousePos.x - mouseOffset.x + "px";
            return false;
        }
    }
}

// make object draggable
function makeDraggable(item){
    if (item) {
        item = document.getElementById(item);
        item.onmousedown = function(theEvent) {
                        dragObject   = this;
                        mouseOffset = getMouseOffset(this, theEvent);
                        return false; };
    }
}

window.onload=function() {
    makeDraggable("img1");
}

//]]>
</script>
</head>
<body>
<div id="div1" >
<img id="img1" src="fig0901.png" alt="Figure 9-1" />
</div>
</body>
</html>
```

This is the most complex example I've included in the book thus far, so let's take the
JavaScript from the top:

- Two global objects are created: dragObject and mouseOffset. The former is the
  object being dragged; the latter is the object's *offset* value. The offset is the object's
  position relative to a container—in this instance, the page. We also capture the
  mousemove and mouseup events for the document and assign them to two event handlers, mouseMove and mouseUp.

- The next is an object, MousePoint. This just wraps the two mouse coordinates: x
  and y. Creating an object makes it easier to pass around both values.

- The next function is mousePosition. This function accesses the target object's
  clientX and clientY values and returns a MousePoint object representing the
  object's x and y locations relative to the client area of the window, excluding all
  the chrome. The parseInt function ensures that the values are returned as
  numerics.

- Following is getMouseOffset, which takes as parameters an object target and an
  event. Once the event object has been normalized past the cross-browser differences, the mouse position of the event is set to the function just discussed,

MousePoint. This is then modified against the object's `offsetLeft` and `offsetTop` properties. If we didn't do this bit of computation, the object would move with the mouse, but there would most likely be an odd jerking motion, and the object would seem to float above, below, or to the side of the mouse. Once normalized, it's used to create a normalized `MousePoint`, which is returned from the object.

- The next function is `mouseUp`, and all it does is turn off dragging by setting `dragObject` to `null`. Following is the `mouseMove` function, where most of the dragging computation occurs. In this function, if the dragging object isn't set, the function is exited. Otherwise, the normalized mouse position is found, the object is set to `relative` positioning, and its left and top properties are set (after again being adjusted for offset).

- The last function is `makeDraggable`, which just makes the object passed to the function into a draggable one. This means adding a function for the object's `mouse down` event, which sets the drag object to the object and gets the object's offset value.

This may seem like a lot of code, but it's actually much simpler than it used to be with the older browsers because most modern browsers share the same properties when it comes to positioning. Again, Google Maps adds an extra element of sophistication by using Ajax to continuously refresh the map, so you never run out of map footage. That concept is a little bit beyond the scope of this book, though. Consider it a future personal challenge.

Size and Clipping

You can control an element's size through six CSS attributes. The first two, `width` and `height`, are the most common and you use them to set the absolute width and height of the element. The other four—`min-height`, `min-width`, `max-height`, and `max-width`—are handy CSS attributes (particularly when working with images), but are not commonly used in dynamic effects. In addition, support for the latter four attributes is patchy among most browsers.

 Actually, an element's `width` and `height` are factors of several attributes, including the element's `border`, `margin`, `padding`, and `content`. Combined, these provide a CSS "box model" associated with block elements—elements that force a line break before and after the element. Read more on the box model at the W3C page, "Box model," at *http://www.w3.org/TR/CSS2/box.htm*.

If the element's contents are too large for the element, you can manage the overflow through the CSS `overflow` attribute, which you can set to `visible` (render all of the content and overflow the element boundaries); `hidden` (clip the content); `scroll` (clip the content and provide scroll bars); and `auto` (clip and provide scroll bars only if some of the content is hidden). In Example 12-5, the `overflow` property was set to `hidden`, to clip the area of the image outside the containing `div` element.

Overflow and Dynamic Content

When an element's contents are replaced dynamically, through either an Ajax call or some other event, the fit of the content within the element could change dramatically. One approach to ensuring that the content is always accessible is to set the overflow to `auto`. If the content is too large, scroll bars are then provided. In Example 12-6, two blocks are given: one with a lot of text and one with a little bit of text. One block is set to allow overflow outside the container; the other block clips. Clicking on the web page switches the content between the two blocks so that you can see how each handles the overflow.

Example 12-6. Changing content and the impact of the overflow setting

```
<!DOCTYPE html PUBLIC "-//W3C//DTD XHTML 1.1//EN"
"http://www.w3.org/TR/xhtml11/DTD/xhtml11.dtd">
<html xmlns="http://www.w3.org/1999/xhtml" xml:lang="en">
<head>
<title>Overflow</title>
<meta http-equiv="Content-Type" content="text/html; charset=utf-8" />
<style type="text/css">
div { border: 1px solid #ccc; }
#div1 { width: 400px; height: 150px; overflow: visible; }
#div2 { position: absolute; left: 450px; top: 10px; width: 400px; height: 150px;
overflow: auto }
</style>
<script type="text/javascript">
//<![CDATA[

function switchContent() {
    var div1 = document.getElementById("div1").innerHTML;
    var div2 = document.getElementById("div2").innerHTML;
    document.getElementById("div1").innerHTML = div2;
    document.getElementById("div2").innerHTML = div1;
}

document.onclick=switchContent;

//]]>
</script>
</head>
<body>
<div id="div1">
<p>
One of the first presentation-specific HTML elements was font, and it's also one of
the older HTML elements you still find, all too frequently, in web pages. It's not
surprising that font and text properties were of such interest in building web
pages. Few changes you can make to an element's style attributes can have such an
effect as changing the text or font properties. </p>
<p>
```

```
Notice I say text or font properties. The font has to do with the characters
themselves: their family, size, type, and other elements of the characters'
appearance. The text attributes, though, have more to do with decoration attached
to the text and include text decoration, alignment, and so on.</p></div><div
id="div2"><p>Smaller item.</p>
</div>
</body>
</html>
```

When the page loads, the large text block overflows the container, but the smaller text block has a lot of whitespace. When the content is switched, the first block contains a little text and a lot of whitespace around it. The only way to alter this is to change the dimensions of the box. Unfortunately, in a real-world example, you may not be able to easily determine the appropriate fit for the new content.

The second box, though, suddenly has a scroll bar to the right, which allows you to scroll through the content. Rather than trying to resize the box by guesswork, a better approach is to set the overflow to `auto` and trigger a scroll bar. This way, the box is relatively stable in the page, other elements aren't continuously being pushed about, large blocks with whitespace don't result, and the content is still accessible. Figure 12-2 shows the page when it's first loaded; Figure 12-3 shows the page after the text blocks have been switched.

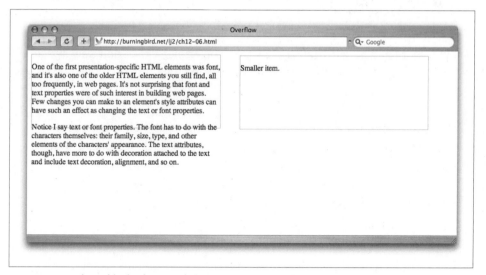

Figure 12-2. A large block of text in the container with overflow set to visible

Another approach to dealing with changing content is to resize the block using the read-only properties `offsetWidth` and `offsetHeight` to determine the actual size of the content. There is a cross-browser difference, though, when using these properties. Internet Explorer includes any border and padding in the block size, whereas Mozilla/Firefox provides just the size necessary for the content.

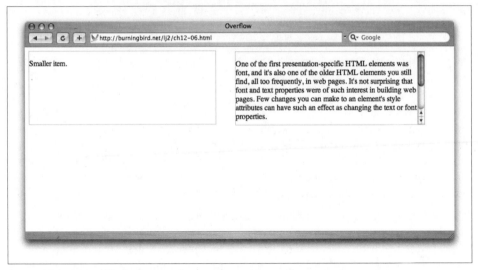

Figure 12-3. A large block of text in the container with overflow set to auto

 You can also access the computed width and height of an element using the getStyle method defined earlier, using `width` and `height` instead of `backgroundColor`.

Though `width` and `height` control the size of the element, they don't always control what's visible of the element. You can control that via the clipping rectangle associated with the element.

The Clipping Rectangle

The CSS `clip` property specifies a shape and the dimensions of that shape. At this time, the only shape the property supports is the rectangle, designated with `rect` and defined by four dimensions: top, right, bottom, and left:

```
clip: rect(topval, rightval, bottomval, leftval);
```

The clipping region constrains how much of the actual element content is displayed. It also requires that the `position` attribute be set to `absolute`.

If an element is 200 pixels wide and 300 pixels long, a clipping region of `rect(0px, 200px,300px,0px)` doesn't clip any of the block—depending, of course, on whether the element has a border or other setting that can alter the effective height and width. A clipping region of `rect(10px,190px,290px,10px)` clips 10 pixels off each side. Note that incrementing the value for the top and left sides or decrementing the value for the bottom and right results in clipping.

From a dynamic web page perspective, you can use clipping to create any form of scrolling effect, whether paired with element movement or not. It can also create the new "accordion effect" that's become so popular with Ajax applications, where clicking on a header seemingly "unscrolls" the content underneath.

Example 12-7 demonstrates a simple use of clipping to create a drop-down animated item. Clicking anywhere in the document either expands or collapses the item, depending on its current state. The example uses a timer to animate the effect; you can also completely clip or unclip the block without the use of the timer if you're not interested in animation.

Example 12-7. Drop-down animation created using a timer and clipping

```
<!DOCTYPE html PUBLIC "-//W3C//DTD XHTML 1.1//EN"
"http://www.w3.org/TR/xhtml11/DTD/xhtml11.dtd">
<html xmlns="http://www.w3.org/1999/xhtml" xml:lang="en">
<head>
<title>Clipping</title>
<meta http-equiv="Content-Type" content="text/html; charset=utf-8" />
<style type="text/css">

#data1     {
           position: absolute;
           top: 100px; left: 100px;
           padding: 0;
           width: 200px;
           height: 200px;
           background-color: #ff0;
           clip: rect(0px,200px,200px,0px);
           }

</style>
<script type="text/javascript">
//<![CDATA[

// globals

var bottom = 200;
var clipped = false;

document.onclick=testItem;

function testItem() {
  if (clipped) {
       unClipItem();
    } else {
       clipItem();
    }
}

function clipItem() {
   bottom-=20;
   var clip = "rect(0px,200px," + bottom + "px,0px)";
   var obj = document.getElementById("data1");
```

```
        obj.style.clip = clip;
        if (bottom == 40) {
            clipped=true;
        } else {
            setTimeout("clipItem()",100);
        }
    }

    function unClipItem() {
        bottom+=20;
        var clip = "rect(0px,200px," + bottom + "px,0px)";
        var obj = document.getElementById("data1");
        obj.style.clip=clip;
        if (bottom == 200) {
            clipped=false;
        } else {
            setTimeout("unClipItem()",100);
        }
    }

    //]]>
    </script>
    </head>
    <body>
    <div id="data1">
    This is the text contained within the div block.
    </div>
    </body>
    </html>
```

When the page is first opened, it contains a longer, yellow box with some text. Clicking in the web page "clips" the box to just the text. Clicking the document again unclips the box.

Notice that rather than get the clipping value directly from the style property to test state, I used a global variable. In Chapter 13, I demonstrate how to create objects and attach both functions and variables to the objects so that you're not strewing global variables all around.

Display, Visibility, and Opacity

An interesting thing about web page elements is that they can be completely transparent and invisible, but still can affect the layout of the page. This is because invisibility/transparency and display/lack of display are not the same thing in CSS.

You can hide an element by setting visibility to hidden, or show it by setting visibility to visible. You also can set the property to inherit, and the element will inherit its visible property setting from the containing element. You can alter an element's opacity until it is completely transparent, making it invisible. However, just as with the visibility property, the element still maintains its position within the page flow.

If an element's `display` property is set to `none`, it's also hidden; however, any effect the element has on the page layout is also removed. To make it visible, you have a couple of options. You can make it visible and have it act as a block-level element (with line breaks before and after the element) by setting `display` to `block`. If you don't want block behavior, you can set `display` to `inline`, and it's displayed in-place and not as a block.

In addition, you can display the element using the default display characteristics of several HTML elements, which include `inline-block`, `table`, `table-cell`, `list-item`, `compact`, `run-in`, and others. It's a rather powerful attribute, and one worth playing around with until you're comfortable with its modifying results.

The Right Tool for the Right Effect

Given all of these ways to hide and display elements, which method should you use for what effect?

If you're absolutely positioning an element and then hiding and showing it based on an event such as a mouse click or form submission, use the `visibility` property. It's easy to use, and an absolutely positioned element is removed from the page flow regardless.

If the hidden content should push down the page elements that follow when it's displayed, such as clicking a collapsed option list when filling out a form, use `display`, switching between a display value of `none` and a display value of `block`.

If you're creating a fade effect or want to deemphasize a page element, use the `opacity` property. You may eventually adjust it so that it's completely transparent, but usually only after an animated fade of whatever duration. Use `opacity` to emphasize and provide visual information. You also can use `opacity` to signal a transition.

 Visual effects for information purposes should also include some textual element so that people using nonvisual browsers or ones with limited visual capability also receive the same level of notification. Never rely completely on a visual effect to provide feedback.

Now it's time for a little live action.

Just-in-Time Information

Some of the best sites I've visited provide some form of help anytime the web page reader requests information. Even if you're asking a person's name, you want to provide an explanation of the privacy controls in place and how that data is used.

You can provide tool-tip style help by setting the `title` attribute of a link surrounding the field label, but this usually constrains how much information you can include. You can also pop up a dialog box with information, which is especially helpful if the information is long and detailed, with a description of options. But for those in-between cases where you have more than a little information but less than a lot, it would be nice to include this information directly in the page.

For the most part, forms take up most of the space on a page, and a lot of text can make the page seem cluttered. One approach is to put the information in the page, but have it show up based on some event.

This is one of the more useful dynamic web page effects you can create, and also one of the easiest. Example 12-8 is the code for the page, including two form elements, each of which has a hidden help block. In the script, when the label for the element is clicked, if any item's help is already showing, the visible help is hidden and the new help block is shown.

Example 12-8. Using hidden help fields

```
<!DOCTYPE html PUBLIC "-//W3C//DTD XHTML 1.1//EN"
"http://www.w3.org/TR/xhtml11/DTD/xhtml11.dtd">
<html xmlns="http://www.w3.org/1999/xhtml" xml:lang="en">
<head>
<title>Just-in-Time Help</title>
<meta http-equiv="Content-Type" content="text/html; charset=utf-8" />
<style type="text/css">
.help { position: absolute;
        left: 300px;
        top: 20px;
        visibility: hidden;
        width: 100px;
        padding: 10px;
        border: 1px solid #ff0000;
      }
form {
   margin: 20px;
   background-color: #dfe1cb;
    padding: 20px;
    width: 200px;
}
label {cursor : help}

</style>

<script type="text/javascript">
//<![CDATA[

window.onload=function() {
   var labels = document.getElementsByTagName("label");
   for (var i = 0; i < labels.length; i++)
      labels[i].onclick=showHelp;
}
```

```
function showHelp(evnt) {
    var theEvent = evnt ? evnt : window.event;
    var theSrc = theEvent.target ? theEvent.target : theEvent.srcElement;

    // hide all first
    var item1 = document.getElementById("item1");
    var item2 = document.getElementById("item2");

    // selectively show right help
    item1.style.visibility="hidden";
    item2.style.visibility="hidden";

    if (theSrc.id == "label1")
        item1.style.visibility="visible";
    else
        item2.style.visibility="visible";

}

//]]>
</script>
</head>
<body>
<form action="">
<p>
<label id="label1">Item One</label>
<input type="text" /><br /><br />
<label id="label2">Item Two</label>
<input type="text" />
</p>
</form>
<div id="item1" class="help">
<p>This is the help for the first item. It only shows when you click on the label
for the item.</p>
</div>
<div id="item2" class="help">
<p>This is the help for the second item. It only shows when you click on the label
for the item.</p>
</div>
</body>
</html>
```

I also added a little CSS sugar to make the page taste better. The form is set with a color background, a help block is outlined in red, and when the mouse cursor is over the input label for each item, the cursor icon is set to the help icon. This typically looks like an arrow with a little question mark, or just the question mark itself. This is also a very inexpensive way to provide a hint to the web page reader. Figure 12-4 demonstrates this hidden help system in action.

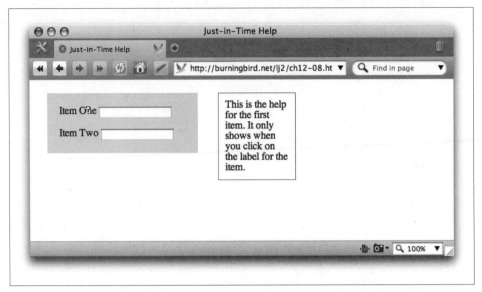

Figure 12-4. In-place help using the visibility property

Revisiting the DOM: Collapsing Forms, Query Selectors, and Class Names

Previously in the book we looked at a couple of different ways to query elements in a web page. The most common method we used was `getElementById`, which gets a specific page element via an identifier. We also used `getElementsByTagName`, which gets all elements via a specific tag name. It would be nice to have some functionality that allows us to get any element via a CSS class name, or even to use CSS selectors, such as the following:

```
div > p:first-child
```

This type of functionality does exist, but it's still quite new and it differs among browsers. Firefox, Opera, and Safari implement a document method, `getElementsByClass Name`, which originated in the work associated with HTML5 and which returns all elements of a given class name:

```
var elems = document.getElementsByClassName('elements');
```

IE8 (in addition to Safari/WebKit) implements another method known as a query selector. This is based on a W3C specification currently in draft format (at *http://www .w3.org/TR/selectors-api/*), which expands on the functionality and allows you to query for elements that match a given selector pattern, such as the following, which is equivalent to the functionality of `getElementsByClassName`:

```
var elems = document.querySelectorAll('.elements');
```

To ensure that the class query selector functionality works across browsers, you can check for querySelectorAll and, if it's not found, use getElementsByClassName:

```
if (document.querySelectorAll) {
    elems = document.querySelectorAll('.elements');
} else if (document.getElementsByClassName) {
    elems = document.getElementsByClassName('elements');
}
```

Now, if document.querySelectorAll is supported, it's used to build the nodeList object, with the list of matching page elements. Otherwise, the getElementsByClassName document method is used to get the same list of nodes.

Being able to get a list of nodes based on CSS selectors is helpful when you don't want to process all elements of a certain type in a page, and instead want to process only those that match a certain CSS selector or class. They'd be especially helpful when implementing a collapsible form.

Having to split forms functionality across many pages is a pain, but a page with too many form elements displayed at once can be unreadable. In addition, in-place editing of data has been growing in popularity: titles for data sections are activated for the person who owns the data, and clicking on these titles opens a form or input fields in which that section of the data can be changed.

Both situations are rich with potential for using a JavaScript-enabled *accordion*: page selections that are displayed only when something is activated, and push the rest of the page's contents down when displayed. Google, Flickr, and a host of companies use this type of collapsible content. Considering that it's also one of the easiest to make accessible, that's not surprising. If JavaScript is not enabled, the event handling associated with the titles that would normally display the content is not active, and the forms don't open. You can add menu items to open a separate page for the form, or perhaps even display them with the noscript tag.

The last example in this chapter, Example 12-9, demonstrates an accordion-enabled form. In this case, it's a stacked set of form-element blocks, all of which are displayed if JavaScript isn't enabled. It uses div elements to make up the clickable labels and collapsible form sections. When the page is loaded, and during the setup routine, rather than access each individual div element within the page and either attach the onclick event or set the element's display property to none, the class query selector functionality just described is used to access all div elements of class elements or class labels and either collapse or attach the event handler, respectively.

Example 12-9. Implementing a collapsible form

```
<!DOCTYPE html PUBLIC "-//W3C//DTD XHTML 1.1//EN"
"http://www.w3.org/TR/xhtml11/DTD/xhtml11.dtd">
<html xmlns="http://www.w3.org/1999/xhtml" xml:lang="en">
<head>
<title>Accordion</title>
<meta http-equiv="Content-Type" content="text/html; charset=utf-8" />
```

```
<style type="text/css">

.label
{
    background-color: #000033;
    width: 400px;
    padding: 10px;
    margin: 0 20px;
    color: #fff;
    text-align: center;
    border-bottom: 1px solid #ffffff;
    cursor: pointer;
}
.elements
{
    background-color: #ccd9ff;
    margin: 0 20px;
    padding: 10px;
    width: 400px;
    display: block;
}
</style>
<script type="text/javascript">
//<![CDATA[

window.onload=function() {
    var elems = null;
    var labels = null;
    if (document.querySelectorAll) {
        elems = document.querySelectorAll('div.elements');
        labels = document.querySelectorAll('div.label');
    } else if (document.getElementsByClassName) {
        elems = document.getElementsByClassName('elements');
        labels = document.getElementsByClassName('label');
    }
    if (elems) {
        for (var i = 0; i < elems.length; i++) {
            elems[i].style.display="none";
        }
        for (var i = 0; i < labels.length; i++) {
            labels[i].onclick=showBlock;
        }
    }

}

function showBlock(evnt) {

    var theEvent = evnt ? evnt : window.event;
    var theSrc = theEvent.target ? theEvent.target : theEvent.srcElement;
    var itemId = "elements" + theSrc.id.substr(5,1);
    var item = document.getElementById(itemId);
    if (item.style.display=='none') {
        item.style.display='block';
    } else {
```

```
            item.style.display='none';
        }
    }

//]]>
</script>
</head>
<body>
<form action="">
<div class="label" id="label1">
Name
</div>
<div class="elements" id="elements1">
<label>First Name:</label><br /><input type="text" name="firstname" /><br /><br />
<label>Last Name:</label><br /><input type="text" name="lastname" /><br /><br />
</div>
<div class="label" id="label2">
Address
</div>
<div class="elements" id="elements2">
<label>Street Address:</label><br /><input type="text" name="street" /><br /><br />
<label>City:</label><br /><input type="text" name="city" /><br /><br />
<label>State:</label><br /><input type="text" name="state" /><br /><br />
</div>
</form>
</body>
</html>
```

The application in Example 12-9 also *gracefully degrades* if neither `querySelectorAll`
nor `getElementsByClassName` is supported: the form sections are not collapsed, and the
page acts as though scripting were disabled. This is also how the application behaves
in IE6.

Clicking the "label" displays the associated section, based on the identifier used for the
label and the collapsed section. You could add several more labels and associated sections, and the JavaScript would not need to change, as long as you use the same class
names and maintain the identifier mapping between labels and elements. Figure 12-5
shows the page loaded in IE8, and Figure 12-6 shows the page with one of the collapsed
sections expanded.

The ability to add any number of new panels to the form may lead you to think how
you can package the accordion functionality into a set of reusable JavaScript functions.
In fact, to simplify the application even further, you could package all of the functionality into one accordion *object*. This leads us to Chapter 13, which covers custom
JavaScript objects.

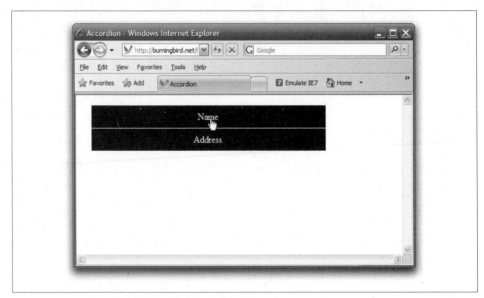

Figure 12-5. An accordion form with all panels collapsed

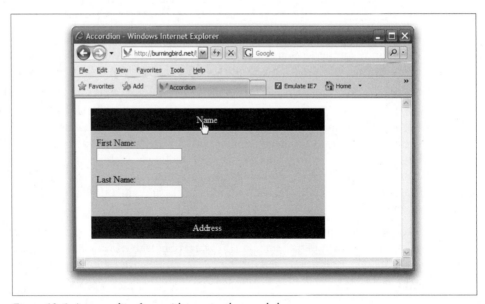

Figure 12-6. An accordion form with one panel expanded

Test Your Knowledge: Quiz

1. Your code tries to access the text color of an element in JavaScript using `obj.style.color`, but no value is returned. You know the font color has been set in a stylesheet. Why is no value returned, and how would you change the application to get a value? Use code to demonstrate your approach by accessing the font color for an element named "name".

2. Given text in a `div` block, how would you change it to display in a 14px font, with a red color and a line height of 16px?

3. If the preceding change didn't work, what could be causing the effect to fail?

4. What are three ways to cause a block to disappear? Demonstrate with code the approach to remove the element completely from the page layout, using the `name` element.

5. If drag-and-drop isn't an effective shopping-cart technique, what dynamic web page effect would be handy for this type of service?

Test Your Knowledge: Answers

1. You can use `getComputedStyle` or `currentStyle`, depending on the browser. Another approach is to set the `style` attribute when the page is loaded.

   ```
   var nameDiv = document.getElementById("name");
   var nameColor;
   if (nameDiv.currentStyle) {
       nameColor = nameDiv.currentStyle['color'];
   } else if (window.getComputedStyle) {
       nameColor =
   document.defaultView.getComputedStyle(nameDiv,null).getPropertyValue('color');
   }
   ```

2. The following is the solution:

   ```
   divElement.style.font="14px/16px";
   divElement.style.color="#ff0000";
   ```

3. If the text in the `div` element is actually contained within another element, such as a paragraph element, and it has different styling, the paragraph style setting will override the outer `div` element's new style setting.

4. To cause a `div` element to disappear, you can either set the width or height to 0, or clip the element completely. You can also set the visibility of the element to `hidden`, or the display to `none`. Lastly, you can move the element all the way off the page, to the top or left. To remove the element from the layout, you'll want to change the display attribute:

```
var nameDiv = document.getElementById("name");
name.style.display="none";
```

5. Rather than using drag-and-drop, attach a mouse click event handler to a link or image that states something to the effect of "Buy me!" When the click event handler is triggered, you can add code to your application to automatically add the item to the shopping cart.

CHAPTER 13

Creating Custom JavaScript Objects

Previous chapters made use of existing objects, defined as part of the JavaScript language or inherited as part of the browser Document Object Model (DOM). This chapter focuses on how you can create your own custom JavaScript objects and package them for reuse across many applications.

The JavaScript Object and Prototyping

An object in JavaScript is a complex construct usually consisting of a constructor as well as zero or more methods and/or properties. Additionally, all objects in JavaScript derive functionality from the standard JavaScript `Object`.

The `Object` itself is not particularly interesting. What `Object` does is provide the framework for creating new objects. Unlike in other programming languages, though, the JavaScript `Object` doesn't provide framework functionality to new objects via traditional object-oriented inheritance and the concept of classes. Instead, JavaScript derives its object functionality from a concept called *prototyping*.

Prototyping

In a language such as Java or C++, to create a class as an extension of another, you define the class in such a way that it *inherits* the functionality of the higher-level object and overrides whatever functionality you don't want.

JavaScript, on the other hand, provides for a constructor, via `Object`, that allows you to create new objects. It is the `Object` constructor that allocates the memory for the object, including all of its properties. The `Object` also provides a `prototype` property that enables you to extend any object, including the built-in ones such as `String` and `Number`. You use this `prototype` to derive new object methods and properties, rather than class inheritance:

```
Number.prototype.add=function(val1,val2) { return val1 + val2; };
var num = new Number();
```

```
num.prototype.add = function(val1,
var sum = num.add(8,3); // sum is 11
```

In earlier chapters, you saw demonstrations of the dynamic nature of JavaScript, and how you can add new methods and properties to objects at runtime. There's a difference between adding a new property or method to an instance of an object and extending the object through **prototype**, though. The following code is not the same as the preceding code snippet because the **add** method now applies only to the object instance, and not to all instances of an object:

```
var num = new Number();
num.add=function(val1,val2) { return val1 + val2; };
var sum = num.add(8,3);
```

When you extend an object through **prototype**, the method or property is available to all instances of the object. When you extend an object *instance* with a new property or method, it's available only to the instance.

The concept of extending objects via prototyping is best explained through a demonstration. Example 13-1 demonstrates how to extend the built-in **String** object by defining a new method, **trim**, using the underlying **Object prototype** property. The **trim** method trims leading and trailing whitespace from the string.

Example 13-1. A first look at JavaScript object creation and prototyping

```
<!DOCTYPE html PUBLIC "-//W3C//DTD XHTML 1.1//EN"
"http://www.w3.org/TR/xhtml11/DTD/xhtml11.dtd">
<html xmlns="http://www.w3.org/1999/xhtml" xml:lang="en">
<head>
<title>String trim</title>
<meta http-equiv="Content-Type" content="text/html; charset=utf-8" />
<script type="text/javascript">
//<![CDATA[

String.prototype.trim = function() {
  return (this.replace(/^[\s\xA0]+/, "").replace(/[\s\xA0]+$/, ""));
}

window.onload=function() {
    var sObj = new String("  This is the string  ");
    document.writeln("--" + sObj + "--" + "<br />");

    var sTxt = sObj.trim();
    document.writeln("--" + sTxt + "--");
}
//]]>
</script>
</head>
<body>
<p>some content</p>
</body>
</html>
```

The application outputs the following to the page:

```
-- This is the string --
--This is the string--
```

Though browsers strip repeating spaces when a page is rendered, one space remains with the first string, which is subsequently trimmed in the second string with the new String method.

With the prototype property, any use of String within the page or pages using this code now has access to this new trim function in addition to the older String object's methods and properties. We haven't created a new object class that's inherited from another so much as we've taken an existing object and extended its functionality. That's the basic difference between a class-based system and one that uses prototyping.

To repeat what I wrote earlier, instead of using prototype with the example, I could have created a static trim function:

```
var str = " this is a string ";
str.trim = function() ...
```

However, only the instance would have access to the function, and I wanted to extend the actual String object itself; hence, the use of prototype. Every object in JavaScript, including those you create yourself, has a prototype property that allows the object to be extended.

How does the prototype property work when the method is accessed? When the method is invoked on the object, the JavaScript engine first looks for the property/method among those associated with the initial object implementation. If it doesn't find it, it then looks within the prototype collection to see whether the property/method exists. Only if the engine cannot find the property or method as part of the global object's implementation or the prototype collection does it search for it locally, attached to the variable.

Of course, extending an existing object has risks because new versions of JavaScript may extend the object with method names similar to your own, but with different behavior. If this happens, your functionality would be overridden, and your applications could fail.

As you create increasingly sophisticated JavaScript applications, you're going to want to package your code into reusable components. The next section covers creating your own custom JavaScript objects and building reusable libraries.

The upcoming version of ECMAScript, most like named Edition 3.1 or 4, will feature a new method on the JavaScript Object: Object.freeze. From my reading, this method should "freeze" an object, not allowing any extensions to the object via the prototype. This allows JavaScript to emulate a class-based language, where classes are immutable (not changeable).

Creating Your Own Custom JavaScript Objects

In the rest of the book, which covers the JavaScript functionality loosely grouped under the term *Ajax*, you'll see how much you must improvise to create objects using JavaScript. At times, Ajax libraries you can download look almost as though they're built in a language other than JavaScript. In fact, many were built specifically to overlay the JavaScript language with other language characteristics, which has advantages and disadvantages.

An advantage to these modern manipulations of the JavaScript language is that the library provides shortcuts for some of the more tedious operations, such as accessing page elements. Laying another language's flavor over JavaScript may also simplify such operations if you use this language as the server-side component in an Ajax application.

The disadvantage is that this effort obfuscates the underlying JavaScript, making the library hard to read, hard to use, and confusing if you're not necessarily up on all the latest language advances.

> One of the best essays I've read on the ambivalence associated with some of the clever and powerful (but obscure) component libraries is "Painless JavaScript Using Prototype," by Dan Webb (at *http://www.sitepoint .com/article/painless-javascript-prototype*).

Returning to the topic of creating objects, we find an old friend—the function—at the heart of the capability.

Enter the Function

For close to a decade now, when you create a custom object in JavaScript, you use functions. There have been some changes in how the functions are written, how private and public properties are defined, and even how those properties are packaged, but fundamentally, if you want to create a new custom object in JavaScript, you start with the function.

> A *private* property or method in object-oriented development is one that you can access internally and only from another method on the same object. You can access a *public* property or method outside the object. I cover both in more detail later in the chapter.

In Example 13-2, JavaScript creates a very simple object, `Tune`, which takes one parameter, a song title, which is assigned to the `Tune` object's `title`. The object also incorporates an array of performers, which you can manipulate via two methods: `addPerformer` (which takes a string) and `listPerformers` (which takes no parameters).

Example 13-2. Creating a custom object

```
<!DOCTYPE html PUBLIC "-//W3C//DTD XHTML 1.1//EN"
"http://www.w3.org/TR/xhtml11/DTD/xhtml11.dtd">
<html xmlns="http://www.w3.org/1999/xhtml" xml:lang="en">
<head>
<title>Tune Object</title>
<meta http-equiv="Content-Type" content="text/html; charset=utf-8" />
<script type="text/javascript">
//<![CDATA[

var Tune = function(title) {
    this.title = title;
    var performedBy = new Array();
    this.addPerformer = function (performer) {
        var i = performedBy.length;
        performedBy[i] = performer;
    }
    this.listPerformers = function() {
        var singers = "";
        for (var i = 0; i < performedBy.length; i++ ) {
            singers += performedBy[i] + " ";
        }
        return singers;
    }
}

window.onload=function () {
    var song = new Tune("Hello");
    song.addPerformer("Me");
    song.addPerformer("You");
    song.addPerformer("Us");
    document.writeln("Song is " + song.title);
    document.writeln("Performed by " + song.listPerformers());
}
//]]>
</script>
</head>
<body>
<p>some content</p>
</body>
</html>
```

In the page, an instance of `Tune` is created using the `Object` constructor, passing in a song title, "Hello." The `addPerformer` method is called three times, passing in three performers: `Me`, `You`, and `Us`. The `listPerformers` method is called, which traverses the array of performers, creating a string from the contents, which is then returned. In the application, the song and the performers are printed to the page.

Going into greater detail, the JavaScript creates a function with the same name as the object, `Tune`. Remember from past chapters that all functions in JavaScript are also objects, so by creating this function you are, in effect, creating your custom object.

Within the function are two properties and two methods. In this example, the code blocks to implement both methods are included as part of the object declaration. Though this isn't a requirement of JavaScript, it is a good practice to make the object easier to maintain and to limit the number of global objects in the application. Still, you can create the function outside the object and just assign the function name to the object member:

```
function externalAddPerformer(performer) {
   ...
}
...
this.addPerformer = externalAddPerformer;
```

Another approach to creating a custom object is to create an instance of the object, and then use the object's **prototype** to assign properties and methods. Example 13-3 demonstrates this approach with a variation on the **Tune** object, but this time I'm using **prototype** to assign a function to an object method.

Example 13-3. Using prototype to assign properties and/or methods

```
<!DOCTYPE html PUBLIC "-//W3C//DTD XHTML 1.1//EN"
"http://www.w3.org/TR/xhtml11/DTD/xhtml11.dtd">
<html xmlns="http://www.w3.org/1999/xhtml" xml:lang="en">
<head>
<title>Tune Object</title>
<meta http-equiv="Content-Type" content="text/html; charset=utf-8" />
<script type="text/javascript">
//<![CDATA[

function Tune (title) {
   this.title = title;
}
function printTitle() {
   document.writeln(this.title + "<br />");
}

window.onload=function() {
   Tune.prototype.print = printTitle;

   var oneTune = new Tune("One Title");
   oneTune.print();

   var anotherTune = new Tune("Another Title");
   anotherTune.print();
}

//]]>
</script>
</head>
<body>
<p>some content</p>
</body>
</html>
```

All new objects in JavaScript inherit from `Object`, which means that all have a `prototype` property, including the custom object, `Tune`. In the example, instead of adding a method directly to the object, a global function is created to print out the song title, and then is added to the `Tune` object using `prototype`.

Using `prototype` is easy and popular. However, using the `prototype` property in this way has risks, not the least of which is the possibility that you'll override an existing method or property, or that another application will override yours. One popular Ajax library, *Prototype.js*, makes extensive use of the `prototype` property to expand functionality on the `Array` object, as well as `Object` itself. One of the problems with using *Prototype.js*, though, is that you more or less have to use this library only, as it doesn't necessarily play well with other applications because of its extensive use of `prototype` to extend the standard JavaScript objects.

 You can access *Prototype.js* at *http://www.prototypejs.org/*.

I used the `this` keyword to assign the title to the object `title` property in both examples. I also used it with the methods in the first example, but not with the `song` array. The use of `this` signals a difference between a public and a private member within a JavaScript object, which I discuss next.

Public and Private Properties and Where this Enters the Picture

Examples 13-2 and 13-3 use the `this` keyword to assign the parameter, `title`, passed during the creation of the object, to a property, `title`, of the object. `this` acts as a reference to the parent object, which is an instance of the new object we're creating. What `this` does is create a public property that is accessible outside the object, as I demonstrated when we printed the song title:

```
document.writeln("Song is " + song.title);
```

The use of `this` is also associated with the two methods, `addPerformer` and `listPerformers`, in the first example. The `performers` array, though, is not assigned to the object using `this`; instead, it's created using the variable keyword `var`. Using `var` rather than `this` makes the property a private one—accessible internally to the object (including to its methods) but not outside the object.

Why have private rather than public variables? Primarily for data hiding—protecting data from direct application access.

Sometimes you don't want application developers to directly access object data, though. They may end up making the object unusable or may inadvertently cause an unwanted side effect. Usually, you'll provide methods to get and set this data, rather than have it accessible as a property. To hide such data in JavaScript, you create it as a private member, with `var`, rather than as a public member, with `this`.

Beginning with the next version of ECMAScript, new functionality known as getters and setters is being added specifically to make it easier to manage private data in JavaScript objects.

Getters and Setters

One of the modifications that will be added to the next formal release of ECMAScript, and that will be implemented in at least a few target browsers, is the concept of *getters* and *setters*. Getters and setters are ways of retrieving and setting data in an object. One approach to add the getter/setter to an object is to add the functionality after the object has been defined.

Example 13-4 duplicates the code in Example 13-3, but instead of sending the title through the object constructor, it uses a getter and setter to manage the data and adds them after the object has been defined.

Example 13-4. Demonstrating the use of getter and setter

```
<!DOCTYPE html PUBLIC "-//W3C//DTD XHTML 1.1//EN"
"http://www.w3.org/TR/xhtml11/DTD/xhtml11.dtd">
<html xmlns="http://www.w3.org/1999/xhtml" xml:lang="en">
<head>
<title>Getters and Setters</title>
<meta http-equiv="Content-Type" content="text/html; charset=utf-8" />
<script type="text/javascript">
//<![CDATA[

// Tune is basically a shell object
function Tune () {

}

// method
function printTitle() {
   document.writeln(this.title + "<br />");
}

window.onload=function() {

   // extend object through prototype
   var t = Tune.prototype;

   // getter and setter
   t.__defineGetter__("title", function() { return "Title is " + this.myTitle; });
   t.__defineSetter__("title", function(tt) { this.myTitle = tt; });

   t.print = printTitle;

   var oneTune = new Tune;
```

```
    oneTune.title = "One Title";
    oneTune.print();

    var anotherTune = new Tune;
    anotherTune.title="Another Title";
    anotherTune.print();
}

//]]>
</script>
</head>
<body>
<p>some content</p>
</body>
</html>
```

The getter and setter are emphasized in the code. You should follow the syntax as it appears in the example, including the use of the two underscore characters before and after the `defineGetter` and `defineSetter` keywords, and the use of `prototype` in the assignment. Following in parentheses is the data member, in this case `title`, and the functions that will set and get the data.

To use the getter and setter, you assign the value for the data field directly, and then access it directly. Notice, though, that the data field you access externally is not named the same as the actual data field. Also notice that I added a string to the title in the getter. This is to test that the getter and setter are working.

 Another approach is to use the getter and setter with an object literal, or the one-off type of object I describe later in this chapter. You can find an example of this approach at *http://developer.mozilla.org/En/Core _JavaScript_1.5_Guide:Creating_New_Objects:Defining_Getters_and _Setters*.

The examples so far have passed basic JavaScript objects (`String`s) as parameters. You can also use custom objects to wrap existing page elements in a form of encapsulation—an effective way to deal with browser differences. The next section covers this JavaScript object encapsulation.

Object Encapsulation

Earlier, I touched on the ability to pass a page object in as a parameter when constructing a new object. The custom object then wraps, or encapsulates, the page object, allowing you to create a set of functionality that hides most of the implementation details. When using a library that has this capability, instead of having to provide all of the JavaScript yourself to change the properties of a page element—say, its opacity—you can just call a method that changes it for you.

If the underlying implementation changes because of what the browser supports, object encapsulation can hide all of the details for managing the new implementation. The applications themselves don't have to change. Hiding browser-specific details makes sophisticated interactive and dynamic applications so much easier to develop.

Additionally, you no longer have to run a continuous set of operations that check whether the browser supports a given functionality. Your code, or the JavaScript library you're using, checks it upfront when the objects are created (usually when the page loads).

Example 13-5 is an application that demonstrates how object encapsulation can work in JavaScript, and how to manage cross-browser differences. The application includes a tiny object library that manages opacity. The page has two `div` elements, each containing an image. Both elements are positioned absolutely in the page: one is opaque, the other transparent. When the page loads, a function is called that creates an instance of the custom object, passing in each `div` element in turn. The first element's `opacity` is set to 1.0 (visible); the second is set to 0 (completely transparent). Clicking the page decreases the opacity of the visible object and increases the opacity of the originally invisible object, creating a transformation effect between the two objects.

Example 13-5. Object encapsulation

```
<!DOCTYPE html PUBLIC "-//W3C//DTD XHTML 1.1//EN"
"http://www.w3.org/TR/xhtml11/DTD/xhtml11.dtd">
<html xmlns="http://www.w3.org/1999/xhtml" xml:lang="en">
<head>
<title>Encapsulating</title>
<meta http-equiv="Content-Type" content="text/html; charset=utf-8" />
<meta http-equiv="X-UA-Compatible" content="IE=EmulateIE7" />
<style type="text/css">
div {
        position: absolute;
        top: 30px;
        left: 50px;
    }
#div2 {
        opacity: 0.0; filter: alpha(opacity=0);
}
#div1 img {
filter:
progid:DXImageTransform.Microsoft.AlphaImageLoader(src=fig0902.png,
sizingMethod='scale');
}
#div2 img {
filter:
progid:DXImageTransform.Microsoft.AlphaImageLoader(src=fig0903.png,
sizingMethod='scale');
}

</style>
<script type="text/javascript">
//<![CDATA[
```

```
    // global
    var theobjs = new Array();

    document.onclick=function() {

        // fade div1
        var currentOpacity = theobjs["div1"].objGetOpacity();

        // end of transform
        if (currentOpacity <= 0) {
            document.onclick=null;
            return;
        }

        currentOpacity-=0.1;
        theobjs["div1"].objSetOpacity(currentOpacity);

        // reveal div2
        currentOpacity = theobjs["div2"].objGetOpacity();
        currentOpacity+=0.1;
        theobjs["div2"].objSetOpacity(currentOpacity);
    }

    function DivObj(obj) {
        this.obj = obj;

        this.getAlphaOpacity = function () {
            var fltr = this.obj.style.filter;
            var indx1 = fltr.indexOf("opacity=");
            var indx2 = fltr.indexOf(")");
            fltr = fltr.substring(indx1+8,indx2) / 100;
            return fltr;
        };
        this.getCSSOpacity = function() {
            return parseFloat(this.obj.style.opacity);
        }
        this.objGetOpacity = (this.obj.style.filter === undefined) ? this.getCSSOpacity:
    this.getAlphaOpacity;
        this.alphaOpacity = function(value) {
            var opacity = value * 100;
            this.obj.style.filter="alpha(opacity="+opacity+")";
        };
        this.cssOpacity = function(value) {
            this.obj.style.opacity=value;
        };
        this.objSetOpacity = (this.obj.style.filter === undefined) ? this.cssOpacity :
    this.alphaOpacity;

    }

    window.onload=function() {

        theobjs["div1"] = new DivObj(document.getElementById("div1"));
        theobjs["div2"] = new DivObj(document.getElementById("div2"));
```

```
  // set initial opacity
  theobjs["div1"].objSetOpacity(1.0);
  theobjs["div2"].objSetOpacity(0.0);
}

//]]>
</script>
</head>
<body>
<div id="div1">
<img src="fig0902.png" alt="" />
</div>
<div id="div2">
<img src="fig0903.png" alt="" />
</div>
</body>
</html>
```

Figure 13-1 shows the page in mid-transformation in Safari. And though there are challenges to using opacity because of IE8's partial support for opacity (discussed in Chapter 6), the application works for all the target browsers (including IE7 and IE8, but not IE6), as Figure 13-2 demonstrates.

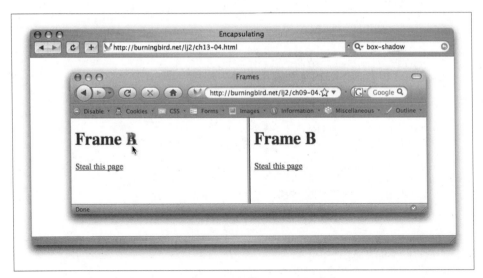

Figure 13-1. Testing the opacity cross-browser implementation in Safari

In the application, to maintain a connection between the page element and the object that encapsulates it, when the new object is created the page element is passed, by reference, to the object. This page element is assigned to a new property on the object, obj. When you adjust the opacity then, you access the page element via this object property. Although the custom object exists, this reference to the page element also

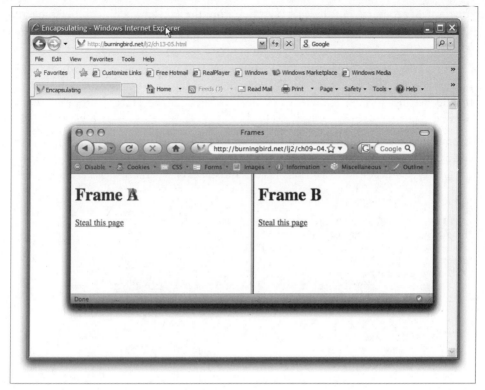

Figure 13-2. Testing the opacity cross-browser implementation in IE8

exists, unless you deliberately delete or modify the object property or delete the page element.

```
theobjs["div1"].obj = null;
```

To better protect against accidental modification of the property, you could modify the code to assign the page element to an internal variable within the custom object:

```
var pageElement = obj;
```

Now, the only functions that can access the custom object's encapsulated page element are those that are methods on the same object:

```
this.pageElement.style.opacity=value;
```

The use of object detection, custom objects, and encapsulation is not as important today as it was in the past when dynamic page effect support varied rather significantly among browsers. However, it's still a great way to hide browser differences, not to mention enforce the old "code once, use many times" philosophy of application development.

It's also an effective approach to use to package functionality into reusable objects even if cross-browser differences aren't an issue. Returning to Example 13-5, notice that the functionality to parse out the opacity value from the filter is a bit cumbersome and dependent on whitespace, which may not be guaranteed across all uses. Compare that with the simplicity of CSS attribute access.

However, thanks to the prototype capability of JavaScript (mentioned earlier) there's no reason why you can't use the CSS attribute setting as a way to store the current opacity setting. In fact, there's no reason you can't set the filter "property" for all browsers, either.

Example 13-6 is a modification of the program in Example 13-5, except this time the code is simplified to pull in the existing opacity setting just from an opacity property on the style object and to set both filter and opacity when the value is changed.

Example 13-6. A simplified opacity encapsulating object

```
<!DOCTYPE html PUBLIC "-//W3C//DTD XHTML 1.1//EN"
"http://www.w3.org/TR/xhtml11/DTD/xhtml11.dtd">
<html xmlns="http://www.w3.org/1999/xhtml" xml:lang="en">
<head>
<title>Encapsulating</title>
<meta http-equiv="Content-Type" content="text/html; charset=utf-8" />
<meta http-equiv="X-UA-Compatible" content="IE=EmulateIE7" />
<style type="text/css">
div {
        position: absolute;
        top: 30px;
        left: 50px;
    }
#div2 {
      opacity: 0.0; filter: alpha(opacity=0);
}
#div1 img {
filter:
progid:DXImageTransform.Microsoft.AlphaImageLoader(src=fig0902.png,
sizingMethod='scale');
}
#div2 img {
filter:
progid:DXImageTransform.Microsoft.AlphaImageLoader(src=fig0903.png,
sizingMethod='scale');
}

</style>
<script type="text/javascript">
//<![CDATA[


// global
var theobjs = new Array();
document.onclick=function() {

    // fade div1
    var currentOpacity = theobjs["div1"].objGetOpacity();
```

```
      // end of transform
      if (currentOpacity <= 0) {
         document.onclick=null;
         return;
      }

      currentOpacity-=0.1;
      theobjs["div1"].objSetOpacity(currentOpacity);

      // reveal div2
      currentOpacity = theobjs["div2"].objGetOpacity();
      currentOpacity+=0.1;
      theobjs["div2"].objSetOpacity(currentOpacity);
   }

function DivObj(obj) {
      this.obj = obj;

      this.objGetOpacity = function() {
         return parseFloat(this.obj.style.opacity);
      }

      this.alphaOpacity = function(value) {
         var opacity = value * 100;
         this.obj.style.filter="alpha(opacity="+opacity+")";
      };
      this.cssOpacity = function(value) {
         this.obj.style.opacity=value;
      };
      this.objSetOpacity=function(value) {
          this.alphaOpacity(value);
          this.cssOpacity(value);
       }

   }
window.onload=function() {

    theobjs["div1"] = new DivObj(document.getElementById("div1"));
    theobjs["div2"] = new DivObj(document.getElementById("div2"));

    // set initial opacity
    theobjs["div1"].objSetOpacity(1.0);
    theobjs["div2"].objSetOpacity(0.0);
}

//]]>
</script>
</head>
<body>
<div id="div1">
<img src="fig0902.png" alt="" />
</div>
<div id="div2">
<img src="fig0903.png" alt="" />
</div>
```

```
</body>
</html>
```

Again, the application works in all the target browsers (except for IE6). How could this be, when IE doesn't currently support `style.opacity` and Opera, Safari, and Firefox don't support `filter` opacity?

All four browsers support the `prototype` object in JavaScript, which means that new properties can be added dynamically to any scripting object. This includes an `opacity` property on the `style` object for IE, as well as the `filter` property for the other browsers. Because the CSS style setting works for three browsers, and the filter setting for the fourth, the opacity change still works for all four. In addition, as the `opacity` setting in the CSS `style` property is so simple to access, it's also used as a "state-saving mechanism" for IE, even though assigning a value to this property doesn't really "change" anything in the page.

Using a combination of prototype and object encapsulation can really simplify cross-browser implementations. As handy as JavaScript's prototype nature is, though, sometimes you may want a more traditional object-oriented approach to development. An example is the concept of class inheritance.

Chaining Constructors and JavaScript Inheritance

JavaScript is not a typical object-oriented language, and you shouldn't push, pummel, or constrain it into one. It has its own strengths, which you should use to your advantage. Still, certain pieces of traditional object-oriented design would be nice to use in applications. In the preceding section, you saw one type of object-oriented design: encapsulation. This section covers another: inheritance.

Inheritance allows one object's methods and properties to be inherited by another object. It's the fundamental power of class-oriented development because one class can inherit from another class, choosing to override whatever functions have a new behavior in the new class.

You can use something similar in JavaScript to emulate this behavior, starting with JavaScript 1.3—the function methods of `apply` and `call`.

 The `apply` and `call` methods are rather tricky, and new developers may find them a little difficult to understand. Don't be surprised if it takes you a little time to wrap your mind around both.

The `apply` function allows you to apply a method on another object, but within the context of a different object, the one that's calling the `apply` function. It takes two parameters: the calling object's context, represented by `this`, and a variable representing an array of arguments for the second object's method. The `call` function is similar

---

to `apply`, except that instead of having to add all of the second object's method arguments to an array, you can list them out individually.

Returning to previous examples, when a function defining a new object is written, it becomes the object constructor and is invoked when the new keyword is used with the function:

```
theobj = new DivObj(params);
```

Both the function `apply` and `call` methods allow you to invoke a method within the context of another object. If used with an object constructor, it chains the constructors in such a way that all properties and methods of the one object are inherited by the containing object. The only difference between the two is the parameters passed; the behavior is the same. The `call` method takes the containing object as the first parameter, identified using `this`, and each argument you want to pass to the constructor of the contained object:

```
obj.call(this,arg1,arg2,..., argn);
```

The `apply` method takes a reference to the containing object and the `arguments` array of the container. If the contained object has two parameters and the container has three, only the first two arguments of the `arguments` array are passed to the contained object:

```
obj.apply(this,arguments);
```

If you're sharing a set of arguments, use `apply`. Otherwise, use `call`.

You can use both functions to *chain constructors* in JavaScript. Example 13-7 uses `apply` and chained constructors to emulate object-oriented inheritance. The first object created, `Tune`, stores information about a song's `title` and `type`. It also has a method that returns a string containing both. The second object, `Artist_tune`, also contains a property for the `artist`, as well as a function to create a string of all properties. The `apply` method is called directly off the `tune` function/object. In addition, once both objects are defined, the `Artist_tune prototype` is assigned the `tune` constructor.

Example 13-7. Chained constructors and inheritance through the apply function method

```
<!DOCTYPE html PUBLIC "-//W3C//DTD XHTML 1.1//EN"
"http://www.w3.org/TR/xhtml11/DTD/xhtml11.dtd">
<html xmlns="http://www.w3.org/1999/xhtml" xml:lang="en">
<head>
<title>Constructor Chaining</title>
<meta http-equiv="Content-Type" content="text/html; charset=utf-8" />
<script type="text/javascript">
//<![CDATA[

function Tune(title,type) {
   this.title = title;
   this.type = type;
   this.getTitle=function() {
     return "Song: " + this.title + " Type: " + this.type;
   }
}
```

```
function Artist_tune(title,type,artist) {
   this.artist = artist;
   this.toString("Artist is " + artist);
   Tune.apply(this,arguments);
   this.toString = function () {
      return "Artist: " + this.artist + " " + this.getTitle();
   }
}

window.onload=function() {
   Artist_tune.prototype = new Tune();

   var song = new Artist_tune("I want to hold your hand", "rock", "Beatles");
   document.writeln(song.toString());
}

//]]>
</script>
</head>
<body>
<p>some content</p>
</body>
</html>
```

An instance of the Tune object is added as a property to the Artist_tune object, which chains the constructors of both together through the use of the apply function. By doing this action, when I go to print the song information in Artist_tune using the method toString, the object context, represented by this, applies with both objects to pull in the artist (from Artist_tune) and song title (from Tune).

Constructor chaining is extremely prevalent within Ajax applications, especially as a way to bind an event handler to an object in such a way that the event handler function not only has a reference to the event object typically passed to the function, but also has a reference to the object context, passed as the first parameter thanks to the intervention of call or apply. I have a small library I use for some of my own effects that uses this approach when binding event handlers to objects when I create object libraries. The relevant code is:

```
bindEventListener : function(obj, method) {
   return function(event) { method.call(obj, event || window.event)};
},

bindObjMethod : function (obj, method) {
   return function() { method.apply(obj, arguments); }
},...
```

Hold on, though; this doesn't look like the object implementation code you've seen in previous examples. That's because my object library is based on a concept I like to call the *one-off object*.

One-Off Objects

When it comes to encapsulating objects, you'll want to use the approaches I described in the preceding section when you want to create multiple instances of objects. Sometimes, though, all you want is just one object, an instance of what I call the *one-off object*. Why one-off? Because you have only one instance of the object—the object itself.

You construct a one-off object from a JavaScript *object literal*, an associative array of properties and methods, all assigned to one variable:

```
var oneOff = {
    variablea : "valuea",
    variableb : "valueb",
    method : function () {
        return this.variablea + " " + this.variableb;
    }
}
```

In the preceding code snippet, the name-value pairs comprising the object literal are surrounded by curly braces, and the whole thing is assigned to a variable, `oneOff`. Since all objects are functions, and all functions are objects in JavaScript, you can add a method to the object literal just like the other static, nonmethod properties. To access the one-off members, the method uses named-array notation, but outside the object, it uses the standard property operator:

```
alert(oneOff.variablea);
alert(oneOff.method());
```

Another approach to creating the same one-off object is to use the following:

```
var oneOff = new Object();
oneOff.variablea = "valuea";
oneOff.variableb = "valueb";
oneOff.method = function () {
                    return this.variablea + " " + this.variableb;
                };
```

You can construct a new object from the actual `Object`, and then add properties and methods to the object instance. You don't use `prototype`, because you're not adding new properties or methods to an underlying object; you're adding them to an object instance directly. The method accesses the parent object's other properties using `this` and just provides a named property.

Here's how to access the properties for the second approach:

```
alert(oneOff2.variableb);
alert(oneOff2.method());
```

The first and second approaches access the object properties in the same way.

The last approach I'll show to create a one-off object creates an instance of the `Function` object:

```
var oneOff = new Function() {
        this.variablea = "variablea";
        this.variableb = "variableb";
        this.method = function () {
                    return this.variablea + " " + this.variableb;
        }
    }
```

Again, this approach accesses the object properties in the same way as the other two.

You can use a one-off object when you need to encapsulate a group of methods and properties into one object, and then reuse this object throughout your entire application. You don't need many instances of the object—just one.

Earlier in the book, I mentioned how you want to avoid globals as much as possible. However, you can't always store whatever information you need in local variables. A compromise between a bunch of single-value global variables and no access to global information at all (except for something such as cookies) is the use of a one-off object library.

Example 13-8 creates a one-off object named `flipper`, which has three methods: `get Style`, `setBackgroundColor`, and `flipColors`. Its purpose is to hold a reference to two `div` elements, and every time the `document` is clicked, the colors for both objects are switched. The object will get the stylesheet setting for a given style, set the background color of an element, and flip the background colors of two elements, respectively.

Example 13-8. A one-off/object literal object that flips background colors given two elements

```
<!DOCTYPE html PUBLIC "-//W3C//DTD XHTML 1.1//EN"
"http://www.w3.org/TR/xhtml11/DTD/xhtml11.dtd">
<html xmlns="http://www.w3.org/1999/xhtml" xml:lang="en">
<head>
<title>One-Off/Object Literal</title>
<meta http-equiv="Content-Type" content="text/html; charset=utf-8" />
<style type="text/css">
div
{
   margin: 20px;
   width: 200px; height: 200px
}
#div1
{
   background-color: #ffff00;
}
#div2
{
   background-color: #00ff00;
}
</style>
<script type="text/javascript">
//<![CDATA[

var flipper = {
   obj1 : null,
```

```
        obj2 : null,
        getStyle : function (obj, jsStyleName, styleName) {
            if (obj.currentStyle) {
                return obj.currentStyle[jsStyleName];
            } else if (window.getComputedStyle) {
                return
document.defaultView.getComputedStyle(obj,null).getPropertyValue(styleName);
            } else {
                return undefined;
            }
        },
        setBackgroundColor : function(obj, color) {
            obj.style.backgroundColor=color;
        },
        flipColors : function()  {
            var color1 = this.getStyle(this.obj1, "backgroundColor", "background-color");
            var color2 = this.getStyle(this.obj2, "backgroundColor", "background-color");
            this.setBackgroundColor(this.obj1,color2);
            this.setBackgroundColor(this.obj2,color1);
        }
};

window.onload = function() {
    flipper.obj1 = document.getElementById("div1");
    flipper.obj2 = document.getElementById("div2");
}

document.onclick = function() {
    flipper.flipColors();
}

//]]>
</script>
</head>
<body>
<div id="div1">
<p>This is first square</p>
</div>
<div id="div2">
<p>This is the second square</p>
</div>
</body>
</html>
```

When the page is loaded, clicking anywhere in the page flips the background colors of the two elements in the page. Of course, you can duplicate this functionality by adding several global functions and variables, but not as cleanly, or safely (in a multilibrary environment). Plus, it's not as easy to package or maintain.

 I gave the earlier encapsulating object a capitalized name, but I gave the object literals/one-offs lowercase names. This is a fairly widespread convention to be able to distinguish among objects that you can instantiate (with new) and objects that are not instantiated.

Of course, this is a lot of work for a single use. Objects, whether literal or not, are usually packaged in separate files to simplify their reuse.

Object Libraries: Packaging Your Objects for Reuse

I contained the examples in the book within one file, and this includes the JavaScript, the CSS, and so on. I did this to make the examples as easy to replicate as possible, and to make the functionality currently being demonstrated easier to see.

For your applications, though, you're going to want to put your JavaScript into a separate file or files, each with a *.js* extension. Packaging the JavaScript separately makes it easier to make code changes and to see what's happening in the code. The next question, then, is how many JavaScript files do you want to create? After all, each adds to the overhead of the page.

A good rule of thumb to follow when packaging your JavaScript is to isolate your objects into different layers of access, processes, or business methods. As an example, I have a set of cross-browser dynamic web effect objects that I use for a set of animation objects packaged in a separate library. The dynamic effect objects are in one file, and the animation objects are in another. By packaging the libraries separately, my applications can access the static effects library without having to also access the animation objects. I can keep my files as small as possible, and then incorporate as many as I need into my web pages.

I also have separate libraries for expanding photos, creating an accordion effect, and using external Ajax libraries for various effects. Each gets its own script tag:

```
<script type="text/javascript" src="flipper.js">
</script>
```

Or, more properly:

```
<script type="text/ecmascript" src="flipper.js">
</script>
```

Of course, if I am using multiple libraries, I'll also want to ensure that my event handling plays well with other applications. Rather than directly assign event handler functions to event handlers, as I do in most of the examples in the book:

```
window.onload=function { ...}
```

I'll use my own packaged-site, one-off object, named **bb**, with its friendlier event handler method:

```
var bb = {
// add event listening
manageEvent : function (eventObj, event, eventHandler) {
    if (eventObj.addEventListener) {
        eventObj.addEventListener(event, eventHandler,false);
    } else if (eventObj.attachEvent) {
        event = "on" + event;
```

```
        eventObj.attachEvent(event, eventHandler);
    }
},
...
}
```

Then, when I want to add an event handler function to an object event, I use the following:

```
bb.manageEvent(window,"load", eventHandlerFunction);
```

Now, it doesn't matter whether other libraries I use also assign `window.onload` event handler functions. I won't override their event handler function assignments.

You can break individual functions into separate files, but you lose the benefits of doing so if you have too many small files, each which must be included. A library for a specific purpose is the best approach: not too much functionality, but not too little, either.

Also, to this point I haven't been trapping errors in the code. So, now is a good time to look more closely at a more sophisticated approach to error handling that is especially important when creating custom objects.

Advanced Error Handling Techniques (try, throw, catch)

Calling functions and testing return values is acceptable in an application, but it isn't optimal. A better approach is to make function calls and to use objects without continuously testing for results, and then to include exception handling at the end of the script to catch whatever errors occur.

Beginning with JavaScript 1.5, the use of `try...catch...finally` was incorporated into the JavaScript language. The `try` statement delimits a block of code that's enclosed in the exception handling mechanism. The `catch` statement is at the end of the block; it catches any exception and allows you to process the exception however you feel is appropriate.

The use of `finally` isn't required, but it is necessary if some operation must be performed whether an exception occurs or not. It follows the `catch` statement, and, combined with the exception handling mechanism, has the following format:

```
try {
...
}
catch (e) {
...
}
finally {
...
}
```

Six error types are implemented in JavaScript 1.5 engines:

EvalError
: Raised by eval when it's used incorrectly

RangeError
: Raised when the numeric value exceeds its range

ReferenceError
: Raised when an invalid reference is used

SyntaxError
: Used with invalid syntax

TypeError
: Raised when a variable is not of the type expected

URIError
: Raised when encodeURI() or decodeURI() is used incorrectly

Using instanceof when catching the error lets you know whether the error is one of these built-in types. In the following code, a TypeError is deliberately invoked and then captured. The exception that's thrown has a message property that you can print to get information about the exception.

```
try {
  var somearray = null;
  alert(somearray[18]);
} catch (e) {
  if (e instanceof TypeError) {
    alert("Type error: " + e.message);
  }
}
```

You can also use multiple tests for the type of error, log the error, and even call a special exception handler—all within the catch block. If you have any functionality that needs to be processed regardless of success or failure, you can include this in the finally block:

```
try {
  var somearray = null;
  alert(somearray[18]);
} catch (e) {
  if (e instanceof TypeError) {
    alert("Type error: " + e.message);
  }
}
finally {
  somearray = null;
}
```

This more sophisticated form of exception handling fits in with object construction because your object methods can throw exceptions using the associated throw statement, rather than having to fuss around with returning null or some other failed value.

You can throw any number of exception types and then process them accordingly in the code that is working with the object.

In Example 13-9, I modified the small opacity object library and related example from an earlier example so that both of the methods that change opacity test to see that the value passed to the function is a number. If the value is not a number, an error, a string literal with "NotANumber", is thrown. This error is then intercepted in the overall objSetOpacity method. To ensure that an error occurs, I deliberately concatenated a string to the number, which converts the whole to a string. I won't duplicate the entire application; just the code, with emphasis on the changed bits.

Example 13-9. Testing the type of a parameter and throwing an error accordingly

```
var theobjs = new Array();

document.onclick=function() {

    // fade div1
    var currentOpacity = theobjs["div1"].objGetOpacity();

    // end of transform
    if (currentOpacity <= 0) {
        document.onclick=null;
        return;
    }

    currentOpacity-=0.1;
    theobjs["div1"].objSetOpacity(currentOpacity);

    // reveal div2
    currentOpacity = theobjs["div2"].objGetOpacity();
    currentOpacity+=0.1;
    theobjs["div2"].objSetOpacity(currentOpacity);
}

function DivObj(obj) {
    this.obj = obj;

    this.objGetOpacity = function() {
        return this.obj.style.opacity;
    }

    this.alphaOpacity = function(value) {
        if (typeof value == "number") {
            var opacity = value * 100;
            this.obj.style.filter="alpha(opacity="+opacity+")";
        } else {
            throw "NotANumber";
        }
    };
    this.cssOpacity = function(value) {
        if (typeof value == "number") {
            this.obj.style.opacity=value;
        } else {
```

```
      throw "NotANumber";
    }
  };
  this.objSetOpacity=function(value) {
    value = "alpha is " + value;
    try {
      this.alphaOpacity(value);
      this.cssOpacity(value);
    } catch (e) {
      alert(e);
    }
  }
}

window.onload=function() {

  theobjs["div1"] = new DivObj(document.getElementById("div1"));
  theobjs["div2"] = new DivObj(document.getElementById("div2"));

  // set initial opacity
  theobjs["div1"].objSetOpacity(1.0);
  theobjs["div2"].objSetOpacity(0.0);
}
```

The methods that set the opacity for the object don't normally return a value; doing so just for error handling is not the way to go. Instead, by throwing the exception, the calling program doesn't have to test the status of the method's returned value, and the methods can trigger the error handling.

The example uses a string literal, but you can also create an object, such as a one-off object or object literal, and throw it. This is a good way to go if you want to pass around more information than just a string message.

Test Your Knowledge: Quiz

1. Let's say you want to create a new `Number` method, `triple`, which triples the current `Number` object's value. You also want this method available for all numbers. What steps would you take to do this?

2. How do you hide a data member with a new object? Why would you want to?

3. Create a function that wants a number argument and returns an error if the argument is of the incorrect type. How would you implement this without having to use the `return` statement?

4. You've seen object detection used previously with events:

```
var theEvent = nsEvent ? nsEvent : window.event;
```

Why can't you use the same type of functionality when dealing with the `opacity` differences?

5. Create a custom object with three public methods—`changeState`, `getColor`, and `getState`—and two private data members, `background` and `state`. Set the data members to on for state, and set a color of `#fff` for the background color. Have the `changeState` method test to see whether the state is `on`, and if it is, to change it to `off` and the color to `#000`. Have the `getColor` method return the color, and the `getState` return the state.

Test Your Knowledge: Answers

1. Use the `Number` prototype's property:

```
Number.prototype.triple = function() {
    var nmToTriple = this.valueOf() * 3;
    return nmToTriple;
}

var newNum = new Number (3.0);
alert(newNum.triple());
```

2. Declare the data member with **var** instead of assigning to `this`. The purpose behind data hiding is to control how the data is accessed or modified.

3. Use the `throw` statement to trigger an error. Then implement `try...catch` in the calling application:

```
if (typeof value != "number") {
    throw "NotANumber";
}
```

4. Unlike with the **event** object, more than just model differences are involved. Not only is the property different, but so is the possible value assigned to the property.

5. Here's one approach:

```
function Control() {
    var state = 'on';
    var background = '#fff';

    this.changeState = function() {
        if (state == 'on') {
            state = 'off';
            background = '#000';
        } else {
            state = 'on';
            background = '#fff';
        };
    }
    this.getState = function() {
```

```
        return state;
    };

    this.getColor = function() {
        return background;
    };
}
```

CHAPTER 14

Moving Outside the Page with Ajax

Ajax originally encompassed functionality that allowed in-page communication between the client page and the server. Its meaning has now grown to also include most dynamic web page effects, including those that used to be labeled Dynamic HTML (DHTML). More than any previous innovation, Ajax has led to a greater interest in JavaScript in general and dynamic JavaScript functionality in particular.

The Ajax examples in this chapter differ from examples in previous chapters in that Ajax requires a server component. Ruby is a popular choice of programming language for Ajax development, but any server-side language that can process the specialized Ajax requests will work. The examples in this chapter use PHP, primarily because out of all the languages it's the most similar to JavaScript, and because it's one of the most common server-side scripting languages in use.

Technically, you don't *need* to use a server-side language to support an Ajax application; you just need the response to be served from a server. So, you could instead use a library of static HTML or XML files on the server that are returned based on the Uniform Resource Identifier (URI) of the request. However, a server-side application processing a request and formulating a response is the common type of Ajax application, and the one I'll be demonstrating in this chapter and the next.

How Ajax Works

Ajax is not as complicated as it may seem at first. A request needs to be sent to the server, a service invoked, and data returned. However, instead of submitting a form and loading a new page with the response, or using an `iframe` and remote scripting (covered in an earlier chapter), Ajax handles all of this activity within the context of the same web page document.

A special object, either Microsoft's older `ActiveXObject` or the more general and standard `XMLHttpRequest`, manages the asynchronous communication between the server and the client. *Asynchronous* means that the request is sent, but the client doesn't have to stop, hold, and wait for the process to finish. Instead, the client provides a function to be called when the state of the request changes.

In this called function, the state of the request is checked, and if the request is finished and doesn't result in a server error, the data returned from the service is processed and is usually output to the page in some form.

To the web page reader, all of this activity looks as though the processing is happening within the page, rather than through client/server interaction. The only visual indicator that server access is happening is if the user is monitoring server requests, or the application provides some indication of the operation.

Now that you've had the 10,000-foot view of Ajax, let's look first at an Ajax application, and then go through its individual pieces in the rest of the chapter.

Hello Ajax World!

One common use of Ajax is to return some data based on a user event, such as when a person picks an option from a selection. In the "Hello Ajax World" application I discuss in this section, the page contains a select list of states, and when the user picks one, cities within the state are displayed as a list, just below the selection.

Example 14-1 contains the web page, including the script used to make the Ajax server call. The page contains a form with one select element, pre-populated with a small group of states.

Example 14-1. First Ajax application

```
<!DOCTYPE html PUBLIC "-//W3C//DTD XHTML 1.1//EN"
"http://www.w3.org/TR/xhtml11/DTD/xhtml11.dtd">
<html xmlns="http://www.w3.org/1999/xhtml" xml:lang="en">
<head>
<title>City lookup</title>
<meta http-equiv="Content-Type" content="text/html; charset=utf-8" />
<style type="text/css">
div.elem
{
    margin: 20px;
}
div#cities
{
    display: none;
}
</style>
<script type="text/javascript">
//<![CDATA[

// global variables
var xmlHttpObj;

function catchEvent(eventObj, event, eventHandler) {
```

```
        if (eventObj.addEventListener) {
            eventObj.addEventListener(event, eventHandler,false);
        } else if (eventObj.attachEvent) {
            event = "on" + event;
            eventObj.attachEvent(event, eventHandler);
        }
}

catchEvent(window,"load", function() {
    document.getElementById("cities").style.display="block";
    document.getElementById("submitButton").style.display="none";
    document.getElementById("stateList").onchange=populateList;
});
// create XHR object
function getXmlHttp() {
    var xmlhttp = null;
    if (window.XMLHttpRequest) {
        xmlhttp = new XMLHttpRequest();
        if (xmlhttp.overrideMimeType) {
            xmlhttp.overrideMimeType('text/xml');
        }

    } else if (window.ActiveXObject) {
        xmlhttp = new ActiveXObject("Microsoft.XMLHTTP");
    }
    return xmlhttp;
}

// prepare and send XHR request
function populateList() {
    var state = document.getElementById("stateList").value;
    var url = 'ch14-02.php?state=' + state;

    // if xmlHttpObj not set
    if (!xmlHttpObj)
        xmlHttpObj = getXmlHttp();
    if (!xmlHttpObj) return;

    xmlHttpObj.open('GET', url, true);
    xmlHttpObj.onreadystatechange = getCities;
    xmlHttpObj.send(null);

}

// process return
function getCities() {
    if(xmlHttpObj.readyState == 4 && xmlHttpObj.status == 200) {
        document.getElementById('cities').innerHTML = xmlHttpObj.responseText;
    } else if (xmlHttpObj.readyState == 4 && xmlHttpObj.status != 200) {
        document.getElementById('cities').innerHTML = 'Error: preSearch Failed!';
    }
}
//]]>
</script>
</head>
```

```
<body>
<h3>Select State:</h3>
<form action="ch14-02.php" method="get">
<div class="elem">
<select id="stateList" name="state">
<option value="CA">California</option>
<option value="MO">Missouri</option>
<option value="WA">Washington</option>
<option value="ID">Idaho</option>
</select>
<p><input type="submit" value="Get Cities" id="submitButton" /></p>
</div>
<div class="elem" id="cities">
<p> </p>
</div>
</form>
</body>
</html>
```

In the page markup, the `cities div` element is an empty element, which will hold the response returned by the request. When the results are returned, this element's `innerHTML` is replaced with the new contents. Figure 14-1 shows the page before the Ajax call.

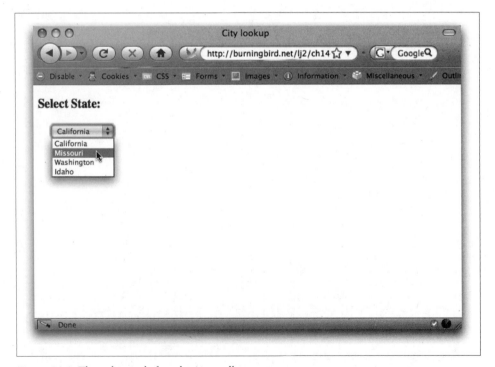

Figure 14-1. The web page before the Ajax call

Example 14-2 lists the server component of the application. Typically, this is a database request to look up cities with more than two states listed. However, in the interest of keeping the example as self-contained as possible, the "cities" are created as a static string, based on the state selected.

Example 14-2. The server component of the Ajax application in PHP

```php
<?php

//If no search string is passed, then we can't search
if(empty($_REQUEST['state'])) {
    echo "No State Sent";
} else {
    //Remove whitespace from beginning & end of passed search.
    $search = trim($_REQUEST['state']);
    switch($search) {
      case "MO" :
         $result = "<ul><li>St. Louis</li>" .
                   "<li>Kansas City</li></ul>";
         break;
      case "WA" :
         $result = "<ul><li>Seattle</li>" .
                   "<li>Spokane</li>" .
                   "<li>Olympia</li></ul>";
         break;
      case "CA" :
         $result = "<ul><li>San Francisco</li>" .
                   "<li>Los Angeles</li>" .
                   "<li>Web 2.0 City</li>" .
                   "<li>BarCamp</li></ul>";
         break;
      case "ID" :
         $result = "<ul><li>Boise</li></ul>";
         break;
      default :
         $result = "No Cities Found";
         break;
    }
    echo "<h3>Cities:</h3><p>" . $result . "</p>";
}
?>
```

Figure 14-2 shows the page after a state is selected.

In the next several sections, I'll go over each component of the page in detail, providing alternatives where appropriate.

The XMLHttpRequest Object and Preparing to Send the Request

Microsoft was the first company to implement XMLHttpRequest, in Internet Explorer, as an ActiveX object. Mozilla followed with a direct implementation of XMLHttpRequest, and other browser organizations have followed since. Though the constructor for the

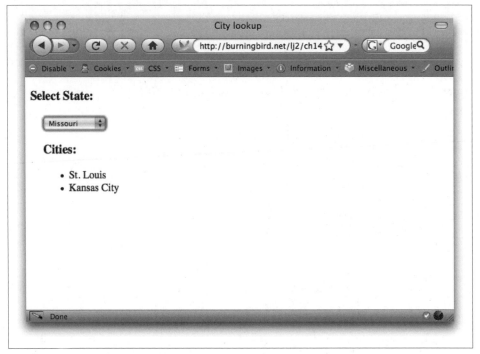

Figure 14-2. The web page after the Ajax call

objects differs between the two formats, both share the same functionality and methods.

 Microsoft now supports XMLHttpRequest, but older versions of Internet Explorer, including IE 6.x, still support only the ActiveX version, which is why we still support this object.

In Example 14-1, the XMLHttpRequest object was a global variable, because multiple functions need to access it, and it can't be passed as a parameter. The first function in the page, then, is the function getXmlHttp, for creating this object.

In getXmlHttp, a local variable, xmlhttp, is set to null. The code first checks to see whether the XMLHttpRequest object is supported as a property of the window object. If it is, a new XMLHttpRequest object is created and set to a local variable. If the page is accessed by older versions of IE, an ActiveX object is created and assigned the same local variable, which is then returned at the end of the function.

```
// create XHR object
function getXmlHttp() {
    var xmlhttp = null;
    if (window.XMLHttpRequest) {
        xmlhttp = new XMLHttpRequest();
```

```
    } else if (window.ActiveXObject) {
        xmlhttp = new ActiveXObject("Microsoft.XMLHTTP");
    }
    return xmlhttp;
}
```

This should solve the cross-browser problem. Or does it?

Object, Object, Who Has the Object?

Example 14-1 demonstrates one way to create an XMLHttpRequest object: using a conditional statement and testing for the object's existence. If the XMLHttpRequest object doesn't exist, it's created as an ActiveXObject, passing in the progID (program ID) of the ActiveX object—in this case, Microsoft.XMLHTTP. However, a possible problem with this is that the object used in the ActiveXObject method call may differ from machine to machine. Among the various versions of the object could be MSXML2.XMLHttp, MSXML2.XMLHttp.3.0, MSXML2.XMLHttp.4.0, and so forth.

You can try to resolve every version of the XMLHttpRequest object, but most Ajax libraries and applications focus on just two: the older Microsoft.XMLHTTP, and the base version of the newer MSXML2.XMLHttp. In addition, because Microsoft throws errors if it attempts to create an ActiveX object that doesn't exist, developers use this to implement the correct version:

```
try
{
    http_request = new ActiveXObject("Msxml2.XMLHTTP");
}
catch (e) {
    try
    {
        http_request = new ActiveXObject("Microsoft.XMLHTTP");
    }
    catch (e) {
        http_request = null;
    }
}
```

If the first object creation doesn't work, the next is tried.

The code is now more robust, but a lot longer. To simplify reuse, the code is enclosed within a function, with the global value set to XMLHttpRequest, or null to signal that it couldn't be created. In the end, the code is modified to include the following function:

```
function getXmlHttp() {
    var xmlhttp = null;
    if (window.XMLHttpRequest) {
        xmlhttp = new XMLHttpRequest();
    } else {
        try
        {
            xmlhttp = new ActiveXObject("Msxml2.XMLHTTP");
        }
```

```
        }
        catch (e) {
            try
            {
                xmlhttp = new ActiveXObject("Microsoft.XMLHTTP");
            }
            catch (e) {
                return xmlhttpl;
            }
        }
    }
    return xmlhttp;
}
```

Of course, any cross-browser problems will soon be resolved because IE7 and later versions support XMLHttpRequest directly. However, until the still popular IE6 disappears completely, you'll need to deal with this complexity.

Now that you have an XMLHttpRequest object, I'll cover the object in more detail.

The XMLHttpRequest Methods

XMLHttpRequest is a rather simple object, with only a few methods and properties. However, it doesn't need to be complicated to provide a rather amazing amount of functionality.

Here are the methods, in the order in which you'll most likely encounter them in an application:

open

    The syntax for open is open(method,url[,async,username,password]). The open method opens a connection to a given URL, using a specified method. Optional parameters are async, which sets the requests to be asynchronous (true and default), or synchronous (false); and a username and password if the server process requires these.

setRequestHeader

    The syntax for setRequestHeader is setRequestHeader(label,value). This method adds a label/value pair to the header in the request.

send

    The syntax for send is send(content). This is the heart and soul of XMLHttpRequest. This is where the request is sent with associated data.

getAllResponseHeaders

    The syntax for getAllResponseHeaders is getAllResponseHeaders(). This returns all HTTP response headers as a string. Among the information included is the keep-alive timeout value, content-type, information regarding the server, and the date.

getResponseHeader

The syntax for `getResponseHeader` is `getResponseHeader(label)`. This returns the specific HTTP response header.

abort

The syntax for abort is `abort()`. This aborts the current request.

Example 14-1 tests the global `xmlHttpObj` to see whether it's set. If it isn't, it calls the `getXmlHttp` function and assigns the results of the function call to `xmlHttpObj`. It still checks the value one more time to ensure that the request didn't fail (i.e., that Ajax is supported in the application environment). Once it obtains an instance of the `XMLHttpRequest` object, it processes the rest of the Ajax request.

When I discussed the `XMLHttpRequest.open` method in the preceding list, I mentioned that the first parameter is the request method used to invoke the service. These are the same HTTP request methods used in traditional client/server applications. The most common methods used with Ajax are `POST` and `GET`, but other methods are also supported, including the following:

GET

Requests data from the server

POST

Posts data to the server

DELETE

Deletes data for the given resource

PUT

Stores data for the given resource

HEAD

Similar to `GET`, but doesn't return the response body (used to obtain information)

Though the different methods are supported on the `XMLHttpRequest` object, there is no guarantee that the HTTP server will support them, which is why Ajax applications primarily use `POST` and `GET`.

When do you use `POST` as opposed to `GET`? The proper answer is that you use `GET` to retrieve a resource and you use `POST` to post data to the server. This is what is known as *the RESTful solution* because it supports the fundamental nature of REST (Representational State Transfer), supported by most web services.

However, to limit access to a service and provide more security for the request, some web services may require `POST`s for retrieving data. In addition, a `POST` supports more data in the request than a `GET`, so there is no absolute rule that you have to use `GET` for data requests and `POST` to update data.

There's no rule regarding use of GET and POST, but you should follow best practices as much as possible, and use GET for accessing data and POST for updating data.

You can remove some of the mystery associated with XmlHttpRequest if you consider that the functionality used to process a form using traditional form submission is the same technology used with Ajax and XMLHttpRequest, with the only difference being that the web page is never reloaded.

In Example 14-1, the request was a GET, so the web page URL has the associated parameters added as part of the URL. If the request had been a POST, the send method would be the following:

```
// prepare and send XHR request
function populateList() {
    var state = document.getElementById("stateList").value;
    var url = 'ch14-02.php';
    var qry = "state=" + state;

    // if xmlHttpObj not set
    if (!xmlHttpObj)
        xmlHttpObj = getXmlHttp();
    if (!xmlHttpObj) return;

    xmlhttp.open('POST', url, true);
    xmlhttp.onreadystatechange = getCities;
    xmlhttp.setRequestHeader("Content-type", "application/x-www-form-urlencoded");
    xmlhttp.send(qry);
}
```

The content-type header is adjusted to the urlencoded form, and a query value is created and sent in the send operation. Other than these changes, the method is the same as the Ajax call with GET.

In addition to the six XMLHttpRequest methods, six properties are associated with XMLHttpRequest, as Table 14-1 shows.

Table 14-1. XMLHttpRequest properties

Property	Purpose
onreadystatechange	Holds a handle to the function called when the ready state of the request changes
readyState	Has one of five values: 0 for an uninitialized request, 1 for an open request, 2 for a request that has been sent, 3 for when a response is being received, and 4 for when the response is finished loading; for the most part, we're interested in a readyState of 4
responseText	Response as text
responseXML	Response as XML, which can then be processed as valid XML
status	Returns the request status, such as 404, 500, or hopefully, 200 (for all is well)
statusText	Text associated with request status

Example 14-1 pulled the data for the web request from a **select** element, which means you have some control over the data. However, it's never wise to depend on the data that is coming from the web page reader as being clean and safe.

One modification to make the query safer is to "sanitize" either the request URL or the query portion. To add this safety factor, you can modify **populateList** to use **encodeURL Component** on the value returned from the form:

```
// prepare and send XHR request
function populateList() {
    var state = encodeURIComponent(document.getElementById("stateList").value);
    var url = 'ch14-02.php?state=' + state;

    // if xmlHttpObj not set
    if (!xmlHttpObj)
        xmlHttpObj = getXmlHttp();
    if (!xmlHttpObj) return;

    xmlHttpObj.open('GET', url, true);
    xmlHttpObj.onreadystatechange = getCities;
    xmlHttpObj.send(null);

}
```

The **encodeURIComponent** method just ensures that the text is safely "escaped" and that no HTML is inserted that could cause problems on the server.

 The use of the **encodeURIComponent** method in the client is only part of the task: the query should also be scrubbed in the server application, as web services are typically invoked from other web services in addition to Ajax calls.

Now that you've made the request, how is it processed when it's returned?

Processing the Web Request Return

Once you've made an Ajax request, the next component of the application is to process the results in some way.

Checking the readyState and status of an Ajax Request

When preparing an Ajax web request, one property you set in the application is **onreadystatechange**. You assign to this property the name of a callback function, to be called whenever a state change is associated with the **XMLHttpRequest** object:

```
xmlHttpObj.onreadystatechange = getCities;
```

A callback function is nothing more than an event handler function, which you should be very familiar with by now. **onreadystatechange** differs from most of the event handler functions in previous chapters in that when the event is fired and when the function is called depend on the server and are outside your direct control. With an Ajax request, the event is a *ready state* change in the XMLHttpRequest object.

In the callback function, getCities, for Example 14-1, two XMLHttpRequest properties are tested before any functionality is implemented:

```
if(xmlHttpObj.readyState == 4 && xmlHttpObj.status == 200) {...}
```

As mentioned in Table 14-1, readyState can have one of five values, but the one that's most interesting to us is when readyState has a value of 4, which means the request is finished and loaded. All web requests should eventually reach this readyState, but not all requests may be successful, which is why you also need to test the status. For instance, if the web service page is suddenly removed, the result would be a status of 404 rather than the desired status of 200. You can try this out for yourself by moving the server page to a different name or location and then trying the Ajax application. Figure 14-3 shows the web page loaded in Firefox with Firebug open, along with the result of running the application with the server page present as well as after it's been moved.

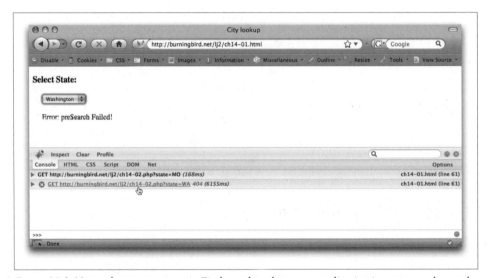

Figure 14-3. Network status requests in Firebug when the server application is present and moved

Because you also want to provide some kind of message to the web page reader if the application fails, you have a second conditional test that looks for a readyState of 4, but a status that is not 200:

```
} else if (xmlHttpObj.readyState == 4 && xmlHttpObj.status != 200) {
```

If this condition is met, you can then communicate with the application user however you deem appropriate. In the case of a successful request, though, the next task is to process the results of the web service request.

Processing the Web Request Result

Many Ajax calls result in data being returned, which then needs to be incorporated into the page. In Examples 14-1 and 14-2, the data is returned already formatted as an HTML fragment, which requires only that you paste it into the web page. This approach is easy to develop if you trust the web service you're using.

 Not all Ajax web requests return text, but most do. If nothing else, the web services return a status, which you can parse to ensure that the Ajax web service request was successful. In Chapter 15, I demonstrate how to process returned data formatted as XML and formatted as JavaScript Object Notation (JSON).

Because the response is being returned as text, it's retrieved from the XMLHttpRequest object via the responseText property, and is just pasted into the page:

```
document.getElementById('cities').innerHTML = "<select>" + xmlHttpObj.responseText
+ "</select>";
```

Again, there isn't anything complicated or complex about Ajax. You can even view the communication process between the server and client if you use a browser/debugger that supports such actions.

Example 14-3 contains a copy of Example 14-1, but with the modifications I discussed in the sections that looked more deeply at the Ajax process.

Example 14-3. A modified version of the "Hello Ajax World" application

```
<!DOCTYPE html PUBLIC "-//W3C//DTD XHTML 1.1//EN"
"http://www.w3.org/TR/xhtml11/DTD/xhtml11.dtd">
<html xmlns="http://www.w3.org/1999/xhtml" xml:lang="en">
<head>
<title>City lookup</title>
<meta http-equiv="Content-Type" content="text/html; charset=utf-8" />
<style type="text/css">
div.elem
{
    margin: 20px;
}
div#cities
{
  display: none;
}
</style>
<script type="text/javascript">
//<![CDATA[

// global variables
var xmlHttpObj;

function catchEvent(eventObj, event, eventHandler) {
```

```
        if (eventObj.addEventListener) {
            eventObj.addEventListener(event, eventHandler,false);
        } else if (eventObj.attachEvent) {
            event = "on" + event;
            eventObj.attachEvent(event, eventHandler);
        }
}

catchEvent(window,"load", function() {
    document.getElementById("cities").style.display="block";
    document.getElementById("submitButton").style.display="none";
    document.getElementById("stateList").onchange=populateList;
});
function getXmlHttp() {
    var xmlhttp = null;
    if (window.XMLHttpRequest) {
        xmlhttp = new XMLHttpRequest();
    } else {
        try
        {
            xmlhttp = new ActiveXObject("Msxml2.XMLHTTP");
        }
        catch (e) {
            try
            {
                xmlhttp = new ActiveXObject("Microsoft.XMLHTTP");
            }
            catch (e) {
                return null;
            }
        }
    }
    return xmlhttp;
}

// prepare and send XHR request
function populateList() {
    var state = encodeURIComponent(document.getElementById("stateList").value);
    var url = 'ch14-02.php?state=' + state;

    // if xmlHttpObj not set
    if (!xmlHttpObj)
        xmlHttpObj = getXmlHttp();
    if (!xmlHttpObj) return;

    xmlHttpObj.open('GET', url, true);
    xmlHttpObj.onreadystatechange = getCities;
    xmlHttpObj.send(null);

}

// process return
function getCities() {
    if(xmlHttpObj.readyState == 4 && xmlHttpObj.status == 200) {
        document.getElementById('cities').innerHTML = xmlHttpObj.responseText;
```

```
    } else if (xmlHttpObj.readyState == 4 && xmlHttpObj.status != 200) {
        document.getElementById('cities').innerHTML = 'Error: preSearch Failed!';
    }
}
//]]>
</script>
</head>
<body>
<h3>Select State:</h3>
<form action="ch14-02.php" method="get">
<div class="elem">
<select id="stateList" name="state">
<option value="CA">California</option>
<option value="MO">Missouri</option>
<option value="WA">Washington</option>
<option value="ID">Idaho</option>
</select>
<p><input type="submit" value="Get Cities" id="submitButton" /></p>
</div>
<div class="elem" id="cities">
<p> </p>
</div>
</form>
</body>
</html>
```

Of course, Ajax is more than just code, as I'll discuss that in the last section of this chapter.

 If you try to run an Ajax application on your local system, you will most likely run into security restrictions. Browsers such as Firefox do not allow XMLHttpRequests on the local filesystem; this prevents stealth Ajax applications from accessing your local filesystem.

Ajax: It's Not Only Code

Ajax functionality is actually quite simple, and you may be wondering why you should even bother with the older client/server model. However, there is more to Ajax than what first appeared in the simple examples in this chapter.

The Dynamic Nature of Ajax

If you want to, you can create an entire website in one page, using Ajax and other JavaScript-enabled functionality based on your web page reader's actions. However, the problem with this is that it becomes increasingly difficult to re-create a specific view of the content.

Ajax, like all dynamic web page functionality, does not create permanent page effects. Such effects have to be re-created each time a page is loaded, or each time a person makes a sequence of movements. They may not be accessible via source, and they may not be printable. There may be no `permalink` to individual pieces, and your web page readers won't have a history of their actions, unless you also add code to account for this lack of default functionality. Most importantly, when your web page reader clicks the back button, instead of being taken in a reverse direction within the Ajax/DHTML display stack, chances are she will be taken completely out of the page.

Entire frameworks have taken on these issues, with solutions such as resolving an anchor-tag release into a sequence of Ajax calls, and in the last section of this chapter, I'll cover some of the more popular Ajax libraries that handle this. However, for the most part, before you look into these, you should ask whether having this capability is essential to your work. You should also question how the use of Ajax impacts the accessibility of your web page.

Ajax Accessibility and Degrading Gracefully

Ajax, like any other dynamic web page effect, makes your page that much less accessible to applications such as browsers for the visually impaired. When you dynamically modify the page contents, the result may not be visible to speech-based browsers, for example.

One of the best pages on Ajax and accessibility is the WebAIM page on the topic, at *http://www.webaim.org/techniques/ajax/*. In addition to covering these issues, it also links to other sites that provide additional information.

Furthermore, because of security or other reasons, people may turn off support for JavaScript. I discussed the importance of degrading gracefully in earlier chapters, but with Ajax, the best way to ensure that an Ajax application degrades gracefully when JavaScript is disabled is to actually provide traditional client/server functionality.

Although the form in Example 14-1 doesn't show in the page when loaded, it does have a submit button, and the form's action is set to call the web service application. When the page is loaded, however, the button is hidden via JavaScript.

However, if scripting were disabled or wasn't supported, the button would show, as demonstrated in Figure 14-4, and the user would be able to do a traditional web service request—press the submit button to take him to another page, where the results are displayed, as shown in Figure 14-5.

The key to degrading gracefully doesn't occur just in the client, though. Whenever there's a possibility that a more traditional web service request will be made, the server should provide formatted data that will "look good" even if the page is accessed directly. Again, I'll demonstrate this more fully in Chapter 15.

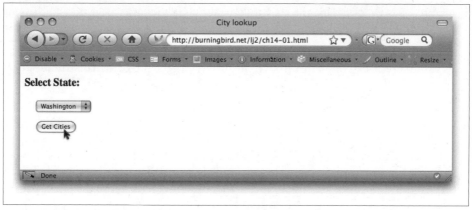

Figure 14-4. Submit button showing when JavaScript is disabled

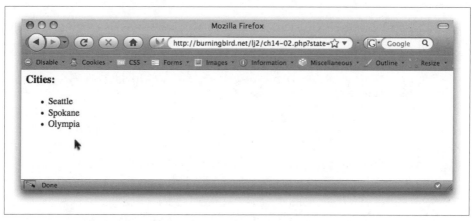

Figure 14-5. Result of traditional client/server web application request

Security and Workarounds

One of the reasons Ajax achieved such quick popularity is because it is relatively safe to use—as safe as most web applications (and requiring many of the same safeguards). The reason for its safety is the JavaScript sandbox and how it impacts XMLHttpRequest.

In the examples in this chapter, the server page is on the same server and domain as the page that made the request to the server. If you tried to put that server on another domain, you'd get an error. Why? Because Ajax operates under the JavaScript same source/same domain rule: you can only invoke services on the same server (domain) as the web page.

Internet Explorer has a setting that allows requests to other domains, but other browsers don't. Firefox supports digitally signed script and cross-domain work, but again, other browsers do not. This means you'll have to either restrict page accesses to one specific domain or find a workaround.

One approach is to work through a proxy. If a proxy is installed on the web server, all calls to the service can be made through the proxy, and the proxy then distributes them accordingly.

What do I mean by a *web proxy*? In Examples 14-1 and 14-2, if the web service to fulfill the city lookup was actually at a different domain—say, *getcitiesperstate.com*—to work around the same-domain policy I could invoke the service request on a page within my domain, which then makes the cross-domain web service request. The cross-domain restriction doesn't impact server-based applications. When the requested data is returned, the application can then process the result and return it to the client page.

To the Ajax application, the web service request is made to, and fulfilled by, a local web service. It doesn't care that the local web service actually had to access a remote web service.

Other web services, such as Google and Yahoo!, encode the web service requests within the script tag rather than using XMLHttpRequest. An example of this approach is the following:

```
<script src="http://maps.google.com/maps?file=api&amp;v=2&amp;key=yourkey"
type="text/javascript">
</script>
```

In addition, you can have your web server rewrite a web request and redirect the calls to a different location. This requires mod_rewrite with Apache and other services with other web servers, but most sites support this capability.

 To toot my own horn: if you're interested in adding Ajax functionality to your website, read my Ajax book, *Adding Ajax* (O'Reilly).

JavaScript and Ajax Libraries

I've mainly used JavaScript directly in web pages to make the examples in this chapter easier to view and re-create. As I mention in earlier chapters, though, you'll typically want to put your JavaScript in separate files and then just include them in whatever web page you're creating that needs the JavaScript functionality.

I've also covered how to work with JavaScript directly, and I haven't used any of the many and excellent JavaScript libraries freely available for developers' use. After all, this is a book on learning JavaScript, not on learning Prototype, Dojo, or jQuery.

In your real-world applications, though, especially those incorporating Ajax functionality, you will want to use external libraries. Most of the libraries have code that is heavily tested, is performance-enhanced, and makes your job a whole lot easier. Even if you're comfortable with JavaScript development, you'll want to use well-tested and developed JavaScript libraries whenever possible.

For instance, I had my own photo-enlarging JavaScript library until the excellent Lightbox (now Lightbox2, available at *http://www.huddletogether.com/projects/lightbox2/*) JavaScript library was released.

If I'm creating a complex Ajax application, I would definitely use an external library to make my life simpler. Here are some of the more commonly used, mature, and robust Ajax/JavaScript libraries:

Prototype
> Commonly thought of as the granddaddy of the Ajax libraries. You can download Prototype and view its documentation at *http://prototypejs.org/*.

Dojo
> One of the most complete and sophisticated of the Ajax/JavaScript libraries, providing functionality for some wonderful and interesting graphical effects. You can access Dojo and view its documentation at *http://dojotoolkit.org/*.

jQuery
> Probably the most widely disseminated of the JavaScript libraries, and included with most of the major content-management systems, including WordPress and Drupal. You can download jQuery from *http://jquery.com/*, a site that also includes documentation for its use.

Other libraries are also available, but these three seem to be the leaders in the Ajax world.

How would you use these external libraries? Focusing on jQuery, which is the one I'm most familiar with, you'd import the script into your web pages using the same functionality you use to import one of your JavaScript files:

```
<script type="text/javascript" src="path/to/jquery.js"></script>
<script type="text/javascript">
      // your own application
  </script>
```

Using an external JavaScript library is no different from using your own code, except that you have to be especially careful in two areas: using the traditional event handler functionality and using global variables.

Using global variables is fairly obvious: if you use a global variable named the same as one in the external libraries, the object in your code will overwrite the object in the library's code, and your application will fail. The problems with using the traditional event handler functionality, though, may not be as obvious. Not obvious, that is, until you run into oddly behaving functionality that becomes a devil of a bear to debug.

If you use a traditional event handler, such as `window.onload`, you risk overriding any of the functionality that's dependent on the `window.onload` event handler within the external library. For instance, if the library attaches an event handler to the `window.onload` event, and you do a direct assignment:

```
window.onload=eventHandlerFunction;
```

your code will "erase" the event handler assignments in the external library.

You're better off using the Document Object Model (DOM) Level 2 event handling I discussed in earlier chapters. However, rather than having to code your own functionality, you'll want to use what's included in the libraries. The three libraries I mentioned provide event handling functionality. As an example, with jQuery, if you want to capture the `click` event for all `div` elements, you could use the following jQuery request:

```
$("div").click(clickEventHandlerFunction);
```

The dollar sign ($) in the code is a popular Ajax technique for designating a function that returns a page element, or a group of page elements, based on some selector criteria. jQuery uses CSS selector syntax to process the request. The following syntax, for example, returns all paragraphs in the page:

```
$("p")...
```

If you want to access an individual element, you use an identifier and then add the hash in front of the element identifier, just as you would in CSS:

```
$("#p1")...
```

If you want to access all elements of a given class, you use this:

```
$(".p1")...
```

Rather fun, isn't it?

To demonstrate how jQuery works at its simplest, the jQuery site has a tutorial that provides a "Hello jQuery" application. I took the tutorial and created it as a separate web application, shown in Example 14-4.

Example 14-4. Using jQuery to create a "Hello World" application

```
<!DOCTYPE html PUBLIC "-//W3C//DTD XHTML 1.1//EN"
"http://www.w3.org/TR/xhtml11/DTD/xhtml11.dtd">
<html xmlns="http://www.w3.org/1999/xhtml" xml:lang="en">
<head>
<title>Hello, World, jQuery style!</title>
<meta http-equiv="Content-Type" content="text/html; charset=utf-8" />

<script type="text/javascript" src="jquery.js"></script>
<script type="text/javascript">
//<![CDATA[

$(document).ready(function() {
   $("#p1").click(function() {
     alert("Hello world!");
   });
 });
```

```
//]]>
</script>
</head>
<body>
<p id="p1" style="background-color: #ff0; padding: 10px; width: 150px">Click to say
"Hi!"</p>
</body>
</html>
```

Be careful if you're creating this example by hand. In jQuery, the `document` is the object passed as the parameter for the `onload` event, rather than the `window`.

Even with this very simple example, especially if you compare it with those in Chapter 1, you can see how using an external library can simplify your code and shorten your development time.

Before you can jump into the ease of using someone else's code, you need to finish the task of learning JavaScript. You're almost at the end of this book's lessons. One more chapter to go.

Test Your Knowledge: Quiz

1. Though it seems to defy the concept of Ajax, an `XMLHttpRequest` can be synchronous (wait for a response). How would you open such a request?

2. Once a request receives a response, it needs to process that response. How do you attach a function to call when the service responds?

3. What are the two states for a successful, and completed, request?

4. In the examples that you can download for the book is a separate subdirectory named *drink*. This subdirectory contains three variations of the same simple—but complete—drink recipe application that originally appeared in my *Adding Ajax* book.

   In the first variation of the application, a drink type is selected from a drop-down selection list, which triggers an Ajax call to the web service, named *recipe.php*. The drink name is attached to the Ajax request. How would you write the code to form this web service request? Assume the drink variable is called `drink`, the `XMLHttpRequest` object is named `xmlhttp`, and the function to process the Ajax return is named `printRecipe`.

5. From the same example, what is one way you could append the HTML-formatted result to a `div` element named `recipe`?

Test Your Knowledge: Answers

1. The third, and optional, parameter of `XMLHttpRequest.open` is a Boolean value. Setting this parameter to `true`, which is the default, creates an asynchronous request; setting it to `false` creates a synchronous request.

2. After getting a reference to the `XMLHttpRequest` object and opening it, assign the callback function to the `onReadyStateChange` property.

3. The `XMLHttpRequest` object's `readyState` property needs to have a value of 4, for completed, and the status property should be 200, for a successful service request.

4. One solution to the web request would be the following, derived from the JavaScript for the first example, *drink1.html*, and its associated JavaScript file, *getdrink2.js*. Note the use of `encodeURIComponent` to scrub the input item, and how the drink is attached to the web service request URL:

```
var drink = encodeURIComponent(document.getElementById('drink').value);
var qry = "drink=" + drink;
var url = 'recipe.php?' + qry;
xmlhttp.open('GET', url, true);
xmlhttp.onreadystatechange = printRecipe;
xmlhttp.send(null);
```

5. Though the example in *drink1.html* uses a fairly complex process, a simple approach to adding the drink recipe to the element is to use `innerHTML`:

```
if(xmlhttp.readyState == 4 && xmlhttp.status == 200) {
   var recipe = document.getElementById("recipe");
   recipe.innerHTML = xmlhttp.responseText;
}
```

CHAPTER 15

Ajax Data: XML or JSON?

In Chapter 14, we looked at a simple Ajax application that called a web service, which returned the result as an HTML fragment. We then pasted the fragment into the web page using an element's `innerHTML` property. Although that is an effective approach, it's limited, especially if you want to further process the returned results. Two other ways to process returned data from web services via Ajax calls are generally more popular: formatting the data as XML, and formatting it as JavaScript Object Notation (JSON).

This chapter looks at how you can modify the application in Chapter 14 to return the result as XML, and as JSON, and discusses when to use one over the other. Rather than pasting a formatted list into the page, you'll use the data from both to create a second selection element, with the cities added as options into the selection.

XML-Formatted Ajax Results

One advantage to returning a response formatted as XML is that the data can be much more complex than simple strings, or preformatted data in HTML. In addition, you can use the same Document Object Model (DOM) methods to work with the web page's elements and to work with the XML document returned in an Ajax call.

The Data's MIME Type

Using XML adds its own burdens, too. For instance, in Example 14-1 in Chapter 14, the result was returned as `html/text`, and the application accessed it through the `XMLHttpRequest`'s `responseText` property. When working with XML, it's important that the server-side application return the property Multipurpose Internet Mail Extension (MIME) type of `text/xml` for the content, or it won't end up in the `XMLHttpRequest` object's `responseXML` container.

If you can't guarantee that the server will return the right MIME type, one other function call on the `XMLHttpRequest` object is `overrideMimeType`, which you can use to override the content type sent via the server. You use `XMLHttpRequest.overrideMimeType` when the content returned is formatted as XML, you want to process the result as XML, and the server application isn't returning the right content header:

```
if (window.XMLHttpRequest) {
    xmlhttp = new XMLHttpRequest();
    if (xmlhttp.overrideMimeType) {
        xmlhttp.overrideMimeType('text/xml');
    }
}
```

However, the downside to `overrideMimeType` is that not all browsers support it, including Internet Explorer and Opera. There's no real problem with Opera, because it returns `responseXML` anyway. However, with the IE limitation, the better approach to ensure that the receiving application gets the data formatted correctly is to ensure, if at all possible, that the serving application uses the proper content type when returning the data.

Generating the XML on the Server

In addition to using the correct content response type, the XML the web service application produces has to be valid XML, including a **root** element that contains all of the other data. Example 15-1 returns XML representing cities based on a web request passing in the state. Note that there are two elements for each city: **value** and **title**. The **value** is what's included within the option, and the **title** is what's printed to the page.

Example 15-1. PHP Ajax application now returning XML

```php
<?php

//If no search string is passed, then we can't search
if(empty($_REQUEST['state'])) {
    echo "<city>No State Sent</city>";
} else {
    //Remove whitespace from beginning & end of passed search.
    $search = trim($_REQUEST['state']);
    switch($search) {
      case "MO" :
        $result = "<city><value>stlou</value><title>St. Louis</title></city>" .
                  "<city><value>kc</value><title>Kansas City</title></city>";
        break;
      case "WA" :
        $result = "<city><value>seattle</value><title>Seattle</title></city>" .
                  "<city><value>spokane</value><title>Spokane</title></city>" .
                  "<city><value>olympia</value><title>Olympia</title></city>";
        break;
      case "CA" :
        $result = "<city><value>sanfran</value><title>San Francisco</title></city>" .
                  "<city><value>la</value><title>Los Angeles</title></city>" .
                   "<city><value>web2</value><title>Web 2.0 City</title></city>" .
                  "<city><value>barcamp></value><title>BarCamp</title></city>";
        break;
```

```
         case "ID" :
            $result = "<city><value>boise</value><title>Boise</title></city>";
            break;
         default :
            $result = "<city><value></value><title>No Cities Found</title></city>";
            break;
      }
      $result ='<?xml version="1.0" encoding="UTF-8" ?>' .
               "<cities>" . $result . "</cities>";

   header("Content-Type: text/xml; charset=utf-8");

      echo $result;
}
?>
```

The XML in Example 15-1 is manually edited, but most programming languages used
to create web services, such as PHP, have libraries that you can use to easily generate
XML. For instance, PHP 5.x and later support DOM XML functionality that's very
similar to what you used in previous chapters in this book. Example 15-2 shows a PHP
page that delivers the same functionality as Example 15-1, but using the DOM.

Example 15-2. The application from Example 15-1 using the PHP DOM

```php
<?php
//If no search string is passed, then we can't search
if(empty($_REQUEST['state'])) {
    echo "<city>No State Sent</city>";
} else {
    //Remove whitespace from beginning & end of passed search.
    $search = trim($_REQUEST['state']);
    $cities = array();
    switch($search) {
      case "MO" :
         $cities [] = array(
                    'value' => 'kc',
                    'title' => "Kansas City");
         $cities [] = array(
                    'value' => 'stlou',
                    'title' => "St. Louis");
         break;
      case "WA" :
         $cities [] = array(
                    'value' => 'seattle',
                    'title' => "Seattle");
         $cities [] = array(
                    'value' => 'spokane',
                    'title' => "Spokane");
         $cities [] = array(
                    'value' => 'olympia',
                    'title' => "Olympia");
         break;
      case "CA" :
         $cities [] = array(
```

```php
                        'value' => 'sanfran',
                        'title' => "San Francisco");
            $cities [] = array(
                        'value' => 'la',
                        'title' => "Los Angeles");
            $cities [] = array(
                        'value' => 'web2',
                        'title' => "Web 2.0 City");
            break;
        case "ID" :
            $cities [] = array(
                        'value' => 'boise',
                        'title' => "Boise");

            break;
        default :
            $cities [] = array(
                        'value' => '',
                        'title' => "No Cities Found");
            break;
        }

    header("Content-Type: text/xml; charset=utf-8");

}

    $doc = new DOMDocument();
    $doc->formatOutput = true;

    $r = $doc->createElement("cities");
    $doc->appendChild( $r );

    foreach ($cities as $city) {
        $c = $doc->createElement( "city" );

        $value  = $doc->createElement( "value" );
        $value->appendChild(
            $doc->createTextNode($city['value']));
        $c->appendChild( $value );

        $title = $doc->createElement( "title" );
        $title->appendChild(
            $doc->createTextNode($city['title']));
        $c->appendChild( $title );
        $r->appendChild( $c );
    }
    echo $doc->saveXML();
    ?>
```

Although it seems as though Example 15-2 is much longer than Example 15-1, the extra complexity would more than pay for itself if you were processing dozens—or even hundreds—of rows from a database query.

Databases such as MySQL also return SQL responses formatted as XML, and you might be able to bypass most of this complexity.

Processing the XML on the Client

Once the server application is finished, you must also change the client-side application built into JavaScript. Example 15-3 is the application from Example 14-3 in Chapter 14, but modified to process XML rather than an HTML fragment. Pay particular attention to the line that pulls the data from the `responseXML` property.

Example 15-3. Client application modified to work with an XML response

```
<!DOCTYPE html PUBLIC "-//W3C//DTD XHTML 1.1//EN"
"http://www.w3.org/TR/xhtml11/DTD/xhtml11.dtd">
<html xmlns="http://www.w3.org/1999/xhtml" xml:lang="en">
<head>
<title>City lookup</title>
<meta http-equiv="Content-Type" content="text/html; charset=utf-8" />
<style type="text/css">
div.elem
{
    margin: 20px;
}
div#cities
{
  display: none;
}
</style>
<script type="text/javascript">
//<![CDATA[

// global variables
var xmlHttpObj;

function catchEvent(eventObj, event, eventHandler) {
   if (eventObj.addEventListener) {
       eventObj.addEventListener(event, eventHandler,false);
   } else if (eventObj.attachEvent) {
       event = "on" + event;
       eventObj.attachEvent(event, eventHandler);
   }
}

catchEvent(window,"load", function() {
   document.getElementById("cities").style.display="block";
   document.getElementById("submitButton").style.display="none";
   document.getElementById("stateList").onchange=populateList;
});

// get XMLHttpRequest object
function getXmlHttp() {
```

```
      var xmlhttp = null;
        if (window.XMLHttpRequest) {
          xmlhttp = new XMLHttpRequest();

          // XML MIME type
          if (xmlhttp.overrideMimeType) {
            xmlhttp.overrideMimeType('text/xml');
          }
        } else {
          try
            {
                xmlhttp = new ActiveXObject("Msxml2.XMLHTTP");
            }
          catch (e) {
              try
              {
                  xmlhttp = new ActiveXObject("Microsoft.XMLHTTP");
              }
              catch (e) {
                return null;
              }
          }
        }
        return xmlhttp;
}

// process service request
function populateList() {
    var state = encodeURIComponent(document.getElementById("stateList").value);
    var url = 'ch15-01.php?state=' + state;

    // if xmlHttpObj not set
    if (!xmlHttpObj)
        xmlHttpObj = getXmlHttp();
    if (!xmlHttpObj) return;

    xmlHttpObj.open('GET', url, true);
    xmlHttpObj.onreadystatechange = getCities;
    xmlHttpObj.send(null);

}

// process cities
function getCities() {
    if(xmlHttpObj.readyState == 4 && xmlHttpObj.status == 200) {
      try {

          // access city selection
          var citySelection = document.getElementById("citySelection");

          // DOM methods can be applied to external XML
          var citynodes = xmlHttpObj.responseXML.getElementsByTagName('city');

          // for every city node
          for (var i = 0; i < citynodes.length; i++) {
```

```
                var name = value = null;

                // find the associated city display name and option value
                for (var j = 0; j < citynodes[i].childNodes.length; j++) {
                    var elem = citynodes[i].childNodes[j].nodeName;
                    var nodevalue = citynodes[i].childNodes[j].firstChild.nodeValue;
                    if (elem == 'value') {
                        value = nodevalue;
                    } else {
                        name = nodevalue;
                    }
                }

                // add new option to selection
                citySelection.options[i] = new Option(name,value);
            }
        } catch (e) {
            alert(e.message);
        }
    } else if (xmlHttpObj.readyState == 4 && xmlHttpObj.status != 200) {
        document.getElementById('cities').innerHTML = 'Error: No Cities!';
    }
}

//]]>
</script>
</head>
<body>
    <h3>Select State:</h3>
    <form action="ch14-02.php" method="get">
        <div class="elem">
            <select id="stateList" name="state">
                <option value="CA">California</option>
                <option value="MO">Missouri</option>
                <option value="WA">Washington</option>
                <option value="ID">Idaho</option>
            </select>
        </div>
    <h3>Cities:</h3>
    <div class="elem" id="cities">
        <select id="citySelection">
            <option> </option>
        </select>
    </div>
    <p>
        <input type="submit" value="Lookup" id="submitButton" />
    </p>
    </form>
</body>
</html>
```

Let's walk through the code to process the return.

First, the DOM function getElementsByTagName is called on the XML returned through the request's responseXML property. This gives us a set of child nodes for each city in the XML. Each child node, in turn, has two child nodes of its own: one for the option's `value`, and one for the option display `title` element.

Instead of assuming that the XML that's returned to the web page is positionally dependent (`value` is always first, then `title`), the application traverses the `nodeList` for `childNodes` and gets the `nodeName` for each. This is compared to `value`, and if a match occurs, its `nodeValue` is assigned to `value`. If not, the `nodeValue` is assigned to `title`. Once the city `childNodes` are traversed, the `value` and `title` are used to create a new `option`, which is then added to the `options` array for the city selection, and the next city is processed.

All of this code is enclosed in exception handling because the DOM functions throw errors that aren't processed as such by the browser. It's a good habit to get into using exception handling when you work with Ajax.

Also notice that the `action` attribute of the form is actually set to the PHP application from Example 14-2 in Chapter 14. This application provides a human-readable response if JavaScript is disabled, which is preferable to the XML-formatted output in this section (or the JSON-formatted option in the next section).

With the approach just demonstrated, no matter how deep the XML nesting is, you can use this process to access the nodes. However, there is an underlying assumption when working with XML: you have to understand the nuances of XML, which is a different "language" from JavaScript. This issue has generated interest in a new format—JSON.

If you're after an attribute and not a node, you can use the DOM `getAttribute` method to retrieve the value from the XML document.

JavaScript Object Notation

As the website that supports it claims, JSON, or JavaScript Object Notation, is "a lightweight data-interchange format." Rather than attempt to chain references as comma-delimited strings, or have to deal with the complexity (and overhead) of XML, JSON provides a format that converts a server-side structure into a JavaScript object that you can use practically right out of the box.

JSON was unleashed (or introduced, depending on your view of the format) by Douglas Crockford, who is the author of *JavaScript: The Good Parts* (O'Reilly). The JSON site is at *http://www.json.org/*.

JSON actually uses JavaScript syntax to define the objects. For an object, the syntax consists of curly braces surrounding members:

```
          object{ } or object { string : value...}
```

For an array, it's elements and square brackets:

```
          array[] or array[value,value,...,value]
```

The values specified follow a subset of the same rules for variables and associated values (strings or numbers) as those defined for JavaScript in ECMA-262, Edition 3. With emphasis on the subset, one major difference between JSON and JavaScript is that JavaScript supports single and double quotes for strings, whereas JSON supports only double quotes.

A Simple JSON Application

JSON, just as with the XML and HTML examples, can be manually encoded, because it is just another text string. However, support is growing for JSON Application Programming Interfaces (APIs) in different programming languages used with web services, and most have encoders that encode or decode JSON-transmitted data.

For our purposes, though, we'll manually create the data structure. Example 15-4 contains a new server application, which provides the server data formatted as JSON. It uses an array of objects as its structure, each with a `value` and a `title` property.

Example 15-4. Working with simple JSON in PHP

```php
<?php

//If no search string is passed, then we can't search
if(empty($_REQUEST["state"])) {
    echo "<city>No State Sent</city>";
} else {
    //Remove whitespace from beginning & end of passed search.
    $search = trim($_REQUEST["state"]);
    switch($search) {
      case "MO" :
        $result = '[ { "value" : "stlou", "title" : "St. Louis" }, ' .
                   '{ "value" : "kc", "title" :" Kansas City" } ]';
        break;
      case "WA" :
        $result = '[ { "value" : "seattle", "title" : "Seattle" }, ' .
                   ' { "value" : "spokane", "title" : "Spokane" }, ' .
                   ' { "value" : "olympia", "title" : "Olympia" } ]';
        break;
      case "CA" :
        $result = '[ { "value" : "sanfran", "title" : "San Francisco" }, ' .
                   ' { "value" : "la",      "title" : "Los Angeles"   }, ' .
                   ' { "value" : "web2",    "title" : "Web 2.0 City"  }, ' .
                   ' { "value" : "barcamp", "title" : "BarCamp"       } ]';
        break;
      case "ID" :
        $result = '[ { "value" : "boise", "title" : "Boise" } ]';
        break;
      default :
```

```
            $result = '[ { "value" : "", "title" : "No Cities Found" } ]';
            break;
    }

    echo $result;
}
?>
```

To use the data structure in the web page, you access the JSON-formatted data from
the responseText property, and then pass it to a function which I haven't yet introduced
in the book: the eval function. The eval function is a built-in JavaScript function that
takes whatever string you pass to it and "evaluates" it; that is, it processes the string
just as though it is JavaScript embedded in the page.

When processing a JSON-formatted string from a web service, the eval function evaluates the structure and assigns it to a local program variable. Example 15-5 is the web
page now adjusted for a JSON data structure.

Example 15-5. Using JSON-structured data between the server and client

```
<!DOCTYPE html PUBLIC "-//W3C//DTD XHTML 1.1//EN"
"http://www.w3.org/TR/xhtml11/DTD/xhtml11.dtd">
<html xmlns="http://www.w3.org/1999/xhtml" xml:lang="en">
<head>
<title>City lookup</title>
<meta http-equiv="Content-Type" content="text/html; charset=utf-8" />
<style type="text/css">
div.elem
{
    margin: 20px;
}
div#cities
{
    display: none;
}
</style>
<script type="text/javascript">
//<![CDATA[

// global variables
var xmlHttpObj;

function catchEvent(eventObj, event, eventHandler) {
    if (eventObj.addEventListener) {
        eventObj.addEventListener(event, eventHandler,false);
    } else if (eventObj.attachEvent) {
        event = "on" + event;
        eventObj.attachEvent(event, eventHandler);
    }
}

catchEvent(window,"load", function() {
    document.getElementById("cities").style.display="block";
    document.getElementById("submitButton").style.display="none";
```

```
      document.getElementById("stateList").onchange=populateList;
});
function getXmlHttp() {
    var xmlhttp = null;
    if (window.XMLHttpRequest) {
        xmlhttp = new XMLHttpRequest();
    } else {
        try
        {
            xmlhttp = new ActiveXObject("Msxml2.XMLHTTP");
        }
        catch (e) {
            try
            {
                xmlhttp = new ActiveXObject("Microsoft.XMLHTTP");
            }
            catch (e) {
                return null;
            }
        }
    }
    return xmlhttp;
}

function populateList() {
    var state = encodeURIComponent(document.getElementById("stateList").value);
    var url = 'ch15-04.php?state=' + state;

    // if xmlHttpObj not set
    if (!xmlHttpObj)
        xmlHttpObj = getXmlHttp();
    if (!xmlHttpObj) return;

    xmlHttpObj.open('GET', url, true);
    xmlHttpObj.onreadystatechange = getCities;
    xmlHttpObj.send(null);

}

// process JSON formatted city list
function getCities() {

    if(xmlHttpObj.readyState == 4 && xmlHttpObj.status == 200) {
      try {

          // evaluate JSON
          eval("var response = ("+ xmlHttpObj.responseText+")");
          var citySelection = document.getElementById("citySelection");
          var name = value = null;

          // process returned data from JSON object
          for (var i = 0; i < response.length; i++) {
            name = response[i].title;
            value = response[i].value;
            citySelection.options[i] = new Option(name,value);
```

```
        }
    } catch (e) {
            alert(e.message);
        }
    } else if (xmlHttpObj.readyState == 4 && xmlHttpObj.status != 200) {
        document.getElementById('cities').innerHTML = 'Error: No Cities!';
    }
}

//]]>
</script>
</head>
<body>
<h3>Select State:</h3>
<form action="ch14-02.php" method="get">
<div class="elem">
<select id="stateList" name="state">
<option value="CA">California</option>
<option value="MO">Missouri</option>
<option value="WA">Washington</option>
<option value="ID">Idaho</option>
</select>
</div>
<h3>Cities:</h3>
<div class="elem" id="cities">
<select id="citySelection">
<option> </option>
</select>
</div>
<p>
<input type="submit" value="Lookup" id="submitButton" />
</p>
</form>
</body>
</html>
```

One of the issues with using JSON concerns the security problems inherent with the eval function. Since any string could be returned, and it operates within the security of the web page, if you're not sure of your web service, you won't want to use eval on the returned value. I guess it's a good thing, then, that we're no longer dependent on eval.

The JSON Object

When the ECMAScript working group announced the next version of ECMAScript, which should be out in 2009, one of the new objects it announced support for was the JSON object, developed specifically to create or parse JSON-formatted data.

One of the first companies to implement the JSON object is Microsoft, with its IE8 beta 2 release. Luckily for us, a JSON JavaScript library, at *http://www.json.org/js .html*, provides a library-based version of the same object.

You can find Microsoft's documentation on the JSON object at *http://msdn.microsoft.com/en-us/library/cc836458(VS.85).aspx*.

What JSON will end up looking like is still to be determined, but you can be reasonably certain that it will have two methods of interest, both of which are static methods accessible directly on the JSON object:

`JSON.parse`

To create a JavaScript object given a string formatted as JSON

`JSON.stringify`

To serialize a JavaScript object into JSON-formatted text

The `JSON.parse` method is quite simple to use in an Ajax application. All you do is call the method, passing in the response text:

```
var response = JSON.parse(xmlHttpObj.responseText);
```

The `JSON.stringify` method isn't quite as simple. It takes up to two parameters for the JSON2 library, and three for the Microsoft object. Focusing on just the first two parameters, the first parameter is the object to be serialized and the second, optional parameter is a replacer function or array that you can use to filter and transform the result. The following example of the use of **stringify** is a variation of an example from the JSON support site:

```
var new objFormattedAsJson = JSON.stringify(myObject, function (key, value) {
    if (typeof value === 'number' && !isFinite(value)) {
        return String(value);
    }
    return value;
});
```

Example 15-6 is a modification of the program in Example 15-5 to include the JSON2 library, as well as use the JSON object. With the incorporation of the library, it works in all of the target browsers.

Example 15-6. JSON City Lookup application, modified to use the JSON object

```
<!DOCTYPE html PUBLIC "-//W3C//DTD XHTML 1.1//EN"
  "http://www.w3.org/TR/xhtml11/DTD/xhtml11.dtd">
<html xmlns="http://www.w3.org/1999/xhtml" xml:lang="en">
<head>
<title>City lookup</title>
<meta http-equiv="Content-Type" content="text/html; charset=utf-8" />
<style type="text/css">
div.elem
{
    margin: 20px;
}
div#cities
```

```
{
  display: none;
}
</style>

<script type="text/javascript" src="json2.js">
</script>
<script type="text/javascript">
//<![CDATA[

// global variables
var xmlHttpObj;

function catchEvent(eventObj, event, eventHandler) {
    if (eventObj.addEventListener) {
        eventObj.addEventListener(event, eventHandler,false);
    } else if (eventObj.attachEvent) {
        event = "on" + event;
        eventObj.attachEvent(event, eventHandler);
    }
}

catchEvent(window,"load", function() {
    document.getElementById("cities").style.display="block";
    document.getElementById("submitButton").style.display="none";
    document.getElementById("stateList").onchange=populateList;
});
function getXmlHttp() {
    var xmlhttp = null;
    if (window.XMLHttpRequest) {
        xmlhttp = new XMLHttpRequest();
    } else {
        try
        {
            xmlhttp = new ActiveXObject("Msxml2.XMLHTTP");
        }
        catch (e) {
            try
            {
                xmlhttp = new ActiveXObject("Microsoft.XMLHTTP");
            }
            catch (e) {
                return null;
            }
        }
    }
    return xmlhttp;
}

function populateList() {
    var state = encodeURIComponent(document.getElementById("stateList").value);
    var url = 'ch15-04.php?state=' + state;

    // if xmlHttpObj not set
    if (!xmlHttpObj)
```

```
        xmlHttpObj = getXmlHttp();
    if (!xmlHttpObj) return;

    xmlHttpObj.open('GET', url, true);
    xmlHttpObj.onreadystatechange = getCities;
    xmlHttpObj.send(null);
}
// process JSON formatted city list
function getCities() {

    if(xmlHttpObj.readyState == 4 && xmlHttpObj.status == 200) {
      try {

          // evaluate JSON
          var response = JSON.parse(xmlHttpObj.responseText);

          var citySelection = document.getElementById("citySelection");
          var name = value = null;

          // process returned data from JSON object
          for (var i = 0; i < response.length; i++) {
             name = response[i].title;
             value = response[i].value;
             citySelection.options[i] = new Option(name,value);
          }
      } catch (e) {
          alert(e.message);
      }
    } else if (xmlHttpObj.readyState == 4 && xmlHttpObj.status != 200) {
      document.getElementById('cities').innerHTML = 'Error: No Cities!';
    }
}

//]]>
</script>
</head>
<body>
<h3>Select State:</h3>
<form action="ch14-02.php" method="get">
<div class="elem">
<select id="stateList" name="state">
<option value="CA">California</option>
<option value="MO">Missouri</option>
<option value="WA">Washington</option>
<option value="ID">Idaho</option>
</select>
</div>
<h3>Cities:</h3>
<div class="elem" id="cities">
<select id="citySelection">
<option> </option>
</select>
</div>
<p>
<input type="submit" value="Lookup" id="submitButton" />
```

```
</p>
</form>
</body>
</html>
```

Now you have access to the JSON capability, and the result is safer.

As you can see, the JSON method is "simpler" than the XML method, though perhaps not as simple as the HTML fragment approach. However, don't let that be the deciding factor when determining which to use. You may have no choice in how the data is sent, and you may have to process the results regardless of the format. In addition, when dealing with increasingly complex objects, using XML with XSLT to transform the XML into viewable material can end up being less work in the end.

If you're working directly with a data structure, such as a relational database, Resource Description Framework (RDF) or Scalable Vector Graphics (SVG), chances are you'll be dealing with XML anyway, so you might as well be consistent in your uses of data.

 One other thing to consider is the use of XML that uses namespaces. Namespaces can annotate an element name to prevent a conflict in vocabularies—for instance, `content:name`. A DOM function called `getElementsByTagNameNS` takes a namespace as one of the parameters, but not all browsers support this, including Internet Explorer.

The point—and I hope I have demonstrated it in these examples—is that Ajax is not a complicated process, and it's fairly simple to use. Most importantly, you have options regarding how your data is transmitted between the server application and the client page.

Test Your Knowledge: Quiz

1. In Chapter 14, I introduced Ajax examples in a subdirectory named *drink* in the examples for this book. The applications take the name of a drink from a drop-down list, and then use Ajax to access the recipe for the drink and JavaScript to display the recipe, as shown in Figure 15-1. The first example processed the drink recipe as formatted HTML. A second example, *drink2.html*, with its associated JavaScript file, *getdrink3.js*, expects the returned data to be processed as XHTML.

   What would be one way you would write the JavaScript to create a `div` element named `recipe`, and using a variety of DOM functions, access the recipe information in the returned XML and format the result as HTML, which is then added to the new `recipe` element? The ingredients would be listed as list items, and the recipe

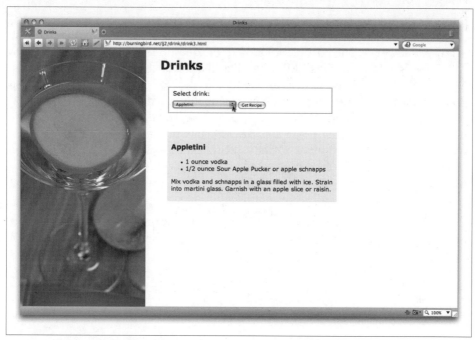

Figure 15-1. Drink application

instruction would be paragraphs, whereas the recipe name would be repeated as an h3 header, just before the ingredients.

The following is an example of the XML you could expect:

```
<recipe>
<title>Appletini</title>
<ingredient>1 ounce vodka</ingredient>
<ingredient>1/2 ounce Sour Apple Pucker or apple schnapps</ingredient>
-
<instruction>
Mix vodka and schnapps in a glass filled with ice. Strain into martini glass.
Garnish with an apple slice or raisin.
</instruction>
</recipe>
```

Note that there is no one right way to answer this question.

2. A third variation of the drink application uses JSON as the format for the returned drink. Keeping in mind the same web page parameters listed in question 1, how would you process data returned in a JSON format, making use of the JSON object?

The following is an example of the JSON you could expect:

```
{ "title" : "Appletini", "ingredients" : [ { "ingredient" : "1 ounce vodka" }, {
"ingredient" : "1/2 ounce Sour Apple Pucker or apple schnapps"}], "instruction" :
"Mix vodka and schnapps in a glass filled with ice. Strain into martini glass.
Garnish with an apple slice or raisin."}
```

Test Your Knowledge: Answers

1. The following is one possible solution to the question. Note the use of the DOM
   methods on the returned XML, as well as the use of element creation in order to
   "build" the formatted content to be added to the web page. One can begin to see
   why Ajax libraries are popular when you see this much code:

```
if(xmlhttp.readyState == 4 && xmlhttp.status == 200) {

        var body = document.getElementsByTagName('body');
        // remove, if exists
        if (document.getElementById('recipe')) {
            body[0].removeChild(document.getElementById('recipe'));
        }
        var recipe = document.createElement('div');
        recipe.id = 'recipe';
        recipe.className='recipe';
        // add title
        var title =
xmlhttp.responseXML.getElementsByTagName('title')[0].firstChild.nodeValue;
        var titleNode = document.createElement('h3');
        titleNode.appendChild(document.createTextNode(title));
        recipe.appendChild(titleNode);
        // add ingredients
        var ul = document.createElement("ul");
        var ingredients =
xmlhttp.responseXML.getElementsByTagName('ingredient');
        for (var i = 0; i < ingredients.length; i++) {
            var x = document.createElement('li');
x.appendChild(document.createTextNode(ingredients[i].firstChild.nodeValue));

            ul.appendChild(x);
        }
        recipe.appendChild(ul);
        // add instruction
        var instr =
xmlhttp.responseXML.getElementsByTagName('instruction')[0].firstChild.nodeValue;
        var instrNode = document.createElement('p');
        instrNode.appendChild(document.createTextNode(instr));
        recipe.appendChild(instrNode);

        // add to body
        body[0].appendChild(recipe);
    }
```

2. The following is one possible solution to the question. The application gets a reference to the body element, and then deletes any existing recipe div element first
   to "reset" the canvas area before appending the new recipe. Your own approach
   could and probably will vary, as this is only one possible solution:

```
if(xmlhttp.readyState == 4 && xmlhttp.status == 200) {

    var body = document.getElementsByTagName('body');

    // remove, if exists
    if (document.getElementById('recipe')) {
        body[0].removeChild(document.getElementById('recipe'));
    }
    var recipe = document.createElement('div');
    recipe.id = 'recipe';
    recipe.className='recipe';

    // create object
    var recipeObj = JSON.parse(xmlhttp.responseText);

    // add title
    var title = recipeObj['title'];
    var titleNode = document.createElement('h3');
    titleNode.appendChild(document.createTextNode(title));
    recipe.appendChild(titleNode);

    // add ingredients
    var ul = document.createElement('ul');
    var ingredients = recipeObj.ingredients;
    for (var i = 0; i < ingredients.length; i++) {
        var x = document.createElement('li');
        x.appendChild(document.createTextNode(ingredients[i].ingredient));
        ul.appendChild(x);
    }
    recipe.appendChild(ul);

    // add instruction
    var instr = recipeObj.instruction;
    var instrNode = document.createElement('p');
    instrNode.appendChild(document.createTextNode(instr));
    recipe.appendChild(instrNode);
    body[0].appendChild(recipe);
}
```

Index

Symbols and Numbers

508 compliance, 16
! (logical NOT) operator, 61
!! (double negations), 31
!= (not equals) operator, 55
!== (strict not equals) operator, 55
" (double quotes), 24
(hash) page fragment symbol, 26
$ (dollar sign)
    Ajax and, 340
    naming variables and, 23
    regular expressions, capturing patterns
        with, 87
% (remainder after division) operator, 42
& (AND) bitwise operator, 45
&& (logical AND) operator, 59, 60
' (single quotes), 24
( ) (parentheses), remembering matches, 87
* (asterisk)
    multiplication operator, 42
    regular expressions, matching characters
        with, 85
+ (plus sign)
    arithmetic operator, 9, 42
    converting strings with, 28
    regular expressions and, 84
    string concatenation operator, 77
++ (incremental) operator, 43
- (hyphen), naming conventions for CSS
    properties, 263
- (minus sign)
    arithmetic operator, 9, 42
    negative unary operator, 43
-- (decremental) operator, 43

. (property operator), 9, 69
.* (greedy match), 85
.*? (lazy star), 85
/ (division) operator, 42
/* ... */ comments, 11
// (double slashes)
    ignoring JavaScript in old browsers with
        CDATA, 13
// (double slashes) comments, 11
; (semicolon), 11
    cookies and, 225
    statements and, 39
< (less than) conditional operator, 9, 57
<!-- ... --> comments, 12
<< (shift left) operator, 47
<= (less than or equals) operator, 57
= (equals sign)
    assignment operator, 40–47
    cookies and, 225
    equality (==) operators, 54
== (equality) operator, 54–57
=== (identity) operator, 54–57
> (greater than) conditional operator, 9, 57
>= (greater than or equals) operator, 57
>> (shift right) operator, 47
>>> (zero fill) operator, 47
[ ] (square brackets), matching characters with,
    86
\ (backslash), as an escape character, 25
    regular expressions and, 84
\n (newline) character
    formatting code and, 40
^ (caret)
    character matches with, 86
    regular expressions, starting lines with, 82

We'd like to hear your suggestions for improving our indexes. Send email to *index@oreilly.com*.

DOM Level 0 (see Level 0 event models)
DOM Level 2 (see Level 2 event models)
domain property, 223
dot (.) (see property operator)
double negations (!!), 31
double quotes ("), 24
double slash (//)
    ignoring JavaScript in old browsers with
        CDATA, 13
double slashes (//) comments, 11
doubleclick event, 146
drag-and-drop, 274–277
Dragonfly (Opera), 130
Duncan, Paul, 228
Dynamic HTML (see DHTML)
dynamic pages, 261
dynamic typing, 19
dynamic/anonymous functions, 103

E

E property (Math object), 92
ECMA-262, 6, 21
ECMAScript, 3
    binding objects, 235
    JavaScript/JScript and, 5
    reserved words/keywords and, 21
Edwards, Dean, 40
Element object, 234, 253
element parameter for callback function, 116
ELEMENT_NODE constant, 248
else keyword, 49
email addresses, validating, 184
EmulateIE7 meta tag, 142
encapsulation, 301–308
encodeURI method, 26, 225
encodeURI( ) method, 316
encodeURIComponent method, 26, 331
ENTITY_NODE constant, 249
ENTITY_REFERENCE_NODE constant, 248
equality (==) operator, 54
equals sign (=)
    cookies and, 225
    equality (==) operators and, 54
error event, 146
error handling, 315–318
escape characters (regular expressions), 84
escape sequences, 25
EvalError type, 316
event capturing, 155

event handlers, 7, 145–164
    Ajax and, 339
    cross browser, 166
    Level 0, 146–156
    this keyword and, 154
Event object, 149–152
eventPhase property (Event), 161
events, 145–164, 166
    bubbling, 152–154
    canceling, 167
    forms, attaching to, 166–168
    generating, 162
    handling (see event handlers)
    inline, 147–156
every method, 116
exec method, 82–84
exp( ) method (Math object), 94
explicit string conversions, 29
expressions (function), 110

F

factory methods, 237
false values, 54
    forms, handling events and, 166
    while loops and, 61
FIFO (first-in, first-out) queues, 97
files (JavaScript), 14
filter method, 116
filter object, 139
Firebug, 124
Firefox
    debugging applications, 124
    object detection and, 138
    Web Developer Toolbar, 18
    Web Developer Toolkit, 129
firstChild property (Node), 245
fixed value (position property), 270
flags (binary), 46
Flash shared objects, 228–231
float property, 263
floating-point numbers, 31
floor method (Math object), 94
fly-in web page effect, 271
focus event, 145, 180
font HTML element, 265
font-family attribute (style), 266
font-size attribute (style), 266
font-size-adjust attribute (style), 266
font-stretch attribute (style), 266

href attribute (<a> tag), 214
href property (location object), 201
HTML, 234
  DOM HTML API, 234
  inline events, 148
HTML API (see DOM HTML API)
HTML5, 242
  DOM storage, 228–231
HTMLBodyElement object, 234
HTMLCollection interface, 239
HTMLDivElement object, 236
HTMLDocumentElement object, 234
HTMLElement object, 235
HTMLFormElement object, 236
HTMLImageElement object, 236
HTMLParagraphElement object, 236
HTMLTableCellElement object, 237
HTMLTableRowElement object, 237
http-equiv meta tag (IE8), 141
Hungarian notation, 22
hyphen (-), naming conventions for CSS
      properties, 263

I

i (case-sensitivity) flag, 82
id attribute
  element properties, accessing, 190
  HTMLElement, 235
identity (===) operator, 54–57
IE8 (Internet Explorer)
  detecting objects for, 136
    DOCTYPE declarations and, 141
  query selectors and, 286
if ... else conditional statements, 11, 49–51
if keyword, 47
iframe element, 203–207
images, 215–217
  reading/modifying properties of, 236
images object, 189
img HTML element
  onload event handler and, 7
  properties, reading/modifying, 236
immutable strings, 77
implicit string conversions, 29
incremental (++) operator, 43
index parameter for callback functions, 116
indexes (Array), 96
indexOf method
  String object, 76

inherit value (position property), 270
inheritance, 308–311
injection attacks (SQL), 185
inline CSS property, 283
inline models (events), 147–156
inline-block HTML element, 283
innerHTML property, 217–219
  Ajax and, 343
input HTML element, 178–182
  regular expressions, validating with, 182–
      184
insertBefore method (Node), 256
insertCell method, 237
insertRow method, 237
instance methods, 73
instances (object), 294
interfaces (object), 235
Internet Explorer, 133
  event handling and, 136
  Event object and, 149
  IE8 http-equiv meta tag, 141
  Level 2 event models and, 158
  Node constants and, 249
  object detection and, 139
  older versions of, 2
  style opacity and, 308
isChar property (Event), 161
italics method, 76
item method (HTMLCollection), 239

J

JavaScript blocks, 47
JavaScript files, 14
JavaScript Object Notation (JSON), 224, 343,
      351
JQuery, 9
jQuery Ajax library, 339
JScript, 4
  JavaScript/ECMAScript and, 5
JSON (JavaScript Object Notation), 224, 343,
      351
JSON.parse method, 355
JSON.stringify method, 355
just-in-time validation, 174, 283–286

K

keyCode property (Event), 151, 161
keydown event, 146

mousemove event, 146
mouseout event, 146
mouseover event, 146
mousup event, 146
moveTo method, 196
Multipurpose Internet Mail Extension (MIME)
       types, 4
   Ajax and, 343
MySQL, 347

N

\n (newline) character, 25
name attribute (<a> tag), 214
name attribute, accessing properties, 189
namespaceURI property (Node), 245
NaN (Not a Number) value, 29
   testing for null/undefined variables and, 35
NaN property (Number), 73
navigator object, 189, 210, 211–214
negative infinity numbers, 31
negative unary operator, 43
NEGATIVE_INFINITY (Number) property,
      73
nested functions, 113–116
new keyword, 70
new method (Date), 91
newline (\n) character, 25
   formatting code and, 40
next property (history object), 209
nextSibling property (Node), 245
Node object, 234
NodeList, 250
NodeList object, 234
nodeName property (Node), 245
nodes, 242
   properties and methods, 245–249
nodeType property (Node), 245
nodeValue property (Node), 245
NoScript, 129
noscript HTML element, 17
NOT (!) operator, 61
NOT (~) bitwise operator, 45
not equals (!=) operator, 55
NOTATION_NODE constant, 249
null variables, 34
number data type, 19, 31–34
Number object, 23
Number.MAX_VALUE property, 73
Number.MIN_VALUE property, 73

Number.NaN property, 73
Number.NEGATIVE_INFINITY property, 73
Number.POSITIVE_INFINITY property, 73
numeric data type, 23

O

object detection, 134–141
object literals, 311
Object object, 293
object.appendChild method, 239
objects, 69–101
   Ajax, 327
   cross-browser differences, detecting, 135–
      141
   custom, creating, 293–319
   encapsulation, 301–308
   functions as, 120
   libraries, 314
   notation, 350–358
   primitive types as, 69–71
octal notation (number data type), 32
onblur event handler, 7
onclick event handler, 7
   this keyword and, 154
one-off objects, 311–314
onfocus event handler, 7
onLine property (navigator object), 211
onload event handler, 7, 145
   this keyword and, 154
onmouseout event handler, 7
onmouseover event handler, 7
onreadystatechange property
     (XMLHttpRequest), 330
onsubmit event handler, 166
opacity property, 138
open method, 8
   window, 192
   XMLHttpRequest, 328
opener keyword, 195
Opera, 130
   object detection and, 138
operators, 39–67
   arithmetic, 41
   bitwise, 45
   conditional, 54–59
   logical, 59–61
   precedence, 44
   unary, 43
options array, 169

options property (select element), 169
OR (|) bitwise operator, 45
OR (||) operator, 60
outerHeight option (window.open), 193
outerWidth option (window.open), 193
overflow (text), 278
overflow CSS attribute, 277
ownerDocument property (Node), 245

P

Packer tool, minifying code, 40
page fragment symbol (#), 26
pageX property (Event), 161
pageY property (Event), 161
parent frames, 199
parent nodes, 244
parentheses (( )), remembering matches, 87
parentNode property (Node), 245
parseFloat function, 32
parseInt function, 32
password fields, 178–182
pathname property (location object), 201
paths (cookies), 224
period (.) (see property operator)
PHP, 345
PI property (Math object), 93
pixelDepth property (screen object), 210
platform property (navigator object), 211
plugins property (navigator object), 211
plus sign (+)
    arithmetic operator, 9, 42
    converting strings with, 28
    regular expressions and, 84
    string concatenation operator, 77
pop method, 99
port property, 214
    location object, 201
position property, 270–274
positive infinity numbers, 31
POSITIVE_INFINITY (Number) property, 73
POST method, 329
post-incremental operator, 43
pow method (Math object), 94
pre-incremental operator, 43
precedence (operator), 44
prefix property (Node), 245
preventDefault method, 167
previous property (history object), 209
previousSibling property (Node), 245

primitive types, 19, 23
    objects, 69–71
private properties, 299
PROCESSING_INSTRUCTION_NODE
        constant, 249
program flow, 47–54
prompt method, 192
property operator (.), 9, 69
protocol property, 214
Prototype
    naming variables and, 23
Prototype Ajax library, 339
Prototype library, 10
prototype property (Object), 293
Prototype.js Ajax library, 299
prototyping, 293–296
public properties, 299
push method, 98
PUT method, 329

Q

querySelectorAll method, 287
quirks mode, 141

R

radio buttons, 175–178
random method (Math object), 94
random numbers, generating, 95
RangeError type, 316
RDF (Resource Description Framework), 358
ready state change, 332
readyState property (XMLHttpRequest), 330
    requests, checking status of, 331
recursion, 111
ReferenceError type, 316
references, passing to functions, 105
RegExp object, 69, 82–84
Regular Expression Library, 184
regular expressions, 69, 81–89
    input fields, validating, 182
    working with, 84
relatedTarget property (Mozilla/Firefox Event
        object), 151
relative, 270
remainder after division (/) operator, 42
remote scripting, 203
removeAttribute method, 253
removeAttributeNode method, 253

removeChild method (Node), 256
removeEventListener method, 156, 158
replace method, 76, 85
replaceChild method (Node), 256
representations of function, 109
reserved words, 21
reset event, 146
resizable option (window.open), 194
resize event, 146
resizeBy method, 196
resizeto methods, 196
Resource Description Framework (RDF), 358
responseText property (XMLHttpRequest), 330, 333
responseXML property (XMLHttpRequest), 330
REST (Representational State Transfer), 329
RESTful solutions, 329
return statements, 106
    forms, attaching event handlers to, 166
returnValue property, 167
RIAs (rich Internet applications), 228
rich Internet applications (see RIAs)
right property (position), 270
round method (Math object), 94
run-in HTML element, 283

S

Safari, 132
    object detection and, 138
same-origin security policy, 222
sandbox, 184–186
    cookie security and, 221–223
Scalable Vector Graphics (SVG), 251, 358
scope, 10
    function, 119
    nested functions and, 114
scope chaining, 114
scoping bubbles, 114
screen object, 189, 210, 211–214
screenX property (Event), 151, 161
screenY property (Event), 151, 161
script HTML element, 1, 3–5
    separate script files and, 14
scroll CSS attribute, 277
scroll event, 146
scrollbars option (window.open), 194
search method, 76
search property, 214

location object, 202
Section 508 compliance, 16
select event, selecting text, 146
select HTML element, 168
selected property, 169
selectedIndex property (select element), 169
self keyword, 195
semicolon (;), 11
    cookies and, 225
    statements and, 39
send method (XMLHttpRequest), 328
sessionStorage object, 229
setAttribute method, 253
setRequestHeader method (XMLHttpRequest), 328
setTimeout method, 207
Shared Objects (SO), 229
shift left (<<) operator, 47
shift method, 98
shift right (>>) operator, 47
shiftKey property (Event), 151, 161
short-circuit evaluation, 60
sibling nodes, 244
sin( ) method (Math object), 93
single quotes ('), 24
slice method, 76
small method, 76
SO (Flash Shared Objects), 229
some method, 116
Souders, Steve, 5
spaces, 40
splice method (Array object), 97
split method, 76, 80
SQL injection attacks, 185
SQRT1_2 property (Math object), 93
SQRT2 property (Math object), 93
square brackets ([ ]), matching characters with, 86
src attribute, 215
    img element, 236
    script element, 4
srcElement object, 137
statements, 10, 39–67
    assignment, 41–47
    conditional, 47
        if ... else, 49–51
    format of, 39
    loops, 61–65
    switch, 51–54

static functions, 103
static methods, 73
static value (position property), 270
status option (window.open), 194
status property (XMLHttpRequest), 330
statusText property (XMLHttpRequest), 330
stopPropagation method (Mozilla), 153
strict equality (===) operator, 54–57
strict not equals (!==) operator, 55
strike method, 70, 76
string data type, 19, 23, 24–30
    converting, 28–30
    escape sequences, 25
string data types
    encoding, 26
String function, 32
String object, 23, 70, 75 81
strings
    swapping with regular expressions, 88
style object, 9, 237, 261–265
    getElementById method, testing for
        support, 136
styleFloat property, 263
sub method, 76
subdomains, 222
submit event, 146, 166
substr method, 76
substring method, 76
sup method, 76
SVG (Scalable Vector Graphics), 251, 358
switch statement, 11, 51–54
SyntaxError type, 316

T

table HTML element, 283
table-cell HTML element, 283
tabs, 40
tan( ) method (Math object), 93
target property, 137
    Event, 161
    location object, 202
ternary operator, 59, 150
test method, 82–84
text, 265–269
text fields, 178–182
text-align CSS text attribute, 267
text-decoration CSS text attribute, 267
text-indent CSS text attribute, 267
text-transform CSS text attribute, 267

text/ecmascript type attribute, 3
text/jsript type attribute, 3
text/vbs type attribute, 3
text/vbscript type attribute, 3
textarea fields, 178–182
TEXT_NODE constant, 248
this keyword, 154
    apply function and, 308
throw keyword, 315–318
tiling, 274
timers, 207–209
timeStamp property (Event), 161
title attribute (HTMLElement), 235
titlebar option (window.open), 194
toElement property (Event), 151
toExponential method, 74
toFixed method, 74
toGMTString method, 90, 224
toLocaleDateString method, 90
toLocaleString method, 74, 90
toLocaletimeString method, 90
toLowerCase method, 76
toolbar option (window.open), 194
top option (window.open), 193
top property (position), 270
toPrecision method, 74
toString method, 71, 90
    Number objects and, 74
toUpperCase method, 23, 76
toUTCString method, 91
traditional models, 147
true values, 54
    >= operator and, 57
    forms, handling events and, 166
    while loops and, 61
try keyword, 315–318
type attribute (script element), 1
type attributes, 3
type property
    Event, 151
    select element, 169
TypeError type, 316
typeof function, 139

U

\u (Unicode) character, 25
unary operators, 43
undefined properties, 139
undefined variables, 34

About the Author

Shelley Powers has been working with and writing about web technologies on topics ranging from the first release of JavaScript to the latest graphics and design tools for more than 13 years. Her recent O'Reilly books have covered the semantic web, Ajax, JavaScript, and web graphics. She's also an avid amateur photographer and web development aficionado who enjoys applying her latest experiments on her many websites.

Colophon

The animal on the cover of *Learning JavaScript*, Second Edition, is a baby black, or hook-lipped, rhinoceros (*Diceros bicornis*). The black rhino is one of two African species of rhinos. Weighing up to one and a half tons, it is smaller than its counterpart—the white, or square-lipped, rhinoceros. Black rhinos live in savanna grasslands, open woodlands, and mountain forests in a few small areas of southwestern, south central, and eastern Africa. They prefer to live alone and will aggressively defend their territory.

With an upper lip that tapers to a hooklike point, the black rhino is perfectly suited to pluck leaves, twigs, and buds from trees and bushes. It is able to eat coarser vegetation than other herbivores.

Black rhinos are odd-toed ungulates, meaning they have three toes on each foot. They have thick, gray, hairless hides. Among the most distinctive of the rhino's features is its two horns, which are actually made of thickly matted hair rather than bone. The rhino uses its horns to defend itself against lions, tigers, and hyenas, or to claim a female mate. The courtship ritual is often violent, and the horns can inflict severe wounds.

After mating, the female and male rhinos have no further contact. The gestation period is 14 to 18 months, and the calves nurse for a year, though they are able to eat vegetation almost immediately after birth. The bond between a mother and her calf can last up to four years before the calf leaves its home.

In recent years, rhinos have been hunted to the point of near extinction. Scientists estimate that there may have been as many as a million black rhinos in Africa 100 years ago, a number that has dwindled to 2,400 today. All five remaining species, which include the Indian, Javan, and Sumatran rhinos, are now endangered. Humans are considered their biggest predators.

The cover image is from *Cassell's Natural History*. The cover font is Adobe ITC Garamond. The text font is Linotype Birka; the heading font is Adobe Myriad Condensed; and the code font is LucasFont's TheSansMonoCondensed.

Related Titles from O'Reilly

Web Authoring and Design

ActionScript 3.0 Cookbook

Ajax Hacks

Ambient Findability

Creating Web Sites: The Missing Manual

CSS Cookbook, *2nd Edition*

CSS Pocket Reference, *2nd Edition*

CSS: The Definitive Guide, *3rd Edition*

CSS: The Missing Manual

Dreamweaver 8: Design and Construction

Dreamweaver 8: The Missing Manual

Dynamic HTML: The Definitive Reference, *3rd Edition*

Essential ActionScript 3.0

Flex 8 Cookbook

Flash 8: Projects for Learning Animation and Interactivity

Flash 8: The Missing manual

Flash 9 Design: Motion Graphics for Animation & User Interfaces

Flash Hacks

Head First HTML with CSS & XHTML

Head Rush Ajax

Head First Web Design

High Performance Web Sites

HTML & XHTML: The Definitive Guide, *6th Edition*

HTML & XHTML Pocket Reference, *3rd Edition*

Information Architecture for the World Wide Web, *3rd Edition*

Information Dashboard Design

JavaScript: The Definitive Guide, *5th Edition*

JavaScript & DHTML Cookbook, *2nd Edition*

Learning ActionScript 3.0

Learning JavaScript

Learning Web Design, *3rd Edition*

PHP Hacks

Programming Collective Intelligence

Programming Flex 2

Web Design in a Nutshell, *3rd Edition*

Web Site Measurement Hacks

Our books are available at most retail and online bookstores.

To order direct: 1-800-998-9938 • *order@oreilly.com* • *www.oreilly.com*

Online editions of most O'Reilly titles are available by subscription at *safari.oreilly.com*

70502